P9-EMP-793

Praise for

The Short and Tragic Life of Robert Peace

"Mesmeric . . . [Hobbs] asks the consummate American question: Is it possible to reinvent yourself, to sculpture your own destiny? . . . That one man can contain such contradictions makes for an astonishing, tragic story. In Hobbs's hands, though, it becomes something more: an interrogation of our national creed of self-invention. . . . [*The Short and Tragic Life of Robert Peace*] deserves a turn in the nation's pulpit from which it can beg us to see the third-world America in our midst."

—*The New York Times Book Review*

"I can hardly think of a book that feels more necessary, relevant, and urgent."

—*Grantland*

"A haunting work of nonfiction . . . Mr. Hobbs writes in a forthright but not florid way about a heartbreaking story."

—*The New York Times*

"*The Short and Tragic Life of Robert Peace* is a book that is as much about class as it is race. Peace traveled across America's widening social divide, and Hobbs's book is an honest, insightful, and empathetic account of his sometimes painful, always strange journey."

—*Los Angeles Times*

"Devastating. It is a testament to Hobbs's talents that Peace's murder still shocks and stings even though we are clued into his fate from the outset . . . a first-rate book. [Hobbs] has a tremendous ability to empathize with all of his characters without romanticizing any of them."

—*The Boston Globe*

"It is hard to imagine a writer with no personal connection to Peace being able to generate as much emotional traction in this narrative as Hobbs does, to care as much about portraying fully the depth and intricacy of Peace's life, his friends, and the context of it all. . . . It is an enormous writing feat . . . fresh, compelling."

—*The Washington Post*

"[An] intimate biography . . . Hobbs uses [Peace's] journey as an opportunity to discuss race and class, but he doesn't let such issues crowd out a sense of his friend's individuality. . . . By the end, the reader, like the author, desperately wishes that Peace could have had more time."

—*The New Yorker*

"Heartbreaking."

—*O, The Oprah Magazine*, "Best Books of 2014"

"Captivating . . . a smart meditation on the false promise of social mobility."

—*Bloomberg Businessweek*

"Nuanced and shattering."

—*People*, "The Best Books of the Fall"

"*The Short and Tragic Life [of Robert Peace]* tackles some important topics: the swamp of poverty; the tantalizing hope of education; the question of whether anyone can truly invent a life or whether fate is, in fact, dictated by birth. . . . [Its] account of worlds colliding will leave nagging questions for many readers, which might be all to the good."

—*The Seattle Times*

"A haunting American tragedy for our times."

—*Entertainment Weekly*, "10 Best Nonfiction Books of 2014"

"Can a man transcend the circumstances into which he's born? Can he embody two wildly divergent souls? To what degree are all of us, more or less, slaves to our environments? Few lives put such questions into starker relief than that of one Robert DeShaun Peace. . . . As Hobbs reveals in tremendously moving and painstaking detail, [Peace] may have never had a chance."

—*San Francisco Chronicle*

"Hobbs chronicles Peace's brief thirty years on earth with descriptive detail and penetrating prose. . . . He paints a picture of a young man who was complex, like most of us, and depicted both his faults and admirable qualities equally. It is up to the reader to decide if Peace was an Ivy League grad caught up in a life of crime or just a victim of circumstances. . . . Hobbs's empathetic narrative gives readers an opportunity to view his life beyond a stereotype."

—*Pittsburgh Post-Gazette*

"With novelistic detail and deep insight, Hobbs . . . registers the disadvantages his friend faced while avoiding hackneyed fatalism and sociology . . . reveals a man whose singular experience and charisma made him simultaneously an outsider and a leader in both New Haven and Newark. . . . This is a classic tragedy of a man who, with the best intentions, chooses an ineluctable path to disaster."

—*Publishers Weekly* (starred review)

"I've seldom read a book as riveting and ultimately devastating. . . . With deftly chosen detail and precision, Hobbs chronicles the obstacle-ridden rise of Robert Peace. . . . Long after finishing the book, I remain haunted by Peace's fate."

—*Psychotherapy Networker*

"Ambitious, moving . . . Hobbs combines memoir, sociological analysis, and urban narrative elements, producing a perceptive page-turner. . . . An urgent report on the state of American aspirations and a haunting dispatch from forsaken streets."

—*Kirkus Reviews* (starred review)

"Peace navigated the clashing cultures of urban poverty and Ivy League privilege, never quite finding a place where his particular brand of nerdiness and cool could coexist. . . . [Hobbs] set out to offer a full picture of a very complicated individual. Writing with the intimacy of a close friend, Hobbs slowly reveals Peace as far more than a cliché of amazing potential squandered."

—*Booklist* (starred review)

"*The Short and Tragic Life of Robert Peace* is a powerful book meant to haunt us with the question that plagued everyone who knew Peace. Hobbs has the courage not to counterfeit an answer, leaving us with the haunting question: Why?"

—*New York Daily News*

"One part biography and one part study of poverty in the United States, Hobbs's account of his friend's life and death highlights how our pasts shape us, and how our eternal search for a place of safety and belonging can prove to be dangerous. Peace's life was indeed short and tragic, but Hobbs aims to guarantee that it will not go unmarked."

—*Shelf Awareness* (starred review)

"The resulting portrait of Peace is nuanced, contradictory, elusive, and probing. . . . At its core, the story compels readers to question how much one can really know about another person. . . . VERDICT: An intelligent, provocative book, recommended for any biography lover."

—*Library Journal*

"If *The Short and Tragic Life of Robert Peace* were a novel, it would be a moral fable for our times; as nonfiction, it is one of the saddest and most devastating books I've ever read, a tour de force of compassion and insight, an exquisite elegy for a person, for a time of life, for a valid hope that nonetheless failed. It is also a profound reflection on a society that professes to value social mobility, but that often does not or cannot imbue privilege with justice. It is written with clarity, precision, and tenderness, without judgment, with immense kindness, and with a quiet poetry. Few books transform us, but this one has changed me forever."

—Andrew Solomon, author of *Far from the Tree*
and *The Noonday Demon*

"Jeff Hobbs has written a mesmerizingly beautiful book, a mournful yet joyous celebration of his friend Robert Peace, this full-throated, loving, complicated man whose journey feels simultaneously heroic and tragic. This book is an absolute triumph—of empathy and of storytelling. Hobbs has accomplished something extraordinary: he's made me feel like Peace was a part of my life as well. Trust me on this, Peace is someone you need to get to know. He'll leave you smiling. His story will leave you shaken."

—Alex Kotlowitz, author of *There Are No Children Here:*
The Story of Two Boys Growing Up in the Other America

"A poignant and powerful can't-put-it-down book about friendship and loss. *The Short and Tragic Life of Robert Peace* takes you on a nail-biting, heartbreaking journey that will leave you moved, shaken, and ultimately changed. In this spectacularly written first work of nonfiction, Jeff Hobbs creates a singular and searing portrait of an unforgettable life."

—Jennifer Gonnerman, author of *Life on the Outside:*
The Prison Odyssey of Elaine Bartlett

ALSO BY JEFF HOBBS

The Tourists

The Short and Tragic Life of Robert Peace

◆

A BRILLIANT YOUNG MAN WHO LEFT
NEWARK FOR THE IVY LEAGUE

JEFF HOBBS

SCRIBNER

New York London Toronto Sydney New Delhi

Scribner
An Imprint of Simon & Schuster, Inc.
1230 Avenue of the Americas
New York, NY 10020

Copyright © 2014 by Jeff Hobbs

All rights reserved, including the right to reproduce this book or portions thereof in any form whatsoever. For information address Scribner Subsidiary Rights Department, 1230 Avenue of the Americas, New York, NY 10020.

First Scribner trade paperback edition July 2015

SCRIBNER and design are registered trademarks of The Gale Group, Inc., used under license by Simon & Schuster, Inc., the publisher of this work.

For information about special discounts for bulk purchases, please contact Simon & Schuster Special Sales at 1-866-506-1949 or business@simonandschuster.com.

The Simon & Schuster Speakers Bureau can bring authors to your live event. For more information or to book an event contact the Simon & Schuster Speakers Bureau at 1-866-248-3049 or visit our website at www.simonspeakers.com.

Manufactured in the United States of America

1   3   5   7   9   10   8   6   4   2

The Library of Congress has cataloged the hardcover edition as follows:

Hobbs, Jeff.
The short and tragic life of Robert Peace : a brilliant young man who left Newark for the Ivy League / Jeff Hobbs.
pages cm
1. Peace, Robert, 1980–2010. 2. Hobbs, Jeff, 1980—Friends and associates. 3. Yale University—Alumni and alumnae—Biography. 4. Working-class African American college graduates—Biography. 6. Drug dealers—New Jersey—Biography. I. Title
E185.97.P38H63 2014
974.9'044092—dc23   2014001213
[B]

ISBN 978-1-4767-3190-2
ISBN 978-1-4767-3191-9 (pbk)
ISBN 978-1-4767-3192-6 (ebook)

Photograph credits: p. 1 courtesy of Jackie Peace, 1985; p. 74 courtesy of Our Lady of Mt. Carmel Elementary School; p. 75 courtesy of Jackie Peace, 1996; p. 122 courtesy of Curtis Gamble, 1998; p. 123 courtesy of Yesenia Vasquez, 2001; p. 202 courtesy of Danny Nelson, 2002; p. 203 courtesy of Adam Stockett, 2005; p. 284 courtesy of Curtis Gamble, 2003; p. 285 courtesy of Hrvoje Dundovic, 2010; p. 332 courtesy of Curtis Gamble, 2003; p. 333 courtesy of Yesenia Vasquez, 2009; p. 402 courtesy of Jeff Hobbs, 2012.

Dedicated to Robert DeShaun Peace
and to his heart, Jacqueline Peace

AUTHOR'S NOTE

◆

I F YOU'RE GOING to tell the story of a man, tell the whole story."
I was sitting in Cryan's Beef & Ale House in South Orange, New
Jersey, with Jason Delpeche, one of Robert Peace's friends dating back
to elementary school. His words were not so much a command as they
were an observation: if the intent of these pages was to recount the life
of a friend who has died—who could neither tell nor defend his own
story—then I had better recount that life well, using all means available.

This story is told through memory, observation, and documentation:
mine, of course, but primarily that of many dozens of others, including
Rob's family, friends, lovers, classmates, teachers, neighbors, colleagues
in the professional world, and colleagues in the drug world. In addition,
many people have contributed to this telling who did not know Rob at
all but have keen perspective on one or more of the many complicated
milieus in which he traveled: lawyers who worked for or against his father, politicians in Newark and the surrounding townships, community
workers, police who patrol the streets on which he grew up, police who
investigated his murder, academics, college administrators, state prison
inmates, state prison employees, and more. I sought out anyone who
might have a shred of perspective not only on Rob's direct experiences
but also on the places and structures that informed those experiences.
The result has been more than three hundred hours' worth of recorded

interviews which, paired with my own memories, eventually became this book. Much of this material is subjective, but so is any human life.

The dialogue that appears in this book was taken directly from these interviews. Though recalling precise exchanges, in some cases from decades ago, can be an inexact science, I am confident that the words I've written reflect very closely the words that were said. In instances where more than one person was present for these conversations, I have fact-checked their accuracy.

Segments relating to Rob's consciousness—his thoughts, feelings, various states of being—came from sentiments he shared with others during the respective time periods in which they took place. I acknowledge that it is impossible to fully understand a man's interior, particularly a man as complicated as Rob Peace, and I included such passages only in cases where the recollections were explicit and specific.

There are moments detailed herein in which Rob was alone or was interacting with someone who has also passed away, and so no one could attest as to what actually happened. Again, I relied on conversations he later had with friends and family. On the very few occasions where Rob never did relate the goings-on both within him and without, I used language to indicate that the content is based on the projections of myself and/or those who knew him well.

Names and some identifying characteristics have been changed.

Part I

—————◆—————

Chapman Street

Rob with his father, Skeet Douglas, in 1985.

Chapter 1

◆

"WHY IS THE AIR NOT ON?" Jackie Peace asked from the back of the car.

"It wears the engine," her mother, Frances, replied from the driver's seat. "You can't bear it for four blocks?"

"He just feels hot to me, real hot." And then, when her mother chuckled: "What's funny?"

"You're a brand-new mama and that's why you have no idea."

"Idea of what now?"

"Babies are strong. They can handle just about anything."

Robert DeShaun Peace, the baby in question, lay sleepy-eyed and pawing in Jackie's arms. He was a day and a half old, eight pounds, ten ounces. When he'd first been weighed, the number had sounded husky to her. Now, outside the hospital for the first time, he felt nearly weightless. The street outside the car was dark and empty on this swampy late-June night in 1980. The last of the neighborhood children had been called inside to clear the way for the hustlers who governed much of the greater Newark, New Jersey, area, and particularly this township of Orange, during the wilderness of the nocturnal hours.

As Frances had noted, St. Mary's Hospital was indeed less than half a mile from 181 Chapman Street, where the Peace family lived. They were parked outside their home within two minutes. Chapman Street was about a hundred yards long, dead-ending on South Center Street to the west and Hickory to the east. These bookends actually protected the 100 block from most of the neighborhood's nightly commerce; dealers found the short stretch claustrophobic, and they were slightly wary of Frances, who never hesitated to march outside at any hour and tell them to get the hell out of her sight.

Jackie carried her son inside, past the rusty fence and weedy rectangle of lawn, up the five buckled stoop stairs, across the narrow porch, and through the open front door, where the ceiling fan made the air cooler. The street had been deserted, but the parlor and dining room were crowded with family. She had eight siblings, enough that she couldn't keep track of who was living in the house at any given time. Still dizzy from labor and first feedings, she didn't bother to count how many were there tonight as she reluctantly let the baby be passed around the living room, from her father, Horace, to her sisters Camilla and Carol to her brothers Dante and Garcia. Then her son was crying, and Jackie took him back and carried him to the room on the second floor where they could be alone, which was all she really wanted right now.

"Swaddle that baby and he'll stop the crying," her mother called as she ascended the stairs.

"I told you I'm not swaddling anything in this heat!" Jackie called in response. And to Carl, who was something like an adopted younger brother, "If you see Skeet out tonight, tell him to get back here." Skeet was Rob's father.

She laid the boy naked in the center of the mattress with a towel spread beneath him, and she lay beside him at the edge of the single bed to let him feed. They fell asleep that way, with her hand pressed against his back, holding him against her. His cries woke her in the early morning, and she raised her head hoping that Skeet would be there—he had left the hospital room abruptly a few hours after the birth, saying he had some "things to take care of"—but she and the baby remained the only warm bodies in the room.

*   *   *

ASIDE FROM A few failed attempts to strike out on her own, Jackie Peace had lived on Chapman Street in Orange, New Jersey, since 1960, when she was eleven. The house had first belonged to her uncle and had been left in her father's name when that uncle died of lung cancer. Back then, the Peaces had been one of two black families on a block of middle-class European immigrants, mostly Italian, and their race hadn't bothered anyone. In that climate, people didn't think much about race, at least not outwardly. They thought about work. They thought about family. They thought about property. Men woke early and rode buses and car pools to the factory jobs that were the lifeblood of the greater Newark economy. Women stayed home and raised children. Neighbors, in silent and efficient understanding, kept an eye on the homes on either side of theirs, most of which were turn-of-the-century clapboards with peaked roofs set atop fourth-floor attics—attics packed with old photo albums and records and dishware, remnants of the passing down of property from generation to generation beginning in the early 1900s. The homes were narrow and close together, but inside they felt big enough, with high ceilings and wide portals between rooms and long backyards shaded by native willow oaks. Police made regular patrols and were known by name.

Central Avenue, a thoroughfare one block south of and parallel to Chapman Street, connected downtown Newark to the pastoral townships farther west: a succession of Italian, Polish, and Jewish grocers, pharmacies, clothing stores, flower shops, funeral homes, and local banks. On the south side of Central Avenue, Orange Park stretched out in ten green, rolling acres shaped like an arrow, its grounds bright with mothers gossiping and children playing. Though dense and urban, Orange could feel very much like a small town where all needs—social, domestic, financial— were proximate and easily sustained. Because factories were the central commerce of greater Newark, and because the workers in those factories lived in places such as Orange, families like the Peaces could feel vital, as if the history of the city of Newark were moving through them.

If Jackie looked east on Central Avenue, in the direction of downtown, she could see in the distance the first of those brick, boxy towers known as "slums in the sky." The federal Department of Housing and Urban Development had erected sixteen of these projects in the 1950s to manage the influx of southerners seeking industrial work—mostly poor and mostly black. These communities had been intentionally segregated by race, in accordance with the common wisdom of urban planners at the time: if people were going to be stacked in such an uncomfortable way, they'd likely be more comfortable stacked with others of their own kind. The towers also served to segregate the urban problems of drugs, violence, and extreme poverty. With such signals largely contained behind those sheer walls and barred windows, people like Jackie and her siblings could drive wide around them, windows up and doors locked.

Jackie's father, Horace, worked at Linden Assembly, a General Motors plant three towns away. She didn't know what he did exactly, only that his work involved simple mechanical tasks that he performed over and over again, all day, every day. She'd always figured this repetition to be the source of his sternness, his absolute insistence on correct manners and etiquette. To him, life was lived successfully by getting the small things right every time. If he grew lazy on the job, he'd be fired and replaced by someone else who wouldn't, any one of the thousands of workers who could do what he did. Likewise, if Jackie or her siblings forgot to say, "May I please . . . ," when asking for something, they'd be slapped—once, hard—on the back of the head. Days were about doing your chores and schoolwork quietly, keeping questions to a minimum. Nights were about staying out of Horace's way—also quietly, which was harder to do as younger siblings (Jackie was the third of nine) kept being born every two to three years. That house came to feel quite small indeed once three people inhabited each bedroom. As the number of bodies increased, so, too, did the financial and physical strain, shared by all except the very youngest, of keeping everyone fed.

Jackie knew from a young age that she didn't want a big family. As a girl, in church and school lessons, she was taught that Love was a boundless and ever-expanding entity. As she grew into her teens and found herself increasingly responsible for taking care of a generation of children she hadn't herself conceived, she learned that there were limitations even to Love. She understood those limitations definitively: her mother out for milk, her father working a second job, her two older siblings gone with friends, and fifteen-year-old Jackie in the living room, tasked with keeping six stir-crazy little brothers and sisters from breaking anything, including their own bones. She didn't have enough Love in her to avoid losing her mind at certain points. And in the back of that mind lay the knowledge that once she'd seen all those children grown and positioned out there in the world, the time would come not long thereafter when she'd be responsible for her parents in their place.

She wanted a family of two children, that was all: two children who would be hers, plus a man capable of fathering and providing for them adequately.

*   *   *

JACKIE HADN'T BEEN told that Carl's friend Skeet might show up, but there he was: not tall but barrel-chested and dark-eyed with a particular coil-like hunch in his posture, the kind of man whose presence was noted by all patrons when he walked into a bar—all except Jackie, even as Skeet approached her directly. She was well accustomed to eluding these sorts, men who relished playing the heavy.

The year was 1979, and Jackie was thirty years old. She'd lost her job at a soul food restaurant on South Orange Avenue, which meant that she'd moved back into her parents' house from the East Orange apartment she'd been sharing with two high school girlfriends. Carl, a friend of the family who had more or less grown up at 181 Chapman Street, felt sorry for her, as she had neither a man nor a baby and was no doubt hearing about it from her mother all the time. Still, Jackie hadn't been leaving the house much lately. Carl considered that a shame, because she was a striking woman with small but intense eyes, a tall brow, an angular chin, thin lips, and short hair (she refused to spend money on a weave) that cumulatively projected an immovable conviction. Carl, when they hung out, got a kick out of the way men would approach her over younger, more classically attractive, easier women; these men seemed drawn to the challenge that Jackie's countenance most surely offered. Jackie was fun, too, and he'd convinced her to meet him at Passion Sports Bar & Café in the Grove Terrace section of Vailsburg, just west of downtown Newark, a conveniently located stopover for the mostly black workers commuting home at the end of the factory shifts. For many, these stop-overs could very easily become all-nighters, and the room grew rowdy around nine or ten o'clock, which was when Jackie and Carl found themselves at the bar, talking about work, money, friends, and how to get her out of the house on Chapman Street.

Carl had met Robert "Skeet" Douglas a few months earlier on a factory demolition job, both grunt laborers who manually cleared the debris too fine for the diggers. They'd gotten along well—Carl was quiet and reserved while Skeet was a witty leader of men. Their acquaintance had led to a loose partnership hustling cocaine. "Making movements," Skeet called what they did, nothing major or particularly dangerous in the great scheme.

At the bar, Skeet eyed Jackie and smiled disarmingly. She ignored him; there were plenty of girls at the bar who would be susceptible to his clearly well-honed charm, girls who didn't know any better. She said she had to get home to make sure her youngest brother had finished his schoolwork.

"What's the assignment?" Skeet asked.

Jackie replied that it was a biography of Frederick Douglass. Skeet proceeded to lay out, from memory, all the key moments and dates of Frederick Douglass's life. The smooth talk vanished as he explained, humbly, that he'd always had a knack for remembering things.

Jackie let him give her a ride home. He happened to live on Pierson

Street, just two blocks north of Chapman. She listened to more biographies on the way; anyone she could name, he knew his or her story. Of his own story, however, she didn't learn much that night, or any of the nights that followed.

*   *   *

"YOU SPOIL THAT child."

Jackie heard these words from everyone. She heard them during her four-week maternity leave from St. Mary's Hospital (in addition to having given birth there, she worked in the basement kitchen), and she heard them after she went back to work. She heard them from her parents, from her siblings, from her friends, and most often from Skeet. "You never put him down. Whenever he wants something, you give it to him. He sleeps in the bed with you!" Skeet would say, not angry but incredulous in a way that only Skeet could get. "Now I see why you won't marry me, because you're married to a six-month-old—"

"There's nothing bad about him feeling safe."

"There's something real bad about him getting everything he wants when he wants it. The boy's never had to struggle for anything in his life."

"If I have my say, he never will."

She talked back to Skeet, and that was one of the reasons he liked her. She didn't know as many facts as he did, and so didn't have the capacity to rebut arguments as he took such pleasure in doing. But she could often shut him up with just a few words, Jackie's basic confidence in her own sense trumping all of Skeet's verbal tricks and back doors. She never let him talk her in circles like he did with Carl; she never let him be right when he was wrong.

The stance that most flummoxed the man was her refusal to marry him, because of the precise and intractable way she'd thought it through. Her older sister Camilla had gotten pregnant at nineteen, married the father, and had the baby. Two years later, the father was gone but the baby remained. Her best friend, Janice, had done the same thing, as had so many others. Jackie believed it wasn't the baby that drove a man to abandonment; she'd observed the bond between a father and his child and knew it to be a true and powerful force. In her estimation, the union of marriage was what ultimately severed the union of family: the arguments over housing and money and time, the ribbing by unfettered friends, the inexorable waning of years and freedom. Men were aggressive creatures by nature, she believed, and as strongly and skillfully as they could push for immediate satisfactions such as lovemaking, they could just as strongly (though less skillfully) push past any obstacles they saw as being in the way of those immediacies.

The baby had not been accidental. She was thirty-one and he was thirty-four; she was strong and he was smart; each enjoyed the other more than anyone else in their orbit; they challenged one another in a positive way; they both had incomes; they were ready. But she'd been clear from the start that she wasn't going to marry him. Knowing that he trafficked in drugs—and intentionally not knowing to what extent, where, or with whom besides Carl—she refused even to move into his home on Pierson Street, which, like Jackie's home, had been in his family for decades. But she still, two years and one child later, couldn't make him see that her decision was for his own good. He could live his life, and all he had to do was help provide, spare what time he could, and treat them well when he was around. She wanted him to expend whatever doting instinct he possessed on the baby, not on her. Of course, this orchestration wasn't entirely selfless. She had her own freedom to consider, too. Before Rob was born, she thought this would mean going out and meeting new people on her own terms, without the curfew of a possessive husband or the baggage of having been abandoned by one. However, the moment she first held her son that fantasy evaporated and a freedom of a different kind coalesced in its place: the freedom to raise her child the way she, and only she, desired. Jackie hadn't been out socially since the birth, and she had no inclination to do so.

People looked down on her with pity and even with scorn for this fundamental, atypical decision. She could bear their opinions, some of which were silent, some not. She had a baby boy, and she never saw a trace of pity or scorn in his eyes.

*　　*　　*

NEWARK AND THE Oranges were not the places Jackie had known as a child. During the 1970s—her twenties—she'd been vaguely aware of the things people talked about when they talked about Newark. There were the riots of July 1967, incited by the alleged brutality inflicted on a black cabdriver by white policemen: five days of burning, looting, sniper fire, and rage, at the end of which twenty-six people were dead, more than seven hundred were injured, fifteen hundred were arrested, and the texture of the city was forever changed. On one of those nights, Jackie and her girlfriends had ventured toward the city; they'd wanted to see for themselves what was going on, like a party they would regret missing (they'd been turned away by National Guardsmen at a checkpoint). There was also much talk about how the communities were no longer defined by the factories where people worked or the countries from which their grandparents had come seeking that work. Instead, they were increasingly defined by skin color: black, brown, or white. But very little of this talk had happened at her own dinner table, where Horace had presided from the contained space his soul inhabited. She'd seen teenagers throwing stones at squad cars and then fence hopping through the backyards of Chapman Street. She'd seen white-black fistfights break out in broad daylight on busy streets, and she'd stepped over the gore of teeth and bloody gum tissue left on the sidewalk in their wake. The men her girlfriends dated were too often angry and muttering about oppression. One of the reasons she took to Skeet later in life was that he never went to that place; he believed with a firm positivity that he didn't need to waste time resenting real or imagined social constructs because he would always be ahead of them. The individual, not the people, was responsible for success or failure. Skeet aimed to succeed.

After the riots came the phenomenon of white flight, which wasn't discussed—not yet—but was observed when she rode the bus to her first job after high school, working in the mail room of Orange City Hall: FOR SALE signs, three and four to a block. In 1973, the western spur of the I-280 was completed, a freeway that channeled beneath the Oranges (just four blocks north of Chapman Street), connecting downtown Newark to suburban enclaves in Morris County and the Watchung Mountains. Transits that had previously taken more than an hour on surface thoroughfares like Central Avenue now took fifteen minutes. In the wake of the racial tensions that had erupted with the riots six years earlier—and that hadn't ebbed much since—this highway provided a corridor by which people who felt threatened or simply uncomfortable near the city's impoverished alignments could coast through them at sixty miles per hour.

One thing her father did talk about, contemptuously, was the crooked real estate market, specifically realtors who profited off the civic unrest by convincing white homeowners that, once one black family moved onto the block, more would follow, and their home's value would only decline if they remained. Jackie did in fact notice—more as a feeling than an empirical observation—that neighborhoods like Vailsburg, Irvington, and East Orange were becoming "blacker": house by house, block by block, moving west from downtown Newark over the span of decades. In 1960, when Jackie's family had moved from Elizabeth, the population of East Orange was 39 percent black and 53 percent white. In 1980, when Rob was born, the population was 89 percent black and 4 percent white, and the area was known colloquially as "Illtown." But as a young woman existing in the day-to-day, Jackie didn't concern herself too much with demographic shifts; she was simply happy to have a job when she could find it, to help pay for fun when she could have it.

Her father, too, was happy to have a job still, because the city's factories were concurrently shutting down in great swaths. All across America but particularly in port cities like Newark, St. Louis, and Chicago, improved transportation capacities caused manufacturing companies to gravitate toward cost-efficient real estate far from urban centers. Japan and China became major exporters of cheaper goods. American companies outsourced jobs to foreign labor. The service economy of the United States grew steadily while the industrial economy tapered and then, beginning in the late '60s, steeply declined. For these reasons and many others, the factories closed, one by one, and the closures came with massive layoffs. Tanneries, glass, plastics, industrial machine parts—over six hundred factories in and around the city, which had made the port of Newark the busiest in the nation for decades, shut down between 1970 and 1980. With public housing already at capacity and unemployment rising steadily, the dangerous side of urban culture began to spill down and outward from the project towers into the spaces left vacant by the fleeing working class: across the wards in the north and west of Newark, and then still farther, into East Orange and, ultimately, past it.

The Peace home lay just over the boundary separating Orange from the traditionally more dangerous East Orange. A half mile west sprawled the affluent neighborhoods like Tuxedo Park and the Seton Hall campus that still made Orange, on paper, a far more diverse and desirable place to live. Because of the technical remove of her address—because Orange was not generally associated with the slums to the east—Jackie couldn't have imagined while growing up that the ethnic grocers on Central Avenue might one day be replaced by liquor stores and check-cashing centers, or that any of the houses on Chapman Street would be abandoned and boarded up, or that the crack of proximate gunfire could interrupt their dinner table talk. But the blight did come, inexorably overtaking Chapman Street, South Essex Avenue, and Lincoln Avenue before the suburbs west of Scotland Road formed the retaining wall that town lines drawn up in City Hall could not. This tide progressed slowly throughout the 1970s, and by the time it was complete, its effects had been sewn into the neighborhood's fabric almost as a given. At any rate, Jackie's physical life had always been based primarily in East Orange, where her friends lived, where she worked and shopped and felt comfortable, and where Skeet Douglas conducted his business. So, too, was Rob's.

During Rob's early childhood, East Orange represented the second-highest concentration of African Americans living below the poverty line in America, behind East St. Louis. The violent crime rate of thirty-five hundred per one hundred thousand people was almost six times the national average of six hundred, and eight times that of adjacent South Orange, which stood at four hundred. The figure meant that any given person in East Orange had roughly a one-in-thirty chance of being violently robbed, assaulted, raped, or killed in any given year; an equivalent person in South Orange, half a mile away, had less than a one-in–two hundred chance of experiencing the same. Horace held his job, though, and the family remained in the house, as they always had, keeping it open to anyone in the family who needed shelter.

Around this time, a resident of the North Ward coined what would become Newark's informal nickname: "Brick City." Depending on whom you asked, the moniker referred to the hardness and resiliency of its people, the bricks that paved many of the older streets downtown, or the easy availability of brick-shaped packages of crack cocaine.

*   *   *

SKEET PLEADED WITH her to stop working, move in with him, let him support her even if she wouldn't let him marry her.

"I'm not moving to your house," she told him.

"Why not?"

"You know exactly."

He looked at her as if she were the most cynical person on earth. "You think I'd ever put my son in danger? Or my woman?"

The kitchen job at St. Mary's was the first in which she earned an annual rather than an hourly wage. The wage still amounted to the national minimum of $3.10 an hour: a little more than $6,000 a year. The work itself was awful, mixing industrial quantities of low-grade animal products into stews ingestible by straw, portioning out endless lumps of

Jell-O onto paper plates from huge vats of it, boiling vegetables to paste. Yet the pride lay in knowing that when she left work, work would still be there tomorrow, and that she'd receive a check on the first and fifteenth of each month. The hospital had a program through which, when the time was right, she could opt to attend night school for a management degree, qualifying her to supervise a kitchen. She'd worked in the cafeteria at Orange High School for credits, so a career in food service represented something like a linear trajectory, more than what many of her friends who ricocheted from job to job had. The money was important, but not as important as the ownership of her life apart from the other lives with which hers was entangled. Fundamental to that ownership was not becoming dependent on a man who dealt drugs, even if she loved that man. Jackie and Rob remained on Chapman Street.

In that house, Rob read. Rather, Jackie read to him, but she felt as if he were reading along with her. With the opening of a book, a shift occurred in his eyes and he nestled an inch deeper into her lap while angling his chin upward, and he seemed to age a year or two. Not a reader herself, Jackie went to the local library for the first time and pulled the popular titles: the Berenstain Bears, Richard Scarry wordbooks, Dr. Seuss, Eric Carle. At a year, he began pointing his index finger at words as she spoke them. At two, he was memorizing simple sentences after he'd heard them once. Always he was entranced by the pictures, the successive turning of pages, the rhythm of his mother's voice. With her job, housing situation, and relationship status, Jackie could sometimes feel as if she had no right to have borne a child. But during those hours, she was meant to be a mother.

Skeet, once he caught wind of the reading obsession, was righteously opposed. In his estimation, a toddler who spent all his time sitting in his mother's lap immersed in fairy tales wasn't getting any better prepared for life. A child, especially a boy, needed to be out and about, around real people, growing skin. "He can do all that when he's with you," Jackie replied. "Me, I'm reading to him." Skeet picked Rob up from day care on the days he wasn't working. He tended to avoid spending time on

Chapman Street, where he often clashed with Horace and Frances—despite or maybe because of his gregariousness, they were suspicious of him, and they also seemed to blame him for the no-marriage clause. Instead, he'd drive Rob around town to show off his son to various friends. These regular rounds were never drug related; he knew better than that. Skeet simply loved people—talking with them, eating with them, helping them fix things—and it wasn't uncommon for him to eat six separate lunches over the course of an afternoon. He wanted to instill that sociability in his son; he believed that being curious about people was one of the few crucial life skills that could be fully nurtured in a place like East Orange.

Jackie's hypothesis regarding fathers and sons had proved correct: the boy had a powerful connection with his father, and Skeet was generous with his time and money. But what she hadn't accounted for was the fact that, by the architecture of her design, the three of them were rarely together. Rob was at day care, or with her and her family, or with Skeet. And so the mannerisms he picked up from each of them appeared abruptly, often abrasively, to the other. The toddler's mind had incredible suction, as his father's did. When he spontaneously recited *Go, Dog. Go!* rhymes in Skeet's car, his father came back to Jackie wondering loudly why his son's head was being saturated by stories involving canines picnicking in tree canopies (dogs around here were often fierce creatures bred for their aggressiveness, not to be treated so lightly). When Jackie put Rob to bed with a book and heard him instead singing himself to sleep with Grandmaster Flash and the Fabulous Five lyrics, she winced. Skeet saw his three-year-old son being bullied on the playground, timid around older people, quiet when other boys were loud; Jackie saw the same son pushing another child at day-care drop-off and grabbing his toy truck.

Like any two parents, they fought. These fights happened mostly on the Chapman Street front porch at night, sitting in the plastic chairs that were chained to the wooden railing, Skeet's cigarette making loops of smoke as he waved his hands around. The neighborhood became

desolate after dark, aside from a few clusters of young men passing periodically, smoking and murmuring. Some of them would offer nods
of recognition to Skeet, a telepathy between men from which Jackie
was glad to be excluded. Jackie's and Skeet's voices would echo off the
cracked sidewalk. She didn't care if these street thugs or neighbors or
her family could hear, so long as Rob, asleep upstairs in their room,
could not. They concentrated on the particulars, the minute details of
books and music and diction and schools. Deeper in their hearts, they
were debating what kind of man they wanted their son to be.

*   *   *

"THE PROFESSOR'S RIGHT over there." The day-care lady pointed to a
set of building blocks, over which Rob, now three years old, crouched
intently.

"The Professor?" Jackie replied.

"You didn't know we called him that?"

Jackie thought she—or, worse, her son—was being made fun of
somehow and began searching for a cutting rejoinder while mentally
mapping out the second-nearest day care.

"It's because he's so smart and he knows everything."

Jackie looked up and saw that the woman was actually serious—that
she called Rob Peace "Professor" in an earnest reference to his intellect.

Professor, she thought to herself. *My boy, the Professor.*

Humbly, she figured that the moniker came simply because Rob
talked so much. He could make her own brain go lumpy with the constant stream of comments and questions. More than any other child
she'd ever cared for, he asked, "Why?" And maybe she was projecting
this, because he was her own, but she felt that he did so not out of reflex
but out of a genuine desire to understand their world and the people
who inhabited it.

On weekends when it was warm, she'd take him to Orange Park
by herself: a blanket, some canned pears and ham, a precious few lazy
hours between the night shifts and backaches of the six-day workweek.

For many years now, the park had been owned by the dealers, and more so as the progression of the 1980s brought crack to the neighborhood. Men—and sometimes women, sometimes boys—sat on picnic tables in groups of two, their feet planted on the benches beside malt liquor in brown bags. Their talk was generally cheerful, and they were un-assuming enough until their patrons approached and a certain gravity fell over the ensuing transaction. The executive of this enterprise was named Day-Day. He was a smooth-faced man in his midthirties, Jackie's age, and he was always on his feet traversing the diagonal footpaths. He never interacted with the dealers, but he was always watching. If you didn't know him, he looked like a guy strolling in the park for exercise and peace of mind. But everyone knew him. Jackie figured he must walk fifteen miles a day within those few acres of city land. He knew Skeet and always paused by their blanket to comment on how Rob looked more like his father each day. On Sundays, he moved his salesmen to the south side of the park and gifted the north side, where the play-ground was, to parents and children.

The playground equipment was splintered, held together loosely by rusty protruding nails. Bits of glass from crack pipes and vials were em-bedded in the dirt beneath the swing set. The park was a highly secure place for people to do drugs after dark, more secure even than homes and apartments. The police didn't make regular patrols because they were too busy answering 911 calls. Policemen were more likely to enter a user's building during the night, answering a domestic abuse call from down the hallway, than they were to make a pass through the Orange Park playground.

Jackie and Rob would eat their snacks on the blanket (never on park benches, because stupefied addicts peed themselves on them), and she'd follow him closely over the jungle gym while her eyes searched always for nails or glass or older, rougher children who had no business on a toddler playground, anything that posed a threat to her boy.

*   *   *

JACKIE ENTERED THE house to raised voices, one of them her four-year-old son's. She walked into the kitchen where Rob and her younger sister Debbie stood on opposite sides of a pool of milk and an empty, upturned carton. He'd spilled it; Debbie was demanding that he clean it up and, once Jackie appeared, that she go buy more. Rob's arms were crossed, his eyes wild. His logic for refusal was that someone had carelessly left the carton open and with the bottom hanging a third of the way over the shelf edge. *That* person should clean it up and buy more. That person was clearly Debbie, judging by her defensiveness. Jackie told her son, not gently, to clean the mess, and he did—huffing and muttering to himself with the fury of the wronged.

"It's just not right," Debbie said, "that in a house with this many people, you've fixed it so you're the only one he listens to."

Too many people were spread across too many years in the house on Chapman Street, and the result was friction. Jackie and most of her siblings were blunt and to the point, like their father. The house could be a chorus of minor discontentments and accusations that became further compacted when Horace took on tenants on the third floor. Because the neighborhood was increasingly unsafe, everyone stayed in the house most of the time, pent up with no energy outlets but to go at one another. Solitude, silence, stillness—these commodities were nearly impossible to find.

Jackie wanted to move, particularly once Rob grew old enough to engage in arguments himself, something he did with particular tenacity. She experienced a spiritual erosion when watching her four-year-old scrap his way indignantly through an argument with an equally indignant adult, and do so with increasing tactical skill. The aggravated environment was no place to nurture qualities like reason and sensitivity. She had the money to move, barely, but nowhere comfortable and nowhere permanent. Renting an apartment in East Orange, the only neighborhood she could afford, was a massive and insecure endeavor. First came the actual search, which meant riding unfamiliar bus lines through neighborhoods that changed from livable to dangerous to mortally dangerous quickly and with no defined boundaries between—a street sign, a dogwood tree, an unthreatening housefront containing a drug den within. Then came the taut negotiations with landlords who were always ultraskeptical because they'd been had so many times before, the rules and restrictions and deposit she'd never see again regardless. Then came the maintenance issues, the expenses of furniture and fixes, the fighting neighbors, the cronies of prior tenants knocking on the door in the middle of the night. And above all, the constant wondering—the fear—of her job going away. Jackie had been through it all a few times before and each attempt had ended with her back home.

And now Rob was about to turn five. She was thinking about elementary school, determined to send her son to a private school. That cost money—not much, but "not much" was relative. She knew that the security required to afford tuition would be a stretch to maintain anywhere else except on Chapman Street.

Skeet tried to make the extraction easier for her by renting an apartment on Chestnut Street, a few blocks from the house on Pierson. His plan was to conduct his business from the apartment and leave the house free and safe for his family. Jackie remained reluctant. She knew that in the deeply layered world of drugs, the nexus of commerce was the person, not the place. And, in the very possible event that Skeet was arrested and sentenced to a few months or years in jail, she had no interest in being knotted to any property bearing his name.

"Look at me," he told her. "I'm thirty-eight years old. Nothing's ever happened to me, and nothing's ever going to. I'm cool." And Skeet was cool about his involvement with the drug trade, as far as she could see.

Jackie didn't like to talk about or even reference obliquely the drugs that Skeet sold. She had never gravitated toward the dealers in high school or the years after, the way many women around her had, enticed by the gifts of coats and jewelry, the bravado and relentless charm, the respect these men commanded from their peers. However, Skeet wasn't like the other dealers. He never flaunted the money he made—which didn't seem like all that much, just enough to even out the math between work paying x and life costing y. He drove a boxy Volvo that had constant problems. He had jobs during the day—nothing permanent, but there was always something; the man wasn't lazy. His friends were for the most part people from childhood, decent-seeming men who'd stayed around and paid attention to their mothers if not always their children. He coached a youth basketball team. He was always casual, never anxious. Most important to him in terms of safety, he didn't try to run with or compete against the younger generation of hustlers, with their codes and protocols always evolving toward brutality. "I got too much respect for human life to mess with all them young 'uns," he assured her. "I stay the hell out of their way." Skeet was loud and sometimes arrogant about his own intelligence and prospects, but he was quiet and conservative about drugs.

What made Jackie wary was the huge extent to which Rob's father was known. To her, it seemed as though everyone living in the three square miles of East Orange—all fifty thousand people—knew Skeet Douglas. Wherever they went out, she heard the constant hoots and waves and incantations of "You call me now!" He told her that this was just the kind of person he was—friendly, with a lot of friends. Jackie knew that friends and friendliness weren't always directly related. Skeet had a huge smile, a beautiful smile, and he bent the truth very well from behind it.

She didn't have to make a final decision on his offer, because the house on Pierson Street burned down. She never found out why. Skeet hadn't called her for a week—rare even for him. She needed to figure out the day-care pickup situation for the month to come, and so she went to the Pierson Street house after work, ready for a fight. The smell of combusted carbon still hung in the air a week after the fire. Skeet was sitting on the front step, hunched over, talking to an elderly acquaintance from the block, his expression one she'd rarely seen on him before: resigned, tired, damned. The house was completely gutted, just an assortment of heavy beams scarred black and ashy objects that had once been furniture. He muttered something about faulty wiring, and she got out of his way.

And the house on Pierson Street just stayed like that, a torched shell, while Skeet moved into his rented apartment on Chestnut Street but continued to pay the property taxes on the now-useless plot of land.

*   *   *

OAKDALE ELEMENTARY SCHOOL was on Lincoln Avenue, just a few blocks west. Redbrick, two stories, with a footprint in the shape of the Chevrolet logo, the local public school looked like a nice enough place to send a six-year-old. When Jackie's younger siblings had gone there, it had been. When Rob began kindergarten, it was no longer. The school's decline wasn't immediately evident. The interiors were generally well maintained, the curriculum in keeping with federal guidelines, the other kids more or less what they were: kids, just barely past toddlerhood. Jackie would walk Rob there and watch him join the stream of children his age going inside with backpacks and lunches, usually turning at the door to wave. But she observed something less tangible in the expressions and movements of the teachers, the laissez-faire attitudes of fellow parents. Most of these children, Jackie felt, were being sent here to be watched for a few hours, not to be taught.

She had gently floated the idea of private school past her parents, and they'd both shaken their heads. He's six, they told her. He's not reading Shakespeare. He's not learning cutting-edge chemistry. Kindergarten was about being with people his age and maybe picking up some simple letters and arithmetic. Paying significant money for an elementary education was silly, considering what she earned. They told her to spend her income on feeding, clothing, and sheltering him. Education was what they all paid taxes for—a whole lot of taxes in this state.

Still, she talked to Skeet about it. Catholic schools, the cheapest of the private options, generally cost $200 a month. If they split it, then Jackie would be paying only a quarter of her own salary toward education: manageable if not ideal. Skeet looked at her and said she was being "uppity." Though he was speaking off-the-cuff, the word carried weight. Where they lived, being known by this label meant that you thought you were better than everyone else around you, that you deserved more, and that—given the opportunity—you would leave this place behind without a second thought. There was shame in thinking like that. Jackie didn't understand what the term had to do with her wanting the best education they could afford for their son, but Skeet had deployed it at just the right moment to make her second-guess.

So Rob went to Oakdale, where by Skeet's reckoning he would learn how to stop being a mama's boy and become a man respected, listened to, and followed by other men. This was more important than humanities and sciences.

The transition to school brought another transition—Skeet began buying Rob things, mostly clothes and music. Jackie resented these purchases heavily, especially coming from a man who refused to pay $100 a month for school, but she stayed quiet about it, which was hard for her to do. The rap group N.W.A. was the worst, with songs like "One Less Bitch" and "Fuck tha Police" that contained not even a nod toward grammatical consistency let alone morality. Skeet worked out in a boxing gym on Halsted Street a few times a week, and a punching dummy soon appeared in the corner of the room she still shared with the boy, a bottom-heavy rubber bowling pin featuring a cartoon white man with a handlebar mustache that righted itself regardless of the force with which it was knocked over. Like a salty manager, Skeet worked with the boy intensely. He taught Rob to swing his arms laterally from wide angles, so that a fist to the temple could be followed by an elbow to the chin.

"Elbows, elbows, elbows," he would chant. "No one ever sees them coming."

It was okay, Jackie told herself in spite of all the ragging she'd endured for spoiling the boy herself. It was okay because there was no denying, or interfering with, the degree to which the son worshipped the father, a kind of worship she hadn't anticipated. Skeet wasn't the type to understand an infant or toddler; he didn't possess the physical and emotional patience required by the very young. As such, the rhythm of Rob's first four years had been mother heavy, with Skeet present to a degree slightly beyond what might be expected. But all of a sudden, to Skeet, the child became a human being who could process situations, who formed opinions about people, who had muscles growing beneath the skin of his chest and back and arms. He looked like his father, too, with the overhang of his brow giving his eyes a hard, caged expression even at rest.

Whenever his father was due to pick him up, Rob waited in the parlor just to the right of the front door. Jackie didn't let him peer out of the glass, which was always shrouded by three layers of curtains to preclude even a sliver of visibility from the street. All the windows on Chapman Street were treated like this to prevent any canvassing by potential burglars; the crack addicts who squatted in the abandoned apartments on Chapman and Center would take anything. But the moment Skeet's Volvo choked around the corner and his footsteps shook the front porch, Rob stood, beamed, and his breaths grew short with anticipation. When his father appeared in the doorframe, Rob would run and drive his shoulders into the powerful man's thighs. Then Skeet would bend over and grab the boy's legs and somersault him upward until Rob was over his shoulders, arms around his neck, and the boy would piggyback on his father upstairs. Then they'd work the punching bag for a half hour, and Skeet would take him out around town. When Jackie got her son back in the evenings—always before nightfall, a steadfast rule—Rob would be talking about the four or five people they'd gone to visit. He gave little in the way of details, not because he couldn't remember but because he seemed to relish these adventures, these characters, shared only with his father. The boy kept them close to the vest, the hours he spent with other men.

* * *

ONE WEEKDAY MORNING in the spring of his first school year, Rob wouldn't get out of bed. He moaned about an aching stomach. He had no temperature, so Jackie was skeptical. But she was also tired and late for work, so she made sure Frances would be around to watch him.

As Jackie opened the front door to leave, she heard him call. Reluctantly, she went upstairs.

"What?" she asked. "You want soup?"

"Your son's sick and you're going to work?" he asked, the question an accusation.

"I don't get personal days."

"Whatever," he mumbled and turned away from her.

She stayed home. As the day progressed, he began writhing and crying, the hardness cultivated under his father's watch slowly crumbling beneath the physical pain. Though Frances told her she was making a fuss over a faker and thus encouraging these manipulations, Jackie took him to the hospital in the late afternoon. After three hours in the ER waiting room—standard, even though she was employed there—she finally harassed their way into an examination room.

His appendix was swelling fast. Late that night, it was removed. The doctor said it could have ruptured at any moment, and Jackie might have saved her son's life that day by not doubting him.

*   *   *

JACKIE KNEW SKEET better than he knew himself. And so she knew that no matter how authentically he presented himself as the tough guy—acidly cutting down the concept of private school, instructing the boy on dirty lyrics and dirtier fistfight tricks, driving Rob around East Orange while giving coded shout-outs to the hustlers—Skeet valued intelligence above all, and the early manifestations of Rob's intellect (picture books notwithstanding) excited him truly. The image became regular and nourishing: father and son crouched over second-grade homework assignments splayed across the coffee table, going back and forth over simple sentence structure and arithmetic. The same intensity with which Skeet could battle her he brought to that coffee table three or four evenings a week.

Skeet harped on particulars that Jackie, in her own childhood, had never even considered: penmanship, consistency of format, and above all, the importance of memory. With an old wisdom in his attention to detail, Skeet would drill Rob heavily on vocabulary, definitions, states and capitals, until the facts became embedded in the cerebral circuitry. She could not believe how patient and tireless they could be, the father and the son, both with the work and one another. She would pretend to be cleaning in an adjacent space, but really she'd watch Skeet as he watched Rob set his lips and point his eyes upward to ponder some elusive connection. And their son—sometimes prompted but usually not—would invariably make that connection. Skeet would grin and squeeze the back of the boy's neck in his hand, then look at the subsequent entry to make sure the handwriting was clean. These quiet, unassuming moments, embedded as they were within her harried days, gave her not only pride but also a simple beauty she'd always sought but never known—made more powerful by the fact that she participated only as an observer. Something positive could happen without her wrangling it through sheer force of will, and it could be shared within the trinity of mother, father, and son.

*   *   *

IN THE SHADED rear compartments of her mind, Jackie had always expected the call to come in the middle of the night, when it would jar her awake from the pleasant seclusion of dreaming.

When the call did come, on August 9, 1987, she was at work, just before the lunch surge on a Sunday. Frances told her anxiously that the police were looking for Skeet. They hadn't said why.

"What'd you tell them?" Jackie asked.

"I said I don't know where he lives or anything about that man."

Jackie asked her to pick up Rob from summer camp at Branch Brook Park, since Skeet now wouldn't be able to.

She kept working, eyes and ears in a heightened state of alertness as she waited for men in uniforms to arrive and pull her aside in front of her coworkers. She thought mainly of what excuse she could give to her boss. After that, she thought about money and time. One of the maintenance staff had a record for dealing; it was all she could do not to ask him about the particulars of a man's being arrested for selling drugs. How much was bail? How much was a lawyer? What was the average sentence? But the police never came, nor did they call. In this moment, more than any other that had come before, she was thankful for the domestic arrangement she'd wrought. Because she didn't share Skeet's name or address, she would be free to manage the consequences this event would have on her and her son's future.

She went home that evening and assumed Skeet's role with home-work; the summer camp assigned short exercises to keep the children busy. She was relieved that Rob, who had turned seven two months ear-lier, didn't ask her why. Jackie was less patient than Skeet when it came to addition and subtraction problems and subject-predicate structure. She did her best, though, and only when Rob fell asleep did she start calling around, starting with Carl.

"When they find him, how long's he going to be away for?" she asked.

"They found him already. He was at Irving's house."

"How long? How long for dealing?"

Carl paused, the silence a reply. Then he told her that Skeet hadn't been arrested for drugs. He'd been arrested for murder. Two, in fact—both young women, neighbors of his in that apartment building on Chestnut Street.

Chapter 2

———————◆———————

FIVE DAYS AFTER Skeet's arrest and three days after his arraignment hearing, Jackie went to Essex County Jail for the first time. She went alone. The jail was a two-story, blue-and-white modular structure made of cinder blocks, surrounded by two concentric rectangles of ten-foot-high chain-link fences. Sandwiched between the Passaic River and the New Jersey Turnpike, the atmosphere smelled of toxic, unfamiliar elements due to the General Chemical plant directly across Doremus Avenue, a towering cistern of polyaluminum hydroxychloride used in wastewater treatment.

Passing through checkpoint after checkpoint—and asked at each what her relationship was to the prisoner, to which she replied succinctly, "He's my son's father"—she felt herself racking up distance from the outside world. She knew only as much as Carl did, which was hardly anything. Her lone hope, aside from the whole situation turning out to be a wrong place–wrong time misunderstanding, was that it would be resolved quickly. She knew that this impulse was selfish; she was thinking about the adjustments she'd have to make to get on with her life. She still hadn't told Rob. That a week had passed without her son seeing his father was uncommon but not truly strange. The boy hadn't asked, but she knew he was attuned to the anxiety coursing through the house on Chapman Street; she knew that the question was coming.

A guard escorted her down a hallway, past the reception room for prisoners held here on lesser offenses, who were allowed to sit in open air across a table from their friends and family. Jackie was led to a narrow room with concrete walls, tight cubicles, low stools, guards stationed on either side of the Plexiglas partitions. Knowing that her son would ultimately come here to visit, she'd hoped the place would be less than completely grim. It wasn't. A buzzer sounded, the steel-reinforced door across from her opened, and Skeet entered wearing bright orange, with his wrists manacled together and palms facing toward her.

She hadn't expected him to be smiling, but the fact that he wasn't jarred her nevertheless. Even during the worst of their arguments over the years, Skeet had been able to grin his way through any conflict. He seemed curiously energized, but the energy was an uncomfortable one: fidgety, pent, his eyes darting everywhere except into her own.

They had fifteen minutes. He asked her if she could find him a lawyer to handle the bail situation and get him out of here quickly. At the arraignment hearing, bail had been set at $500,000. That amount had to be lowered if he were to get out, plan his defense, talk to some people, and see his son.

He didn't seem to comprehend yet that his charge could not be evaded through guile and charm. She wanted to tell him this, tell him that people—*two young women*—were dead, and he might very well be sentenced to pay for their lives with his own. Instead, she said she didn't know any lawyers and didn't have the money for one anyway. She spoke clearly and directly, leaving no room for Skeetesque rebuttals. The maintenance man at Jackie's workplace had told her in the intervening days about lawyers and the hours they billed. This was a capital case. Good lawyers would be beyond unaffordable; bad lawyers would be ill equipped for the task. And even the cheapest lawyer around would find a way to bill five figures, minimum. He'd told her that contacting the public defender's office might be the best option. Skeet could get lucky by being assigned one who truly became invested in the client. Not likely, but possible.

She tried as hard as she could to look at him and not see a man who had killed others, to commit herself to the idea of innocent until proven guilty.

"How's our boy?" Skeet asked.

"He's good," she replied. Soon their allotted minutes were up, too few for him, too many for her.

*　　*　　*

THE MURDER VICTIMS, sisters Charlene and Estella Moore, had been in their twenties. Charlene's infant son had been in the apartment, along with a third woman who had been shot in the face and arm but survived. (Jackie's underlying hope was that this woman had witnessed the violence and would clear Skeet's name; she didn't know yet that the survivor, Georgianna Broadway, had identified Skeet as the murderer in the hours following the shootings.) Jackie couldn't help visualizing the scene. She had no context, and so, while lying wide awake in the middle of the night, she would make up scenarios that varied in detail but all shared the same expressions of disbelief or denial among the victims, the same pleas of "Don't" or "Why?" and the same silence that must have settled in the moments after, interrupted by the unharmed and suddenly motherless baby's cries. She would think these thoughts and, when morning came, stare at her own son and hold him tight, to the point where he'd squirm away and say, "Ma, c'mon now." As he'd grown, he'd become less responsive to physical affection in the way boys did once toughness became a desirable quality.

Rob was very tough, and he had been making a name for himself in neighborhood football games on weekends. These games were played in the street, with the lines of parked cars forming sidelines (these sidelines were considered "in play," such that one could be pushed or tripped or outright tackled against one). Rob was neither fast nor agile, but he had broad shoulders with premature muscle mass. He was known to hit low, drive upward from the hips, and flip other boys over his shoulder and onto their backs, knocking the wind out of them on the glass-

littered asphalt, sometimes causing a fumble and always inciting cheers
from onlookers up and down the street—especially when he punctuated
the hit with the words "Patent that!" (He didn't know what a patent was,
but the expression was used among his father's friends when something
clever had been said.) This permissible violence was unique in that it
elicited respect from the victim rather than calls for retribution. Neighbors would watch from second-floor windows, and Rob imagined that
these were the upper decks of the Meadowlands, where the New York
Giants played, and he was Lawrence Taylor, a Giants linebacker so athletic and mean that NFL coaches were currently reinventing their entire
offensive philosophies, not to stop him but simply to slow him down.

East Orange, with congested traffic and little in the way of street
greenery to oxygenate the atmosphere and provide shade, could feel poi-
sonously humid during the late summers. Visible waves of heat clung to
the blacktop. Men walked around bare chested with their shirts hanging
like rags from their low-slung belts. Malt liquor in tall, cold glass bottles
was passed around groups of stoop-sitters, often offered as refreshments
to the boys playing football. A positive energy coursed through the
neighborhood, because up and down and across the grid of residential
city streets, everyone was outside. Plumes of dark smoke that smelled of
seasoned meat rose above the houses from backyard cookouts. Elderly
women opened their front windows wide and sat there all day behind
fans that blew across bowls of ice cubes. Cards, dice, checkers, jacks,
jump rope, hopscotch, craps, step dance–offs, stickball, handball, basketball—one could not turn a corner without encountering a game being
played, often with the elderly cheering on the young, dispensing their
peanut gallery wisdom gained from decades of playing the same games
on the same blocks. Because of all these crowds, it was the safest time of
year, even if one of the least physically comfortable, to be outside. This
was the time of year when Skeet and Rob, wearing matching sleeveless
undershirts, would normally walk from Chapman Street to Taylor gro-
cery, where Skeet bought ice cream for Rob and cigarettes for himself,
and then just keep walking together, farther and farther east, into the

center of East Orange, stopping multiple times on every block to chat with people Skeet had known his whole life as well as people he was meeting for the first time. Skeet was not old but certainly not young, and he enjoyed that temporal in betweenness. He could watch a hoops game from the sidelines and comment on the sloppiness or talent on display with the other retired veterans, or he could take his shirt off and enter the game himself and usually hold his own. Despite the heat, this time of year had always been Skeet's favorite, and so it had always been Rob's, too.

A memory, which must have seemed innocuous at the time but which ultimately Rob would hold close, began with a Yankees game that two strangers were listening to on their stoop as Skeet and Rob walked past. Skeet asked what the score was; it was close. They stopped and listened to a few at bats. Someone else walked past and began chatting and listening, too. Teenagers who lived in the house came outside to convene with their friends. The game remained tight. The crowd of listeners grew, overflowing onto the sidewalk, then the street: middle- and lower-middle-class people who worked and raised families in this neighborhood, whose primary desire was for their children to have better opportunities than they had, and who had long since accepted the fact that, though they represented the majority population of East Orange, their home would always be characterized by the few thugs and dealers whose presence kept them inside on most other evenings like this. The radio's owner kept turning up the volume. Suddenly a glass of lemonade was in Rob's hand; he didn't know who'd put it there. Late afternoon became early evening, and amiable sand-colored light slanted across to the east side of the block and made the houses there momentarily luminous. The temperature dropped, only a couple degrees but just enough. And as the game ended with a Yankees win and the cheers erupted and the back-talking Yankee haters scowled, Rob looked around at the crowd of people that had amassed here together and felt the kind of kinship with his world that his father had always spoken of but that Rob, overprotected as he was, had never before known.

That day had been in August 1986, one year ago. Now, in the middle of August 1987, Rob's football game ended with the side mirror of a car being taken off by someone's shoulder. The boys dispersed quickly, and Rob walked back to Chapman Street. Over the past week, more than a few acquaintances had asked in passing where his father was, and Rob was eager to see him and have a day together like the one that had culminated in the Yankees-themed block party.

Jackie couldn't tell him. Not that day, not the day after, not the day after that. She let her son call the apartment on Chestnut Street and get no answer. She lied and said that Skeet had taken a last-minute trip to see extended family, knowing that every hour that passed increased the likelihood that one of the kids on the street would hear the gossip and take it upon himself to tell Rob that his father was locked up. Lord knew that the concept wasn't exactly new or novel among Rob's peers.

Frances urged her to tell him before the school year started. "Don't put it all on him at once," she said. "Summer's over. Father's locked up. It's too much for a boy his age."

"I know, I know," Jackie replied, and still failed to tell him.

A few days before first grade began, Jackie found him alone in the front living room, past dusk, kneeling on the sofa with his elbows perched on the headrest, pressing his face against the window to peer up and down the block. He crouched in the expectant way he did whenever he knew that Skeet was en route. The ceiling fan creaked and wobbled on high speed above his head. She'd told Rob many times not to situate himself this way. Stray bullets didn't actually concern her, though this was sometimes the reasoning she used. She just didn't want him to become too interested in the daily and nightly rhythms of their block; she didn't want him to know all the loiterers and hustlers by name, the way Skeet always had. She told him to sit back, away from the window, and then she initiated the hardest conversation she'd ever had with her son.

Afterward, she didn't remember what exact words she'd employed to explain what had happened. She'd told him that the crime was murder—

but not how many victims and not that they were women. She'd told him where his father was and that she had no idea how long he would be there. She'd told him that he could visit when he was ready.

The boy nodded throughout and picked at his thick, coarse hair with thumb and index finger, saying less and less as his face tightened into an almost sepulchral mask. Unusual for him, he never asked, "Why?" The question he kept asking instead was, "When is he coming back?"

At that point, Jackie had no idea. All she could say was, "Soon. He'll come back soon."

* * *

TWO ARMS OF the criminal justice system—the county prosecutor's office and the office of the public defender—had already begun moving. As usual, both moved glacially, the former a little less so.

Thomas Lechliter, the Essex County prosecutor assigned to the case, immediately began interviewing the police officers who had first encountered and searched the crime scene and the detectives investigating the murder that had occurred there. He did not need much time to assemble the police department's version of the events that unfolded between the night of Friday, August 7, when Georgianna Broadway, Estella Moore, and Charlene Moore convened at the Moores' apartment for a night of liquor and cocaine, and the morning of Sunday, August 9, when Robert "Skeet" Douglas was arrested in a friend's home near Branch Brook Park, the loaded murder weapon reportedly tucked into his belt.

Late on that Friday night, Georgianna Broadway and her roommate, Deborah Neal, went to visit the Moore sisters at 7 Chestnut Street in East Orange. The four women took turns holding Charlene's four-month-old baby boy, they drank cocktails and malt liquor, they danced and complained about work and men and poverty—until midnight, when Georgianna took Deborah home to the house they shared on Palm Street. Georgianna then proceeded to 17th Avenue in Newark, one of the most dangerous areas of the city, to buy $40 worth of cocaine. She returned to the Moores' apartment at around one fifteen. At that point, Estella left with a man named Mervin Matthews to go drink at a nearby bar. Georgianna and Charlene sat together in the dining area. Georgianna drank Colt 45 malt liquor; Charlene drank rum and Coke. Both smoked cocaine while the baby slept in the crib in the bedroom. Georgianna smoked regularly, and so her highs lasted only fifteen minutes. For four hours, while Charlene nodded off, Georgianna had hit after hit, until $40 had been cooked into her respiratory and nervous systems. The baby cried but fell back to sleep.

When Estella came home with Mervin at five thirty on Saturday morning, Georgianna asked if she could sleep there. She'd been up for twenty-four straight hours that had begun with a full workday. In the bedroom, with the crib at their feet, Georgianna and Charlene curled up together, backs to the door. They slept.

On his way home, Mervin Matthews stopped to buy cigarettes and realized he still had Estella's keys, so he returned to Chestnut Street at six o'clock to return them. He encountered Skeet Douglas standing in front of the entrance of the complex with another man. Mervin knew who Skeet was and assumed that he had interrupted a drug transaction, so he tried to slip past them casually, but Skeet entered the building with him. Skeet's apartment, 2D, stood perpendicular to the sisters in 2E at the end of the hall. The two men went into their respective doors. Estella was still awake, Charlene and Georgianna sleeping, but Mervin stayed only a minute or two. When he left, Skeet joined him again on his way back outside, saying that he was waiting for a pickup to take him to Newark International for an eight o'clock flight to North Carolina, where he had family—though he carried no luggage.

Georgianna woke up at seven thirty, groggy and cotton mouthed and with an angry pulsation in her head, all that pleasure she'd stoked fewer than two hours ago replaced by deep aches and pains. She heard voices down the hallway, probably from the kitchen, a man and a woman. Charlene still slept soundly beside her, the baby asleep in the crib. When Estella came into the bedroom, Georgianna asked her for some food. Estella brought her leftover Chinese from the refrigerator. Georgianna then requested salt. Estella, apparently too distracted by whatever exchange was happening in the kitchen to be annoyed, went and grabbed the salt, which would be Estella Moore's final movement on this earth. She returned to the darkened bedroom with a salt shaker and what Georgianna would later describe as a "scared look."

Then the bedroom door opened. Five shots were fired immediately, in quick succession. Estella fell first, onto the floor, a single bullet embedded in her brain. Charlene, who had rocketed upward out of her sleep, fell next, into mortal repose behind Georgianna, bullet holes in her chest and head. Georgianna felt a kick in her arm and a sharp sting beneath her chin as the bullet ricocheted upward off her humerus bone, and she fell backward off the far side of the bed without ever glimpsing the shooter.

At nine thirty, 911 dispatch received a call from Deborah Neal's home on Palm Street. Georgianna was there with Charlene's baby, wearing Estella's blood-soaked trench coat. The police and an ambulance arrived at the same time, and before Georgianna was taken to University Hospital she told Officer Alfred Rizzolo that "Skeet" shot her in apartment 2E of 7 Chestnut, and there were two dead bodies at the location. None of the responders understood why Georgianna, critically injured, had chosen to drive there on her own, why she hadn't sought a neighbor's help on Chestnut Street, why she hadn't gone straight to East Orange Hospital, less than a block from the building where she'd been wounded.

Three police officers pulled up to the Chestnut Street address at nine forty. They proceeded inside with caution. The doorway to 2E was wide open, and the inner hallway was spackled with blood. They found the bodies in the bedroom, still very warm. They searched the apartment according to protocol and found no weapons, just the remnants of the previous night of drinking and drug use, an infant's playpen, Georgianna's Chinese food barely touched on the bedside table. Because the dispatcher had alerted them to the possible suspect residing in 2D, they moved on—carefully—into Skeet's apartment, the door to which had been ajar when they'd arrived.

In 2D, they found absolute squalor, which the lead officer, Michael Brown, would later liken to that of an unclean, unsupervised child: dirty clothes everywhere, filthy dishes and rotten food, naked lightbulbs, and torn, stained furniture. Since there was no sign of any physical struggle or burglary, they could only assume that this was how the suspect lived day to day. On a table, they found scales, glass bowl pipes, a razor blade and spoons dusted with cocaine residue, a bag of marijuana, a plastic container of cocaine, an empty black gun holster on a chain buried beneath dirty clothes, two black cestuses (fighting gloves weighted with iron studs), and a thick Rolodex.

By now, investigators and medical personnel had begun arriving, including Captain John Armeno and Detective Sergeant Alan Sierchio. Without a warrant, they were permitted only to "look around" the apartment, specifically for weapons. They found no firearms, but Captain Armeno did gravitate toward a conspicuous framed photo lying on its side on a built-in shelf. In the photo, Skeet Douglas wore a bright green tuxedo complete with top hat, and—bizarrely—he was swinging a bejeweled cane. Armeno immediately sent this photo to University Hospital, where Georgianna was lying on a gurney in the emergency room, in critical condition due to shock and blood loss. She had been intubated and couldn't speak. But she remained conscious, and when asked whether she knew the person responsible for the shootings, she nodded. The officer took out the photograph and asked her whether the pictured person was the shooter. She nodded again and began to cry. Later, she would admit that she had never actually seen who pulled the trigger, but she would claim to have recognized Skeet's voice talking to Estella in the kitchen. She'd met Skeet once, a week before the murders, when he'd come over to the sisters' apartment to fix their faulty door.

That same afternoon, Detective Sergeant Sierchio used this exchange to obtain an official search warrant for 2D and access Skeet's Rolodex. A short time later, Frances Peace received the call inquiring as to Skeet's whereabouts, and she relayed this to both Jackie and Carl.

The following day, using information gleaned from Skeet's Rolodex, Detective Sergeant Sierchio and three uniformed officers knocked
on Irving Gaskins's third-floor apartment door. Mr. Gaskins, seventy-
eight years old and a longtime friend of Skeet's family, lived on 13th
Street in Newark proper, a few blocks from Branch Brook Park, where
Rob was currently enrolled in the summer camp. They were admitted
entry by a woman. In the apartment, a group of children played on the
floor. Mr. Gaskins was hooked to an oxygen tank due to a combination of emphysema, diabetes, and heart disease. The suspect, Robert
"Skeet" Douglas, was seated nearby, and after a brief, charged confrontation during which Mr. Gaskins begged the police not to shoot—
because a stray bullet might explode his oxygen tank and harm his
grandchildren—Skeet was put in handcuffs. According to the police
report, the arresting officers found a .38 caliber Taurus Spesco revolver
tucked in Skeet's pants, loaded with six rounds of ammunition, with
five more live rounds in his pocket. In the days following, ballistics
experts would confirm that striations on the bullets removed from the
murdered women's bodies exactly matched those within the flute of
this revolver, and in turn the revolver had unique markings etched
on the outer surface of the barrel that matched the holster found in
Skeet's apartment.

At his desk in the prosecutor's office, Thomas Lechliter reviewed
dozens of transcripts and reports, photographs, and inventory lists,
and he constructed a clear narrative of the murders. As he did so, his
confidence grew that not only would this evidence lead to a conviction, but also that a conviction would represent justice in the world. In
other words, the defendant was guilty. He did not overlook the many
loose ends presented within the story: the single witness who had been
inebriated, strung out, severely overtired, and hungover at the time of
the murders, and who had identified a suspect, by voice only, whom
she had encountered once in her life and never spoken to directly; the
very odd time lapse between when the murder was said to have taken
place—seven thirty—and when Georgianna's roommate had first called

the police two hours later (the warmth of the dead bodies upon police arrival did not help explain that, either); a suspect who, though a known drug dealer, had neither prior convictions nor any history of violence; the less-than-kosher initial police search of apartment 2D, the tuxedo picture illegally taken from the scene, and conflicting police statements as to when the gun holster had actually been found—before the warrant was issued or after (because the holster had been concealed by dirty clothes, finding it before the warrant would have required more than the quick, noninvasive search granted by law); the fact that not one of the interviews conducted so far had alluded to anything resembling a motive.

All of these questions would be sufficiently answered, Lechliter was sure, before the case went to trial. In the meantime he had the murder weapon, found on the suspect's person at the time of arrest, and that was really all he needed to win. That, and for Skeet Douglas to obtain legal representation, so that the requisite filings, hearings, appeals, motions, pleas, movements, selections, and—ultimately—the trial of *State of New Jersey* v. *Robert Douglas* could commence.

* * *

JACKIE TRIED TO hold her son's hand on the bus ride to Essex County Jail, but he wouldn't let her. He gazed out the windows at autumnal Newark flashing past. Most of the other passengers were women in their late teens and early twenties en route to see boyfriends, husbands, brothers. The rest were older, probably parents. Rob was the lone child.

Jackie hadn't wanted to bring him so soon, but Skeet had been adamant. He'd used so many of his daily fifteen minutes of phone time— minutes that were supposed to be used to contact lawyers—to call her instead, demanding to see his son, that she'd finally given in. "I'm his father, he loves me, he can see me as I am," Skeet told her. "I'm not guilty and I'm not ashamed."

At the jail, Rob walked the same path she'd walked a few times already, past the same checkpoints and the same gatekeepers, until he was watching his father through the glass. Never before had their likeness struck her so strongly, and it loosened valves within her, the ones that kept her darker feelings contained. Even here, the boy emulated his father, the way he held the handset loosely to his ear, his other elbow propped on the counter, head angled down, words spoken in a low mumble.

Skeet asked, "How are you doing, little man?"

Rob told him about street football, summer camp, and first grade starting at Oakdale. Skeet promised that he would call him every day, that he would be here whenever Rob was able to visit, that he would be home very soon.

"Hey," Skeet said, just before their time was up, "you know I didn't do anything wrong, right? You know I'm innocent?"

"Yeah," Rob replied, his confidence unwavering. In that moment, Jackie almost believed Skeet, too.

*   *   *

SCHOOL BEGAN, and Jackie tried to treat the changing days and seasons normally, for her son's sake. She walked him to school, bused herself to work, and met him back at home. She was worried about his learning progress, both because his teachers were less than inspired and because of the emotional trauma he was enduring. With Skeet's help and his own motivation, Rob had always been able to bridge the gap between his own drive and the lack thereof at Oakdale Elementary. Jackie tried to fill Skeet's role doing homework, but she wore out easily. After long days taking orders in the kitchen, she didn't generally have the strength to give orders at home. Over the following months, Rob began gaining weight—"husky," she started calling him—and acting lazy. Coming home and seeing her seven-year-old splayed on the sofa, half asleep with his books unopened and watching junk on TV, reminded her of every man around the neighborhood whom she wanted nothing to do with. And yet she hadn't built up the heart to push Rob forward from this event the way Jackie was pushing herself forward. Usually, she simply dropped on the sofa next to him and watched whatever he was watching. Whenever she felt sorry for herself, she tried to think of Skeet, seven miles away, alone in a cell. Whenever she felt really sorry for herself, she thought of the Moore sisters.

Then she was in the school principal's office, with Rob sitting hunched beside her, his blood still hot, muttering breathy little resignations to himself, "I don't care if they kick me out, that boy's a fool."

In the winter of first grade, Rob had had his first fistfight, on the front steps outside Oakdale Elementary. Fights weren't uncommon, and the faculty didn't treat them very seriously. But they'd still called Jackie at work. To her chagrin, no one at the school asked for a disciplinary meeting. So Jackie demanded one herself, left work, and walked to Lincoln Avenue. Throughout the curt discussion that followed (she felt the administrators were humoring her so they could go home), she visualized the scene: two seven-year-old bodies in winter coats tumbling down the concrete steps into dirtied snowbanks, arms flailing and profanity in play, while fellow students and young male passersby from the surrounding neighborhood chanted encouragement ("C'mon, li'l man, kick his ass!"). They were two little boys pretending to be men.

On the walk home, after chewing him out, she thought to ask why he'd thrown the first punch. This wasn't an act of the boy she knew.

"He called me a nerd," her son informed her.

"You keep going like this," she said, "and you've got nothing but disappointment coming to you . . ." She went on, but a part of her heart was pleased. Members of her family had been called a lot of things over the generations, but she was pretty sure "nerd" had never been one.

Rob ultimately expressed the appropriate sentiments to project shame. She sensed that he, like the principal, was humoring her so that she would leave him alone, and then he could wait for his father to call from jail, so he could tell the man how he'd won the fight. The other boy had come away with a black eye. Rob had only a bruise on his shoulder from hitting the steps.

* * *

AFTER HIS ARREST, Skeet was assigned a public defender. Their initial meetings did not involve the events of August 8 at all but rather Skeet's finances. The lawyer filed a plea of not guilty, but that was his only legal motion over the course of the fall; in January 1988, the public defender's office wrote Skeet in prison to say that they were denying him representation, due to his failure to prove indigency. They referred to the house he owned on Pierson Street, which according to "reliable real estate brokers in the area" had a value of between $70,000 and $110,000. The letter also cited a pending civil action, from a car accident Skeet had been in years earlier, in which he still had an expectation of financial recovery (the insurance claim for damages and lost work was $3,174). Skeet began appearing in court without representation, and the judge advised him that if he truly could not afford a lawyer, he could appeal the public defender's decision. This process took almost a year, a year of nearly cosmic miscommunications and misunderstandings between Skeet, the public defender's office, and the appellate court—and a year in which the defendant remained lawyerless, his witnesses uninterviewed. The public defender's office accused Skeet of intentionally mailing the wrong forms and failing to read the case studies they had cited; Skeet accused them of misinformation and outright sabotage. He complained about lack of access to the law library, functioning copy machines, stamps, and envelopes. A recent legislative change, in which indigency came to be decided by the judiciary branch rather than the public defender's office, caused additional confusion as Skeet continued sending appeals to the wrong office without being notified of the change. In nine hearings spread over eleven months, Skeet fought not for his innocence but for his right to someone capable of pleading his innocence.

On November 2, 1988—a year and three months after the murders—his case was once again taken up by the public defender's office. The entire delay boiled down to a single overlooked form and the proper submission of a photo of Skeet's burnt-out property on Pierson Street, which Jackie took.

Almost five months later, on March 28, 1989, Skeet's newly appointed attorneys filed a motion to set "the dates for the filing and hearing of all pretrial motions"—in other words, a motion to schedule further motions. After more conferences, this date was set for August 7, 1989, exactly two years after the Moore sisters' final evening together. The hearing of pretrial motions commenced September 6 and continued into October. During that span, Irving Gaskins, in whose home Skeet had been apprehended, passed away. Due to the prolonged legal confusion, Gaskins had never given a formal statement to the defense attorneys that could be presented in a trial. According to Skeet, Gaskins had been prepared to testify that the murder weapon and ammunition had not, in fact, been found in his belt—that the police had planted it on him. After all, what killer would fail to get rid of his weapon in the span of a full day following his crime? What sensible human being would carry a loaded gun around a sick, elderly man and his grandchildren?

On February 22, 1990, Skeet's lawyers filed a motion to set the trial date, asserting that in addition to the loss of key witnesses and inability to properly strategize a defense, the long delay between arrest and trial might give the impression to the jury that the defendant's guilt was not really at issue, just the punishment he should receive. On March 9, a trial date was scheduled for September 10. On that day, now three years and one month after the murders, jury selection began for *State of New Jersey* v. *Robert Douglas*.

Three years: three years during which Skeet waited in jail along with all the other accused murderers and rapists and pedophiles of Essex County—like a new, warped incarnation of the neighbors he'd once spent his afternoons chatting up along the avenues of East Orange; three years, or more than eleven hundred days, on each of which he was permitted one hour of exercise and fifteen minutes of phone time, calls made collect at extremely high prison rates; three years, or 160 weeks, during each of which Jackie took Rob to see his father; three years during which Skeet, on days when he didn't need to speak with his lawyers, called his son on the phone to go over homework problems; three years during which Rob grew from a child of seven to a boy of ten; three years during which this boy went about his daily life, knowing full well that Thomas Lechliter and the State of New Jersey were building their case against his father for the death penalty; three years during which Jackie waited in dread to learn whether or not Rob would be called to testify in this regard.

He was called to do so, once in the winter of 1990, at the hearing to confirm that the death penalty would be sought. For ten minutes the nine-year-old—fully aware that his father's very life might be at stake in his words—answered questions from Mr. Lechliter.

"Have you ever been to your father's apartment on Chestnut Street?" Lechliter asked.

"Just outside the front, sir," the boy replied.

And, later on: "Have you ever seen your father using drugs?"

"No, sir."

To the extent that he could, Rob used his responses to declare over and over that his father was a nice man who cared about homework and would never hurt anybody. Lechliter managed to sway the judge toward the death penalty regardless.

*   *   *

AT OAKDALE ELEMENTARY, Rob led the math league and spelling bee teams to area competitions where they were typically routed by more affluent schools in South Orange and Montclair. He took these defeats to heart, scowling and stomping around the house for days afterward. Already, he and his more motivated classmates were learning that no matter how badly they wanted to succeed, they seemed to lack some element that would put them on equal footing with peers growing up just a few miles away. Of course, they figured that the element was money.

In addition to such socioeconomic awakenings, her son now officially hailed from a single-parent home. He was far from alone in this regard; of the roughly sixty thousand people living in East Orange in the late 1980s, 25 percent were under eighteen years old, and 67 percent of those children lived in single-parent homes. More than ten thousand children in the three square miles Rob Peace inhabited shared his new situation, whether through abandonment, death, or imprisonment. But for the most part, families in the area tended to break up very early, before long-term memory imprinted and the children had fully formed their attachments. These children had never had involved fathers and so they didn't know, as Rob knew, what it felt like to love and be loved by one—and then have him ripped away.

The only positive effect Jackie observed was that in a high-crime area such as East Orange, where murders were relatively common, no one crime stood out to the extent that it generated much gossip or judgment. People close to the Peaces knew what had happened, of course, but the event wasn't otherworldly enough to send shock waves of "Oh my God, can you believe . . . ?" coursing through the surrounding blocks. Jackie had worried about Rob in this regard at first—his association by blood to an alleged killer of women—but found that there was no need. He didn't seem to experience any exclusion, name-calling, or dirty looks. No one cared, not really. What did worry her was when Rob would come home smirking with an ugly sort of pride. He'd tell her how someone—an older kid at school whose dad knew Skeet, or a random set of guys trolling the neighborhood in the evening, or Carl—had lauded his father as some kind of noble rebel-warrior and considered him above all a victim of the white establishment. "Shame how they did him like that," they would say to the boy. And worse: "You have to carry his name on proud, little man."

To avert this name carrying, Jackie had to make a change.

During the year after Skeet's arrest, she began attending night school to become qualified as a kitchen supervisor. Consequently, for six months she saw her son for less than an hour in the mornings. This huge sacrifice proved worthwhile when, upon completion, she landed an administrative job at University Hospital and a raise of $2,000 a year. Instead of cooking the food, she was now responsible for ordering, tracking, keeping inventory, and delegating work to others. She skimped on clothes, food, and all luxuries, both for her and Rob. She took a second job sweeping hair off a salon floor. And after two years of this—of Rob enduring ridicule for wearing clothes he'd outgrown while eating yellow rice with black beans most nights, often by himself or with his grandparents—Jackie had saved enough to send her son to private school on her own. This time, no one questioned her desire to do so. She was forty-one years old.

In September 1990, just as his father's murder trial began in the courthouse downtown, Rob entered the fourth grade in a private Catholic school. During the months to come, the remainder of Skeet's life would be decided upon by a jury of his peers. In a certain way, Rob's life would be, too.

Chapter 3

———————◆———————

M T. CARMEL ELEMENTARY SCHOOL stood on East Freeway Drive overlooking the I-280. As the mostly poor, mostly black and Hispanic students filed in and out, they could look down the steep embankment at the cars whooshing past, carrying suburban commuters from their bucolic homes to their downtown jobs and back again. The modest brick building was sandwiched between a church and a nursing home. On a grass lawn directly behind it, nurses took turns jumping rope while the octogenarians in their care looked on eagerly, clapping out revolutions—and also creating a kind of neighborhood watch that kept loiterers and dealers away (the interstate off-ramps provided convenient locations for white-collar commuters to buy drugs quickly, without venturing into the hood). Mt. Carmel, kindergarten to eighth grade, cost $200 a month. Most of the teachers were elderly white nuns, of whom Skeet would disapprove. But unlike before, or possibly ever again, he had no say in the matter. Jackie was paying about a third of her monthly salary—now around $600—in tuition, plus additional expenses for clothes, books, and supplies. She was also taking a big risk by hoping this sacrifice would mean something. If Rob turned out like any other rough boy in the neighborhood—if her son wasn't special like she believed he was—she feared the disappointment that would follow too much striving on her part. At the very least, she was confident that

47

he was now among people who saw beyond who and where they were. Uppity or not, Jackie saw beyond.

Rob was a quiet boy who, with his broad chest and wide shoulders and constant glower, strutted around the school as if someone had just stolen something that he wanted back. With only eighteen students per grade, he stood out. He wore boots with untied laces, and the belt of his pants hung halfway down his backside (he still took care to make sure his shirt was tucked in, in accordance with the dress code). He received A's in every subject.

The heavy burden Rob carried was clear to all around him. But whatever plagued him specifically, he didn't speak of it, and his self-contained bearing inhibited his classmates from asking (they were, after all, ten years old, though many were growing up much faster than they deserved). And as Rob gradually made friends and ingratiated himself with his teachers—through work ethic and graciousness, if not his demeanor and appearance—he never mentioned the trial unfolding downtown throughout the fall of 1990. Rob's first months of private school were his father's last months of being presumed innocent.

*   *   *

AFTER MORE THAN three years of waiting, the weeks-long jury selection began. Though the jury ended up being composed of eight blacks and four whites, the defense attorneys still complained of racial bias since the composition did not adequately represent the area in which the crime had occurred. In turn, the prosecution chose its jurors based on the strength of their belief in the death penalty.

The actual trial spanned a single week in November 1990. Mr. Lechliter's opening statement painted an intimate, detailed rendering of the morning of August 8, 1987, with multiple references to the infant in the apartment. Then he called a parade of policemen who'd been at the scene of the crime. One after another, these officers described the arrangement of the bodies of the two women, the disarray of Skeet's apartment and the drug paraphernalia found there, the photo corroborated by the single witness, and the moment when Skeet had been apprehended, armed with the loaded murder weapon, sitting among children. Lechliter's strategy seemed to be to imprint his narrative on the jury through force of repetition, as nine different policemen answered more or less the same two dozen questions over the course of three afternoons. During cross-examination of the State's witnesses, Skeet's public defenders focused almost exclusively on details of positioning, needling each officer to recount, practically down to the square inch, where he had stood during every moment of the crime scene investigation. Even the judge seemed to grow prickly during these lengthy, sometimes redundant exchanges.

A ballistics expert for the prosecution then explained why the spent rounds found at the crime scene could have been fired only by the gun found on Skeet at the time of arrest.

And then Georgianna Broadway, who had recovered from her wounds, took the witness stand. Though her foggy memory and misunderstanding of hearsay laws muddled what the prosecution intended to be a highly dramatic moment, her testimony still concluded with her pointing to Skeet Douglas and identifying him as the murderer. "Him right there. He killed Stella and Charlene."

After six days, Mr. Lechliter rested his case. He had not pressed any of his witnesses to present a motive to the crime (nor had the defense pointed out the lack of one). He had based his case on the same set of facts he'd learned of in the days following Skeet's arrest: a witness placing the defendant at the crime scene, a less reliable witness pointing to him as the shooter, and a murder weapon owned by and found on him.

The witnesses for the defense numbered three: an old friend of Skeet's from junior high basketball, the mother of another childhood friend, and a neighbor from Pierson Street. All served strictly as character witnesses, asserting Skeet's basic kindness and aversion to trouble. After each witness spoke, Mr. Lechliter approached for the prosecution's cross-examination and asked a single question: "Were you in Apartment

2D of 7 Chestnut Street on the morning of August 8th, 1987?" to which each witness replied no. The defense's case lasted less than an hour.

And yet the jury reported they couldn't reach a consensus despite deliberating for a longer time than the trial proper had actually taken. Maybe Georgianna's choppy testimony had interrupted the prosecution's story (the jury had requested a reading of Georgianna's transcript multiple times during deliberation). Maybe the stark visual contrast between nine white policemen testifying against one black man proved hard to overlook. Maybe one of them believed the defense attorney when, in his closing statement, he asked the jury to *consider* the possibility that, in an area long known for police corruption, one or all of the arresting officers might have conspired to plant the weapon in Skeet's belt.

The judge directed them to deliberate for at least another day, noting that one of the jurors had reported sick during one day of deliberation. He sternly insisted that a verdict should be reached.

When the twelve citizens finally emerged, they did so with a verdict: guilty on each of two counts of first-degree murder, as well as one count of aggravated assault on Georgianna Broadway and possession of an unregistered handgun.

On December 13, 1990, after more than four dozen appearances at the courthouse over the previous three years, Skeet came back for the sentencing. The state sought the death penalty, but Skeet received a life sentence in Trenton State Prison. He would not be eligible for parole until 2020, thirty years hence. Near the end of the hearing, Skeet was given a chance to make a statement. He stood up before the court and cleared his throat.

I respect my lawyers and I have a lot of respect for them and I think they're fine gentlemen, but as far as in a professional capacity sometimes, well, from my understanding a crime is committed, the police reports are taken and all investigations go at that point and from that point and if those police reports are erroneous then people are going to have erroneous investigations and they're going to try to defend based on that. I have a lot of respect for Mr. Lechliter, I know he's just doing his job, but he wasn't there and if they say this is the designated defendant then it's his job to win the case, you know, but the truth never came out. It's win or lose and unfortunately my lawyers lost, but justice wasn't done and the truth never came out during that trial and I think a better effort could have been put forth . . . From the beginning, as I said, I did not commit this crime. I know the jury has determined that I'm guilty of the crime. I really don't know anything about what happened in that room. I was not there. I did not commit the crime. I was arrested and unfortunately the only gentleman that could really tell the truth, since I did not take the stand, under the advice of my attorneys, was Mr. Irving Gaskins and he died. I did not have the weapon on me, that's completely fabricated . . . [Gaskins is] the only one that could tell what happened at the time of my arrest, that I did not have a weapon on me . . . I don't know why I'm accused of this and I never saw the photographs of the actual crime scene until court. I don't understand how a person could come in a doorway and shoot someone whose right side is facing the doorway and she is shot on the opposite side and there was no testimony elicited from the medical examiner as far as the person that's supposed to have fired the shots. Someone evidently fired the shots, but where they could have been standing for this lady to be shot from someone coming from one direction and the entrance wound, contact entrance wounds are coming from the opposite direction. I just don't understand that and it was never brought out in the trial . . . I mean it seemed like Miss Broadway was laying on that side and that's the side where the shots came from. I mean, something is not right here and I've been convicted of this—

At this point, the judge stopped him and said, "I know that you have sustained throughout the trial and today your innocence and as you can see I'm struggling. I really don't know. I'm sitting here with the verdict and I don't know . . ."

Skeet finished by saying:

I have a ten year old son. His mother has been very gracious. He's been coming to the jail every week for three and a half years. This whole thing is unbelievable. I know I've been convicted. As I said from the beginning, as God is witness, I'm innocent of this crime. My heart goes out to the family of Charlene and Estella Moore . . . but I have a family and my son's a beautiful child and when I was out there I spoiled him. I was with him everyday. I thank God that he's a very brilliant child. He's a straight-A student and he sings in the choir at church and . . .

Finally, Skeet trailed off, shook his head, and sat. Rob and Jackie were not in the audience, and hadn't been at all throughout the trial. This, like the prison visits, had been Skeet's decision. He hadn't wanted either of them to see him in this most vulnerable position. After gearing his entire existence and child-rearing philosophy around friends, Skeet's fate ultimately lay at the mercy and judgment of strangers.

* * *

JACKIE CONSIDERED THAT maybe it was a good thing Skeet would be gone for a while, considering that the Mt. Carmel uniform would have given him an aneurysm: pink shirt, brown slacks, with a purple-and-pink plaid tie.

Two evident types of children walked through the neighborhood each afternoon. The kids who went to school walked in cheery clusters, many wearing simple bicolored uniforms and carrying backpacks. They walked slowly to and from the bus stop, savoring one another's company, none eager to part ways and return home to whatever awaited them there.

The other kids walked in much smaller groups, usually two but never more than three. During the summer they wore wife-beater undershirts, and during the winter they wore baggy coats that they shouldn't have been able to afford. Whether these children actually sold drugs or simply wanted to project an association with people who did, Jackie felt sorry for them—sorry for the fact that ten and twenty years down the road, assuming they were not incarcerated or dead, they would be doing exactly the same thing they were doing now. These kids, mostly boys, mostly fatherless she presumed, would pass by the schoolkids, leering. The schoolkids, whose safety came from numbers, would quiet for a moment and walk on. Jackie saw this dynamic almost every day on the corners on either end of Chapman Street, but only as she edged farther into her forties did she begin to see the power in it: half the generation already lost, the other half just trying to get home each day.

Just after Skeet's conviction, Jackie splurged on a gift for her son: the *A* volume of the Encyclopaedia Britannica. She bought it from a door-to-door salesman, with a spontaneity rare for her, and she began saving extra so that every few months she could furnish another volume.

Her faith in her son's promise began with his intense interest in books, a passion that could not be taught, not where they lived and not with Jackie's work schedule. These books were gateways, not just in abstractions of the mind but to real-world opportunity. They led him to as many school academic squads as he could fit into his schedule and subsequent competitions in the tristate region. Unlike Oakdale, the Mt. Carmel teams were actually capable of winning. Rob began bringing home ribbons, certificates, and small plastic trophies. He placed them all in a cardboard box beneath his bed. He joined a traveling church choir at St. Mary's. Rob never said much about these extracurriculars, aside from asking for rides to and from places and small amounts of money for travel fees. "Industrious," the nuns at Mt. Carmel called him. "Focused . . . advanced . . ."

Jackie, Frances, Horace—everyone who loved Rob—feared the effect that Skeet's conviction would have on the boy's energy, his intelligence, and above all his spirit. After news came of the sentencing, and after they made their final visit to Essex County Jail before the transfer to Trenton State, Rob turned inward and ceased to ask questions, perhaps because the first question he'd asked about his father back in August 1987—"When is he coming home?"—had finally, irrefutably been answered. His family could only hope that he was pushing at his own pace through this uniquely protracted process of losing a father. They believed he was strong enough to do this on his own, and they hoped he wouldn't lose sight of the bigger picture; they hoped he wouldn't get mired in self-pity. Self-pity was hard to avoid in East Orange, and once it took hold of a person, it was harder to shed. Jackie knew that. Her rule for herself, in the event of loss or strain or bad luck, was to take a night to feel sorry for herself, typically with a strong drink next to her bed. The next morning, she flushed the sorrow out with her hangover.

In her son's case, she was confident that the new friends who surrounded him at Mt. Carmel, many of whom had lost fathers themselves and possessed the sympathy needed to relate one situation to another earnestly, would be sufficient to move her son forward.

She didn't know that Rob hadn't told his friends anything about his father. As far as any of them knew, the man had simply never been around, a typical enough story that Rob could wholly elude their attention and whatever support they might have given.

*   *   *

A SIGNAL EVENT in Newark history had occurred four years earlier, in 1986, when Sharpe James had been elected mayor. A former alderman, he'd campaigned on a platform of jobs, improved low-income housing, and attracting development money back to downtown Newark. Over the next twenty years, Mayor James would govern a generation of Newarkers. He presented himself as a different sort of politician, who had lived his whole life among residents, who wore jogging suits in public, and who knew and cared about the people on the individual level. At the time of his election, Newark proper was 52 percent African American, and the African American community for the most part adored Sharpe James. Skeet Douglas, in the eight months between James's inauguration and his own arrest, was one of those people, and the mayor had been a fixture in Skeet's neighborhood conversational rounds.

At the time, more than one in three people in Newark lived below the poverty line. The violent crime rate was so consistently high that a 1996 *Time* magazine article dubbed Newark the most dangerous city in America. The public high school graduation rate was below 60 percent, and in some outlying areas, such as East Orange, less than 10 percent of residents held a college degree. The city had lost 130,000 residents since the 1967 riots. The Ironbound District, once a busy, ethnically diverse commercial center northeast of the train station, was now a seedy stretch of shuttered storefronts inhabited by squatters. Some of the oldest companies in the city's downtown, such as Prudential Insurance, were trying to move; attracting workers had become too difficult. The city had gone so far as to construct enclosed "skyways" two stories above the ground, so that employees in the city center could walk from building to building without having to set foot on the street.

These larger socioeconomic problems persisted through Mayor James's first term, while he sorted through the complicated, land mine–laden pathways toward revitalization. His primary goals were to raze the project towers built by Mayor Addonizio's administration in the '50s and replace them with small-scale public housing and middle-income units, and to bring a performing arts center and sports arena downtown. But as he worked toward these and other aims (while also committing the first of more than fifty fraudulent acts that would lead to his own indictment years later, in 2007), he offered many of his residents a symbol. Here was a dignified black man of resonant conviction, born and bred here, who'd gone to college and worked his whole life and now, in his early fifties, had entered public service to *serve the public*. In fact, an acquaintance of Jackie's had asked Mayor James for a job during one of his rallies downtown, and a week later she was hired as a school crossing guard.

Rob heard this and other stories, and in his own ten-year-old way came to worship James, who in 1990—while Rob began private school and Skeet began his lifetime prison sentence—easily won a second term in office. His face brightened when he or Horace or one of the nuns at Mt. Carmel spoke of the mayor. The Oranges were their own townships with their own city halls and did not fall under James's jurisdiction. But Newark cast a long shadow. To a boy like Rob, growing up on Chapman Street and never attending a school beyond walking distance, that cluster of earth-toned towers a mile and a half to the east, surrounded by a network of tall steel cantilever bridges spanning the Passaic River, represented a beacon, a diverse population center where commerce, education, and potential converged. And Sharpe James was the standard-bearer.

Jackie was surprised when her son suddenly began watching the news, just to hear what the mayor said. In fifth grade, he composed a biography of him. He asked her to take him to speeches downtown, which were held whenever Mayor James cleared a lot for a new office building or appropriated money to hire more police officers.

She didn't know what the term "surrogate father" meant exactly, but years later she would agree—"Mm-hmm, I suppose that's right"—when asked if Sharpe James might have been Rob's first.

*   *   *

WITH SCHOOL TUITION effectively canceling out the pay raise Jackie had obtained, and with Skeet no longer contributing to the day-to-day, Rob saw how she struggled. There were, as ever, the constant night shifts. There were the ramen noodles and cans of beans and bags of rice in the cupboard. There were the increasing arguments at home about who was responsible for what share of annual property taxes, roughly $3,500 per year. There was Jackie's contracting social life and the beeline she made for her bedroom upon returning home from work, where she immediately fell asleep. There were the aunts and uncles and cousins he'd grown up with who, in steady succession, left New Jersey for better opportunities in Ohio, Florida, Atlanta, or elsewhere in northern New Jersey (of Frances and Horace's nine children and five grandchildren, only Jackie and Rob remained on Chapman Street). There was the decade of age Jackie had on the mothers of almost all his friends, and in the latter half of that decade a doubling of the financial and emotional burden she carried. Though she hadn't wanted to marry Skeet, and though he hadn't left them intentionally, the aura of abandonment intractably clung to her.

Despite the attachment he felt to his father, Rob came to scorn abandonment above all things, and as he turned eleven and fifth grade began, he aggressively assumed the role of husband to his mother. She would find dinner plates covered with foil in the fridge when she got home late, leftovers of whatever Rob had cooked for himself that night. Sometimes she would wake up around midnight, after a few hours' sleep, and he would be in the rocking chair beside her bed, reading. He began working odd jobs on weekends for people he knew through his father—raking leaves, shoveling snow, painting—for a few dollars per gig. Always, he divided these earnings and left half on the counter for his mother. If he made $6.50 over a weekend of helping move furniture, and his employer gave him an extra fifteen cents for a candy bar on the way home, Rob factored the tip into his wages, rounded up one cent, and left $3.33 for Jackie. He became competitive with himself, trying to earn more each week than he had the last. He could always find people in Skeet's orbit to call on, always carve out additional hours with which to bring in money. He logged these earnings in a pocket-size notepad beside his bed, maintaining neat columns of what he'd made alongside what he wanted to make. Jackie let him do this not because she needed the money or didn't want him to spend it on himself, but because she saw the feeling of empowerment that taking care of her gave him.

Above all, whether at work or school or home with her, Rob strove to project confidence and strength while refusing to show weakness or insecurity. And Jackie wanted to stoke that quality, which she considered a greater embodiment of manhood than any football heroics or rap lyrics or fashion statements or even academic awards. Also, she didn't have the heart to inform him that, however mature he may have felt, he was not yet the man of the house.

But still she saw the anger in him, a gradually thickening shade just behind the sometimes impenetrable veil of his eyes. She knew that any anger could be dangerous, and that this particular variety, seeded so deeply during Skeet's three years in jail awaiting trial—nearly a third of her son's life by the time it was finished—was especially destructive. But its source came from a time and place from which Jackie had already willfully moved on, and she didn't have the heart to revisit it. She could only hope that over time, Rob's feelings would fade, the way all of anger's counterpart emotions—hatred, sadness, love, joy—tended to do.

* * *

. . . Later Jack and Ralph had an argument and Jack went off into the forest. Jack and the hunters went hunting again. They invited Ralph and the others to the feast. During the feast, Simon ran out of the woods, and the hunters killed him. The next night Jack, Roger, and Maurice stole Piggy's glasses. Ralph, Piggy, and Sam 'n' Eric went to retrieve his glasses. This action resulted in Piggy's death. Ralph was now alone running from Jack and the savages. Jack set the whole island on fire which flushed Ralph out. Fortunately a military group saw the fire and were waiting at the beach. Ralph fell at the officer's feet and told him the story.

Conflict: Man vs. Man and Man vs. Himself, because the boys fought each other and the savages within themselves.

Voice: The story was written in the third person point of view because the author, William Golding, is narrating the story.

Tone: The tone of this story is the adventure, nothing happy or sad about it (with the exception of two deaths).

For the most part, Mt. Carmel's English teachers let students choose their own books from a predetermined list rather than assigning specific titles to all students. Rob opted for the classics, relatively dense books with big themes often rooted in mortality: Jack London's *The Call of the*

Wild ("Conflict: Man vs. Man and Man vs. Himself, because Buck had to prove to his owners as well as himself that he was a leader"), John Steinbeck's *The Pearl* ("Conflict: Man vs. Man and Man vs. Himself, because Kino fought many people and the emotions of shooting his son"), Mark Twain's *The Adventures of Tom Sawyer* ("Conflict: Man vs. Man and Man vs. Himself, because Tom fought many people in the story and his own bad judgment"). He always made a cover for his book reports with crayon illustrations and large elaborate lettering (the above excerpt, written on *Lord of the Flies* in sixth grade, received an A along with a note scrawled diagonally by the teacher, "I would like you to share this with the class!"). He wrote succinct sentences, each leading quietly into the next, short on adverbs and adjectives, penned in cursive perfected under Skeet's watch. His teachers were accustomed to grading book reports composed of a few poorly punctuated and often illegible sentences, and Rob quickly found himself singled out, often prodded to read his work aloud to the class. His ability to consume and digest pages was iconoclastic at Mt. Carmel. As his teachers gradually learned through parent-teacher meetings with Jackie, he read these books and wrote these reports with minimal help from her, as on the nights she wasn't working he tried to finish his homework before she came home from the day shift so that the two could hang out.

His real passions were math and science, subjects in which hard conclusions were calculated from known variables by way of clear, logical processes that were largely absent from his life. The key component of middle school math was "showing the work," mapping the pathway between questions and answers. His teachers graded the format and logic of the problem solving with the same weight as the solution itself. At first, Rob took issue with this and would repeatedly write only the answer. His fifth-grade math teacher was fairly convinced he was cheating on his homework by using a calculator, that he wasn't learning how to problem-solve (in fact, Rob wouldn't own a calculator until freshman year of college). She sent home a note to Jackie.

"I'm not cheating," Rob told his mother adamantly.

"I know," she replied. "Just do what she says and show your work."

"It's just a waste," he replied, as if the world were conspiring to get one over on him.

"A waste of what?"

"Paper, pencil lead . . . *my time.*"

Talking to Rob, like talking to his father, could be beyond frustrating when he had a firm opinion on a matter. "Just *do* it how they want it," Jackie said, and then something occurred to her. "How do you get the right answers without writing anything down anyway?"

"I do it in my head," he replied.

Jackie won, and Rob began to painstakingly write out every step of his problem sets, often making little notes in the left margins explaining what he did, as if the teacher grading might not be up to speed. As the math advanced from fifth grade to eighth grade, from long division to algebra and geometry, so did these sheets of calculations, often with extra loose-leaf paper stapled to the back. As in English, his work was often displayed on a bulletin board. Rob was not as proud of these accolades as his teachers thought he should be. He rarely cracked a smile. They were mystified by his nonchalance that bordered on apathy. Most kids his age, especially those from suboptimal circumstances, received a significant confidence boost from public praise. In contrast, Rob would turn away from his work on display, as if it were all he could do not to tear it down.

Rob had always been what most would describe as a nerd. With the loss of his father's persistent street influence, the nerd was permitted to flourish unbridled beginning at age seven. Like his father's, Rob's brain had a huge capacity to store facts. Unlike his father, however, Rob developed an outsize work ethic and attention span: he was able to open a book and read straight through until he finished it, or study the science texts until all the relevant facts were embedded. His mother encouraged this. His teachers marveled at it. The other boys in his orbit, at least those who were not his close friends, were less impressed, which engendered the fundamental struggle of Rob's adolescence: being a fatherless boy in East Orange was hard, but being a nerd was harder.

The struggles of losing a father—emotional, social, financial—were helped by the fact that they were shared with so many of his peers and thus provided a common bond through individual hardship. Without necessarily trying to, Rob would draw these particular boys to him. Though they communicated in typical kidspeak over typical topics— football, girls, complaining about school—a genuine, mature tenderness manifested in their interactions that touched Jackie deeply. Most of Rob's friends were good boys in their hearts. They called her "Ms. Peace," had fine manners, and didn't talk back. And they were always around, either on the street or on the porch or in the house. Her son, though now fatherless and in some ways motherless considering her hours, was hardly ever alone. She'd always wanted her son to have a sibling, and now, on weekends, she felt as though he had more than one. These relationships, the way the boys talked often of brighter futures, drew forth faint music from Jackie's heart, allowed her to feel that she was doing well in the parental intricacies she could control and doing her best in those she couldn't.

But being academically gifted presented a different struggle entirely, because unlike fatherlessness, Rob was isolated in it. His schoolwork— the unbroken succession of A's year after year, the solitary hours spent obtaining them—was an aspect of his life that could not be shared. He had his close friends to whom grades did not matter at all, but the rest of the kids at Mt. Carmel did not know what to make of this young, hard-looking upstart whom most of the nuns adored. So many of them treated him with suspicion, and their suspicion bred scorn. Private school could be even worse in this regard than Oakdale; because Mt. Carmel presented a more competitive environment, the academic structure could also breed more negativity. Periodically Jackie would come home at the end of the day to find her son sitting alone in the dark, sulking, and she knew something had happened that day, some cruel name had been applied to him. These were some of the rare moments when he still permitted her to embrace him physically, and a part of her was grateful for the ridicule her son endured so quietly.

And then there were the various arenas he had to navigate outside school, on the street. Walking from Mt. Carmel to Chapman Avenue, Rob would pass the Center View Plaza apartment project on Center Street (which had neither a view nor a plaza, but always a steady stream of hustlers walking in and out), followed by four blocks of houses inhabited by people who'd known his father, and then Town Liquor and the teenagers hanging outside. Sometimes he might cut across Pierson Street to pass the burnt shell of his father's old house. But whichever route he took, loud music played, drug deals were transacted, threats were dealt. Some people would tell him how sorely his father was missed, while others would step in front of him and aggressively try to create conflict, something Rob learned to avoid by naming someone he knew in the projects, constructing a human bridge over the social gaps between them. This happened almost every day while Rob—wearing the pink shirt and purple tie—made his way home along with whoever was walking with him that day.

Starting in seventh grade, he was usually walking with Victor Raymond. Victor had grown up in Bridgeton, a working-class, ethnically split town in southern New Jersey. When he was eleven, his parents both passed away from illness within months of each other, and he lived with his seventeen-year-old brother, the aptly monikered "Big Steve," who gave up a college football scholarship in order to work, pay the mortgage, and raise Victor. Then the state involved itself and declared that Steve, himself still a minor, could not be considered a legal guardian. So Victor moved north to live with his aunt in her apartment on Center Street adjacent to Orange Park, about a quarter mile from the Peace home. She sent him to Mt. Carmel, where Victor was taken with the quiet boy who sat in the back, somehow found a way to make the school uniform look thuggish, and scored 100 percent on every test. Rob took Victor under his wing, invited him to play in his football games, helped him study, and provided an unvoiced assurance that, though Victor was reeling from the loss of his parents and the vastly different climate in Orange, everything would be okay.

The first time Rob called Victor's apartment to hang out, his aunt answered the phone, heard the deep, drawn-out voice on the other end, and asked Victor, "What is a grown man doing calling and asking for you?" Victor told her that this was the kid he'd been talking about, the one with the best grades.

Rob and Victor were eleven, then twelve, then thirteen years old and feeling their minds expand exponentially each year. At the same time, they commuted daily through a slum populated by people they knew and liked but who never seemed to change at all. In order to make these transits safely, they had to be seen as fully a part of the streets and their residents. If they happened to be carrying any money, they would spread the bills around their bodies—tucked inside socks, back pockets, and underwear—leaving a few dollars in their wallets so that in the event they were mugged (which they were three times during middle school), they could hand over their wallets and plead their case: "This is all I have, take it." They carried their book bags everywhere, slung over their shoulders, so that they seemed to be going to or from school and thus not threatening anyone's turf. In addition, for Rob, this meant talking like the people talked, quoting the lyrics they quoted, playing football the way they played, and never letting them forget that he was Skeet Douglas's son. Not relevant in this arena were the Catholic principles of patience, pacifism, and conflict resolution taught at Mt. Carmel; nor was Rob's widening knowledge of American literature, human biology, European history, and algebra.

Victor watched Rob begin to develop and hone the system of neural switches—the subtle, never-ending calibrations of behavior and speech—that enabled him, at intervals throughout the day, to be an ideal student, the stand-in provider on Chapman Street, and just another mouthy kid parlaying on the corner of Hickory Street and Central Avenue. Further subsets existed within each of these roles, a complex network of personalities, each independent of the others, that Rob had to assume. In school he listened attentively to the nuns and their Christ-centric lessons. He was a steady sounding board for the personal lives of

Victor and the rest of his friends. Though he was not a leader by nature, he became one by the example he set, and he assumed this role dutifully; he spoke slowly, enunciated clearly, and the faculty often deployed him to resolve conflicts among the students. At home he was obedient to his rapidly aging grandparents, mindful of the chores Horace still assigned a generation after his own children had performed them. He was enthusiastic about rendering his day to Jackie when she had the energy to listen, and quiet when she did not. To the extent that he was allowed, he participated decisively in matters of time, property, and especially money. And on the streets outside, he knew everyone by name; he never lowered his head to scuttle past the hustlers, as most of his classmates did, but engaged with them as people. During football games he continued flipping ball carriers over his shoulder and not helping them up. He walked with his head raised and his chest puffed out, spoke fast and commandingly, and he took to being called by his middle name, DeShaun and later just "Shawn," in much the same way that his father had opted for "Skeet" over their shared given name.

Each day, he was all of these people. But at any given moment, he walled off all but one. This existence was fracturing, but it was the only way to integrate his ambition and intellect in a milieu in which neither had currency and in which both could get him hurt.

He had a title for this all-encompassing process: he called it "Newark-proofing" himself.

*   *   *

Rob and Jackie kept visiting Skeet after he was transferred to Trenton State Prison in January 1991. Jackie would borrow her parents' car and endure an hour of monotony on the New Jersey Turnpike before taking the I-295 spur west into Trenton. The prison rose ominously from the surrounding neighborhood of short, narrow row houses and wholesalers. Whereas Essex County Jail was surrounded by chain-link fencing, Trenton State was wrapped by an unbroken brick-and-concrete wall that exuded permanence, like a coffin the size of a city block. This wall was twenty feet tall but rose to seven stories in some stretches, a fortress on the scale of the medieval structures Rob had been reading about in history books. Manned turrets resembling airport towers were spaced at fifty-yard intervals, dwarfing the steeple of the Church of God of Prophecy across the intersection at Cass and 2nd Streets. On the Cass Street end of the prison, which was the stretch Rob and Jackie drove along to reach the visitor parking lot, a colorful panoramic mural depicting a baseball game ran along the wall for its entirety of two hundred yards. Directly on the other side of this wall, attached to it, lived New Jersey's death row inmates.

If walking into Essex County the first time had felt to Jackie and Rob like a passage into purgatory, then the entryway to Trenton State was hell. A hundred Essex County Jails could fit into Trenton State. Through barred windows in the visitor hallways inside, they could glimpse the first inmate buildings across a concrete courtyard, six stories high and a hundred yards long and perforated by rows of tall, narrow window slits. They wondered how many six-by-eight cells could fit into that building, and how many more similar buildings there were, and which building—which cell—was now inhabited by Skeet. Fully contained from the surrounding neighborhood, which looked not unlike East Orange, the grounds had their own order, with buildings fanning out from a central security hub. The men who lived there followed a specific schedule, designed in accordance with rehabilitation guidelines of the time. Trenton State felt like a warped college campus, and it seemed that a person could not achieve a greater state of anonymity, of meaninglessness, than to become one of the nineteen hundred inmates. The visitors moved along slowly in a line to the point where Jackie stopped and let Rob see his father alone, as she would from now on, knowing that the long trip wouldn't be worthwhile to her son if his conversations with his father were monitored. She would sit in the waiting area and try not to think about the smell, which even here in the far fringe of the facility was a mixture of sweat, garbage, food of far lesser grade than what she worked with at the hospital, blood, feces, rot, guilt, resignation—a smell akin to the monotonous inevitability of death.

On the long drives back to Newark, often as dusk and then night fell, she'd talk to Rob about the week of school coming up, what Victor was doing tomorrow, and what was going on with the girl Rob had a crush on—everything but the man Rob had just seen. Rob would humor her, only rarely mentioning the various legal appeals that Skeet had slowly begun moving forward. Her son deeply, firmly believed that his father had been falsely accused by witnesses, set up by police, positioned to fail by the system, and wrongfully convicted by the jury. This Jackie knew and regretted, because she saw nothing more hopeless that her son could waste his ample mind worrying about than his father's past or future. The past had happened; the future was literally locked in place. Neither could inform the present in any meaningful way. Her son, still such a boy complete with a boy's terrible optimism, was not yet capable of understanding this kind of permanence, as Jackie did. Like many other aspects of their reality, she figured that her son would be best served by learning about this on his own, in good time.

But still she dutifully took him to Trenton State, and these visits very much marked the passage of time during Rob's middle school years. The transit, the arduous entry process, the waiting room, the interstate rest stop fast-food counters all added up to a singularly endless day for her—usually her only day off of the week. But to the boy, the actual time spent with Skeet must have seemed much too short. Each time Jackie parked on Chapman Street and entered the house afterward, she would feel relieved; no sooner could she experience that relief than Rob would ask when they could go back.

"Soon," she would tell him as she went to work making dinner. "Maybe in a couple weeks."

A few days would pass, and Rob would start talking about heading down to Trenton this coming Sunday, after church. Sometimes she would be able to put the next visit off for two weeks, three, but never more than four. Rob was persistent in almost everything he did, and visiting his father more than the rest. For all the toll they took on her, the prison visits seemed to energize her son. Maybe this energy came from the way Skeet kept him up to date on his legal processes and enabled Rob to feel like an adult participant in contrast to the way he'd been largely removed from the actual trial. Or maybe he just liked to lay eyes on the man and be heartened by the fact that prison, during these first years, was not enough to break Skeet Douglas. If not surprised, exactly, Jackie was herself struck by how *himself* Skeet remained after his conviction. The trial had burdened and frustrated him to the point where communication had been hard; Skeet had simply come to exist on a lower wavelength than she. The verdict, while not the one any of them desired, seemed to have released all that pressure and given him a return to his true form. When she did go in to see him now, maybe every third visit or so, he grinned and talked vibrantly about new friends inside while asking questions about old friends outside. He was clearly hopeful about his sentence eventually being overturned. She didn't know to whom he was talking—she was no longer privy to his legal undertakings, as Rob increasingly was—but Skeet took with him to Trenton State a hopefulness that was not contagious to Jackie as it clearly was to their son.

In the meantime, Rob seemed to expand through adolescence in every manner. His bones elongated and thickened; muscles followed. Basic math and reading begat abstract problem-solving and reading-comprehension skills. Boy-girl crushes became full-fledged, impassioned romantic pursuits. And his perspective of adults and adult behaviors—no doubt accelerated by his interactions with his father—matured to the point where he fully considered himself one, though he had not yet completed middle school.

*   *   *

IN THE FALL of 1993, Jackie lost her job due to mandatory cuts at University Hospital. She'd been stretching their finances thin lately, trying to spoil her son a little. She'd bought him a used bike so that he could ride to his friends' homes. She'd bought some new clothes to accommodate a recent growth spurt. She'd been trying to nourish him better with fresh produce instead of canned. Because of these efforts, she had no savings to carry her through a job search. After two weeks, her severance pay ran out, and unemployment insurance covered only the essentials. She had to take Rob out of Mt. Carmel and send him back to Oakdale.

"Okay," he said casually. "It's okay, Ma. We'll do what we need to do." He began leaving 100 percent of his work earnings on the counter for Jackie, which she found when returning home late each day after busing around the city applying for jobs.

Public school was much different in eighth grade than it had been in third grade, in terms not just of physical violence but also emotional stress. From his first day back, Rob had to put more energy into navigating his fellow classmates in order to avoid being jumped or robbed, and this left little reserves with which to maintain his grades, to glean at least some new knowledge from the limited amount being dispensed in those classrooms, some of them packed with more than forty kids at a time. Mt. Carmel was not a high-end private school, but it was far enough removed from Oakdale to make for a surreal contrast. The disparity wasn't strictly financial, as Mt. Carmel ran on a smaller operating budget per student than the publicly funded school and had no subsidies for books or supplies. The difference lay in the attitudes of both students and teachers. When Rob told Jackie casually that kids were dealing drugs—and a lot of them—at Oakdale, she knew two things immediately: she had to get him back into Mt. Carmel and place him in a private high school next year.

A part of her had been thinking that he could go to Orange High, just like Jackie had, and easily make it into their gifted student program. But in the wake of these Oakdale revelations, she took the bus to Orange High between job interviews, in the middle of the school day. There, she stood on the sidewalk on South Orange Avenue and looked up the short rise to the building that she'd entered every day for four years in the mid-1960s. Aside from the food service supervisor program she'd attended after Skeet's arrest, this had been the last place she'd gone to school. Jackie was forty-four years old; high school had been a quarter century ago. The place looked different now, and not simply because of the profane graffiti sprayed across its walls. It appeared to her that those hundreds of kids perched on the steps and leaning out of windows and milling around the yellowed lawn were training not for college or jobs but for their destiny as loiterers, hustlers, and single mothers. Jackie felt very old in that moment. But the natural question—what had happened to twenty-six years?—occurred to her only once, fleetingly, because its answer was obvious. Her son had happened. Many of her decisions had turned out poorly, many of her circumstances were more precarious now than they'd ever been, and most of her dreams had fragmented. But her son remained, and he was bright and he was strong and he loved her to world's end. Jackie understood now, looking at her old high school, that she would never leave this place, Orange, like most of her siblings had. She was part of the asphalt fabric on which she stood. She also understood that, with a few more years of determination and sacrifice on her part, Rob *would* leave. He would do so in spectacular fashion. She could almost—*almost*—visualize it, through the massive outlay of effort that sat between this stark moment and that prescient one.

A few weeks later, Jackie found a job with a health care company that managed hundreds of nursing homes and posthospital rehabilitation centers around the country. She was placed in the food service department at the Summit Ridge Center, in West Orange. The job was a demotion from management back to kitchen work, but her employer pitched itself as a strong company in an expanding field with room to grow, and all these terms appealed to Jackie, who'd never had experience with a single one. She enjoyed riding the bus daily west toward the suburbs rather than east toward the city—to see her neighborhood open up and give way to fields and woods and ranch homes sprawling across half-acre plots along Route 501, to see where all those former neighbors she'd grown up with had moved during the '70s while the Peace family had stayed put.

The work starting out was worse than the hospital, and the kitchen had a hierarchy—of which she started on the bottom rung—that was jolting, having come from a place where coworkers generally tried to have fun and help each other by sharing car rides, covering shifts, being interested in the lives around them. She had a hard time falling in with the big-corporation cost-consciousness that led to her cooking food for the patients that she would never let her own family eat. But she was able to transfer Rob back to Mt. Carmel.

Christmas that year was very thin. Jackie could manage no more than some homemade baked goods and stocking stuffers. Rob didn't seem to mind; he told her that he considered the used bike, which she'd bought him last spring, to be like an early Christmas present, plus the encyclopedias (Jackie had gotten up to the G volume before losing her job). A few of her siblings came home for the holiday to sit in the living room with Horace and Frances. The house had been feeling too quiet lately, hollow in a way, and Jackie missed the chorus of arguments that used to resonate through the halls and stairways. She was worried that without anyone to engage him at home while she was working, Rob would reach farther and farther outward for stimulation, to people and locales where she had less control, if any at all.

That year, at age thirteen, Rob learned how to drink alcohol and smoke marijuana. Absent was any ceremonious "first time" that would later be fondly remembered as a rite of passage. These two crutches were a standard aspect of the stoop culture on and around Chapman Street, and the matter was as simple as Rob, goaded by the older boys with whom he played football, climbing three steps onto a neighbor's porch, swigging from a bottle of beer, malt liquor, or E&J brandy, and then filling his lungs with a joint. And he liked it. The alcohol, since he had no tolerance for it, immediately brought forward a kind of blissful stupidity, a state in which words poured forth from his mouth free from analysis or reservation, and he must have found ease in laughing with others without weighing the relative meaning of what they had said. And then came the marijuana, with its immediate dilution of stress, and each of the five senses grew more receptive to minute pleasures in the air, in the sounds, in the faces. Under these influences his father's trial and his mother's dreams must have seemed suddenly very far away, and far less a part of him than they actually were. This state of mind was easy to enter, particularly with the advent of spring and warm weather when the whole neighborhood for a mile in every direction came out onto the stoops.

Rob couldn't afford to buy alcohol or marijuana himself, but one of the benefits of remaining so well known in East Orange—and being Skeet's boy—was that wherever he went, there were people, mostly men, who wanted to take care of him and who didn't have much else to do. Rob would have to walk only a couple of blocks west along Central Avenue into East Orange, past Harrison Street and Evergreen Place. He'd make a left on Burnett Street, and in three blocks he would be on Chestnut Street, near the building where his father had lived, where the Moore sisters had been murdered by someone Rob believed in his heart was not his father. And here he would be summoned onto stoop after stoop, asked how he was, asked how his father was doing, and ultimately asked if he wanted a sip or a toke.

Victor Raymond accompanied him on a few of these excursions. At first Victor was impressed by the extent to which his best friend was a part of the neighborhood, treated as an adult by all these other adults who seemed so cool and wise. He drank and smoked a little himself. Sometimes there were girls around, and he and Rob would take turns trying to talk to them, practicing lines. Always, they heard music, about which Rob was increasingly passionate. He devoted much of his time to memorizing rap lyrics of groups like A Tribe Called Quest: breaking them down, analyzing them, internalizing the words as poetry.

But Victor quickly and alarmingly noticed that for his friend, these walks were more than time-wasting little adventures, boys doing things they shouldn't be doing and hoping not to get in trouble later. And these people whom Rob kept introducing him to with pride—dozens of people—were not so cool, not so wise. These were grown men and women who sat on their front porches all day in various states of inebriation listening to music. Rob threw himself into these gatherings with an intensity not evident in anyone else, which Victor struggled to confront directly. Rob knew who was having car trouble, who was looking for a job, who was behind on rent. He knew everything about everyone, it seemed to Victor, and was able to store each separate personal story in that cavernous brain of his. Like a math or science problem, Rob was always trying to get inside these people, figure them out, learn their problems, provide solutions.

Most disturbing to Victor was the almost professional means by which Rob hid these vices from his mother and grandparents: saline drops for the eyes, spearmint gum for the breath, aerosol deodorant for the clothes, and a preternatural ability to carry himself with as much controlled composure high as he did sober.

Victor much preferred the Caribbean Festival in Prospect Park, Brooklyn, to which he and Rob took the train together every year to walk with the brightly dressed crowds down wide, blockaded avenues far from those they lived on, drinking mango juice and eating jerk chicken off skewers and meeting smiley strangers with melodic island accents. That was his favorite day of the year, and that was the Rob Peace he liked best.

*   *   *

THE PRIVATE HIGH schools were all well known: Seton Hall Prep, the Immaculate Heart of Mary, Essex Catholic, and St. Benedict's Prep. Simply put, these schools sent students to college, and—more important in most cases—they were affordable. Each accepted one hundred to two hundred freshmen a year, roughly six hundred placements for the ten thousand or so teenagers of greater Newark seeking the opportunity. Each had tours, interviews, and entrance exams. About half the students at Mt. Carmel applied, guided through the process by the nuns. Some of these children had never written a personal essay before and were stymied by questions like, "In two hundred words or less, describe yourself."

Victor was already committed to attending St. Benedict's, the only all-boys school. He'd geared much of his last two years around applying: writing letters to the faculty there, going to soccer and baseball games, attending community open houses. Rob and Jackie toured each of the schools, and she could tell immediately that he gravitated toward St. Benedict's, too—her last choice, due mainly to geography. Seton Hall and Immaculate had relatively expansive campuses in suburban West Orange and Wayne, respectively, whereas St. Benedict's was a compact building in central Newark, on Martin Luther King Jr. Boulevard, in the exact opposite direction of her new job. Traffic would be terrible during both rush hours, and the neighborhood immediately surrounding the school was sketchy at best, with adjacent basketball courts and fast-food restaurants tailor-made for hustlers. The school was two blocks from the courthouse in which Rob's father had been convicted of murder.

But she empowered her son to choose, and she figured he based his decision on staying close with Victor and on the matter of diversity. St. Benedict's was the least diverse of the four schools: the student body was 89 percent black and Hispanic. The school had a much more generous financial aid program than the others due to its strong and successful alumni network. The tuition was $8,700 per year against an overhead cost of $16,000 per student, along with further financial aid available based on need.

Rob was wait-listed at first. No one understood why but figured it had to do with the financial statements, which Rob had undertaken himself—maybe he'd left them incomplete, maybe he'd fudged a little. Victor, who had been accepted with a B average at Mt. Carmel, told his aunt. The next day she went to the school personally, sat down in the headmaster's office, and said she would raise a stunning amount of hell if they didn't accept Robert Peace. Jackie received the acceptance letter the following week—which left her anxiously waiting to learn what aid they would offer. That envelope came in the late spring, after a long day of work during which she'd been yelled at constantly by her boss, an irritable white man who supervised the kitchen at Summit Ridge. St. Benedict's offered Rob a tuition of $4,000 per year: a $500 down payment followed by monthly installments of $388 if she opted to pay only during the nine-month school year, or $291 if she wanted to pay continuously year-round.

The decision was a hard one and involved a lot of math that Rob helped her sort through. She'd been paying $200 for Mt. Carmel, but with her recent pay cut that tuition was already gouging the food budget. The extra $90 per month and additional three months of payments would begin encroaching on utilities and other basic costs. She'd have to ask her parents to pay the full property taxes this year, and probably for the next four if she wasn't promoted.

"You'll get promoted soon," Rob told her, "I know you will. And I can get a real job."

She kept looking at the numbers he'd written in his lined composition book, where he kept track of his own wages.

"Ma," he said with conviction beyond his years, "we'll do this. It's important. It'll be all good. You can bring home food from work. I'll eat whatever."

"Yeah," she said, "you'd eat horse meat if it was put in front of you with ketchup. And that's just about what I'm serving these days."

She took his arm, about to give him a hastily prepared speech about focusing on work and taking advantage of this coming opportunity. But she said nothing. Rob didn't need to hear it; he already knew.

Rob (second row, third from right) and Victor Raymond (second row, sixth from left) with their seventh-grade class at Mt. Carmel. Jackie made many sacrifices to send her son to private school, which she could only hope would prove to be worth it in the end.

Part II

---◆---

Prep

*Rob and Jackie celebrating Christmas during
his junior year of high school.*

Chapter 4

───────────◆───────────

F OR ROB, the summer of 1994 lasted all of three weeks: three weeks
of sweltering heat and football games and stoop hopping around
East Orange, sometimes drunk and often high. Then, during the second week of July, the incoming freshman class of St. Benedict's showed
up for "Summer Phase," which in their collective minds was akin to
summer camp but would prove to be something different entirely. One
hundred and forty fourteen-year-old boys passed through the small vestibule on Martin Luther King Jr. Boulevard, bookended by automated
double-locked doors that were controlled by the guard in the adjacent
glassed-in security station. They filed beneath the sign in the lobby that
read in bold gray letters WHATEVER HURTS MY BROTHER HURTS ME,
and down a hallway of classrooms to the gymnasium, known as "the
Hive" in reference to the school mascot, the Gray Bee. Here, they lined
up in rows with sleeping bags and duffels at their feet.

This group came from forty different towns and sixty middle schools
in and around Newark. The boys represented all economic backgrounds
but were weighted toward lower and lower middle class. They stood
there and took each other in, some loose and cracking jokes among
already-formed small groups, others stiff and nervous and alone. Even
before Friar Edwin Leahy, their new headmaster, made his lofty speech
about the trust and unity they would have to build in order to succeed

here and in life, the incoming students intuited that the next four years were crucial, that there would be no do-overs or second chances. They had all gone through the rigorous application process; they had chosen this school knowing all the challenges ahead of them; they were committed to becoming men here. Summer Phase officially began with the singing of the school song. After that weak and discordant effort, the group was divided into eighteen colors, with eight boys randomly assigned to each group. These colors would account for a large part of each student's identity over the next four years. Rob was tagged maroon, which at the very least trumped the pink to which he'd never grown accustomed.

Summer Phase entailed full academic days, followed by sports games and evening group activities, and then the gym lights clanked off over the boys as they whispered in their sleeping bags on the floor. The gym had been built in the 1940s and never renovated; the hardboard basketball court was bowed and splintered, and mice could be heard in the walls. The boys did everything in their color groups—classes, meals, even toothbrushing. In between structured activities, they were required to learn the first and last name of every other student in the class before week's end, as well as memorize the lyrics to five school songs, which were to be sung in the hallways between classes for the duration of freshman year. They had to leave all their belongings in the gym, fully exposed; no locks were permitted inside the school. At the end of the week, they took a test in which they wrote the name of each classmate, as well as the names and dates of every headmaster in the 126-year history of St. Benedict's. Only then did the students formally receive gym T-shirts and shorts in the colors they had been assigned.

The purpose of these various structures was obvious to the freshmen: memorizing names and songs fostered discipline and loyalty, the color assignments kept the boys from forming their own cliques, the schoolwork gave them a preview of what to expect come fall semester, the unsecured belongings built trust, the overnights implanted a feeling of shared experience—of family. And yet a greater aim loomed behind all this effort that would be apparent to the boys only years later, after they'd left St. Benedict's and begun navigating the challenges of adulthood: trouble, and staying out of it.

Friar Edwin Leahy and the elderly Benedictine monks who ran this school knew that before they could teach math and history, before they could coach soccer and baseball, before they could take attendance or host parent nights—they had to preempt the problems to which this group of boys, most of them urban, many living with minimal family guidance, was prone. Through decades of experience, the faculty had learned the many forms these problems took. Fights, theft, and negative attitudes were the most common. Beyond those lay the more disruptive tendencies of emotional abuse inflicted on peers, dealing and using drugs, or dropping out of school entirely. The preventative measure the school deployed against these lurking obstacles was a combination of keeping the boys very, very busy while fortifying them with school pride: an inoculation, so to speak, administered primarily through force of repetition and a borderline invasive control over the most precious asset in their lives: their time.

Rob went through the Summer Phase largely unnoticed by anyone, including Victor, who had been assigned to a different color group. He stood out only once, near the end of the week when summer reading assignments were given: *The Adventures of Huckleberry Finn* by Mark Twain, *A Light in August* by William Faulkner, and *Chesapeake* by James Michener. While the other boys emitted disbelieving laughter at the sheer weight and thickness of the combined pages, Rob sat cross-legged on his bundle of blankets, opened the cover of *Chesapeake* (888 pages), and spent the hour before lights-out quietly reading. He'd already read the two other books on his own, for fun.

A rumor had also begun circulating that there was a boy in the class who knew the lyrics of every Bone Thugs-n-Harmony song, every single word to every single song. Because these songs were typically so fast-paced they sounded like a random spewage of consonants and vowels, learning one song, let alone all of them, was a feat that inspired awe in the freshman class. They began asking around: "Who's the Bone Thugs kid?" He was Rob Peace.

*   *   *

St. Benedict's Preparatory School for Boys was founded in 1868 by a group of Benedictine monks, and over the next ninety-nine years it expanded from a church and small schoolhouse to a group of structures spread over a full city block. During the postwar boom in Newark, the student body came to be composed primarily of the white sons of affluent white men in the area, the leaders of the city's corporate and manufacturing sectors. Headmaster Edwin Leahy graduated in 1964 and left for divinity school, planning to return to St. Benedict's afterward and teach English.

Then the 1967 riots happened, the thickest of the violence in the second police precinct, right outside the school's redbrick walls. While the live-in monks fortified themselves within, the city center was decimated, not just in terms of property but also in attitudes and in trust. The racial tension left in the aftermath of the riots was compounded by the assassination of Martin Luther King Jr.—who later gave name to the very street St. Benedict's was built on—in April 1968, followed by Robert Kennedy's in June, and the expansion of American involvement in Vietnam, which manifested itself in a draft that summoned by force of law many hundreds of young, uneducated black men from their homes in and around Newark. A racial awakening occurred in these homes, in the town halls, and in the streets of downtown. The St. Benedict's faculty—most of them elderly, pacifist white men who wore dark red robes and grew thick white beards beneath their spectacles—was not equipped to adjust to the tension, nor were the school's traditional students prepared to commute from their suburban homes into the city center, the crucible of unrest. More than a dozen teachers left for cushier positions at wealthier monasteries. In 1972, the school found itself unable to reach a sustainable attendance. The doors closed with no promise of reopening, even as a church. This was the state of the school when Friar Leahy came back.

He was twenty-four years old, skinny and pale and relatively green. He was also fearless, ambitious, and direct. He saw that the school closure had more to do with the energy, or lack thereof, of the monks than with any new social reality that had taken hold of the city. So he recruited a group of young, fresh, liberal divinity school graduates, and he led the movement to reopen the school in 1973, not as St. Benedict's Prep but as a smaller, religion-focused educational venture. This effort actually exacerbated rather than alleviated the anger within the African American community. At a town hall meeting that spring, Friar Leahy fielded a question from a young black mother in the crowd. She said, "How come you can call the school St. Benedict's *Prep* when it's all of you around, but now that it's all of us around you don't call it *Prep* anymore?" Her remark seemed to exemplify all the social issues in the country that seemed impossibly complicated. In 1974, Friar Leahy reopened the St. Benedict's Preparatory School for Boys with a new mission to serve young men from the urban districts within and immediately surrounding the city. The transition didn't occur overnight, nor did it always occur smoothly. And yet, quicker than any of the monks expected, and in the middle of one of the most tumultuous decades in Newark's history, something happened that many residents in the city, both white and black, had previously dismissed as a progressive fantasy: the African American community of Newark took ownership of the school.

Nurturing this change was not easy. From a business standpoint—with tuition covering just half of the per-student overhead—nobody could make sense of the budget, and Friar Leahy spent two-thirds of his time on the phone or in meetings, beggar's hat in hand, tasked with raising $1 million a year just to cover operating costs. But the school grew, thanks to an alumni network predating the school's reinvention that remained extremely loyal (and extremely wealthy) even though the student body was suddenly unrecognizable to them.

By the time Rob and Victor arrived in 1994, Friar Leahy was raising $5 million per year from a reliable network of corporate and individual donors. The school had a pool, an auditorium, a sports complex with a turf field and synthetic track, a science wing with sufficient chemistry and physics equipment for each student to run his own individual experiments, a computer room with a row of Apple IIc's, and a library with six thousand books.

But even though the school had modernized and flourished, the biggest challenge these teachers faced each fall was still the same challenge that had existed in 1973, two decades before Rob ever walked onto the grounds: how to minister to the often crippling emotional trauma caused by the suboptimal home lives of so many students, and in doing so, free their cognition—and their potential—in full.

* * *

ROB'S FRIENDS FROM the neighborhood—the ones he played ball, drank, and smoked with—cracked themselves up in the weeks leading up to the fall term: his school had fencing, water polo, and chess teams—but no football. They wondered loudly how a badass like Rob Peace could have chosen an all-boys prep school like that over a real school like Orange High. They made Jesus jokes. They made pussy jokes. They made gay jokes. Rob had no grounds to fight them over it, because in his eyes these friends were more or less right to laugh. Matriculation at St. Benedict's posed problems.

Through a special application process with the Orange Township school board, Rob and Victor acquired waivers to play on Orange High's football team in the fall while attending St. Benedict's during the day. They went to two-a-days in the August heat; the players spent the first practice on hands and knees in full pads picking glass from broken bottles out of the field. Rob played running back and linebacker in the JV squad's first scrimmage the week before the school year started. Some of his upperclassman teammates had been playing with him in the street games for five years, so he didn't have to prove himself the way many freshmen did. Other teammates knew him as a guy who liked to chill and get stoned around East Orange, and they were amazed at his intensity, his desire for collision.

For the first three weeks of school, he would catch the bus downtown at six, get to school by seven, go through the school day, catch another bus to Orange High at three, be on the field by four, practice until six, catch another bus home, and read until he fell asleep. The schedule left him with little energy to socialize at school, where most of the boys were still in the process of checking one another out, projecting confidence while feeling insecure in their new surroundings. Between classes, freshmen were required to walk with their right shoulders touching the wall at all times while singing the school songs in a predetermined order. The upperclassmen maintained discipline in this regard, and they were quick to call out any freshman they saw breaking rank with a smack on the back of the head. The students stayed with their colors throughout the day, from convocation in the morning to classes to meals to gym. Each of the eighteen colors had its own president and vice president in the senior class, tasked with addressing any behavioral or academic problems that arose within the group. Entering the school, the freshmen could roll their eyes at this manufactured brotherhood and its hierarchy reminiscent of British imperialism. But day by day, the system had a way of drawing them in. An individual young man could easily get lost among five hundred other young men in the school; among twenty-five wearing his same color and obligated to look out for him, he couldn't.

Rob did get lost, and not by accident. Because of football, he was able to feel like he could come to St. Benedict's each morning and take advantage of its curriculum and facilities without buying into its philosophies. He showed up on time, sang the songs, and went through the motions without ever fully engaging with them, as if he were in on the joke that his friends from the neighborhood were in on. And the moment classes ended each day, he was out the door, on the bus, then on the field, in pads, standing among the boys he lived with, bashing his head against theirs.

Immediately, the smartest kids at St. Benedict's stood out; the school encouraged this by posting grades in the hallways. The majority of this subset commuted from the suburbs, where they had attended private middle schools and their families were intact. Their good grades were, in the oversimplified view of less fortunate peers, a given. For the students of lesser means, part of the sacrifice of coming to a school like St. Benedict's was the knowledge that they would never be among the smartest in the class.

Which was why, when cumulative GPAs first went up halfway through the fall of freshman year, and Robert Peace was listed along with three other names at the top with 4.0s, guys were confused. Nobody knew much about Rob yet, just that he did the football thing and lived west of downtown and strutted around with a dour expression on his face while referring to himself as "Shawn." Once his grades were made public, a collective perception formed of a wealthy, well-educated black kid from the suburbs who walked around acting like he was from the hood.

The year might have continued like that, with St. Benedict's being a school Rob attended rather than an ideal he was a part of, if not for the clumsy bureaucracy of the Orange School Board. A month into the football season, an administrator filing insurance forms noticed that two names on the football roster weren't registered in the Orange system. The next day, as they hustled out onto the field for practice, Rob and Victor learned that they could no longer play football due to the insurance liability. Rob took it hard, but Jackie had no patience for her son suddenly moping around. She'd disapproved of the football situation anyway—her son busing all over town among the transients, not taking full advantage of his own school campus that she was stretching herself thinner than ever just to pay for, all so that he could participate in legalized violence alongside boys she wished he didn't know anyway.

"What am I going to do now?" he mumbled.

"St. B's has sports teams," she replied. "Lots of them. Find one and join it."

He laughed. "Like what, *fencing?*"

"Well, you wear a helmet, just like in football."

"Mom, please."

"You want to play football?" Jackie said, feeling an energy surge that was rare for her these days. "Because I'm sure as hell fine to take you out of that school and send you to Orange High. You can play as much football as you want there."

He thought about her words and looked away, momentarily silent. And Jackie smiled; as with his father, she rarely got the last word in with her son.

* * *

WAYNE RIDLEY HAD graduated from St. Benedict's in 1990, and he'd started teaching and coaching there the year before Rob arrived. He'd grown up in Irvington, just west of downtown Newark, in that gray area between the heavily policed city blocks and the outlying wilderness where the neighborhoods truly began to fray. He coached the swim team, and in the late fall of 1994 a powerfully built but still soft freshman approached him about joining.

"Sure," Coach Ridley said. "You in shape?"

"Yeah."

"Come out this afternoon and swim some laps."

Rob didn't reply. His limbs were a little short for a swimmer; he had muscle there, but no litheness, no grace.

"You have something else you need to do? Because you came to me, here."

"No," Rob said, "it's just that I don't swim."

"You don't swim?"

"I mean, I don't know how to swim."

During practice that day, while the team swam their daily 240 laps— six thousand yards, or a little less than four miles—Rob lowered himself into the half lane adjacent to the wall. Coach Ridley began guiding him through the physical dynamics of freestyle, breaststroke, backstroke, and butterfly. He understood the toll this took on the boy's pride: splashing slowly and clumsily while the pool teemed with two dozen boys his age cruising swiftly through the water. And Rob came off as a particularly prideful kid. Ridley didn't expect him to last more than a few days—especially when Rob ditched the second practice, claiming that he had sprained his back as a result of sneezing while simultaneously grabbing milk out of his refrigerator at home. But he came back, and by the end of the winter swim team season he could handle himself capably enough in the water to come out for the polo team the following fall.

Swimming and water polo were "cool" sports at St. Benedict's, and Tavarus Hester was the prized recruit of the freshman class. Tavarus was short and scrawny but a natural and experienced swimmer. He had grown up in East Orange with a single parent. His was a rare case in which the mother had abandoned the family—she would disappear for stretches of six months or a year throughout his childhood, and she fled for good when Tavarus was twelve. He and his older brother had been raised by their father, a good man, a good parent, Tavarus's best friend. In the spring of eighth grade, Tavarus's father died suddenly of cancer. He'd gone to the doctor with a persistent stomachache one afternoon, and three months later was buried. Tavarus's admission to St. Benedict's with significant financial aid had been the last positive thing that had happened before his father died. Tavarus now lived with his aunt and grandmother, provided for by Social Security checks, and he'd entered St. Benedict's in a conscious state of not giving a fuck about anything except drinking, smoking—and swimming.

Tavarus had been assigned to Rob's color group, so he knew him a little better than the rest of their classmates. During the fall of freshman year, he'd sensed an anger in Rob that ran parallel to his own. So when football was taken away, he told Rob to come swim. He tried to explain how there was something cathartic about being in the water. You stared down at the thick black line scrolling steadily beneath you, and all you heard was the rush of water past your ears, and a life that at times felt cosmically complicated was reduced to the simplest elements: oxygen, buoyancy, propulsion.

Rob listened, and because he did, through swim team practice that winter and water polo the following autumn, he met the four friends who would compose the daily heart and rhythm of his life until its end.

*   *   *

DREW JEMISON GREW UP in Montclair, a middle-class suburb northeast of the Oranges. His father had left when he was four, but his mother's boyfriend, Snow, had been a steadfast presence since then—not a father exactly, but the next best thing. Drew was massive, with a booming voice that belied his relatively soft sensibilities. He wasn't a brawler because he didn't have to be; just by standing up straight he projected an assurance of never being confronted about anything. He played goalie, his wide shoulders and long arms all but blocking the whole net.

Julius "Flowy" Starkes was tall and almost cartoonishly thin, with a long face that gave him an ever-present hangdog expression. He and his twin sister, Tess, had grown up in the worst of poverty, their father killed by violence and their mother troubled enough to practically destroy their formative years, yet functional enough that social services had never intervened in their home on 18th Avenue off the Garden State Parkway. They lived in the very center of greater Newark's web of drugs and violence, a place where lethality hovered close by always. People called him Flowy for his ability to exist casually in a grid of blocks where men and boys could be killed simply for walking down a street they didn't live on. He was all good with everyone; he just flowed. The last words he remembered hearing from his father, without much momentousness, were, "You ain't gonna live to see twenty-one." But his uncle was the dean of discipline at St. Benedict's, and Flowy had chosen to apply to and pay for St. Benedict's fully on his own, using Social Security checks for supplies. He'd undertaken this mainly because he'd known that going to public school, with girls, would sentence him to fatherhood by age sixteen, and he wanted to evade that pattern, one from which he himself had been born. At six five and 150 pounds soaking wet, he was awkward in the hallways, barely able to wedge himself behind the classroom desks. But in the pool, he was in control, and with a sharp scissor kick could elevate his body from the water up to the waist and extend his long arms still higher for towering, indefensible shot angles.

Curtis Gamble was an amiable leader in the school immediately. He was curious, easygoing, hilarious: the boy who knew how best to spend each hour. His mother was white, his father was black, and they were both schoolteachers. Their home on Smith Street in East Orange was about a mile southeast of Rob's and would provide a refuge and a family for the rest of the newly formed crew—particularly Tavarus, Flowy, and Rob, none of whom had ever known truly what those two words meant. Curtis, with his relatively comfortable circumstances and laid-back approach to life, served as a model, the person they all wanted to be more like, the son they wanted to raise themselves someday.

The boys knew very few of these details about one another at first; they didn't talk about their lives, their histories, their problems. Instead, they talked about music. They talked about what they wanted to eat. They talked about weekend parties that may or may not have been happening. They talked about practice and their hard-ass teachers and coaches. They talked about the momentary wants and obligations of their daily lives, the way all boys did. But their unvoiced pasts, the way their stories bridged and intersected and illuminated each other, formed the foundation upon which their bond grew—as well as the fact that they were members of what they assumed to be the only all-minority water polo team in the country, maybe even the world.

When semester grades were posted freshman year, with Rob's name again clustered at the top of the list with a 4.0, he noticed that Tavarus was on the other end of the spectrum with a 0.7. Rob had known that Tavarus was struggling emotionally, but he didn't know how badly until he saw the atrocious figure. Without mentioning the grades or alluding to any personal issues that spawned them, he organized a weekly study group after swim team practice. Rob didn't need the group, and indeed spending nights helping his friends catch up actually hindered him from getting farther ahead. But he observed the depressive pattern Tavarus was in, and here was a tangible way to help.

Usually Curtis's mother would pick up the boys downtown and bring them home to Smith Street. She would make sure everyone was fed—a laborious and calorically expensive task with five high school boys swimming the miles that they did, but she could tell there was minimal nourishment occurring in their own homes. The basement, adjacent to a laundry area, was cramped and penned in by metal storage shelves and boxes of old clothes. But it had a refrigerator stocked with soda, and the boys made it into a clubhouse of sorts, cramming themselves into the stuffy subterranean space with their books nestled on their laps. There, for hours on end, Rob would tell them what they had to know in each of their classes, including the ones he wasn't taking himself. Curtis's father was usually upstairs watching the news or prepping his lesson plans for the following day at school. To Rob and Flowy, his simple and constant presence was something to marvel at and, perhaps, envy. To Tavarus, Mr. Gamble was like a mirage of some kinder present day than that which he'd been granted. Then Mr. Gamble would speak, making abstract-sounding statements that almost always started, "When you all head off to college . . ." He spoke as if this, college, were a given.

The house at 34 Smith Street (incidentally, less than a block from where Georgianna Broadway and Deborah Neal had shared their house) was within walking distance of all except Drew's. The house—specifically, the basement—became the physical center of the boys' lives, where any or all of them could be found at any given hour when they weren't at school, and sometimes when they should have been. They were comfortable there, warm, fed, far from conflicts. On the foundation of this sudden, unexpected stability, the boys built a brotherhood, a family structure that was easy and permanent and good.

*   *   *

MILLIONS OF LEAVES fluttered overhead. Water flowed along a ravine beneath them, from snowpack in the Catskills a hundred miles north. On either side, woods stretched out, impenetrable. Ahead and behind, the packed dirt of the trail meandered steadily, definitively through them. The air was sweet and washed and full of oxygen, though slightly tainted by the odor of 150 boys marching through it in a line two hundred yards long. Once in a while they would crest a rise and the view would open up, and still all they saw were more trees and maybe a distant church steeple to mark a town isolated in all the nature.

The fifty-mile hike along the Appalachian Trail, from High Point State Park to the Delaware Water Gap, was the physical and metaphorical completion of their first year of high school. Most complained about the heavy packs, blistered feet, mosquito bites, and the too-fast pace set by Coach Ridley up at the front of the column. Rob, who had been elected leader of his subgroup of eight students, was quiet during the walking phases but turned vocal during the camp setup and cooking. He seemed to derive a purpose and efficiency from what they were doing—carrying their own load as they covered a specified number of miles each day—that eluded most of his classmates. When they finally boarded the bus to go home, they were pumped full of endorphins and the once-a-year glee that accompanied the beginning of summer. Back in Newark a few hours later, its neighborhoods could not have felt more claustrophobic. Many of the boys had never before registered the fact that their hometown had the smallest proportion of open space per person of any city in the country.

That summer, Rob went to the public pool at Columbian Park four days a week to train with Flowy and Tavarus. They would swim a hundred laps and throw the ball around, shooting on a homemade net kept afloat with empty milk jugs. Afterward, they would go back to Curtis's house, eat, play video games, and do schoolwork since St. Benedict's held a Summer Phase to keep the students engaged.

Tavarus was tapped to go on a retreat to Maine, at the estate of Charles Cawley. Mr. Cawley, Class of '55, was the CEO of MBNA bank and the largest benefactor of the school. Of the $5 million Friar Leahy raised to keep St. Benedict's running each year, Mr. Cawley gave roughly half, sometimes more if needed. Every summer, the banker opened his vast property to twelve students: four top students, four average students,

and four academically poor students. All were deemed by school counselors as coming from "troubled" circumstances (which was why Rob,
who exhibited no outward signs of hardship at home, was not selected).
The idea was to reward good work while providing incentive for those
falling off. Tavarus was among the worst of the latter selection, and between the catered sit-down lobster dinners and fishing trips and lectures
on economics given by credit card titans, he managed to start a fistfight.
That night, still heated and snarling under his breath, he was ordered to
call home and explain what he'd done. He called Rob instead.

"What happened?" Rob asked, sounding very much like the stern but
patient father Tavarus had lost.

Tavarus explained: the kid had made a comment about his shoes,
they'd started having words, one thing led to another, Tavarus wasn't
about to let himself be punked, etc.

"Wait, wait, wait, hold up," Rob said. "You're getting served steak and
lobster, getting to sleep in your own bedroom with your own bathroom
and a *maid*—and you're starting shit over some words about shoes?" Rob
made a *psha* sound. "Don't be such a bitch, T."

When he phrased it that way, Tavarus felt pretty much like a bitch.

"Just chill," Rob told him. "Don't let the stupid shit get to you. Think
about the big picture."

The retreat, a comprehensive immersion in the lifestyle of the haves,
was transformative for Tavarus. When he returned, with Rob's guidance
and encouragement, he signed up for extra summer tutoring at the school
and in the evenings let Rob coach him on how to study—specifically
how to take quality notes in class and then focus on the meat of each
subject without going cross-eyed from the details. When Curtis's father
spoke of college, Tavarus had never allowed himself to feel included
in that particular brand of long-term thinking. And as a 0.7 freshman-
year GPA was a deep, deep hole to be tasked with digging himself out
of, he still didn't. But in some long-dormant part of his consciousness,
now stirred by his friend Rob, he saw it: a campus far from here with
grassy quads and matching eaved buildings, with Tavarus himself walk-

ing through it carrying an armload of books. This image was grainy, but the resolution became sharper and more detailed with each hour spent in awe of Rob. During their first year, Tavarus had figured his friend to be naturally gifted, as if all he had to do to maintain that 4.0 GPA was open his eyes each morning. Over the course of that summer, he learned how doggedly Rob worked, the sheer volume of pages he read, the meticulousness with which he notated those pages. In Rob's small room on the second floor of the Chapman Street house, a three-shelf bookcase was packed with black-and-white composition books, the front and back of each page filled with single-spaced notes from various classes. Tavarus thought, *Damn, this is how you go places.*

*   *   *

A BIG DRAW of the water polo team was that there were only three squads, including St. Benedict's, in all of New Jersey. For competition, the team had to travel most weekends to tournaments in Pennsylvania, Connecticut, and Massachusetts, where the school would rent four doubles at a Motel 6 or Super 8 and the players would pack in seven and eight to a room.

During an early-season trip in the fall of sophomore year—Rob's first on the team—one player had managed to bring along a six-pack of Bacardi Breezers. To enthusiastic hollers, he handed them out, but Rob refused his. He panned around the room of young black men sitting on cheap hotel mattresses, sipping on their pink carbonated lady drinks.

"You look like a bunch of pussies," he cracked.

Flowy responded, "You're so hard, you bring the party supplies next trip."

The following weekend, Rob opened his duffel bag and pulled out a dime bag of weed as well as a fifth of E&J Brandy. He poured the liquor into small plastic cups from the lobby. Tavarus, who also had more than a bit of experience with drinking and drugs, was the only excited one. All the other boys sniffed the stuff, made faces, looked around to confirm that they were not alone in their apprehension. But they were trapped in this room now, with pride at stake as Rob Peace watched them expectantly. He was already rolling a small blunt, sliding his tongue across the cigarette paper and tweedling the package back and forth between his thumbs and index fingers.

"This gonna make me sick for the game tomorrow?" Drew asked.

"Game's not till the afternoon," Rob replied. "And you're big as hell. You'd have to drink this whole fifth to get sick."

"Smells nasty," someone else said.

"That's why you down it fast." Rob took a shot, exhaled a sated breath, poured another.

Dutifully, without toasts or fanfare, the boys downed their shots. The brown, lukewarm spirit tasted toxic and burnt, like a zipper of fire being ripped down their throats. And yet even this first shot, before Rob finished rolling the joint and sharing hits, seemed to soften the world around them while at the same time hardening their own interiors. Once the weed entered into the proceedings, time itself began to thin out and grow gentler. They chanted rap lyrics and talked sports and mostly just laughed so hard that they were sure Coach Ridley would knock down the door and kick them out of school—which, because they were stoned, made them laugh harder. The next day, though Rob was not yet a strong enough swimmer to make the starting rotation, they won their JV game.

After that trip it was clear that Curtis may have been a leader of men, but Rob was the Man, a guy who could *hook you up*. And indeed, not long after that a few classmates approached him quietly in the hallway with a question (this as they walked single file, shoulders pressed to the wall, singing): Can we buy some weed off you?

"Hell no," Rob said, and instead told them to talk to Tavarus, who was able to get real quantities of marijuana through his older brother. Tavarus was living in a one-story, two-bedroom home on Halsted Street with his grandmother, aunt, and numerous cousins. Rob knew how badly he needed the money, which was why he was surprised a few days later, when Tavarus slipped him a twenty-dollar bill in passing.

"Kickback," Tavarus said quietly. "Thanks."

Rob had the money changed at a store on the way home and left half for his mother, just like he always had. Twenty dollars for a referral was not bad at all.

*   *   *

CURTIS PULLED ROB and the rest of the team out of the pool during warm-ups. "There's a fight. Shit is *real*."

With towels around their waists, they ran to the skyway connecting the school to the faculty parking garage across the street, from which they could see all the way down Martin Luther King Jr. Boulevard. What they saw wasn't a fight so much as a riot, with a few dozen students and some teachers from St. Benedict's lined up across from a phalanx of students from the nearby public school, Central High. The Central kids would often venture down toward St. Benedict's at the end of the school day to taunt what they saw as overprivileged prep schoolers, call them faggots and pussies and bitches. This had been a problem for years, and Friar Leahy addressed it from time to time during morning convocation. He told his boys to keep their heads down and maintain their perspective, and never to forget that words were just words. But words mattered, more so in Newark than many other places. In a world where income and possessions were limited, words represented dignity, pride, self-worth. And just as they had with Tavarus at the Maine estate, words electrified that day and became clenched fists cracking against chins, brains colliding against crania. Teachers from St. Benedict's—the young ones who'd gone to school here not long before and were still in tune with these tensions—came outside to break it up, only to become involved themselves. Rob's crew watched the melee from one story up and fifty yards away, aching to take part—Rob more than the rest, watching his classmates be inexorably overcome by the greater numbers from Central. He headed for the stairs, his musculature tensing in full. Curtis grabbed him by both shoulders from behind.

"You don't even have shoes on."

Rob looked down at his gym shirt, the towel around his waist, his bare feet on the cold concrete. "Fuck," he said.

Flowy murmured, "I'll go down there. I know those boys. I'll talk."

They went inside and got dressed. Rob and Flowy intended to find familiar faces in the Central High group, and pacify. But by that time the police had already arrived, and seven people were in handcuffs. Still, Flowy wandered up to the front steps of Central at the end of the day, founds some guys he knew, tried to sort out what exactly had happened, and ensure that everyone was cool.

The next morning, Friar Leahy assembled the entire school in the gymnasium and lit into students and faculty alike for two hours. He gave sermons every Sunday in the church that adjoined the school, and the one he gave that day was full of fire and brimstone, rendering a vivid version of the future begotten by what had happened: prison, poverty, and early death—a future that many of the boys saw around them every day. The friar's voice, hoarse to begin with, faded to an angry, condemning rasp.

Afterward, a rumor began spreading that Friar Leahy was going to retire in the wake of this, that he couldn't go on leading people who wouldn't follow him.

Rob, Curtis, Flowy, and Tavarus set a meeting in his office, and they begged him to stay. They promised to corral the student body and bring guys back in line. With Rob speaking for the group, he told Friar Leahy that if he were to leave, they would leave, too. Because they still had two years and change, and they wouldn't go to a school where Friar Leahy wasn't the headmaster.

Friar Leahy had in fact never harbored any thought of leaving the school he'd built, but he indulged the boys their pleas because they were so sincere. What struck him most about the meeting was that he'd never heard Rob Peace speak so much at one time, and he saw in the speech a kind of quiet leadership that came along rarely. Later that year, he asked Rob to lead the freshmen on the Appalachian Trail in May, a task normally given to juniors.

During the hike, a rainstorm moved in quickly, in the middle of the night, shrouding them in total blackness and flooding the campsite with runoff beneath the sharp strikes of lightning and resounding thunder. While everyone scrambled for shelter from the lashing winds, communication along the line of campsites was lost, and Rob's group of twenty-four freshmen became isolated from the rest. Their cheap tents collapsed. The freshmen, though just a year younger than he, were mortally scared. More than a handful of them had witnessed gunfights in their neighborhoods, seen dead bodies sprawled on concrete. But this, the raging of nature, was completely new and terrifying. Rob had everyone hold hands—"Just do it," he growled when one student gave it a homosexual slant—and he led them down off the exposed mountainside like children. They left everything except rain gear so that they could move fast. They ended up in a small town off the trail, two dozen black kids huddled in the front yard of a rural house at three in the morning while Rob knocked on the door and, very respectfully and politely, asked if he might use the phone inside. After Rob called a faculty coordinator back in Newark to let him know they were okay, the homeowner asked if the boys wanted to stay in his garage until the storm let up. Rob declined; now that no one was going to be struck by lightning or washed down a mountainside, he wanted his group to get through this on their own.

The next fall, a new addition came to the Class of '98 in the tall, pale, goofy form of Hrvoje Dundovic. He'd come alone from Pula, Croatia, fleeing the economic malaise that had gripped the country since the Balkan conflict of 1992. He was living with a host family in East Orange, an arrangement made through the St. Benedict's alumni network. Having come from a suburban seaside enclave in a nearly all-white country, he could not have ended up in a more alien environment. During nights and weekends, he rarely went outside. At school, the cultural divisions were amplified by the fact that this was a particularly tight-knit class that had been together for two years already. Three months into the school year, he had yet to hear anyone, including teachers, pronounce his name correctly (HIT-of-way). He did, however, join the water polo team. He'd grown up playing water polo, which was one of the reasons he'd landed at St. Benedict's. His strategy to fend off homesickness was to listen to his Walkman all the time and lose himself in the songs he'd grown up listening to in his bedroom back home.

"What you got in there?" Rob, now one of the leaders of the varsity team, asked out of the blue. He nodded toward the music player.

"The Misfits," Hrvoje answered in his thick glottal accent.

Rob motioned with his hands, and Hrvoje slipped off the headphones and passed them over. Rob's eyes went wide with distaste upon hearing the screechy wail of Glenn Danzig, the metallic confusion that was the guitar and drums. "What the hell kind of music is this?"

"Prog rock," Hrvoje answered. "Or some call it punk."

"Damn, that is awful." Rob walked away shaking his head and laughing.

Hrvoje assumed this exchange would be the end of their acquaintance, but the next day Rob came back to hear more, Black Flag in the Walkman this time. Rob knew what prog rock was now; he'd looked it up in his Encyclopaedia Britannica the night before. He had memorized the dates, the important figures in the movement, the intellectual thinking behind the sound. From then on, the two of them sat together on bus rides, Rob willing himself to develop an appreciation, if not a taste, for punk rock while he coached Hrvoje through the lyrics of his own favorites: DMX, Nas, Tupac. An image that would be remembered always by the team was Hrvoje, standing in front of the bus aisle while Rob goaded him on, both hands folded into hang-ten signs and jabbing at the air, singing Tupac's "Hail Mary" in his Croat accent.

Rob, Tavarus, Drew, Flowy, and Curtis called themselves the Burger Boyz, because between class and practice they could typically be found at the Burger King around the corner. Rob never bought food for himself. Tavarus would spring for him on occasion, a culinary version of the kickbacks he still gave to Rob for shepherding marijuana business his way. Most of the time, Rob was content to suck on ketchup packets from the condiment bins, sometimes a dozen in one sitting. He told his friends that he did it for the salt, and he would segue into a chemistry-based explanation of the NaCl exchange necessary, on the cellular level, to drive the body through the workouts to which Coach Ridley subjected them. But his friends knew he was concerned about money. They'd all been to his house, registered the austerity of it, the way the lights or the heat would be shut off from time to time. By now, they called Jackie "Ma." Sometimes she would bring home surplus food from work, which was a long fall quality-wise from the homemade spaghetti and casseroles Mrs. Gamble made for them, but the boys were always gracious. The only other food option at Rob's house were the rows of Oodles of Noodles in the cupboard, bought from the Price Cutter on Springfield Avenue.

They all were poor, but Rob seemed to hold his poverty closer than the rest of them, to feed off it like he fed off the ketchup packets: a nutritionless condiment that powered him through miles and miles of water. He didn't joke about being poor the way most did; he didn't outwardly resent it, either. Rather, he carried it with him under vigilant guard: the one pair of school shoes he shined obsessively, the earnings figures still recorded in the composition book beside his bed, the encyclopedias he kept dusted, the refusal to spend money on anything personal, not even weed, which he'd been procuring through Carl, whom Rob called his uncle, since Carl had been the most constant male presence on Chapman Street since his father's imprisonment. His friends figured that he contained whatever anxiety he felt because he alone knew that he would one day overcome it, and not even too long from now.

*   *   *

THE WATER POLO TEAM was strong their junior year, in the fall of 1996. Rob, now the lead butterflyer on the swim team, played in the "hole," the basketball equivalent of a power forward. At five eleven with a barrel chest and short but muscular arms—as well as the ability to absorb and dole out punishment—he was naturally suited to the role. The offense ran through him as he hovered five yards in front of the opponent's goal, shrugging off defenders who would alternately lock their forearms under his armpits to pull him underwater, dig their nails (unclipped specifically for this purpose) into the flesh of his neck, angle their kneecaps to take shots at his testicles underwater, where the refs couldn't see. Rob, often deploying the covert elbows that his father once schooled him on, was adept at shrugging these defenders off so that he could pull in a pass, take a shot himself, or kick the ball out to Flowy or Hrvoje on the wings. Tavarus, small but quick enough to cover the full width of the pool, played defense along with Drew in the goal. A big part of their game was the intimidation inherent in a team of muscular, razor-mouthed, dark-skinned (all except for Hrvoje, who looked like a pale, skeletal specter among them) inner-city boys walking into the pools of the privileged majority, there to play rough and win games dirty if need be—and talk more than their share of smack while they did it. If parents in the stands weren't complaining to the refs about their language, then the Gray Bees figured they weren't talking enough. The team carried with it an unbridled quality, some primal mixture of arrogance and competitiveness and zeal.

They won their first tournament at Lawrenceville, near Princeton, and came in second at their next, at Wesleyan University in Connecticut. Ultimately, they would come two wins shy of winning the Mid-Atlantic championships, and Flowy would be selected to the All-Regional First Team. A referee pulled him aside one weekend and told him that if he was interested, he could pull strings to put Flowy on track for a scholarship to UMass. On the nights in motels between the games, the boys—with Hrvoje now a part of their group—would drink and smoke, listen to music, and play spades deep into the night before playing their hearts out the following day. During the week, they would practice until after six, watch game film at Coach Ridley's house until eight, go to Curtis's house and study until ten, at which point Mrs. Gamble would drop each of them back at his home. When she'd first begun doing this, Flowy had asked her to let him off on South Orange Avenue, a well-trafficked thoroughfare, rather than enter the narrower, darker side streets of his neighborhood on 18th Avenue. She'd told him not to be silly; she'd lived in East Orange for over three decades and knew how to check her mirrors.

At school, they began working with college guidance counselors—
even Tavarus, who in two years had raised his 0.7 GPA to 2.1. Flowy
was extremely aware of the financial realities that lay between him and
something like college—which, unlike St. Benedict's, could not be paid
for with a few hundred dollars' worth of Social Security each month—
but that referee's voice made a resonant echo in his head: *scholarship,
scholarship, scholarship.* Curtis, the only one whose parents had gone to
college, was already listing party schools, particularly in Atlanta; Morehouse appealed to him. And Rob was thinking about Seton Hall, eight
blocks from his home and his mother. His counselor told him that he
should apply wherever he wanted to apply—that with Rob's grades and
his leadership accolades (not to mention a combined SAT score of 1510
out of 1600, placing him in the ninety-ninth percentile nationally), it
couldn't hurt to visit a few of the top-tier schools, if only to see what
they looked like. The school organized and paid for these visits, which
would begin the following summer before senior year. Rob went ahead
and signed up for the Ivy League tour; he didn't take the prospect seriously, but he would travel anywhere given the free opportunity.

Junior year, as the Burger Boyz would remember it, ended with a
party. Rob walked the mile to Curtis's house, where Tavarus and Flowy
met up with them. They took a few hits of weed together and then all
walked west as the sky darkened, their crew looking the same as any
other group of young men trolling around East Orange that night.
They said hey to anyone they passed, people they knew and people they
didn't. They smoked continuously and drank from brown-bagged bottles of Cisco wine, past the Seton Hall campus and into South Orange,
where the wide streets curved beneath blooming cherry blossom trees
and the green lawns were lit by yellow lights embedded in the mulched
gardens. They ended up at Columbia High, the public school servicing
this wealthy area. Rob's friend from Mt. Carmel, Jason Delpeche, went
to school here and had invited them to a dance. Drew met them in the
gymnasium. There were supposed to be girls there. The Burger Boyz
tended to do well with girls.

Except tonight's party sucked: a few dozen kids pressed against the wall of a cavernous gym, with parent chaperones eyeing those who ventured to dance too closely. They couldn't believe that they'd walked three miles to be there and would have to walk three miles home. Curtis made a call from the lobby pay phone and learned of a party down the street, at some kind of dance studio, so the five of them took off. They didn't realize they were being followed until a hundred yards later. Back in East Orange, trailing footsteps would cause the backs of their necks to tingle in apprehension, their eyes to begin scanning for an alley down which to escape. But behind them now, almost all the Columbia High students were walking as if in formation, just as the freshmen had done on the Appalachian Trail, confident that Rob, Curtis, Tavarus, Flowy, and Drew would lead them somewhere they all wanted to be.

They landed at the next party and immediately became its center, cluster-dancing in slow motion under strobe lights, surrounded by girls, sneaking outside for hits of marijuana, feeling the excited beating of their own hearts as the culmination of the last three years together, three years that had formed them somehow, without any of them being aware. In the fall of 1994, they'd been boys, followers of other boys. Now, in the spring of 1997, they were young men, leaders who had earned the right to strut the way they did. And three, ten, twenty years from now? On that night, they were confident, even arrogant, that they would rule the city of Newark.

Chapter 5

———————————◆———————————

Coach Ridley stood across from the seething, wild-eyed boy as their last volley of charged words ricocheted off the tiles of the pool. He couldn't believe this was happening, that he'd allowed what had been intended to be a quiet, sensible conversation to reach this pitch—and at seven in the morning no less.

St. Benedict's opened its pool to the neighboring public in the mornings, mostly city employees swimming a few laps before work. Rob had been lifeguarding for a small wage his junior and senior years, which meant getting to school no later than five thirty to open up the pool.

Coach Ridley had figured that this early, quiet hour would be as good a time as any to broach a topic that had been bothering him for many weeks now, and so he'd waited for all the swimmers to finish, leaving Rob alone to close down the pool. As the boy went about his succession of tasks—spooling in the lane ropes, stowing away the kickboards— Coach Ridley approached and asked Rob outright why he smoked so much marijuana, why he would jeopardize his lungs, his mind, his future that way. His intention was to have a reasonable conversation in the manner that St. Benedict's teachers were trained to confront their students' out-of-school lives: nothing accusatory, nothing tense, nothing to drive a boy farther away. But Coach Ridley—though he'd spent so many hundreds of hours in this very same chamber with Rob, though he'd taught the kid to swim, though he'd opened his own home so the Burger Boyz could study film—had no idea of the vast reservoir of anger within Rob Peace. And somehow his very earnest questions about Rob's drug use had fully loosed this anger.

Now Coach Ridley was standing there, his own temples pumping with blood, hearing Rob scream, "I haven't had a father since I was seven years old! What makes you think I need one now?"

This was the first time Coach Ridley had ever heard the kid mention his father. He replied, "I'm not trying to be your father, Rob. I just care about you."

But Rob was already stalking out of the pool, his bare feet slapping the wet tiles. During his five years of teaching, Coach Ridley had never lost control of an interaction so completely. Rob didn't show up at water polo practice for the rest of the week.

At St. Benedict's, academics represented only a fraction of the faculty's responsibilities. Test scores were in many ways secondary to the task of instilling confidence in kids not primed to believe in themselves and confronting rampant emotional issues resulting from the loss of a parent, usually a father. The school's emphasis on sports went a long way, particularly rarefied sports like water polo, fencing, and lacrosse. The expansive counseling system was a fundamental part of the curriculum, as well as the teacher rotation—without overtime pay—that kept the school's doors open on weekends to students seeking a quiet place to work away from harried homes. But there remained limits to what infrastructure could accomplish, because the biggest mistake a counselor could make in addressing emotional problems was to call attention to those problems outright. In troubled cases, the key was to locate a tangential entry point, something like a back door through which counseling could be administered without the boy feeling as though he needed extra help.

The first telltale sign of difficulty at home tended to be academic: a disengagement with the classroom and subsequent falling grades. While heartbreaking to watch, this process presented a tangible opportunity to find that back door—as had been the case with Tavarus freshman year, when the Maine retreat had successfully aligned his touchy consciousness with the potential he'd forgotten he had.

But there were the rare students bright enough to maintain high grades no matter what they were struggling with internally. As Coach Ridley learned that early winter morning of 1998, Rob Peace was one of those students. All the anger Rob felt—at his father's imprisonment, his mother's weariness, his own poverty that tasted like ketchup packets—only seemed to fuel his merits as a scholar and leader, and hide itself behind those ever-rising attributes.

The following Friday night, while Coach Ridley was packing for a water polo tournament—and trying to figure out who could play the hole position in Rob's place—Rob called him at home. He asked when the bus was leaving tomorrow. Coach Ridley, aware that Rob knew very well what time the bus left, told him to be at school by eight in the morning.

"Cool," Rob said. "Cool." Silence followed, but neither hung up.

"How are you feeling about the games tomorrow?" Coach asked.

"Strong. I think we can run the table."

They talked for an hour, about game strategy against the talented Exeter Academy team, about the New York Giants, about random school gossip and events. They talked about everything except what they'd talked about earlier in the week.

Rob was on fire at the tournament, scoring multiple goals in each of their four games. They lost to Exeter in the semifinals but won their consolation game to take third place overall. And Coach Ridley never confronted Rob again about marijuana. He figured that here was a fundamentally good kid of spectacular mental faculty, and that if he could do as well as he did while relying on a little cannabis to metabolize his anger, then maybe it was best not to meddle, not now.

*   *   *

IN THE SECOND week of their senior year, Rob was elected group leader, the president of all the eighteen color groups, each of which had its own president and vice president. He was in charge of the convocation each morning, resolving conflicts among the underclassmen, and, above all, disciplinary measures. One of his first actions was to make boots illegal in school. Because of the uniforms, many students utilized footwear as fashion statements. Sneakers weren't allowed, and so kids wore big construction boots with the laces untied—just like Rob had worn at Mt. Carmel. Rob decided that these boots were a distraction in the hallways and in class, with the heavy thumps they made and the fights they sometimes caused. He took plenty of flack for this policy decision, but he didn't care. The rule went into effect.

When he wasn't at school, he was with Curtis, whose father had died during the summer between junior and senior years: an assault of cancer similar to that which had taken Tavarus's father four years earlier. Alone or all together, the Burger Boyz reneged on their silent agreement to steer their talk clear of the hard stuff, and they wondered what beef God had with the fathers and sons of East Orange. Curtis's father, though sometimes gruff, had provided a beacon for the group, as well as a motivator, a constant stream of eyes-on-the-prize mentality. While thugs, junkies, and vagrants trolled up and down Smith Street at night, Mr. Gamble had always been home by six, available for help with homework or a verbal ass-kicking for any of the five boys who merited one. And now he—just like Tavarus's father, just like Flowy's, just like Drew's, just like Rob's—was gone.

Losing a father was more than a singular devastating event. It marked the beginning of a struggle, a lifetime struggle made harder by the conscious awareness that it would always be so, that no achievement would ever nullify the reality of such an absence. The single thing that did help—to cope with if not to overcome—was friendship, to which these boys clung fiercely.

Through all the various periods of tragedy during their four years together, Rob had yet to reveal anything about his own father. He visited Skeet once a month—more often if his sports schedule permitted—in secret. These visits encompassed more than a father and son divided by Plexiglas, striving to remain in tune with one another's day-to-day.

Rob had in fact been spending a vast amount of time helping his father legally prepare for his long-awaited first appeal, which Skeet had been engineering for five years now.

During the summer between sophomore and junior years, Rob and Tavarus had both interned at a real estate firm run by a St. Benedict's alumnus, mostly doing title research. They'd spent much of each day in the Office of Public Records downtown, cross-referencing tax maps with parcel numbers and property values and transfer deeds, making sure that there were no title irregularities capable of deep-sixing an acquisition (Newark real estate was characterized by its irregularities). The Essex County Law Library was just across Springfield Avenue from the Office of Public Records, and during lunch breaks Rob began spending time there, studying capital murder cases and all the various elements of his father's trial that, increasingly as he grew older, plagued him. Once his junior year of school began, he would finish his homework and then—while his classmates watched TV or talked on the phone or slept—spend a late-night hour with these dense tomes of legal jargon, filling up notebooks with any shred of precedent that might help. As a teenager beginning in 1996, Rob had taken it upon himself to do what the public defenders had failed to do in the fall of 1990: prove that Skeet was innocent. Through his junior year, the following summer, and the first semester of his senior year, in the midst of the trail hikes and early-morning lifeguarding and his group leader responsibilities and high school romances and his first college applications, Rob worked on behalf of his father.

And on December 2, 1997, midway through Rob's senior year of high school, he helped Skeet file a petition for postconviction relief. Representing himself, Skeet argued that his constitutional right to a speedy trial, granted by the Sixth Amendment, had been violated. At the center of this strategy was Irving Gaskins, the man in whose home Skeet had been arrested and who had passed away a year before the trial. Gaskins had been interviewed at the time of the arrest, stating firmly that Skeet had possessed no weapon. But he hadn't been asked to give a formal deposition to Skeet's lawyers before his death, and so this testimony never came forth in the trial. Skeet blamed the public defenders for insufficient representation in this regard, as well as for "severely prejudicing" Skeet's case due to the nearly yearlong period during which the office denied him representation following his initial arrest. Once Skeet had been granted representation, his lawyers had also opted not to file a "speedy trial motion," which he argued further protracted the proceedings.

One of Skeet's public defenders from his trial testified during the postconviction relief hearing that December. Ironically, he did so on behalf of the State, making the case that he had represented Skeet more than adequately, that three years between arrest and trial was not uncommon for a capital crime and had been necessary in order to plan his strategy, and that Gaskins's statement, even if it had been recorded, would not have affected the outcome of the trial given that Gaskins would have spoken of what he had not seen (the murder weapon) rather than what he had. The lawyer argued that the long pretrial process had in fact spared Skeet's life, as it had granted the defense time necessary to "prepare a list of mitigating factors" and escape the death penalty.

But on that day, the presiding judge sided with Skeet and said, "Based upon the defendant's claim of a violation of his Sixth Amendment right to speedy trial, and as a consequence thereof, the indictment which charged him with murder and other offenses has been dismissed." The judge stayed the decision for fifty days to permit the State to appeal, meaning that Rob's father was not yet an entirely free man. Nevertheless, ten years and four months after the murders of the Moore sisters, Skeet came home.

*   *   *

ROB AND CARL STOOD on either side of Skeet as they walked past the final guard station and into the main parking lot beneath an overcast Trenton sky. The redbrick wall behind and above them cast its long shadow over the rows of vehicles. They burrowed into their coats, walked quietly to Carl's car, and headed for the turnpike. Rob had spent many nights preparing to fill his father in on how Newark and the world had changed in the last decade: the Gulf War, Bill Clinton, the razing of four project towers by Mayor James, the breakouts of rap artists like Nas and Outkast and Tupac and the Notorious B.I.G. (he'd made a mix tape for the drive), the murders of the latter two. He knew his father thrived on asking questions, and he was ready to provide everything Skeet wanted to know, share all the information that time constraints had precluded during their half-hour visits over the years.

But Skeet's thirst for human data was limited to only one human: his son. School, sports, his friends, his girlfriends—he drilled Rob with rapid-fire questions, and Rob was startled. As a kid who had geared much of his life around the concerns of others, he was neither accustomed to nor comfortable fielding inquiries about himself. Rob grew increasingly quiet in the backseat as Carl bucked along South Orange Avenue. Skeet had lived his whole preprison life within a mile of this road, but he hadn't laid eyes on it in a decade. He didn't lay eyes on it now, craning his body instead to face his son, their too-similar faces just inches apart, breathing the same air, no more barriers between them.

The fifty-day stay the judge had granted loomed even now. Mr. Herman had left them with no doubt that the State would eventually file its counterappeal of the postconviction relief ruling, and when it did so, Skeet would almost certainly have to return to prison until the appeal was ultimately decided. They didn't know how long the State would take to prepare this counterappeal; they hoped that the approaching holidays would delay the motion, since lawyers had families, too. In the meantime, Rob was fueled by the prospect of reintroducing his father to the neighborhood the same way that his father had introduced it to him so long ago. All those hours in the law library, all those commutes to Trenton State, all those nights lying awake and alone in his bed—and here was the culmination: he and his father entering the house on Chapman Street together.

But the reality of Skeet's homecoming in no way resembled Rob's fantasies.

Skeet moved into the third floor, in a room directly above Rob's. Immediately, the house felt crowded. For the first few weeks before Christmas, Skeet didn't leave. He paced around, ate, read, and continued barraging Rob with questions. He seemed self-conscious about venturing out the way he'd once relished doing, reluctant to confront any of the dozens of neighbors he'd counted as his extended family.

"Everyone's been asking about you," Rob implored him. "Let's take a walk around."

"Uh-uh, uh-uh," Skeet replied. "It's too damn cold outside."

Day after day, his father kept himself surrounded by four walls nearly at all times. Maybe he needed time to acclimate. Maybe he felt vulnerable, disconnected, no longer the Man in this domain. Maybe his father knew that the second he ventured outside he would begin to attract old friends who were exactly the types of people he couldn't be seen around right now. Maybe he would also attract people who had known the Moore sisters, people not above their own brand of retribution. Maybe, after a decade in a cell, he needed those walls on all sides just to breathe.

Jackie kept herself busy and largely apart from the son and his father during these first weeks. She'd convinced her parents to let him stay there temporarily, at least through Christmas, for Rob's benefit alone. But she had no role to play between them, not anymore. Even if she did have one, Jackie wouldn't have had the energy to fill it. She was tired to a degree never before known to her. She'd watched her son's body grow strong from swimming, his mind oiled and tight from the rigorous curriculum he'd designed for himself (which now included college-level calculus and chemistry classes at Essex Community College). She sometimes felt that her own body had withered in inverse proportion, that her own mind had become diffuse and good for little besides calculating stew ingredients according to serving size. Her hair was graying, her posture was slouched, her knees were shot. She hadn't been able to save any money in four years and had relied on her parents' savings to get her through a few lean months. She'd taken Rob to school at five thirty for his lifeguarding job as often as she could. In her parents' Lincoln, she'd picked him up at Curtis's near midnight after study marathons. She'd skimped as little as possible when it came to his education. As much as she could, she'd tried to shield him from the strain this placed on her. The fact that her son was thriving, that he was on course for college, had sustained her. And now, on the home stretch of senior year that she'd always envisioned as a time of vital decisions and valuable reflections on the eighteen years of life she and her son had lived together, she was instead worried about Skeet. She worried about whether he would actually find another place to stay like he'd assured her. She worried about him eating more than his share. She worried about him distracting Rob from schoolwork, something that no one prior had ever been able to do. But she had never worried that having his father at home would make her son unhappy.

Skeet tracked the boy's movements obsessively. Anytime he left that month—to hang with Curtis on Smith Street, to go to the mall in Union with a girl, to work out with Tavarus and Flowy at the pool—Skeet met him at the door, wanting to know exactly where he was going and with whom. And when he returned, Skeet would be there waiting for a detailed rendering of what he'd done while away.

Rob had been living more or less as an adult, responsible for his own time, for years now. He'd constructed his own social network, his own schedule, his own way of life. And he'd done all this with aplomb, ascending to the pinnacle of the St. Benedict's community as well as the precipice of a college education. Through it all, Rob had spent time every day for ten years wondering what it would be like to have his father back. Against the image of this father waiting almost desperately by the front window for him to show up (and Rob could remember waiting in that same place himself as a seven-year old), he was spending his days remembering fondly what it was like being his own man, with no one hovering or questioning or living vicariously through him.

Christmas arrived, and various extended family members came home from Georgia, Florida, and Ohio. The Peace clan, almost all of whom had begun their lives in this house, congregated there once more. Rob had organized the reunion himself, calling, cajoling, offering to help pay for airfare; he'd been obsessed with a family Christmas. Now Rob seemed to locate the happiness that he'd found so elusive in the weeks since his father's release. He cooked and passed around trays of food. He decorated the house. He invited Victor and his aunt over, and Victor would remember for the rest of his life the degree to which Rob resembled his father. Presents were relatively few, but Rob gave his parents both imitation-leather coats that he'd bargained for in the fashion district of Manhattan. Skeet held up his coat and nodded thanks, but no one saw him smile. It was as if he knew that he'd never wear it.

Just after the second semester of school began in January, the State filed its counterappeal to the postconviction relief ruling. As stipulated by the judge's prior stay, Skeet returned to prison. Once more, Rob walked with his father across a prison parking lot, this time to Essex County, to await another verdict.

*　　*＊　＊　＊

NEAR MIDNIGHT, a sharp breeze rolled across Orange Park. The swing set creaked near the bench on which Victor and Rob sat. Victor couldn't recall seeing his friend cry in eight years of knowing him. Had their positions been reversed, Rob most likely would have told him to "quit being a bitch." But Victor wasn't going to say that. His friend spent so much time being rough, hard, guarded, that this moment felt almost precious, and Victor wished he knew what to do or say.

They were sharing a joint, both leaning forward with elbows on knees. Orange Park remained a relatively safe place to smoke, because the police still didn't make regular patrols and because the boys knew by name all the young dealers who operated here—had grown up with many of them. They were left alone to work their way through this new problem, rare in the sense that it belonged to Rob.

In early spring of their senior year, college acceptance letters had begun trickling in to the school. Rob had been advised to apply to nine colleges: three "stretches," three "good bets," and three "safety schools." He'd ultimately chosen to apply to six, in order to save Jackie money on application fees: Johns Hopkins, Yale, Penn, Columbia, Seton Hall, and Montclair State. Earlier that day, Rob had received his third response, from Montclair. The state school had offered Rob a full merit scholarship. The Ivy League did not award merit-based scholarships, only need-based. Columbia, in New York City, had turned him down—Rob felt because that was the one application on which, in the financial aid attachment, he'd mentioned his father's status as an inmate. Johns Hopkins, his first choice after all the college visits, had accepted him but with only partial financial aid. He'd made the mistake of listing the house on Chapman Street as an asset, which had shaded his and Jackie's circumstances in ways he hadn't foreseen, as it had once done for his father in pursuit of public defense. For the general essay question, "Write about a challenge you have overcome," he told the story of the storm on the Appalachian Trail and shepherding underclassmen down the mountainside at night.

Now, he was crying, trying to hide it, digging his index finger into his eye as if there were a bug in it.

"I don't know what I want to do," he murmured.

"You have to go to Montclair, you go to Montclair," Victor responded. "I know it's not an *Ivy* and all, but it's not a bad college."

Rob shook his head. "You know you want to fly planes, right?" Victor had been learning to pilot small planes throughout high school with a group called the Young Eagles, and he'd already accepted admission to Daniel Webster College in Nashua, New Hampshire, which had an aviation program. "But I don't know *what* I want to do."

"You're going to do whatever the hell you have to do," Victor told him, and he ventured laying a hand on Rob's thick shoulder as his friend took a deep drag of marijuana and handed the joint back. "Just like you're doing now."

Rob nodded. The problem was not as simple as money, though money was the most powerful variable in that it basically didn't exist. The other element—the one drawing forth these tears—had to do with potential, of which Rob knew he possessed a vast amount but didn't know where to focus it. He excelled in math and science but remained passionate about books. He'd valued his real estate internship and the complicated minutiae that accompanied the property acquisition process—with profits lying in gathering more information than competitors, in being less lazy. He'd been fully immersed in his father's legal battles, and despite the sobering undercurrents of his father's time at home he still held on to the exhilaration of his role in achieving that time. He loved gaining knowledge in any subject, and he was unnerved by the onset of this first consequential decision of his life—the realization that from this point on, the choices he made would begin closing doors as well as opening them. He told Victor, though not in so many words, that he wished he weren't as smart as he was; he wished his horizon might be narrower and thus more easily navigable. Considering his academic pedigree, Montclair State represented a narrow horizon indeed. But that's where he was going to go—even after Yale and Penn accepted him over the next two weeks, with aid packages similar to that offered by Johns Hopkins. He owed it to his mother not to take anything more from her; this debt was unspoken, and unknown even to Jackie herself.

The senior banquet was held in mid-April, in the gymnasium. On the same bowed floorboards on which the class had rolled out their sleeping bags during Summer Phase in 1994, the school arranged two dozen tables with linen and silverware. The cafeteria staff prepared steak, salmon, and Caesar salad. The students had been prepped for their best behavior: no slouching, elbows on the table, jokes. Colin Powell, then the secretary of defense, was the guest of honor. Louis Freeh, the head of the FBI, was there as well, along with an army of Secret Service agents. The banquet was a formal celebration for parents and an awards ceremony for students, but it was also a fund-raising event, a chance for the school to show off its finest to alumni donors and high-profile guests.

Charles Cawley, the MBNA CEO, sat at Table One with Friar Leahy, Mr. Freeh, and General Powell. He was bald, with thick white tufts of hair over each ear, his napkin tucked into his collar over a polka-dot bow tie while he sipped vichyssoise. Though he appeared in the flesh only once or twice a year, his was an everpresence among the students. From behind the scenes he had played a direct or indirect role in each of their lives.

As group leader, Rob gave the keynote address. He'd rehearsed at home with his mother, and his deep voice didn't falter as he spoke of this journey they were near to completing, the reliance they'd placed on one another along the way, the gift of manhood that the St. Benedict's tradition had imparted to them. He was striking to all: muscular, focused, commanding. But what struck Charles Cawley was not Rob's speech but Friar Leahy's introduction. The headmaster spoke of a boy who woke up at four-thirty six days a week to lifeguard at the pool, who taught himself to swim as a freshman and now was among the top ten butterflyers in the state, who led quietly and by example, who spent hours each week officially and unofficially working as a math tutor, who would have been valedictorian if a C in freshman art class hadn't knocked his grade point average down to a 3.97—third in the class—and who had grown up with nothing and now had college acceptances to Hopkins, Penn, and Yale.

At the end of the dinner, Rob was polishing off his chocolate cake when he felt a hand on his shoulder. He looked up into Charles Cawley's face, stood politely to shake his hand and shrug off compliments on his speech. Then Mr. Cawley took a dinner napkin with a phone number scrawled on it from his pocket, and he pressed it into Rob's hand. He said, "You can go to college wherever you want."

Rob glanced at Friar Leahy, who was watching the interaction with a knowing, contented expression.

"Thank you, sir," Rob said, not fully understanding.

"Congratulations, son," Mr. Cawley replied, and he returned to his seat.

A few minutes later, Victor found Rob in the bathroom. For the second time in a month, his best friend since elementary school was crying in front of him.

That night, Rob gave the napkin to his mother and told her what had happened. She figured he'd misunderstood something. Then she called the number the next morning and learned that Rob had been granted a blank personal check from Charles Cawley to cover all his college expenses, no questions asked.

She didn't have time to marvel or celebrate. She didn't even have time to confront her initial reaction, which was to spurn charity and politely decline, write a respectful letter to Mr. Cawley saying that this offer was too generous, and they would be fine making do on their own (she knew that Mr. Cawley was rich; she didn't know that, with an annual salary approaching $50 million, he was one of the best-paid executives in the country). Rob actually called Friar Leahy at home to express this sentiment, and the headmaster told him directly, a little harshly, even, that Mr. Cawley had chosen to make this offer, an offer he had never made to any other student in twenty-five years as a benefactor to the school. Rob had a responsibility to accept it, and to earn it. "Yes, Father Ed," Rob replied.

His heart was set on Johns Hopkins. Jackie knew people in Baltimore, knew the city and its rhythms, knew that it wasn't too dissimilar from Newark. Its science program was top tier, and during visits Rob had appreciated that the boundaries between the university and surrounding lower-class neighborhoods were less clearly demarcated than they were at other urban schools like Penn and Yale. The student body, too, felt more diverse. Rob spoke often of "real people" with his friends, by which he meant people who struggled, like they all did. On the Ivy League campus visits, any sense of daily or long-term struggle had seemed airbrushed. At Johns Hopkins—and maybe he was only imagining this because of the Ivy League stigma absent in Baltimore—Rob believed the average student had worked harder and sacrificed more to be there.

The April postmark date for the Hopkins acceptance and room deposit arrived. Rob and Jackie had the signed documents—and the $500 deposit—sealed in a yellow manila envelope, ready for her to drop off after work.

A dreaded day among industrial food service workers was the random health standards inspection by state regulators, which happened at the Summit Ridge facility on April 10, 1998. A group of five inspectors wearing white smocks arrived and spent the full afternoon checking the kitchen, the ingredients, the workers. Jackie received a mark for wearing a hairnet that didn't meet the code in the density of its meshing. As punishment, her supervisor made her stay to oversee the full three-to-eleven shift, though she'd previously arranged for two half shifts. She'd borrowed her mother's car for the post office run that day, and after getting off work at eleven fifteen she headed straight for the I-280 to Jersey City, where there was a post office that stayed open until midnight. But it was Friday night, and she got caught in a snarl of Manhattan-bound tunnel traffic. She made it to the post office ten minutes late. Jackie knocked on doors and banged on windows. Finally, she scribbled, "Urgent, please postmark for April 10th!" on the front of the envelope addressed to Johns Hopkins, slipped it in the mailbox, and drove home hoping that one day wouldn't make a difference.

Hoping wasn't enough to get her son to his first college choice. A phone call the following Tuesday confirmed that the folder hadn't been postmarked in time, and Rob had automatically been placed at the end of the waiting list. As a small consolation, they assured her that the room deposit would be returned immediately.

Her son didn't hold it against her. They spent a meal bitching about her supervisor at work, and then they began assembling acceptance materials for Rob's second choice, Yale University.

*   *   *

Robert D. PEACE
Nickname: Shawn, FOD, Ropert, Wideback
Activities: Swimming (1,2,3,4); Water Polo (2,3,4); Math League (3);
 Trail (1,2,3); Honor Code (4); Overnight (2,3,4); Senior Group Leader;
 Group Leader of DS (3); Lacrosse (1)
Favorites: Peace Family, CSP, Victor, DA BURGER BOYZ, real people,
 and knowledge
College/Future Plans: Attend College (unknown) and accomplish many things

The yearbooks had been published before Charles Cawley made his offer, but Rob appreciated the fact that Yale wasn't listed on his page. He was embarrassed enough by the way his mother had been telling everyone she knew where he was going to school. She'd even submitted the information to the community page of the East Orange paper, bought many copies, and posted the small blurb on the bulletin board at work as a subliminal *fuck you* to her supervisor.

"Ma, I'm gonna get curbed," Rob said to her. She asked him what the term meant. He told her not to worry about the specifics, but to know that it wasn't something you wanted to have happen to you.

She said, "I've been quiet about my son for eighteen years. I can let people know you're going to college."

"You don't have to advertise *Yale*, though," he replied. "People are already talking shit."

"Let them talk. And watch your mouth. Anyone busy talking about you isn't going to Yale I bet."

But she saw how serious he was, and she stopped advertising to the extent that pride allowed her.

Her mother, Frances, was sick with the early stages of emphysema. At graduation that spring, known as "Walking," Jackie sat in the back in case Frances needed to step away for a coughing fit. She listened to the valedictorian speak, less eloquently in her opinion than her son had spoken at the senior banquet. She watched her son walk in his broad-shouldered strut to receive his diploma.

Afterward, milling in the crowd, she began to see familiar faces flitting in and out of view: estranged siblings, old neighbors, Skeet's friends and relatives, boys Rob's age from the Orange High football team, people she hadn't spoken to or thought of in years. She needed a moment to realize that they were all there for her son, and another moment to understand that Rob, unbeknownst to her, had maintained relations with all these people, people she'd been too busy or tired to keep in touch with herself. He'd listed "Peace Family" first among his favorite things in the yearbook, and he'd made sure everyone he'd ever considered a part of that family was there that day, everyone except his father.

The summer of 1998 was the last hurrah, and Rob and his friends treated it as such. Flowy, whose scholarship aspirations had been quickly doused along with any hope of affording college (he did not even apply), took a few weeks off before a coach at St. Benedict's helped him secure summer work as a lifeguard for the Department of Parks & Recreation. Everyone else was going to college: Victor to Daniel Webster College; Tavarus to the University of Georgia–Clarkson; Drew to Johnson C. Smith, a small university in North Carolina; Curtis to Morehouse. They took the bus downtown for nostalgic lunches at the Burger King by school. Rob got a tattoo, a sphinx on his right biceps. Victor had drawn the picture during a Fourth of July cookout, and Rob was sufficiently taken by the image to have it inked permanently on his skin. They barbequed in Curtis's backyard and, when his mother wasn't home, they drank a lot and smoked more. They talked about a future in which each of them would congregate here again, in the homes and blocks they knew, with four out of five of them holding college degrees. They would get jobs and then get better jobs. They would save money and buy property and then make profits to buy better property. They would sleep with many women until each found the woman who suited him, and then they would marry and have families and be true to those families. They would teach their sons to swim and send them to St. Benedict's, where Friar Leahy would lecture them about manhood at convocation each morning and Coach Ridley would run them through six-thousand-yard swims at practice each afternoon (ten thousand yards during holiday double sessions).

They would be businessmen, landlords, leaders. They would take care of their parents and each other. They harbored little doubt that this future, this collective trajectory, would be earned and actualized. They felt that in light of all the struggles they'd endured, nothing ahead of them would feel very hard at all. Only time lay between now and then.

In August, as Rob was getting ready for one more Appalachian Trail hike with the underclassmen, Jackie gave him a piece of mail, with a Wilmington, Delaware, return address.

The letter began, "Dear Robert, looks like we're going to be roommates . . . ," and briefly described a guy who was going to run hurdles on the Yale track team and major in English. He professed to be relatively clean, quiet, and excited about college (except for the quiet part, these were lies). In the letter, he suggested that they talk on the phone before leaving for New Haven, so that they might suss out who was bringing what to furnish the room. The letter was from me.

A week or so later, I came home from my summer job at a preschool for mentally challenged kids, where I helped with sports like kickball and floor hockey. I was turning around for track practice in preparation for the Junior Olympic Championships in Seattle that year when my mom, in the kitchen, shouted that one of my roommates, Robert, had called. She was cooking dinner for six, meat-starch-vegetables, as she'd done most every evening of my life. Above the kitchen table, more than a dozen photos of me and my siblings playing sports were arranged in a sprawling shrine. My little brother was watching *The Simpsons* on TV in the next room.

Later that evening, I called Rob back. Jackie answered the phone.

"Hello?"

"Hi, this is Jeff, is Robert there?"

"Jeff who?" Her voice was curt, I felt, and bordering on suspicious.

"Jeff . . . Hobbs."

"How do you know Shawn?"

"I . . . think we're going to be roommates." She remained silent, as if needing more information to complete the explanation. "At . . . Yale?"

"Oh yeah, yeah, yeah. You're the one that sent that letter?"

"Yes, Mrs. Peace."

"Let me get Shawn."

While I waited, I heard adult voices in the background, three or four, arguing about something. Then Rob muttered at whoever was there to keep it down before he picked up the phone. "Hello?" That he was black was basically the first thing I learned about Rob Peace, evident in the first syllable of the first word he spoke. His voice was deep, as if created by a stone friction far down in a subterranean larynx. His speech had a viscous cadence, heavy on *o*'s and lacking in hard *r*'s, and he had a particular way of not responding to sentences—of embedding long silences into our conversation—that left me slightly uneasy.

The Orange, New Jersey, address meant little to me. My older sister's college roommate was from a nearby town, and she came from a wealthy Italian family; as far as I knew, all of northern New Jersey was affluent, siphoning fortunes out of Manhattan. I learned over the course of our conversation that Rob had gone to a prep school, he "played a little water polo," and his favorite pastime was hiking the Appalachian Trail. Nothing he said shaded him as anything other than well-off and overeducated: a typical rarefied Yale applicant. And yet there was something serious behind his voice, contemplative and world-wise. I told him that my older siblings—my brother a Yale graduate two years earlier, my sister going into her senior year at Yale—had advised organizing beforehand who would bring what to the room to prevent overlap. Rob told me he had a TV and side table; I said I could bring a stereo and a few lamps. Neither of us seemed interested in prolonging the conversation; an inherent awkwardness existed in talking to someone whose face you'd never seen and with whom you would be living in tight quarters for the next nine months. "Later," he finally said and hung up.

A few weeks later, Rob spent a day making rounds to his friends' homes. He spent another day visiting his father in Essex County Jail, where Skeet was still waiting for the postconviction relief hearings to begin (the first hearing wouldn't take place for another eleven months). Then Rob loaded up his grandparents' car—TV, one large canvas duffel bag of clothes, backpack full of books, one side table—while his mother sat on the porch keeping watch, as it was foolish to leave a packed vehicle unattended for even a moment. Rob embraced Frances and Horace. Then Jackie drove him the ninety miles to Yale.

After more than two hours they rounded a bend in the interstate, and New Haven, similar in scope and appearance to Newark, coalesced into view. They joined the slow stream of cars, packed with the material existences of more than a thousand other freshmen like Rob, and then stop-started along Temple Street, between the centuries-old alternately Gothic and Georgian buildings in which he would now live alongside the hundreds of already-arrived students now jaywalking around their car in flip-flops. They rode mostly in silence, both exhilarated by what this new commute signified and frightened of the pending moment, not far away now, in which they would have to say goodbye.

Before graduation in 1998, Rob won the St. Benedict's Presidential Award, the school's highest honor. Teachers such as Abbot Melvin (left) and Friar Leahy (background) were beyond proud of how far the student had come in four years, and how far he was set to go from there.

Part III

―――――――――◆―――――――――

Class of Oh-Deuce

Rob studying at his usual spot in Yale's Pierson College dining hall during exam week.

Chapter 6

───────◆───────

I ENTERED MY NEW HOME, a quad on the fourth floor of Lanman-Wright Hall, with both of my parents trailing behind me. My dad carried a small table, my mom an armload of new sheets. Dad was in a lousy mood; the four-hour drive from Delaware had been followed by thirty minutes jockeying for a parking spot near the eastern gate of Old Campus, the gorgeous, sprawling quad in which most Yale freshmen lived—and now he had to contend with the stairs. After listening to him swear and honk as if the hundreds of other packed cars had no right to be there, barging in upon Jackie and Rob was jolting. They were just sitting in the common room, almost submissively still—resigned, even. For a moment, the harried commotion that accompanied twelve hundred eighteen-year-olds moving into a single building over a four-hour time window ceased entirely, replaced by the feeling that we'd interrupted a moment whose gravity lay far beyond me.

His single duffel bag had been tossed on the floor in the left-hand bedroom, and a small, bunny-eared TV was lying on its side in the common room. Random handprints marked the film of dust coating the blank gray screen. Rob wore jeans and a T-shirt, and his close-cropped hair made his face look very young, which belied his deep voice as he shook my mother's hand first, officiously, and said, "Pleasure to meet you, Mrs. Hobbs." Then he shook my father's.

"Chuck Hobbs," Dad said. He appreciated a firm handshake, and I could tell he approved of Rob's grip. I had no idea what weight might lie within that grip on Rob's part. My Dad was handsome and fit, and when he wasn't trying to park a car he was gracious and kind. Whereas Rob's father was an inmate, mine was a surgeon. Dad's primary advice to me in preparing for college was to take easy intro classes the first semester. ("Christ," he said, "I took some philosophy course my first semester of college, thinking it'd expand my mind or something, and it just about killed me.")

To Jackie, Dad said, "How are you doing today, ma'am? Bad traffic?"

"Wasn't much," Jackie replied, a little glumly. She had gray in her short hair, a slight underbite that gave her a miffed expression, and very little interest in engaging with the Hobbses even as her eyes seemed to probe each of us.

Rob nodded in my direction and said, "'Sup." We performed a half handshake, half hand slap gesture at the level of our waists. I put my bags on the floor, not sure whether etiquette called for me to move into the room Rob had already chosen or wait for our other two roommates.

In the self-centered context of my arrival at college, I never thought to wonder where Rob's dad was. I was too eager to peek into the bedrooms and confirm that the rumors of their dimensions had been true. Everyone downstairs was comparing them to prison cells. With measurements of seven by twelve, they were actually larger than the six-by-eight cells at Trenton State.

My mom was heartened that my rooming situation would include some diversity, and she became overly chatty with Rob: "Have you thought about what classes you're taking?" "So you play . . . water polo?" "I guess all these stairs will keep you boys in shape!" Rob humored her politely. After a time, she occupied herself with measuring all the windows for curtains she was planning to make on her sewing machine and bring with her on Parents' Day in two months. My dad and I plowed through a half dozen trips to the car for clothes, school supplies, lamps, and tables. Each time we entered the room, Rob and Jackie seemed to be in the same curious state of doing nothing, not even talking. When the transfer was finished, Dad and I were both sweaty and stiff, and he was eager to beat the traffic home. He shook my hand and made a quick exit so as to hide reluctant tears; my mother embraced me, letting her own tears flow, and left as well: both parts of the ritual I had witnessed in this same dorm between them and my older siblings and so understood well. We felt nostalgic and perhaps a bit gloomy—this moment was a milestone that represented aging for them and the removal of childhood cushions for me—but not traumatized. We all knew that life hadn't actually changed all that much.

Once they were gone, I realized that Jackie was now sitting on the windowsill overlooking a stone courtyard. Below her, a herd of students milled around, introducing themselves with a breathy, manic energy, exchanging hometowns and entryway assignments. Some were dressed in a style akin to business-casual; others wore PJs. Almost all were white and cheery and well-heeled, some veterans of mass move-ins after four years at elite boarding schools. Music played from speakers facing outward from someone's window: Guns n' Roses' "Sweet Child o' Mine." Jackie had barely moved all afternoon and had yet to appear anything other than impassively observant—judgmental, even, and I felt compelled to perform for her somehow, to show that her son would not be living with just another wealthy legacy kid (though I was both wealthy and a legacy). I offered to get her some water, to remove bags from a chair so that she could sit, to make a pizza run. She declined each outreach: "Nah, nah, I'm all right." Rob, too, seemed to be studying our surroundings and the people newly inhabiting them, the subtle negotiations already taking place over bunk assignments, bathroom stations, and furniture arrangement, the wide-eyed marveling over the bedroom sizes. He must have been thinking about Summer Phase at St. Benedict's, his 140 classmates with their sleeping bags in the Hive, tasked with memorizing one another's names by week's end.

Our other two roommates arrived. Dan Murray was a white guy from Seattle, his father a doctor like mine. He wore preppy clothes and carried a plastic water bottle with him at all times. He spoke very fast and in a high voice, such that it was impossible to understand him at first. Ty Cantey was "blackasian" (black father, Japanese mother) and he ran the four-hundred-meter hurdles, my event. He hailed from San Jose, California, where his father was a NASA engineer. A nearly flawless physical specimen, with chest and arms chiseled like a Greek sculpture, Ty had me intimidated before I even set foot on the track that year. The reasoning behind our "random" rooming assignment was clear: Ty and I were together because we both ran track, Ty and Rob were together because they were both African American, and Dan had been tacked on as a white suburban kid like me to fill out the quad. Ty and I ended up sharing one bedroom, because we figured we'd be waking up early for practice and track meets together. Dan and Rob took the other room. Unstated but thickly understood was the fact that the "right" thing to do was to mix our races. Rob and Ty both claimed the bottom bunks; Dan and I politely ceded them. Dan had gone on the weeklong FOOT trip, an Appalachian Trail hike for incoming freshmen. Ty had participated in PROP, an orientation retreat for minorities during which they'd stayed at a nearby camping ground and played games like capture the flag. They had both already made friends, had begun to construct social lives here in a way that Rob and I hadn't. They flitted in and out of the dorm while Rob and I mostly stayed put, neither of us ready to join the fracas outside.

Rob set himself up in the room silently but directedly, never asking permission or guidance on where to put things. For decoration, he pinned two pictures to the wall. One was of him and his mother at his St. Benedict's graduation. The other was of him, Curtis, Tavarus, Drew, and Flowy standing over a smoky grill in the backyard of 34 Smith Street, making "East Side" hand gestures: the right hand extended palm in, fingers splayed except for the overlapping middle and ring fingers to form a warped E. With their baggy jeans, ribbed undershirts, and skullcaps, they looked like a gang. As I spent the late afternoon organizing my desk with tchotchkes and pictures of family, he walked his mother downstairs to her car. Their goodbye, which took place among the honking lines of expensive foreign cars still coming and going, must have lasted forty-five minutes.

*   *   *

THE FIRST WEEK of college, in my recollection, was a collective celebration of freedom. By day, this took the form of endless ceremonial speeches, extracurricular bazaars, and focus groups on sexual education. By night, more than a thousand eighteen-year-olds, many of whom had never truly "partied" before, engaged in some serious binge drinking. The shared bathrooms began to exude a vomit stench onto the stairwell landings. We lined up outside entryways and frat houses waiting for our rations of stale keg beer. We crowded into Yorkside Pizza and Rudy's Bar hoping to not be carded, which we always were. It was as if all of these kids had spent so long working so hard to get here that the reaction to actually being here was to become idiots. The RA fixed a paper bin filled with hundreds of multicolored condoms to the bulletin board in each entryway; the bins were empty by the following morning, prompting a sign that read ONLY TAKE IF YOU ARE ACTUALLY GOING TO USE THEM! Kids sectored off into giddy groups that seemed preordained: the Manhattanites, the Midwesterners, the Californians, the Northeastern boarding schoolers, the internationals. Already coursing through the freshman class was the confident recognition—fostered in no small part by the university—that we were the elite, and these four years would be our passageway to flourishing in whatever arena we chose, and in the midst of that passage we were entitled to celebrate our status freely, often sloppily.

Rob wasn't sloppy. When he was in the room, he methodically paged through his Blue Book, the three-inch-thick paperback of course listings, with an almost menacing seriousness. He spoke in mumbled monosyllables as we gradually furnished and decorated: "Huh," "Yeah," "Cool." Sometimes I would pass him in the courtyard, sitting on a bench or a stone pillar smoking cigarettes, usually alone.

The Yale student body, much like St. Benedict's, was divided into groups within the group in what was called the "residential college system." Though almost all freshmen lived on Old Campus, our social lives were tagged to one of twelve colleges situated around the university, each with its own distinct architecture, dining hall, library, and "master"—a designated professor who lived in a home affixed to the dorm, there to provide guidance and oversight. We were in Pierson College, a Georgian building that wrapped around a grass courtyard on the northwest corner of campus. The first time the one hundred members of the Pierson Class of '02 congregated together, we were on the slate patio outside the dining hall. Rob stood on the fringe, wearing baggy jeans, Timberland boots, and a "skully," a tight, thin piece of black nylon fabric in the shape of a stingray, the wing tips of which he bound at the base of his cranium. He was smoking a cigarette, his back turned to us. The classmates who hadn't met him yet clearly figured him to be a dining hall worker or part of the maintenance staff. He did nothing to dispel this notion. In fact, he seemed to take pride in it. Like his mother on move-in day, he harbored little interest in interacting with the rest of us. Though I'd made an effort to be friendly enough, I kept my distance in those moments. An uncle had advised me not to get too chummy with my roommates early on, because it was easier to become better friends than to extricate yourself from someone you didn't like.

In a way that at the time felt natural but perhaps a bit too deliberate, I thought having a black roommate was fortunate. Though my high school was demographically the opposite of Rob's—90 percent white— I was a national-caliber hurdler and had spent my summers traveling and rooming with mostly black runners at Junior Olympic meets. As a result of many long, cramped van rides, I had a familiarity with popular hip-hop artists of the day, I was conversant in certain strands of street lingo ("That's *tight!*"), and I knew how to play spades. Overall, I considered myself quite the "honorary black man," a title with which my old teammates had laughingly graced me. In the dining hall, I would seek out Rob and sit with him. To the extent that I could, I tried to subtly intimate how well qualified I was to be his pal, dropping small hints as to my comfort level among urban black males, omitting or outright lying about certain details that might undermine the claim. I told him I'd grown up "near Philly," when in fact I had grown up in an eighteenth-century farmhouse on fifteen acres of rolling rural hills in Chester County, thirty miles from the city. I consciously failed to mention that I'd attended private school beginning in prekindergarten, and that my parents, who had been married for almost thirty years, had invested their entire lives (not to mention their finances) into taking care of their four children—removing all uncertainty from our formative years. The two Labradors, the trips to Florida each spring, the sports camps, the annual late-summer mall trips for new school clothes, the pool behind our house—none of these flourishes of my life seemed to come up. Whether out of sensitivity or amusement, Rob never clued me in to the fact that, despite a few track meets, we hailed from different worlds, different families, different perspectives—different everything. I would learn that on my own, over the course of many months and never at my friend's behest. In the beginning, we were able to laugh over the fact that I was a white guy who ran sprints and he was a black guy who played water polo. Our friendship coalesced slowly, very slowly, from there.

"What's your dad do?" I asked once during those first days.

He finished chewing and swallowing his food—Rob filled his tray with massive heaps of sustenance, heavy on protein, and he lowered his face very close to the plate while eating, such that he was always looking up from beneath his fierce brow—before replying, "He's in jail."

"Oh," I said. "Oh, sorry. I didn't—"

He shrugged and glanced away. "It's all good," he said, and then, unprompted, "Manslaughter." I asked nothing further.

As he'd done in high school, he kept to himself the fact that the State of New Jersey's counterappeal to Robert Douglas's Sixth Amendment ruling began in earnest that October with another back-and-forth of motions to begin hearing arguments. The first hearing would not be held until the following March, and the process would stretch on into June, effectively encompassing Rob's entire freshman year of college.

*   *   *

MY OLDER BROTHER had spoken of it when he'd first left for Yale in 1992: how the black kids ate and hung out only with each other, how some kind of racism, or reverse racism, coursed through "their" social dynamic. Twelve years old at the time, I'd nodded energetically at his keen cultural observation, wondering what it would be like to live out there in the "real world" (Yale, at the time, seeming to me as such). Six years later, my white classmates and I noticed pretty much the same thing. Yale intentionally fills its dining halls with long, narrow tables intended to spur discussions with new people during mealtimes. But once two black classmates sat down at the end of the table, and were joined by three more, and four more after that, from a distance their conversations tended to be loud, a little profane, punctuated with tics of diction and dialect not our own. These groups seemed to cordon themselves off from the majority, and if a white kid ventured to sit there, he looked conspicuously progressive, performing for the rest of the dining hall as if to say, "Look at me! I'm sitting with the black kids so I'm definitely not racist!"

This self-segregation, and the self-consciousness it engendered in the white kids, was most evident at lunch and dinner, but it extended to classrooms, libraries, and particularly weekend parties. Though rarely spoken of—certainly not by whites—the dynamic remained a quietly understood aspect of this strange new milieu in which we lived. In college we were asked to become part of (and most of our parents paid small fortunes for us to become a part of) a manufactured civilization, a city-within-a-city that trumpeted a long list of lofty ideals inscribed in Latin on the stone archways. As freshmen, we wanted to take ownership of our new place within this structure, to begin leaving our mark as the Class of 2002. At the same time, we emulated the upperclassmen and their established social pretexts, begotten from the upperclassmen before them, and we succumbed easily to pressure—academic, of course, but social even more so. White students went to frat houses, one of five popular bars, outdoor quad parties; black students did something else, of which we knew little except that rap music was most likely playing very loud.

The beginning of our first semester entailed much desperate scrambling: we scrambled to choose our classes, most with at least vague notions of future majors; we scrambled to find extracurricular groups to be a part of (sketch comedy troupes, film societies, social activist committees, etc.); we scrambled for friends and social lives that—though we weren't necessarily aware of it then—would define us for the next four years. We were inclined to engage with cultural presentations like drama school plays, guest lectures, and singing groups—to immerse ourselves in "the Yale Experience" colorfully advertised in our orientation materials (these inclinations would fade quickly, as all we really wanted to do was get decent grades and find free drinks; "Thursday is the new Friday" was a de rigueur expression). We sought out the adventures that, we all assumed, would form the basis for conversations at our tenth reunion in fourteen years: "Didn't we once . . . ?" "Remember that time when we . . . ?"

Above all, we did our best to define—and in most cases redefine—ourselves. Jocks, intellectuals, humorists, student leaders, partiers, stoners, debaters: an electric feeling manifested that here, now, any one of us could be any person he wanted to be. No one knew what anyone else had been like in high school, and during the fall of 1998 we walked to classes and to parties and to meals on a blank slate. These first weeks were an ephemeral, transitional time, a collision of nervousness and self-consciousness and ambition and independence and confusion and bravado that sparked a collective blossoming—and in some cases, wilting—of twelve hundred teenage identities.

I had no awareness of this then (of course I didn't, even though I lived with two black men and spent four hours every afternoon training with my racially mixed track teammates), but a deeper transition affected people of color in this dazed context. Before course selections and extracurricular sign-up sheets—before bags could even be unpacked in rooms—black students had to situate themselves within their own race. The process was complicated, conflicting, usually silent, highly fraught—and wholly invisible to their white classmates, most of whom had never actively had to consider the role of race in their lives, most of whom tended to see black culture as monolithic. Hence the "black tables" in the dining halls, viewed by the people sitting there as a filial group of like backgrounds and interests—West Coast or Caribbean Islands or Brooklyn, say—but viewed by those watching from afar as inherently exclusive. Others were seen as "acting white" when they sought out the majority-centric opportunities (an expansive humanities curriculum, a capella groups, or, as in Rob Peace's case, the water polo team). A latent variance also existed within the demographic, among black students of affluent backgrounds, lower class, and all the gradations in between. Rob, being both black and poor, was in the minority of the minority. Of our class, 12 percent were black. Of that subset, 20 percent had grown up at or below the poverty line—about thirty classmates who could relate directly to where Rob had come from. And since he'd come from a city where he had been in every way a member of the majority, the transition was unsettling, and it must have inspired some level of resentment.

However, Rob was incredibly skilled at not showing how he felt.

He was also skilled at concealing who he was and who he wanted to be. In high school, he had been all things: an athlete, a leader, an academic, a partier. In college, he went about his days so very quietly, slipping in and out of the room with a head nod and a "'Sup," his canvas book bag slung over his shoulder—the same book bag his father had bought him for Oakdale, scuffed and threadbare, which he'd taken everywhere in the neighborhood to Newark-proof himself. At meals, he usually sat alone near the entrance, at a small round table just behind the station where Jacinta Johnson, one of the dining hall ladies, swiped our ID cards. Jacinta was an overweight, light-skinned, red-haired African

American woman in her forties who had a grandmotherly aspect. Rob usually kept a textbook open in front of him but he talked to her over his shoulder, and he made her laugh a lot. When I sat with him sometimes, his reserved demeanor and the open textbook elicited the question, "Is it cool if I sit here?" as if I might be intruding on intensive study or simply a desire to be alone—which was a desire that I myself valued highly, as solitude could be hard to find in college. He would shrug and say sure, and his dialogue with Jacinta would continue as he paged through the textbook and I opened a paperback from a Shakespeare's tragedies or romantic poetry class, *King Lear* or Wordsworth. During that time, I didn't know him well but I appreciated the quietude that surrounded him. Any other table in the dining hall carried the threat of having to perform for new acquaintances, to prove how clever or worldly or socially connected you were in the context of conversations about foreign policy, Ptolemy, the best bars on campus. With Rob, there was no judging, no need to hone any aspects of personality or tout knowledge. I could just sit, read, maybe joke about our roommate Ty's weird sleeping hours and weirder culinary routines (he would eat half a dozen microwave soy burgers at midnight, run five miles, and then go to the library until seven). An added benefit came with knowing that no one else would venture to sit with us, both because Rob always chose the smallest table and because our classmates still kept their distance. I hailed from a small school and a small town, and the social onslaught had been intimidating. Rob provided a buffer of which I, selfishly and without truly asking if I was welcome, took advantage.

Then he met Zina. I wasn't privy to their brief courtship, or really to any part of Rob's social life. From my perspective, one day our dorm room was what any dorm room shared by four eighteen-year-old males was: a shambles of clashing furniture and clothes and books, but habitable and generally peaceful. The next day, this girl was camped out on our futon (which she'd folded out into bed mode, such that it took up half the common room) along with half her possessions. And she was not just any girl. Everything about her—her towering bun of coiled hair, her skirts that ballooned around her sprawled legs, her various moisturizers and conditioners, her high and ceaseless voice—consumed space and oxygen. She was a senior from Jamaica, and though she had an off-campus apartment she took up residence on the fourth floor of Lanman-Wright Hall, such that she seemed to be there at all hours, even when Rob was not. I observed from this too-close vantage point as, over a span of less than a month, they succumbed to the dating tendency common among college students—they behaved as though they were married.

I'd already observed this among others in our class: with college just weeks old, a few couples had formed who ate breakfast together in their sweatpants while reading the *Yale Daily News*, clasped hands while walking across the quad between classes, held court during dinner as if this were their home and they were hosting a society party, studied in adjacent library cubicles, and planned their weekends solely around each other. I could easily see why this happened; we were on our own for the first time, and people wanted to feel like legitimate adults. And then, in almost every case, the inevitable parting happened, impelled by the realization that they were not in fact adults, that codependence actually impinged on these precious four years of freedom. For those on the outside looking in, the subsequent breakup always presented good fodder for speculation (as the newness of college began to wane that semester, so did the compulsion to discuss "serious" topics, replaced by that old reliable: gossip).

Rob and Zina were different, carrying something more consequential in their dynamic that precluded gossip and left one only to watch, often bewildered. They fought all the time. As in a marriage, their fights began with little things (our messy room, him not calling when he said he would, etc.) that escalated into big things (suspicions of cheating, he being fundamentally an asshole, she being fundamentally a bitch, etc.). Because Zina had neither pitch control nor self-awareness about being overheard, Dan and Ty and I were privy to these fights with an intimacy none of us desired (I soon began to study in the library). They sounded

scripted, like the domestic arguments policemen overhear in TV proce-
durals before they burst into a project housing drug den.

"Robert, you just smoke and eat your face off and don't do nothing,"
she yelled at him. She was in her spot in the common room; he was in
his bedroom, with a door closed between them.

"Shut up, I'm trying to read."

"You're not reading! You're just sitting there all fucked up in your
pigsty room!"

Rob said what I, overhearing from my top bunk, had been wanting
to say for quite some time (Zina nagged me about the mess, too): "You
think the room's too messy, get the fuck out and go back to your own
room."

And so on.

I asked him once, with carefully premeditated phrasing, "What do
you and Zina do for fun?" Meaning: Why are you with this woman?

In response, he showed me a leather jacket he'd been wearing
lately—real leather, and the only possession of his that he seemed to
take good care of, always folded and hung. I hadn't realized that it had
been a gift from Zina. He said, "She's a real woman, not like these other
Yalie bitches." Then he laughed and brought out the Facebook (this was
before Facebook.com; the Facebook was a paperback room listing of
the entire freshman class, with head shots, that boys spent hours comb-
ing through with highlighters to note those they would like to sleep
with, realistically or not). Rob had marked a handful of pictures, not for
himself but for me. The "Freshman Screw" dance was coming up that
weekend, in which one's roommates arranged your date for the night.
"Which one you into?" he asked.

I looked over his listings and happily saw that he'd taken the task seriously, and the girls he had in mind for me were by and large attractive.
After I ranked them, we huddled over the book together for the benefit
of our other two roommates. Rob had it in his mind to "screw" Ty by
setting him up with a less-than-desirable face.

Rob and Ty got along well. They were both taking intro biology together, the precursor to premed classes. Like Rob—like almost all the students now surrounding us—Ty was a fantastic student accustomed to straight A's in high school. Unlike Rob, he was tremendously competitive and pulled all-nighters with a particular pride, intent on being at the top of the class. Rob, who was laid back about schoolwork, had no problem with Ty's academic approach. Rob's problem had to do with the "thug" persona that Ty nurtured with near-equal intensity. He wore a heavy jacket with FUBU (an acronym of "For Us, By Us," alluding to black people) printed in huge red letters across the chest, and he came to be referred to as "T-Money," or, as he signed off on his emails, "T$." He talked "hard" and seemed to loop every other story about high school around to some fight he'd been in, some girl he'd slept with, some bad neighborhood he'd hung out in. Ty had grown up in the suburbs and spent money freely. He bought new clothes frequently to the point that they burst out of our shared closet and onto every hangable ledge (including the FUBU jacket, which Rob told me cost upward of $300, noting that the "For Us" part of the slogan did not apply to poor black people), and he ate a lot of take-out food from the overpriced delis on Elm Street, because the dining hall food— already paid for in his tuition, roughly $25 per day—was unappealing. He considered himself quite the ladies' man, kept his shirts ironed and his Tommy Hilfiger cologne stocked. Obsessed with his physique, his desk was rowed with industrial-size containers of GNC products like creatine and whey protein powder; he sometimes lifted weights in the Pierson gym at three in the morning. He was friendly and funny, but he was all but incapable of daily chores like laundry, bathing, disposing of half-eaten soy burgers (squirrels began sneaking into our common room for leftovers). Rob, who had been responsible for his own household since 1987, didn't like it. So when Ty was pounding his chest about someone who'd "punked" him and who had a "beatdown" coming his way, Rob just laughed and said, "T, we both know you ain't gonna do shit, so quit fronting."

This word "fronting" was important to Rob. A coward who acted tough was fronting. A nerd who acted dumb was fronting. A rich kid who acted poor was fronting. Rob found the instinct very offensive, and in college he saw it all around. He felt as though people were in a constant state of role-play before teachers, before each other, even before Jacinta in the dining hall (some students would pass her briskly as if in training for futures filled with ignorable service workers, while others would stop and chat with perky but manufactured curiosity). When he spoke contemptuously of this, about midway through that fall, I was surprised. For the last two months, because of how he carried himself, I'd figured him to have nothing more than marginal interest in all but a few of his peers. I learned that he tracked the people surrounding him with the observational intensity of the novelist I aspired to be. And he was not above judging them, often harshly.

"It's like nobody's real here," he said, to Zina, late one night. Ty was at the library. I was in bed with the door closed. Rob and Zina were in the common room, curled together beneath a blanket. "It's like you can't have a real conversation with anyone."

"You're real, baby," she told him and made a cooing sound as the sheets rustled and the futon creaked.

"You, too," he replied.

I didn't overhear any more, because I'd buried my head under the pillow in the event of imminent lovemaking. But I thought about those words often, along with other more oblique references to what he saw as a fundamental flaw in the social construct we now inhabited. I didn't know then the degree to which surviving his childhood had necessitated his own brand of fronting, the many different masks he wore on Chapman Street, at St. Benedict's, in East Orange; I didn't know about the Newark-proofing he had mastered. I'm certain that, if presented with this question, he would have argued very precisely that what he did growing up—what he still did when he went home—had not been fronting at all. He would have argued, and I would have believed, that his various manifestations of self represented the height of authenticity, that he was each of those people. "I'm not fronting," he might have said. "I'm just *complicated*."

*   *   *

PARENTS' WEEKEND CAME a few weeks before Thanksgiving. As we scrambled to clean our room and fabricate the impression that we were in fact self-sufficient and responsible adults, Rob stowed a few books and clothes into his backpack.

"You making a break for Zina's place?" I asked.

"No, Newark," he replied. He pronounced the city name very fast, and with no accented syllables: "nwerk." I'd grown up near Newark, Delaware, which we called NEW-ark in our hybrid tristate dialect, a tic that Rob considered a sacrilege. ("Nwerk-nwerk-nwerk," he'd spent the fall drilling me. "Say it three times fast, try not to sound like such a honky.")

"Your mom isn't interested in the big football game?" I asked jokingly.

"She has to work all weekend," he replied, not joking.

In a kind of reverse commute, as thousands of parents descended on the campus, he took the Metro-North southwest along the string of Connecticut commuter towns, through the Bronx, and into Manhattan's Grand Central. Then the subway shuttled him to Penn Station, where he boarded the Path train to Newark, and Flowy picked him up. The transit took about two and a half hours, and he would make it dozens of times over the next four years.

They smoked marijuana at Flowy's apartment for a bit. Flowy had performed well enough lifeguarding that the job was secure for the following summer. Between seasons, he was working for a landscaper blowing leaves. He'd rented an apartment with his girlfriend, LaQuisha, on a marginally safer street a couple blocks from where he'd grown up, near Vailsburg Park. The building was filled with loud neighbors and hallways that were busier at two a.m. than two p.m. But on the fifth floor, he had a nice view east toward downtown. From above, East

Orange looked quite peaceful, particularly on autumnal evenings like this one. He asked Rob how school was going, and Rob rolled his eyes. "You know," he said.

"How the hell do I know?" Flowy laughed. "I don't go to no Yale U."

"The work isn't much harder than St. Benedict's, but the people"—and he paused to make one of his *psha* sounds—"the people are hard to take. Sometimes I just have to check out."

"How do you have time to check out at a school like that?"

"That's the thing," Rob said. "At St. B's, we had *no* time. Between work, lifeguarding, school, practice, film, homework, home shit, any spare time we had we just used it to sleep. Remember?"

"True. I remember sleeping on stairs, sleeping on the bus, sleeping on the benches by the pool."

"Exactly. But in college, you don't have but three, sometimes even two hours of classes a *day*. Food's cooked for you, all the food you want—and boy, I *kill* those buffets. Rent's paid for. Utilities, too. No family around to see. You can only study so much"—Rob would get straight A's in a schedule that included advanced calculus, 200-level physics, and a religious studies class in Buddhism—"and the rest of the time is just that, *time*. I've never had that before. So you know, I'll go to my boy's house, smoke out a bit, just chill . . ."

They talked about their families and friends for a while, how Curtis by all accounts was the king of campus at Morehouse, but Tavarus and Drew were both struggling academically and, in Tavarus's case, financially. Tavarus had spent months assembling a package of loans to pay for college and now was looking at the interest rates and decades-long payment plan and wondering how a college education could possibly be worth it.

"How're you making it work?" Rob asked Flowy. "Food, rent, all that?"

"Hustling on the side, a little bit," Flowy said. "You know."

"You got a good connect?" Rob asked. A "connect" was a bulk supplier who provided marijuana to small-time dealers like Flowy, selling it to them for less than they could sell it for but assuming less risk. "He's cool?"

"Yeah, he's good people." And then Flowy thought of something. "People must smoke up at Yale, right?"

"Hell yeah," Rob said.

"Could be an opportunity."

Rob began thinking as well.

Flowy offered to drive him to Chapman Street, two miles away. Rob opted to walk. Dusk had fallen, and Flowy watched from the window as his friend trudged off slowly through the hood. He was wearing the leather jacket that Zina had given him, and Flowy thought that was a mistake, something the young punk dealers making the first cash of their lives would do to flaunt it. Others would see the leather and think he had money on him. He wondered if Rob had grown so accustomed to his new surroundings, the poshness and security that Flowy imagined often while triangulating heaps of leaves in front of high-rise apartment buildings, that he'd lost that acute awareness of the details necessary to stay safe. But he didn't say anything. Rob, more than most, could take care of himself.

Yesterday Rob had walked about the same distance from our room to Science Hill for biology class: past Sterling Memorial Library and its four million books, across the marble stones of Beinecke Plaza with its sculpted memorials paying tribute to Yale students lost in both world wars, beneath the forty-foot golden dome of Woolsey Hall, past the university president's mansion on Hillhouse Avenue toward the modernist twenty-story building around which were clustered eleven different science labs, each of them larger than St. Benedict's. Today, he walked through the network of dealers who governed Vailsburg Park, along Central Avenue, a few blocks from where the Moore sisters had been killed, and then to Chapman Street. Along the way, he passed small houses, tall project towers, struggling businesses gating their doors, and poor people going wherever they were going, heads angled down. And with every step some sector of his consciousness must have wondered how he'd gone from this world to that, why he'd gone, for what larger purpose. He was stoned, and perhaps this softened the impact of his feet, the impact of these questions. And maybe it also stoked the idea that there was money to be made at Yale, which would carry none of the hazards that it carried on the streets he was walking.

He made it home without incident and watched TV with his grand-parents until Jackie got off work at eleven. The two of them ate dinner together at midnight, pork chops that Rob had bought on the way home and cooked with rice. He knew that she'd cried for the first two months he'd been away. He'd spoken to her on the phone nearly every night, short murmured conversations that he took into his bedroom with the door closed. I'd been affected by the way he said goodbye as he emerged: "All right, Ma, you're my heart," with an earnestness that belied his de-meanor. This made me feel guilty for all the times I'd hurried off the phone with my own mother (still working on those curtains, asking for further window measurements), saying briskly, "Later, Mom."

While the rest of us toured our parents around campus that week-end, energetic with pride as we key-carded our way through the gated archways leading into catered buffets and ultimately congregating at the football field for the weekend's game, Rob sat on the porch and smoked cigarettes with Jackie before making the rounds of old friends. He stopped by St. Benedict's to have lunch with Friar Leahy and observe an off-season water polo shoot-around, giving in to the impulse to bark commands at the players. His Ivy League association caused him to be treated by former classmates, kids he'd led on the Appalachian Trail, as a conquering hero. After that, he visited his father at Essex County and, most likely, got up to speed on the appeal situation. By that time in early November, Skeet was still standing by while Carl Herman submitted the long succession of preliminary documents, many of them recycled from the successful PCR hearing. They were accustomed to the admin-istrative lag times by now, but the waits carried a more expansive kind of anxiety than either of them had before known; in Skeet's and Rob's eyes, the man had been freed, his conviction overturned on no less an authority than the Constitution of the United States, and yet here they were again, battling the legal army of a state-sponsored apparatus that seemed intensely focused on keeping him imprisoned.

My own father had been sending me letters, which arrived in my post office box each Thursday. He'd made this effort for my two older siblings during their first semesters at Yale. Dad was not the most emotive man, and he wrote these messages on small yellow Post-its, a few illegible sentences along the lines of, *Hope your classes aren't too bad and practice is going well. Grandma came over for dinner on Sunday. Mom made lasagna. Hang in there. Dad.* Attached by a paper clip would be a small news article from the local paper about my high school football team. As the weeks went on, the meaning of these letters evolved from nostalgic to something more powerful. They became the primary, tangible reminder that home still existed. While I moved through the trials and tribulations of this much-hyped college experience, the inconsistent loops and falls of my dad's handwriting still took minutes-per-word to decipher and my mom still made lasagna when Grandma came over. The world might be big and layered, but my life within it was small, secure, rooted in old simplicity.

Marijuana, I believe, served the same function for Rob: a bridge, spanning far more distance than my own, between the world he'd come from and the world he found himself in. I had no idea how much he smoked, and just like he had in his mother's house, he hid it well. He smelled more thickly of chlorine from water polo practice (the initiation for which had found him wearing a toga in the middle of the Commons dining hall, singing "Express Yourself" by Madonna) than he ever did of weed. He never smoked in the room. Scents could not cling to his leather jacket. He seemed zoned out fairly often, crouched over a textbook with the TV on and music playing loud, but I just figured that was a quirk: in order to focus he needed to create an excess of noise to shut out. Track practice was year-round, so Ty and I were catching the three o'clock shuttle bus out to the athletic complex a mile from campus, where we spent the fall running endless wind sprints across a grass intramural field, known as the Flats, that stretched a quarter mile toward a hillside of fiery autumnal leaves. We trained for two hours and then took the bus back to the campus gymnasium to lift weights for another hour, then had dinner before returning to the dorm around seven to work. These were four hours every day during which we were completely checked out from the campus, loosening our bodies from our minds—and four hours that, I later learned, Rob spent getting high with a new group of friends who lived off campus, doing pretty much the same thing.

People called it the Weed Shack: a two-story clapboard house on Temple Street, two blocks west of campus proper. Sherman Feerick, a junior, was the leaseholder, and four or five others lived there with him. Sherman had grown up in Montclair and been a football star. He was an intelligent talker, and he talked nonstop. When he'd first met Rob, he'd said, "So you're the new one," meaning the single token poor African American male Newarker admitted to Yale each year. The two men were drawn to one another, the way Newarkers living outside Newark tended to be. Their shared knowledge of the very particular milieu made for a strong bond, and so did the fact that Sherman consumed—and sold—weed. After his conversation with Flowy about possibly selling on campus, Rob ran the idea past Sherman, out of a respect more than a desire to have questions answered. Rob told him that Charles Cawley sent the tuition checks directly to the school, but that didn't account for books and lab equipment, which approached the level of his entire high school tuition. He told him that his mom was in bad shape—tired, poor, and now alone. He shrugged casually and said he could use a little money. And Sherman, rather than feel like his own earnings were threatened, began steering a little business Rob's way, just like Rob had done for Tavarus in high school. He schooled him on how to stay under the university's radar, which was practically effortless as long as you weren't stupid.

Rob became a fixture in the Weed Shack's living room, where a bong or a joint was perennially lit and shared by whoever happened to be hanging there. Those sunken couches and scavenged chairs provided a safe haven for students to get stoned and say what they really felt about Yale, about Yalies, about the Yale Experience. Their criticisms could get acidic, coalescing into a kind of groupthink that—for Sherman, at least, looking back years later—went far beyond what the actual reality merited. That a Yale education was a rare and coveted gift remained always a part of the big picture, but few things were easier for a group of young men to lose sight of than the big picture. Some of their grievances were common to the point of cliché: the school tailored itself toward rich kids, legacies, phonies; the financial aid packages were basically for good PR and entailed more paperwork than any 300-level class; the social hierarchy in place was more vapid than high school; the professors outsourced the actual teaching to TAs a few years older than the undergrads while they focused on their own research. Other complaints were more nuanced, invoking deeper, historical elements of the minority condition. PROP—the minority orientation week that Rob had not attended—had included seminars on how to take notes; "Like we need to learn how to hold a pencil," Sherman said. The Af-Am House was hidden on a small footpath on the edge of campus, tucked away behind the Art & Architecture building on York Street, smaller and more remote than the cultural centers for Asians, Hispanics, Jews. The university proper refused to give any official sponsorship to the annual Af-Am Week, in which black students from all over New England came to campus for a long weekend of lectures and parties. This place, they collectively opined, was racist.

Rob, by all accounts, had never thought much about race. While he had painstakingly devised methods to navigate the different groups of people in his life, almost all of those people had been black. Uncharacteristically for the average black student coming to Yale, he'd never contemplated, let alone practiced, the fine intricacies of living in a socioeconomic atmosphere not his own. New friendships with people who railed against those intricacies—loudly, profanely—had him thinking about race very much. Typical of Rob Peace, though not of Sherman and the others, he did so intellectually rather than angrily.

"Say a white boy takes a wrong turn and comes to my hood," he once said. "Now he's in the minority—nobody wants him there, unless it's to rob his ass—and more than anything he has to think about how to protect himself, how to get out. There's no weaker situation to be in than that, and this boy isn't getting anything productive done until he's out, back among his own people. But we take a wrong turn and end up at Yale, for the first time in our lives we *don't* have to worry about protecting ourselves. And we were all able to get enough shit done to be accepted here—so imagine what we can do when you take all the crazy hood shit out of the equation and we can just focus on the business at hand. So what if it's annoying as hell? Instead of sitting around here bitching about it, maybe we just accept that it is what it is, and know that we have the capacity to get way more from them than they'll ever get from us."

He took a mighty pull from the bong and sat back, eyes closed, exhaling a hypnotic plume of smoke into the air above him.

A weeklong Thanksgiving vacation was coming, which he would spend in reunion with the Burger Boyz. He would also meet Flowy's connect so that he could bring back a few ounces of weed to sell in eighths to his classmates during the harried weeks preceding final exams. This he would do quietly, away from his own living space and invisibly to his roommates.

Chapter 7

◆────────────◆

A WINTER EVENING AT Yale could have a spectral quality. The un-
touched snow in the center of the Pierson College quad tamped
the urban noise while brightening the halos cast by half a dozen gas
lamps. On the bells of Harkness Tower, the Guild of Carillonneurs
played the *1812 Overture*. The students had for the most part retreated
to their rooms, and each of the few hundred windows embedded in
the brick façade emitted a warm light suggesting comfort, focus, and
industry within. As I walked the thirty yards between the dining hall
and entryway D—still faint from a track practice that had left me dry-
heaving beneath the bleachers in Coxe Cage—it was easy to forget that
we weren't actually existing in the New England of colonial times, when
these structures had in fact been built.

Our sophomore dorm room was less tranquil, looking as though a
bomb composed of dirty laundry, CDs, and aluminum take-out food
containers had detonated. I flicked on the lights, and Rob materialized
out of the dark. He'd been sitting in a wooden chair in the far corner,
head bowed, one hand hanging over his broad chest while the other
picked at his frayed, newly grown cornrows. The room was thickly per-
fumed with incense. In a charged flurry one night a few weeks earlier,
we'd written some of our favorite verses in permanent black marker on
the white walls. One of my contributions had been the last line of Ten-

nyson's poem "Ulysses": *To strive, to seek, to find, and not to yield.* Above it, Rob had written a stanza from a Ludacris song that detailed having sex with a woman on the fifty-yard line of the Georgia Dome. Rob sat just beneath those lines, his exhalations audible and weighty. His dining hall uniform was unbuttoned over a ribbed sleeveless undershirt. His face was angled down and away but his body resembled a dark, clenched fist.

The second half of freshman year had passed uneventfully. We'd cemented our friend groups, grown accustomed to the academic cycle, and in some ways come to see this place as our home. Rob and Zina had broken up, and my initial urge to celebrate had been tempered by how truly depressed Rob had become in the weeks after. He'd begun working in the Pierson dining hall for $8 an hour in the spring of freshman year—starting in the dish room, same as Jackie—and when I came to eat he would take a break to sit with me behind Jacinta until she told him, smilingly, to get his ass back to work. While I had gone home for the summer to the same job I'd had in high school, Rob had remained in New Haven for the first half to work on the custodial staff during Yale's reunion weekends, and then he'd spent the second half at home with Jackie and his friends. In June, Skeet's postconviction relief had been overturned when the judge sided with the State's counterappeal, and Rob had stood by while his father was transferred to Trenton State once again, a year and a half after Rob and Carl had walked out with him in December 1997.

These labors, duties, paychecks, and heartbreaks were six months of Rob's life, and I knew little about most of them. What I did know was that the tentativeness with which I had first regarded him had faded, if not into total comfort then at least close enough. I knew that Rob had also, beginning with fall reading week and progressing through the winter and spring of freshman year, become one of the leading drug dealers on campus.

By this time, midway through our second year, I would typically come home to a mirthful tribal circle carved out of his bedroom—a safe haven for misfits and trendsetters alike to pass around a joint and download their days, Rob presiding with his trademark grin and barbed bons mots. Never before had I found him as I had now: alone and miserable and sitting wide-awake in the dark.

"Yo, Rob," I said. He barely raised his reddened, watery eyes. "Everything cool?"

He mumbled some ambiguous syllable.

"You want the lights back off or . . . ?"

With true, unadulterated vitriol, he replied, "I just hate all these entitled motherfuckers." He was talking more to himself than to me, as I was more or less one of those entitled motherfuckers. In other words: the majority of the Yale student body, clusters of them now passing back and forth in front of our first-floor window with their books and winter coats, the Ivy League version of the hustlers walking Chapman Street at night.

He picked up a physical chemistry textbook from the floor and began to read. And I retreated into my bedroom to spend a few hours in the Congo with Marlow in search of Kurtz. Aside from the audible friction of a page being turned, Rob gave little suggestion of life unfolding in the next room.

After a time, the chemistry textbook thumped closed and the TV came on: one of his beloved kung fu movies. I put my own book down and deferred the essay I was to start writing tonight in order to join him. He was watching a bootleg VHS of *Snake in the Monkey's Shadow*, which he'd brought back from his last trip home along with a gallon-size ziplock packed with dry marijuana and orange rinds. The film—grainy and nonsensical, definitely not worth the $2 he'd paid for it—lightened his mood to the point that he asked me if it was okay for him to smoke. I nodded, and he lit up. He looked older and rougher when inhaling a joint, pinching it between thumb and index finger with the live end cupped in his palm, breathing in with fast intensity and out with painstaking slowness. Apropos of nothing, he said, "So you wanna know what happened?"

The incident had occurred in the dining hall, where Rob worked five nights a week. A group of guys on the crew team (that association implying that they were white, rich, and had landed at Yale by way of elite New England boarding schools) had stood up to leave without busing their trays to the window ten paces away. Rob had told them— courteously, he wanted me to be sure—to take care of their trays so he could wipe off the table, which itself had been left a crumby, puddled mess. The guys had mumbled something about being in a rush and kept walking, leaving plates heaped with half-eaten food for Rob to dispose of. They probably hadn't realized that he was a student. They failed to say thank you to him or any other staff workers on their way out.

Each rendered detail accumulated in the telling and restoked Rob's ire: the disrespect, the avoidance of eye contact, the smirks, the preppy clothes, the slovenly mess, the food haphazardly wasted, the fact that these guys had no doubt forgotten the interaction the moment they'd passed by Jacinta and exited the dining hall to begin their nights—a keg party at the Zeta Psi house, presumably, since it was Thursday and that was what the crew team did on Thursdays. And Rob, in his starched white uniform and with a hairnet over his cornrows, had stood over the remnants of their dinners and watched them leave. Beneath the tall portraits of prominent alumni, the dining hall was bright with talk and laughter, rendering him helpless to do what he wanted to do, what most any of his neighborhood friends from Newark would have done: pin each of them facedown on the hardwood floor and stomp the backs of their heads until their teeth popped out—"curbing," a process he had refused to explain to his mother but that he described in detail to me now, including the satisfying squelching sound of teeth relinquishing attachment to gums. I didn't ask whether this portrait came from firsthand experience. He couldn't even call them what later, to me, he would: motherfuckers. All he could do was bus the three trays, so that Jacinta or Roslyn or Jimmie—his colleagues and friends, full-time dining hall employees—wouldn't have to. Then he'd put his fist through the wall in the dish room. He showed me the resultant swelling in three knuckles. I asked if he'd get in trouble for that, and he replied that one of the cooks had promised to patch up the hole with plaster before the manager showed up, so Rob wouldn't get fired.

I thought the story ended there, but Rob kept going, protracting these events into the future: his desire to find the guys, get them off campus, and carry out retribution away from the faculty overseers, blue-lit emergency phones, and campus police who maintained the pervading atmosphere of complete safety, even invincibility. Though he didn't say so in words, he seemed intent on proving, to himself and to them, that no one was invincible—that, Yalie or not, anyone could and should be held to account for the kind of person he was. I got the sense that where he'd grown up, this wasn't a matter of etiquette or debate.

"You . . . can't do that, Rob," I said, and he looked at me chagrined, his face saying, *Why the hell not?* My answer: "I mean, you just can't."

"I know, I know," he finally said. "What, you thought I was serious?" In fact, I had known he was.

I was still struggling to equate the irritating but unremarkable encounter he'd described (I had doubtlessly forgotten to bus my own tray once or twice, though I didn't admit that now) with the profound anger still coursing through him, a few hours and a few joints later. I felt guilty for being unable to do so, for lacking the empathy required to connect a careless prep school slight to a fundamental flaw in the social construct in which we lived. All I said was, "That sucks, dude."

He shook his head and smiled for the first time that night, a smile approaching the broad, remarkable grin that had come to characterize him on campus. He knew I could never understand, and he was kind enough not to hold my sheltered obliviousness against me. This had become the rhythm of our friendship at Yale: he would share with me the smallest fragment of his world and then step back into the whole of mine.

We watched the movie's climactic fight, a murdered ninja sensei being avenged by his protégé. My mind drifted back to my English paper and the track meet this weekend and some girl who wasn't emailing me back. His mind went somewhere else, a place I couldn't access, a struggle rooted in a youth he never spoke of, a struggle he seemed to feel—with a possessiveness closely related to pride—was his alone to bear.

*   *   *

HE DIDN'T HIDE his drug dealing anymore, and he conducted much of it in our room. A few times a night there would be a knock on the door, and a student would murmur, "Hey," and slink past me into Rob's room, where he would execute their commerce via the lower right-hand drawer of his desk. If the buyer was a friend, he or she might stay and smoke with him. Some nights these gatherings would grow to four or five people who fit themselves in as best they could, sitting hip to hip on his bed, on stacks of textbooks, on the heavy black trunk in which he kept his bongs, weed, and ledgers. I didn't know where he hid his cash or how much he actually made, only that cash was all he used to buy anything (though he bought very little). One of these purchases was a desktop computer, which a grad student had dug out of a lab closet and sold to him for $200. We'd come to college during the time when everyone began owning computers. For those who couldn't afford one, Pierson College maintained a dark, usually empty room of desktops in the basement, known as the "computer ghetto." Rob had spent many hours down there, and he was proud of his new machine; he cleared space for it on a desk in the common room and said we were all welcome to use it. He quickly found that the model was at least six years out of date, incapable of supporting basic word-processing programs, let alone Excel and the Internet. When he also learned that the grad student, who had made it out to Rob as though he were buying it from the biology department, had actually pocketed the money himself, Ty and I spent a full afternoon talking him out of the inclination to beat up the guy. He ended up propping the computer in our nonfunctioning fireplace, as some sort of totem to his naïveté.

With this computer screen watching like our version of the eyes of T. J. Eckleburg, the mixing of people from all walks of life that university pamphlets displayed in glossy photos but was rarely observed on campus manifested itself in his stoner circles. Blacks, Hispanics, grungy kids wearing hemp hoodies and beards, thespians and athletes, an Australian with long blond hair who was famous for walking around barefoot—they all gravitated toward Rob Peace's room, the place where judgments were few, laughter was steady, and weed was always available.

"Don't you worry about living with a drug dealer?" friends would often ask. Coolly, as if I had the faintest clue as to what I was talking about, I would shrug and smile and say, "It's just Rob, it's what he does. He must need the money and he would never be dumb about it." Honestly, I was more worried about the way he cracked his joints every afternoon after water polo practice in a disturbing ritual: he would drop his bag and stand in the middle of the room, then point his face to the ceiling and arch his back grotesquely, such that his torso was nearly parallel to the floor. Starting with his top vertebrae, the bones popped one by one down his spine. He would twist at the hips, and the left socket would sound off, then the right. He brought each arm across his chest and pulled with the opposite hand to accomplish the same with his shoulders. Knees, ankles, elbows, wrists, and for the finale, the machine gun pop-pop-pop of his fingers. I wasn't worried about him getting busted for marijuana. I was worried about him dislocating his hip or ending up hunchbacked. Since he never seemed to spend any of the money he made, I figured he must be using it for tuition, or saving up for graduate school, or helping Jackie—whom I hadn't seen again since we'd moved in a year and a half before but whose aloofness still stayed with me.

The four of us had decided easily to stay together as roommates after freshman year, an agreement consummated with guy-ish head nods and shrugs. But Ty had a serious girlfriend, Adanna, the daughter of a wealthy Los Angeles gastric surgeon who specialized in stapling stomachs (Rob called her "Predator" for her long, thin dreadlocks, and gently mocked her wealth). She had drawn a single room in the lottery, so Ty effectively lived with her. Dan had fallen in with a popular crowd, kids who found a way to party each night of the week and were fond of saying, "Ninety percent of what you learn in college happens *outside* the classroom." And so, in our dorm room, Rob and I tended to be alone, quietly coexisting for the most part, sometimes talking about girls, football, food. "Buuuuuullshitting," he called what we did, fondly, and we did it all the time. Though we spoke about nothing much at all, this was how I learned about the football games of his youth, the afternoon with his father listening to a Yankees game on a stranger's front stoop, Jackie and his grandparents and Victor, and the deep role that marijuana played in his life: "I smoke a blunt, and I can hang out or study or just chill," he said dazedly, "and it's like nothing matters, not even time, and for a couple hours I can just *be.*"

He once looked up from across the room and said, "You know what I like about you, Jeff?" Having been curious about this for some time but somehow afraid to ask, I asked. "Because it's aaaaall good with you. You just read your books and write your stories and don't give a damn." A low-level pride coursed through me upon hearing his observation. In a world where defining yourself felt unnecessarily complicated most of the time, I thought that being "all good" was a pleasingly simple way to do it.

By virtue of proximity, I felt more involved in his life than I ever would have predicted during the first months of college. When he and Zina had broken up—after my initial relief had subsided—I'd consoled him with comments like, "She's about to graduate anyway; the long-distance thing never works . . ." (The incident in the dining hall was the second time he'd put his fist through a wall; the first had been at an Af-Am House dance party, when he'd seen Zina grind-dancing with a senior, flaunting herself in front of him.) We'd chosen our majors at the same time—mine was English language and literature, his molecular biophysics and biochemistry. Because of friends on the track team as well as Rob, I felt relatively in sync with the black community and would regularly show up at the Af-Am House dances to be schooled on how to move my hips from side to side without overinvolving the shoulders, how to lose or at least soften my white man's overbite and the irresistible tendency to snap my fingers with the beat. Those friends called me "Da Jeff" and, like Rob had once done with Hrvoje Dundovic on water polo bus rides, goaded me to belt out the lyrics to songs like "Shake Yo Ass." I was a source of amusement and happy to dance (literally) in that role. Although there was something disingenuous about me being there—like a benign joke we were all in on—I found it far easier to loosen up in that situation than I did with more preppy classmates, among whom existed a pressure to align with a specific kind of humor and overall social affect. The black students of our year anointed themselves the "Class of Oh-Deuce," and from time to time a call-and-response chant would break out during a dance party, with one person yelling, *"Oh-WHAT?"* and the rest of us responding, *"Oh-DEUCE!"* over and over, with vitality and pride.

I didn't smoke marijuana at all at the time. I was so obsessed with track—with literally and metaphorically running around in circles for hours each day—that I didn't even permit myself caffeine. Never a part of Rob's stoner group, I lived unassumingly on its fringe. As I began to recognize the faces and names of his more regular customers, we all developed a low-key rapport, sometimes even pausing to converse for a minute or two in the common room before they entered Rob's room to get what they'd come for. I was quick—far too quick, not to mention self-righteous—to judge these people as "wastoids" (though Rob seemed to smoke more than any of them, I somehow never included him in this blanket mental term). But I never dug any deeper than the shallow surface; I never pulled back far enough from my seemingly comprehensive breakfast-classes-lunch-practice-weight-room-dinner-library-sleep schedule, as well as my own perception of how they spent their free time, to consider that each of them—just like Rob, just like me, just like any one of my friends—possessed a nineteen-year-long story that had culminated in them being here, now, at Yale, buying pot from my roommate.

Raquel Diaz was almost as colorful in dress as she was in attitude, befitting her hometown of Miami. (Her Puerto Rican family pronounced the English *y* sound as *j*, and when she'd been accepted to Yale the house erupted with exclamations of, "Raquel is going to *jail*! Raquel is going to *JAIL*!"; she struggled not to project undue symbolism onto the dialectical mishap.) A dense tangle of long, reddish-brown, tightly curled hair burst from her scalp at all angles. She was the kind of person around whom you had to be careful about the opinions you expressed, because if she disagreed, she would let you know it. She was like a beautiful tropical bird, all smooth placid feathers one moment, and the next a quick-striking chaos of talons and beak. She'd met Rob during the second or third night of college, when she found him stoned to the point of passing out while her friend, a beautiful future actress from Morocco named Lyric Benson, performed something like a belly dance above him. Raquel's father, a Cuban opera singer and Santero, had stormed out of their home when she was six months old, following a fight with her mother. He'd never returned. Her barrio upbringing had been rife with anxieties similar to those Rob had experienced with a single, poor, minority mother. Like Rob, she had controlled these stresses by excelling in sports and academics. However, unlike Rob, Raquel was temperamental and unpredictable, and at Yale she found few socially acceptable means by which to vent her various frustrations. Increasingly as college wore on, she vented them to Rob, often in the boiler room two stories beneath the college's ground floor, where they met to share a blunt after dinner a few nights a week. While the heavy machines around them pumped heat to a few hundred students above, she found in Rob Peace a strange blend of an older brother's strength and a sister's sensitivity that she'd never encountered before: someone with whom she could just chill and worry less about the tuition installments her mother might not be able to send, and exchange gripes about the people around them without judgment. They were at Yale. They had "won." But they both learned the hard way that "winning" didn't mean they wouldn't encounter problems—problems that some herb and good company went a long way toward resolving.

Daniella Pierce grew up in a biracial family in Oakland, California—

she and her mother were white, her father and her two siblings were black—and she'd gone to a predominantly black public high school. In the auditorium on their first day of freshman year, the principal had instructed the students to look at the person sitting on their right and left and understand that one of them would not graduate. This had proven to be the case. She'd left for Yale a few weeks after her high school boyfriend—black—had gone to prison for dealing, and she brought that conflict, among many others, with her. She wore baggy clothes, spoke with urban intonations, and went out exclusively with black men— including Rob "for a minute." Academics were particularly hard for her, and she spent most days feeling unfit to be a part of this student body. She was majoring in psychology, but no matter how many hours she invested, no matter how much extra help she sought, she felt destined to struggle academically. Like many students accustomed to being the smartest kids in suboptimal high schools, she came to Yale and for the first time felt stupid. Also like many students, pride prevented her from seeking out the infrastructure of tutors the Yale system had in place (ironically, the affluent kids from prestigious high schools—those who needed it the least—often took the most advantage of these utilities to sharpen their already-honed academic skills). But then, while stressing about a test late at night and seriously considering transferring to a California state school, two strong hands would land on her shoulders and begin gently massaging her muscles, and that deep, assuring voice would say, "It's cool, Daniella, it's cool." And in those moments, with Rob standing behind her, she could permit herself to believe, if only fleetingly, that it was.

Perhaps the most frequent presence in Rob's room was Oswaldo Gutierrez. He'd grown up in Newark's predominantly Puerto Rican North Ward, in a small, chaotic home owned by his grandparents and populated by transient uncles and cousins. He was slight in stature, but he had a sharpness to him somewhere in the hard-to-pin layers between his wiry physique and elusive personality. Though he was always polite to me as he ducked beneath my arm that held open the door, he seemed to keep an invisible fence raised around him, complete with a sign that read, "We're fine, but we're not the same, so don't get too close." Oswaldo was, in a word, guarded. An uncle who worked for a Colombian drug cartel was paying his tuition. The disparities between the house he'd grown up in and the towers he now lived in clung to him constantly. He found himself angry all the time, judging his classmates and what he saw as their blithe existences, their wide-open futures that didn't involve taking care of a sprawling, violent, dysfunctional family. In Rob, he found a man who harbored many of the same feelings but was able to do so seamlessly (at least outwardly so), with a smile and some profane but harmless shit talk over a blunt.

Rob had many friends. Danny Nelson was technically his boss in the dining hall, a slight student from the Bronx who walked around campus with his earphones in, often alone; from a distance he looked to be shuffling along gloomily with his head pointed straight down to the ground, but up close you could see that he was actually dancing in a kind of fox-trot, with a subtle smile aimed at no one. Yesenia Vasquez was Oswaldo's girlfriend and an aspiring poet. Nick Crowley, our hall mate freshman year, played on the lacrosse team. Rob had friends from the water polo team, friends from the Weed Shack, friends from his science classes. Alejandra, Cliff, B.J., Arnoldo, Linda, Maria, Chris, Josh, Candace, Anthony, Pablo . . . so many names that I eventually ceased keeping track. In contrast to the unnervingly quiet kid with whom I'd first shaken hands in Lanman-Wright Hall, Rob had become something of a beloved presence on the Yale campus, and not simply because he sold drugs and hung out. He had a natural curiosity about the stories of those around him paired with a brain that was quick to draw insights from within each of these stories. And Raquel, Daniella, and Oswaldo were the people who became most intimate with his own story. With Raquel, he would talk about family. With Daniella, he would talk about classes. With Oswaldo, he would talk about home. With each of them, he would talk about Life: where it was now, where it needed to get, and how to bridge that gap, which sometimes seemed gaping. They'd made it to Yale, but once there they were all surprised to learn that they hadn't Made It, not yet.

I respected the fact that these friendships with Rob were far deeper than my own, and I made it a point never to intrude. I was attuned to the worth of each one, and I felt that, if I were to make an overt effort to take part, I would be thieving somehow. But still, as time passed and I watched their various bonds strengthen, I felt jealous.

I didn't have any real grounds to feel that way, especially since, as a friend, Rob saved me twice sophomore year. The first time was on Halloween. Through a friend who played the flute in the Yale Symphony Orchestra, I'd gotten a job as a "bouncer" at their annual midnight Halloween show. The atmosphere was more like a Kiss concert: Woolsey Auditorium became a throng of drunk people in elaborate costumes, bodies hanging over the balconies, all waiting anxiously for the curtain to rise on the symphony (it says a lot about Yale that this was one of the most anticipated social events of the year). My job was to make sure no one snuck in the side door to the right of the stage. A hundred ticketless students were outside pounding to get in, and I had to make sure no one went out those doors, either, because if they pushed them open, the inflowing tide would prove impossible to stop. Fire code violations would surely follow. I took this responsibility seriously, standing in front of the door in a black T-shirt, with my arms crossed and a dour expression intended to convey impassability.

For most of the night, I politely turned back errant and inebriated students, who regarded me as some meddling asshole before turning to seek another exit. Then a tall, muscular guy—another heavyweight rower—walked toward me with some momentum. I sidestepped to block him. "Sorry, can't go out this way." He ignored me and juked the other way. I blocked him again; this time his chest collided with my still-crossed arms. He backed up three steps and barreled toward me. From high school football, I knew how to lower my center of gravity, the way Rob once did in the street. We thudded together and I gave no ground. Suddenly his fists were thumping against my chest and shoulders, and I returned in kind, exhilarated by my first collegiate fistfight. Because he was so drunk and I wasn't, I performed adequately, at one point connecting an almost-uppercut to his jaw. He ceased bothering with punches and tackled me instead, and we tumbled through the door I'd been enlisted to keep shut, down five concrete steps, onto Beinecke Plaza. We stood, gathered ourselves. I hollered, "Get him outta here!"— but to little effect, because he'd now been joined by two rowing team-mates and all three were bearing down on me while the kids who'd been pounding to get in stepped back, amused, reducing my thoughts to, *Oh fuck, this is going to be embarrassing.*

Then they stopped. The two newcomers put their hands on my combatant's shoulders and pulled him away, and they headed off while he gave me the finger and slurred a few profanities. Thinking my firm countenance had something to do with their retreat, I puffed out my chest, feeling quite the badass. Then I heard Rob behind me: "Damn, son, didn't know you had it in you!" From the balcony a few moments before, he'd seen the initial altercation and hurried down. All he'd had to do was stand behind me, feet set and fists clenched and with what I imagine now to be a taut grin on his face, to send the crew guys packing. He helped me close the door; the incoming stream ceased upon his appearance.

"Thanks," I said, pain beginning to settle in the kidney area.

"You know I got your back," he replied. The following week, the flutist who'd recruited me left a fruit basket for my efforts.

The second time Rob saved me had to do with a girl. She was a fresh-man on the track team; her father had in fact run track with mine at Yale in the late '60s, and so my mom had prompted me to check in on her during the first week of school. I remembered her vaguely from track team reunions when we'd been children and was surprised to find that she was very beautiful. We saw each other at the track every day, went to a lot of the same parties—she was half black and so could hang out with both demographics—drunk-kissed one night, and began dating. I felt very much in love and so fell into the pattern I'd once smirked at in which I tried to pretend that we were married, or at least engaged. This behavior carried on blissfully (I thought) through the first semester: weekend trips to Manhattan to stroll hand in hand through Central Park, clothes left in one another's bureaus, sweet "I love you"s whispered across the pillow while listening to Sade ballads in her bed at night. Then in January, after a friend told her, "Jeff Hobbs, he's like *marriage material*," she quickly dumped me—divorced me, I felt, as I fell into a pathetic spiral of self-pity. The breakup was the hardest thing I'd ever experienced in my life, the saddest and most all-consuming.

Rob hadn't seemed to think much of it; maybe he'd made a "Fuck dem hos" comment here and there to "get my head right." Then, a few long weeks later, he'd found me at two o'clock on a Saturday night in our common room, having just composed a long, driveling email to her with which I was quite satisfied: *What we had was so special . . . you'll never find another guy as good as me . . . blah blah blah.* Rob looked over my shoulder and understood the gravity of the situation, in terms not so much of my feelings but of my dignity, which at the moment was nonexistent. Before I could hit Send (my finger reaching for the button, convinced this bunk would bring her hurrying back that very night), he physically pulled my chair away from the desk. "Nah, nah, nah," he said sternly. "You want to share your feelings with someone? Share them with me."

And I did. For forty-five minutes, I outlined the complex (I thought, again) feelings churning within me, waxing on about the family I wanted to have with this girl, the nice home we'd have in Chatham, New Jersey, where she'd grown up—Chatham being one of the posh commuter towns ten minutes west of East Orange—and the three children we'd raise who would all run track for Yale, and this entire idealized future I'd constructed in my head. He indulged me with patience, sincerity, sans laughter, despite the urge he must have felt to laugh. I asked him if he knew what it was like to have a woman you loved inhabit every single one of your waking thoughts, and most of your dreams. "Yeah," he replied soberly. "I do."

He kept nodding with appropriate sympathy, even as he informed me that I was acting like a girl in every way. Then he said, "Jeff, you're a good dude, too good to be bothering with this bullshit." I nodded glumly. "I'm gonna fix you up with someone, someone fine. Stay tuned."

He did, and that helped, and I slowly recovered from what had seemed at the time to be a cataclysmic, irreparable heartbreak. (Epilogue: I did end up hitting the Send button after Rob went to bed, and needless to say the email did not accomplish what it had been designed to. When Rob learned this, he fell onto the couch and laughed his ass off.)

* * *

MOLECULAR BIOPHYSICS and biochemistry was not for the faint of heart. Embedded within an expanse of various sciences—chemistry, geology, engineering, astrophysics, etc.—MB&B garnered, on average, twenty-five students per class out of five hundred to six hundred total science majors. For premeds, the most common major was intercellular, molecular, and developmental biology (IMDB), which was basically an elevated extension of high school biology. For those planning on medical school, a primary goal of these classes was to get good grades, good MCAT scores, and acceptances to good med schools. Students and advisers designed curricula around these ends, and so most students steered far clear of MB&B and its many dizzying prerequisites: advanced calculus, theoretical physics, physical chemistry (commonly known to be the hardest course of all the Yale sciences), as well as each of the core classes that the IMDB majors took. Those who majored in MB&B were either smart and confident enough to know they would get A's anyway, or sufficiently interested in the subject not to worry about their GPAs. Rob was both. His classmates at Yale, as his classmates had at St. Benedict's, knew him as a guy who would sit in the back of class, often looking stoned or simply bored, taking notes but rarely speaking. Then, when the time came to take a test or give an individual presentation, he would "kill it," making the others wonder what they were doing wrong.

Because of its immense difficulty, MB&B was in some ways free of the hypercompetitiveness that prevailed in the various premed tracks. I'd gotten a small dose of this freshman year when I took intro biology. From English classes, I was already well accustomed to students talking tediously regarding their keen insights into *The Canterbury Tales* or Pope's *The Rape of the Lock*, leaning back with legs crossed and eyes pointed upward as if divining their words from on high. But I'd never before experienced the thickly layered pressure of a Yale science lecture hall, during which a few hundred students craned forward while writing every word uttered by the professor, sometimes recording on MP3 players as well. The atmosphere was stifling, more uncomfortable than the chairs in the lecture hall, which themselves were particularly narrow and lacking legroom in order to accommodate the masses. You could almost sense a shortage of oxygen in the air, as well as a collective constriction of the lungs consuming that oxygen. These students felt that their futures were at stake in each class and each test, and one missed word, one minute less spent drilling the textbook pages, could mean the difference between Harvard Medical School and someplace lesser, like, say, Vanderbilt. (As a result of this experience, the only other science class I took to fulfill graduation requirements was Geology 101, otherwise known as "Rocks for Jocks.")

Rob didn't give any ground to the anxiety coursing through the students around him. He simply went to class, did his work, got A's. That he did so while smoking (and dealing) copious amounts of marijuana only made him more of a marvel; he wasn't just smart, he was *cool*. Rob would have said that the weed and the grades were directly related, because being high helped him study free from the nervousness that racked his peers. He chose the MB&B track mainly out of curiosity; he wanted to know how things worked, and MB&B spanned everything from the most intricate proteins within the human body to the workings of the cosmos over billions of years (think Stephen Jay Gould and Stephen Hawking designing a college major together). The choice of major spoke to what Rob had put last on his high school yearbook list of favorites: "knowledge." He liked to say, almost dreamily, that there were more chemical interactions taking place in the human body each second than there were stars in the universe.

He and Oswaldo started a small study group together, more or less a science club. Once a week, as Rob had done with the Burger Boyz in high school, he, Oswaldo, and a few others gathered to talk about science. Unlike in high school, his task here was not to catch his friends up but rather to immerse himself in what interested them and to discuss the long-term applications of their schoolwork, whether it was med school or a PhD or working in a lab. They talked about the financial repercussions of each option—particularly vital to Rob and Oswaldo, both of whom carried with them the expectation of providing immediately for their families upon graduation. Med school had the biggest long-term upside, but the amount of debt one had to take on in the short term—mid–six figures for a top school—was intimidating. A PhD program led to a teaching career, but that meant living in the petty, racially complicated world of academia forever. Lab work was perhaps the most intellectually fulfilling, but options were limited, as was the prospect of making any real money. Because they were just sophomores when they started the group, the life talk could remain cozily abstract; they still had plenty of time to figure it all out. Mostly, they reveled in having a safe environment in which to fully celebrate their nerd-dom, which for all their lives—on the streets of Newark certainly, but also in unexpected ways at Yale—they'd been compelled to camouflage. As word of the study group leaked and more students began trying to join, kids Rob didn't know as well, he began to disengage from it. Early junior year, he stopped coming altogether.

At the same time, he began working in a lab at Yale Medical School headed by a famed molecular chemistry professor, performing research under the guidance of two PhD students. He began as a lab assistant: sterilizing beakers, recording data, getting coffee. Because of his disciplined promptness and curiosity, he quickly graduated to running his own low-level experiments, primarily in crystal diffraction. His work mostly involved trial and error, and he failed more often than he succeeded in achieving the desired results. His experiments dealt in the scope of atoms; one too many or one too few, and the reactions fell apart. But unlike most other realms of his life, in a lab with sufficient funding he could always go back to the beginning and try again, which he did with a determination that had the graduate students above him fearing for their jobs.

Social life, academics, lab work—the days and weeks and months and, ultimately, the years passed with an increasing fluidity. Whether he identified with his chosen university or not, the truth was that Rob Peace was a Yalie, and he seemed to grow more comfortable with his status as such. At points along the way, we sometimes wondered how much money he was actually making selling weed. Hundreds of dollars a month? Thousands? More, maybe? We couldn't keep track of the customer traffic coming in and out. We did know that Yale students would pay whatever he asked, no haggling. We knew that every other weekend he would make a trip to Newark, sometimes just for the day, and return with two gallon-size ziplocks of pot in his backpack to carry him through until the next re-up. (He was always in a good mood upon his return, as if nourished.) We knew that each night he spent fifteen minutes or so with his ledger and, as he'd done with menial jobs during childhood, kept careful track of money he'd made, money he expected to make, money he needed to outlay. We knew that he'd quit his dining hall job and worked in the lab for free. We knew that he sold pot to townies, grad students, and even professors in addition to classmates. We knew that his business seemed to steadily ratchet upward from month to month, and that this was the main reason he lobbied us to move into an apartment junior year, a two-bedroom still paid for in tuition as university housing but located in an apartment building across the street from Pierson College proper, outside the gates and so technically "off campus." What we didn't know, we didn't ask and instead made assumptions: he must be sending money home to his mother, he was saving for graduate school, he kept everything on the DL, or "down low," he knew exactly what he was doing.

Oswaldo felt differently, and he didn't keep his opinions from Rob the way most everyone else did. Unlike many of our classmates who bought from him, Oswaldo didn't see anything "cool" or "thug" about dealing drugs. Dealing, to him—and as it had been to Rob's father—was a practical matter of economics, of calculating and compensating for shortfalls. As such, you had to be smart. And a smart dealer didn't work out of his Yale dorm room. He didn't carry ziplocks of weed in his backpack across campus. He didn't prop the entryway door open with a phone book so that he wouldn't have to get off his lazy ass to let customers in. Oswaldo had been dealing, too—after his cartel-associated uncle was put in prison, his assets were frozen and thus unavailable for tuition payments. But Oswaldo was quiet about it. He worked off campus and in small quantities, just enough to help out. He also maintained a work-study job in the library. Oswaldo was flummoxed by the fact that his friend could be so quiet, almost embarrassed, about his academic acumen, yet so damn loud and proud of his status as a premier campus drug dealer.

"I've never met anyone so smart but so fucking dumb," he told Rob.

Rob just shrugged, laughed, and replied, "Don't worry about me."

Less skeptical were Victor, Tavarus, and Flowy, each of whom visited a number of times. Victor came the most often, busing down from Daniel Webster two or three times a year. His older brother, Big Steve (when he got up from the couch, the springs failed to rise with him), would come up from New Jersey. They seemed like smart guys, kind, easygoing, and nonconfrontational. They did not fit the mold of the stock characters I imagined him hanging out with on his Newark trips (where I envisioned the re-up transactions occurring on dark, barren sidewalks in the middle of the night). They were always smiling and laughing, usually over a blunt and a 1.5-liter bottle of E&J. They carried no cynicism or condescension regarding Yale; they seemed, above all, proud of their friend for being here. They would listen to music in the room with little interest in recruiting girls to join, always inclusive of me and Ty. (Dan left our quad after sophomore year; considering that he lived physically in the bedroom where Rob kept his stock and entertained his friends, I didn't blame him.) Rob told them that I had "pull" with girls—an utter lie that I gladly played along with. Their visits were just like any visits between high school friends on a college campus: booze, weed, empty pizza boxes littering the floor beneath bodies passed out on the couch. Big Steve typically vomited at some point, and because of his immense size it could be difficult for him to make it to the bathroom in time. The pizza boxes, it turned out, did not make for adequate receptacles.

One night sophomore year, they returned to the room swearing and hyped up with rage. Rob had a large black welt on his forehead.

I asked what happened. "Some fool just hit me in the street, turned tail, and ran away," Rob growled.

"Who?"

"Don't know. Wasn't a Yalie."

"Why'd he do it?" I asked, thinking of my own comical fistfight, knowing that I was incapable of producing a bruise like that on a man while visualizing the kind of person who could.

"Thought I was someone else."

I believed this story of mistaken identity, and I participated in their collective anger.

"We should find the guy," I said, thinking that was the thing you said in this situation—but definitely not thinking that the three of them would put their coats back on and head for Victor's car to troll the streets of New Haven, looking for retribution. Unlike Ty—unlike most anyone I'd ever known—Rob wasn't in the business of chest-thumping. Words, for him, meant deeds. Otherwise, he would just be fronting.

"You coming?" he asked. The writer in me wanted to go, as here was an opportunity to cross boundaries somehow, as well as prove to my friend that I was "real." But the sheltered college student was terrified of the prospect manifesting in their narrow, glaring eyes. Very rarely, real violence had infiltrated the campus. There'd been a gang-related shootout at the intersection of York and Chapel Streets the year before. Every few months a student walking alone at night on the edge of campus was mugged or even beaten. There'd been a heavily publicized stabbing death a few months earlier, along with bulletins that warned us to walk in groups after dark, know where the blue-lit emergency phones were, stay on campus at all times.

I did go with them, pride ultimately trumping good sense. In Victor's old Lincoln, we drove widening concentric circles around campus. That there was no way we'd ever find this guy became quickly apparent (a relief to me), and yet hours passed quietly, elongated, each of us peering out at the deserted streets and darkened, crooked clapboard houses in which most of the population of New Haven, aside from the five thousand Yale undergrads, lived. Rob would slow the car when we passed small groups of men on the sidewalk, studying each of their faces until one of them invariably turned and spread his arms and said, "The fuck you want?" At around three thirty, long after what we were doing had become more of a ritual than an actual undertaking, I murmured, "Hey, Rob, doesn't seem like we're gonna find this asshole. Maybe we should just head back to . . . campus?" He gingerly fingered the welt on his head and replied, "Yeah, getting low on gas anyway. Motherfucker."

On that night and on all the less eventful others, I was envious of the degree to which these three men knew each other, their shared history and easy way of spending a weekend together, as if no time at all had separated these visits—and the understated yet automatic way they had one another's backs. I had never had a male friendship like that; I couldn't even conceive of how to build one. Though I didn't understand this at the time, the fact was that it hadn't been built. Like the organic compounds Rob worked with in the lab, their friendship had evolved over time, experience, and an inexorable atomic pull. They called each other "brother," and in the context from which they came, a brother was someone who would die for you—not as a verbal phrasing meant to suggest a deep kinship but in actual fact should the need arise.

Tavarus and Flowy were more guarded when they came, just once, during Af-Am Week of junior year. Their offishness may have had to do with their circumstances at the time: Tavarus had just dropped out of college and was back in Newark, living with his brother in a run-down apartment above and beneath Section 8 recipients and neighboring a significant drug den. He was trying to get his foot in the real estate business, building off that high school job doing title research; his poor grades and dropout status from two years of college did not aid him. Flowy had torn two ligaments in his knee when he'd slipped lifeguarding, and he hadn't worked in a month. They were both in one of life's ebbs, unsure about anything, wondering how they'd been riding such promising trajectories at St. Benedict's just two and a half years before. They must have experienced some reserve in seeing Rob with his towers of books, his spacious, paid-for apartment, his thriving business, his white roommate with the crew cut and Yale Track & Field T-shirts, his stable of female friends who happily came by to spend three hours rebraiding his cornrows just for the pleasure of his company. With melancholy faces, they spent the afternoon in our living room, arms folded and shoulders hunched as if they'd been called into the master of discipline's office at St. Benedict's. They were polite enough, but no effort of mine could extend a conversation past two or three exchanges. Flowy spoke in a quiet mumble without spaces between his words, and with something like a southern twang. I couldn't really understand him anyway.

Because of Af-Am Week, parties were happening everywhere, and the racial mix of crowds on the quads was, for this long weekend, evenly split between white and black. I stayed in to read, and I was in my underwear, brushing my teeth, when they returned and Rob said, "About to be a couple people rolling through," as he picked stray clothes off the couch. Flowy and Tavarus, as opposed to earlier, were now giddy and active after the four hours they'd spent out. They cycled through the CDs fanned across the top of our stereo, some of which were mine, albums by the Wallflowers and Faith No More that rarely made it onto the air in our room. Suddenly "Throw Dem Bows" by Ludacris, a hard-driving song with its own dance that I knew and liked, was playing at full volume.

The door was open and people were streaming through, and not just a couple as Rob had advertised: a dozen, then two, then three, until the apartment was jammed, mostly with strangers from other schools. Daniella Pierce was the only other white person. I was still in my underwear, more or less hiding in the bedroom Ty and I shared. Rob, Tavarus, and Flowy were in the middle of the room, "throwing bows" with the bass line like a black urban version of the chicken dance. To them, this moment must have recalled that party at Columbia High School, when everyone had followed them to the dance and they'd felt like the absolute center of the world. I tried to hang out, but the situation was overwhelming, short on familiar faces, and with all the noise and crowd—there were probably another forty people outside the apartment building waiting to get in—I had no doubt that the campus police would show up eventually. And if the campus police were to show up in our room, smell the weed inside, enter and look around, open Rob's lower right desk drawer or his black trunk . . .

For the first time, our room didn't feel safe to me, and it felt less so when Rob caught me as I was leaving, gestured toward my laptop on the desk, and said, "You probably should put that away if you want it to still be here tomorrow."

The cops did show up, I learned the next day. Rob had known they would, but he'd also known (or so he claimed) that all they would do was disperse the crowd outside, tell him to turn the music down and keep the front door of the building shut. Any further action would have caused undue racial tension, which had happened many times before during Af-Am Week, and which (or so he claimed) Yale was in a constant state of trying to avoid.

He was so happy during those weekends with his boys, carefree and kinetic, exhibiting a pride that was rare to observe in him and elevated by the pride his friends had for him. His attitude in their presence resembled mine during Parents' Weekend, eager to show off the life he had carved out of this place and his ownership of that life. And while he played down certain aspects of Yale—the girls were generally unattractive, the guys were stuck-up, most of the parties were "lame as hell"—he relished the brief windows he was able to give the East Orange set into New Haven—or "New Slavin'," as he sometimes called our adopted city.

But the happiest I ever saw Rob in college wasn't when his friends visited. He traveled to Costa Rica during the summer after sophomore year. In addition to his custodial job cleaning up campus after graduation, the lab work that continued into the summer, and a month on Chapman Street with Jackie, he'd gone to visit a friend, an international student at Yale. When school began again, I asked him how the trip had gone. He folded his hands behind his head and looked up toward the ceiling, not smiling exactly but with a far-flung expression, a shedding of anxiety so total that he might have been a Buddhist monk at the door of nirvana. He told me about smoking a blunt alone on a black sand beach on the Pacific Ocean. "I hiked through three miles of jungle to the beach . . . the sand was so soft, so *fine*, volcanic . . . the water blue like you've never seen blue before . . . sky . . . mountains . . . and I rolled a blunt and just sat there, for hours, alone . . . and it was so damn peaceful."

That trip inspired a passion for travel that would underlie the rest of his life and in college lead him to begin planning a postgraduation trip to Rio de Janeiro, which research and word of mouth had led him to see as the perfect balance between urban and scenic and cultural pleasures. The first thing he did, two years in advance, was begin taking Portuguese classes so he could speak the language.

But before that trip, he had to graduate. The certainty of that event was shaken severely when the master of Pierson College called Rob into his office to address the not-small matter of the drugs he'd been selling.

Chapter 8

---◆---

Drugs: The unlawful possession, use, purchase, or distribution of illicit drugs or controlled substances (including stimulants, depressants, narcotics, or hallucinogenic drugs); the misuse of prescription drugs, including sharing, procuring, buying, or using in a manner different from the prescribed use, or by someone other than the person for whom it was prescribed.

This entry in Yale's *Undergraduate Regulations* fell under the list of infractions punishable by expulsion, as ruled by the Executive Committee, a group of seven faculty members and three undergraduates responsible for the "fair, consistent, and uniform enforcement of the Undergraduate Regulations."

As Rob entered the Pierson master's office in February of his junior year, he was fairly certain that he was walking into an arraignment of sorts, which would be followed by a conjoined trial, judgment, and sentencing under the committee. Whereas his father's conviction had taken three years, he figured his would take in the vicinity of three weeks. Then he would be gone.

"The block is hot." The expression was used in the drug trade, meaning that the police were sniffing around—not to an extent that should cause panic but a warning to be alert. Rob had said these words, lightly, when I'd found him rifling through his belongings a few days earlier. His black trunk was open in the middle of the room, and he was packing it with bongs, bowls, one-hitters, weed, ledgers, and cash as his pet python, named Dio, meandered lazily around the mulch carpet of its glass tank. He'd bought the two-foot reptile in the fall. Every week or so, I would drive him to a pet store ten minutes away for snake food: a live mouse. I'd watched Dio's very first feeding with Rob and Ty, like a live Discovery Channel show. Rob dropped the mouse into the tank, and the snake let it exist for a few minutes, just hanging out behind a small log while the rodent frantically pawed at the glass wall. When Dio did decide to move, the act happened fast: a quick, precise strike that kicked up mulch and ended with the mouse—a white, adorable little thing—wrapped tightly in two coils of Dio's body, asphyxiating, one of its eyeballs loose from its socket. The actual ingestion that followed was grotesquely prolonged, Dio's jaws dislocating to encompass five or six times their normal span, the mouse passing through them in slow, millimeter increments. Rob watched the entire process silently, hypnotized. Afterward, the snake didn't move for days as the lump inched down its body by way of peristalsis.

"What are you doing with all your . . . stuff?" I asked, speaking of the black trunk being packed tight with drug paraphernalia.

"Taking it to a friend's."

He didn't seem too worried, certainly not enough to make me worry. The relocation of incriminating items was just precautionary. This had happened once before sophomore year, and the police had never come. No one came this time, either. What did come was a letter, with a red warning stripe on the envelope and a message three sentences long:

Dear Robert,

You are hereby required to meet in the Master's office tomorrow afternoon at 4 pm. If you have standing obligations, a note can be acquired from the Master's office excusing you. Please be advised that this is an important matter, and failure to appear will result in immediate disciplinary action.

So they knew about his dealing, and the fact that he'd received a formal letter rather than an email suggested that they meant business. Most likely a customer he didn't know well had been caught smoking and betrayed the source. Or maybe Oswaldo had been right, and Rob had been too cocky, had just assumed that because he'd never been in trouble, he never would. Either way, he was out.

The master's office was directly across the street from our apartment building, no more than twenty steps away. After walking hundreds or even thousands of miles through the dangerous streets of East Orange in the course of his life, after spending dozens of hours on Metro-North trains with a backpack full of drugs, those twenty steps must have been the most anxious of Rob's life. What would he do once he was expelled? He would have to tell Raquel, Daniella, Danny, and Oswaldo, friends who had depended on him to get them through their own harried Yale years. He would have to tell Jacinta in the dining hall, who knew what he did and had constantly warned him to stay safe. He would have to tell Charles Cawley, to whom he'd been sending his transcripts following each semester, with handwritten notes describing his experiences and continuing gratitude. He would have to tell Jackie and subject her to yet another phone call at work during which she would learn that the most important man in her life had failed her.

He must have been thinking about these conversations as he entered the office and waited in one of the three wooden chairs, alongside students there to drop a class or apply for a part-time job. Then the receptionist told him to go in.

The master of Pierson College was a short, bald Slavic literature professor. He was considered one of the "coolest" masters, both because of his patient manner that had helped uncountable numbers of students endure the various pressures they felt Yale placed on them, and because of the annual Jell-O wrestling match he took part in on the Pierson quad. The dean of Pierson College was a petite woman with a sharp German accent, whose job it was to handle things like class schedules, academic conflicts, and discipline. Both had always been kind to Rob and checked in with him often over the years—too often, he sometimes complained, as if they felt he needed extra attention for some reason.

Rob slung his backpack over the chair and sat. He said hello to each of them politely and waited for his due.

The meeting lasted twenty minutes, and Rob said very little. The administrators took turns speaking about the seriousness of this infraction, the short- and long-term consequences, the fact that Rob was such a talented guy, so intelligent, so much better than what he was doing. The master focused on the emotional aspect of it, the disservice Rob was doing himself, the opportunity he was squandering; the dean spoke about the institutional side, the Yale ideals Rob had betrayed, the damage it could cause both other students and the university itself. Rob didn't deny anything. He didn't cite financial strain as an excuse. He didn't explode with self-righteous indignation as he had done with Coach Ridley. He nodded his head and kept saying, "Yes . . . Yes . . . Yes . . ."

In the end, they asked him to give his assurance, under the honor code of Yale University, that he would stop dealing drugs entirely. "Yes," he replied one more time, and he thanked them for their guidance and discretion. He finished by saying, "I'm sorry."

They let him go. There would be no Executive Committee hearing. There would be no police. There would be no expulsion. And Rob went straight to water polo practice, for which he was thirty minutes late.

Rather than dampen Rob's growing air of untouchability, this brush with authority only elevated it. "It looks bad for the university if someone like me goes down like that," he told Oswaldo the following night, with a grin and a shrug. "They don't want to mess around with it." They were in Oswaldo's room in Trumbull College, a Gothic building next to the library. Oswaldo was flustered, bordering on angry. Exactly what he had warned his friend would happen had happened, and yet here was Rob in his leather coat, acting like the Man when he should have been preparing to present his transgressions before the Executive Committee.

"Get the fuck out of my room," Oswaldo said. "I have to study."

"Damn," replied Rob. "Chill. I'm gonna keep it on the down low for a minute."

"I can't deal with your dumb shit anymore," Oswaldo said. "You do dumb shit and you know it's dumb shit but it's the same dumb shit you grew up around so you do it anyway. I'm done."

Oswaldo was dealing with his own shit, in fact, shit that would land him in a white room in Yale's Psychiatric Institute a few weeks later. His brain had begun to crumple under the weight it had to bear: his spiraling family in Newark; his affluent, oblivious classmates whose constant whining about how hard their lives were made him want to turn a gun on them; the daily financial planning involved in keeping up with his tuition payments and the growing debt load in his name; the ever-approaching moment when graduation came and he would be faced with trying to keep his life moving upward—and all of this before he even cracked a textbook to study for his 400-level psychology curriculum. Fantasies of turning a gun on the people around him evolved into turning a gun on his forehead, and suddenly he found himself walking around a nether region of New Haven in the middle of the night, struggling to recall his own name let alone what he was doing here, in the grip of a full-fledged psychotic break. Luckily, his girlfriend had sensed that something was wrong, notified his dean, master, and campus police, and they were able to find him.

Rob visited him in the psychiatric ward almost every day and sat across a table from him in a monitored room for as long as he was permitted, excursions that were similar to a prison visit in purely physical ways: the security checkpoints, the cameras affixed to the ceiling, the bolted metal doors, the space between you and the person sitting across from you just a few feet and yet signifying so much more. Rob would look at his short, rail-thin friend, the friend who had always counseled him wisely if not patiently, and whose counsel he'd refused to take. Now that friend was twitchy and not making much sense at all. Rob would just nod and give him a general update of what was happening on campus and say, "Trust me, you're not missing anything." His staidness paired with the ability to not treat Oswaldo like a psychiatric patient— sparing him both the hesitancy of speech and overenthusiastic bursts of innocuous information that visits from other friends entailed—was its own form of therapy.

Raquel Diaz firmly believed that "going crazy" was a luxury of the wealthy, because poor people like her had too many responsibilities to bother with mental health episodes. Though her consciousness was frayed just as Oswaldo's was, she didn't permit herself to seek help. Her grades remained stellar, but her mother couldn't afford the tuition anymore, her classmates seemed to find new and original ways to enrage her, and her boyfriend of two years had had his own psychotic break and had recently been stalking other women and trying to become a rapper. So she took her junior year off to work as an au pair in Italy and then visit China, an opportunity that the college master helped her secure. The hiatus from school was intended to salvage her brain, reassemble her finances, and place some much-needed distance between herself and this campus—to regain a level of perspective that would see her through graduation. Her friends and roommates let her know that this was a shortsighted decision that would delay her life by a full year, remove her from close friendships, and waste so much of the work she'd already put in. When Rob showed up, she was filled with self-doubt and overwhelmed with the task of packing up her room at the end of sophomore year. They spent a full day organizing her possessions, with Rob lugging her furniture down to the basement storage rooms. Throughout, he told her not to worry about what anyone else was telling her, not to worry about anything at all except getting herself right.

"You do what you have to do," he said more than once that day, and she did, knowing that while she was gone Rob would continue doing what he had to do—not only in terms of dealing and consuming marijuana, but also by carrying whatever burdens he had to carry alone, and walking with order and strength, and striving to help those around him do the same.

*   *   *

AT THE END of junior year, Rob began receiving cryptic emails from phony Hotmail accounts. *We are watching you. We know where you are and we are coming. Be prepared. Tonight is the night when it will happen.* Rob wasn't alarmed, paranoid, or impelled to think that he needed to start watching his back again. In fact, he was amused, because the emails meant that he was being "tapped" for a secret society initiation.

The most famous society was Skull and Bones, referenced in the biographies of both Bush presidents and movies both highbrow (*The Good Shepherd*) and lowbrow (*The Skulls*). There were many other societies: Wolf's Head, Scroll and Key, Mace and Chain, Book and Snake, Berzelius, and on and on. Each was composed of twelve seniors chosen by the class preceding them. The oldest societies occupied heavily gated, windowless, sepulcher-like buildings dotting the campus. Being tapped for any society, particularly the older, more secretive ones, was considered an exclusive honor, like a badge that said you had made an impression on this campus during the previous three years. Admission was quietly coveted by many. I, for one, was surprised when Rob went ahead with the initiation for the group that had chosen him, Elihu, named after the university's founder, Elihu Yale. A secret society was in essence yet another version of the manufactured friendships that Yale was, in Rob's view, constantly foisting upon its students. My roommate had always felt, loudly at times, that he had his real friends and didn't have time for facsimiles of friendships. As such, he was not primed to give a shit about another construct asking for his time. Maybe he was curious. Maybe, in a pragmatic way, he was thinking ahead to the future career contacts such an association promised. Maybe he had become more of a Yalie than he'd ever admit.

Initiation was protracted over three weeks in the spring. The specifics varied from society to society, but they typically involved seniors wearing masks and dark robes walking across campus like so many Grim Reapers to perform minor hazing rituals that took place in various chapels, with an almost celebratory emphasis on the cultishness of it all. Like learning the school songs at St. Benedict's, Rob had to memorize verses written on papyrus scrolls that detailed the history of Elihu, the school's third-oldest secret society. He had no trouble doing this, mumbling the words with an exaggerated detachment from the proceedings, a contrast to peers who did the same thing with trembling, anxious, humbled whispers. Then came Tap Night, when the campus erupted with a few hundred inebriated students assigned tasks for the night: breaking into classroom buildings to steal chairs, climbing campus monuments to sing songs in their underwear, etc. Rob was asked to lie on his stomach in front of the library and challenge any passing campus police to an arm-wrestling match.

"Nah," he said. He'd grown up in a neighborhood in which policemen were constantly checking him out, and in which policemen, in his eyes, had set up his father for life in prison. "You can't get me to do that." In the end, they couldn't.

The following week, he and the eleven other new members of Elihu were invited to the society-owned property, a Federal-style house on the New Haven Green, to drink and receive their pins, with hoods and masks removed. Every Thursday and Sunday night throughout senior year, this group would meet here for a few hours, the goal to open up fully to people who otherwise would have remained merely acquaintances or strangers—to actualize, in a way, the Yale experience in which so many different people of so many different backgrounds were "tapped" to live in these cordoned-off city blocks together. Rob seemed more interested in the fact that he would now have access to the house, which through generous alumni contributions had its own housekeeping service and was kept fully stocked with high-end food and booze year-round. The newly tapped members each owed $100 to the treasurer, Laurel Bachner, a Manhattanite from the Upper East Side and a Dalton School alum. Rob's check bounced initially, and he seemed to forget about it after that. She was nervous about confronting him; an inherent discomfort existed between a rich white girl approaching a poor black man regarding money he owed. She'd never known anyone in her life who couldn't keep $100 in the bank. He'd already made a few cracks about her spoiled upbringing, and she was prepared to cover his dues herself to spare them both the confrontation. Just before she did so, Rob stopped her on campus and slipped her the money in cash. "Sorry about that," he said. "The bank changed my account number for some reason. That was why the check bounced."

The Elihu retreat at the end of that year took place at the New York Governor's Mansion in Albany; a senior member of Elihu was the governor's daughter. Oswaldo, recently out of the psychiatric ward and doing his best to catch up on his classes before year's end, still took a moment to pull Rob aside. "Don't be a fool," was his advice, meaning: don't bring a bunch of weed, don't drink too much, and in general don't get all messed up. Rob was going to the *Governor's Mansion*, and Oswaldo felt that he needed to treat the experience with respect. Rob was representing their kind of people, and if he "got stupid," he would only be reinforcing stereotypes. In the wake of his breakdown, Oswaldo had become hyperattuned to the way he, and people like him, were perceived. For his first three years at Yale, he'd been frustrated by these perceptions, feeling that they were inescapable, allowing that caged feeling to overwhelm him. The perspective granted him by two weeks of near total isolation had led him to believe that he—and in a much bigger way, Rob—had only propagated the ignorance of their peers. Because they *did* get stoned all the time, they *did* get angry, they *did* dress like thugs, they *did* talk shit about a college education that might set them up for fulfilling lives, they *did* set themselves apart. For Oswaldo, the issue had ceased to be a philosophical and historical one, and instead had come to revolve around a simple goal: to graduate from Yale without making that task harder than it needed to be. After all, that was the point of college—not freedom, not alcohol, not relationships, but to *obtain a degree*.

After sitting in FDR's wheelchair that was on display in the museum sector of the Governor's Mansion, Rob ended up doing all three of the things that Oswaldo had warned him against, and Saturday night of the retreat found him passed out on the pool table, an empty bottle of the governor's whiskey clutched in his hand. With that, his initiation into the secret society, perhaps the most rarefied and exclusive component of Yale, was complete.

*   *   *

My head was wedged between the tubular metal arm of our futon frame and the windowsill of a second-floor stair landing.

"*Pull,*" I grunted, "don't push. *OW!*"

"Sorry, my bad." Rob laughed, and then the pressure eased off my skull.

We were moving into the dorm again, early September of senior year. For what would be the last time, we were rummaging through the basement storage rooms for our scuffed and dented furniture, hauling each item up the shoulder-width basement stairs and then angling it around the landings, smashing our fingers and torquing our elbows and laughing throughout. We were in the grip of a too-conscious awareness that everything was suddenly a "last." The last New Haven fall with leaves all afire, the last coed intramural football games, the last tailgates, the last naked parties (one Yale staple in which Rob did not take part), the last time we would all be catching up on our summers, which at this point many had spent in internships related to their chosen career paths. Beginning with the transport of furniture, we began to embrace these "bright college years" with an energy that hadn't existed before the light at the end of the tunnel began flashing so closely, beckoning us while at the same time warning us to turn back.

We'd been back in school for a little over a week when the Twin Towers fell. I was buying toothpaste at a CVS up Whalley Avenue when I heard the urgent newscast over the radio behind the cashier, not totally following what was happening. A half hour later, in the dining hall for lunch, some students were crying. Others were shaking their heads, bewildered. Still others were already intellectualizing the event. Another fifteen minutes passed before someone actually told me that the World Trade Center had been reduced to rubble, and the Pentagon had also been hit. The master walked solemnly from table to table, asking students if their families were all safe. My two older siblings lived in Manhattan now, and my parents happened to be in the city while my dad attended a surgical conference. Phones were down but I was able to email my brother in his SoHo office, where his window had given him a clear view of the bodies plummeting from the upper floors. Between the first and second towers falling, my dad had volunteered to board a bus filled with doctors from the conference, heading toward the site to set up a triage center. We didn't learn until the evening that the bus had been rerouted to Chelsea Piers, but that very few patients came in due to the severe nature of the event: the majority of affected people were either psychologically traumatized but physically unharmed, or else dead. There wasn't much in between.

Ty, Rob, and I gathered in our half-assembled room to watch the news, the endless replay of the second building turning to smoke. Ty kept talking animatedly about the goddamn terrorists, how we should kill them all. At one point a plane flew low overhead, its engine reverberating through the dorm, and Ty's girlfriend screamed mortally and tried to climb under the futon. Rob sat forward, elbows on knees and hands clasped between them. He said very little that I can remember. Then he stood and we went together to the candlelight vigil held in front of the library, during which the president of the Arab Society gave a powerful speech. Afterward, Rob went off alone, I assumed to the Weed Shack or Oswaldo's or somewhere comfortable for him to speak his mind about the day's events, or maybe just to study, which was what I did.

He went to Anwar Reed's house. Anwar was a "townie." He'd grown up in New Haven and now lived with two pit bulls three miles east on State Street, one of those downtrodden regions of New Haven that students avoided. Anwar hustled; that was how he and Rob had met. He was also quiet and kind, low-key, and never made fun of Rob's association with Yale, whose ornate structures had always towered in distant but clear view, seeming to mark the capital of a foreign country. Anwar was planning to join the army, and Rob went there to talk about the day's heavy consequences on Anwar's future.

Unbeknownst to me, from the beginning of freshman year Rob and Oswaldo had been drawn away from Yale via their friends on the dining hall and custodial staffs, outward into the city of New Haven. Rob considered these excursions a much-needed dose of reality, the social equivalent of an antidepressant. Anwar's yard had a view of East Rock, particularly striking at sunset when the last rays enriched the limestone frontage. He hosted a lot of barbeques in that yard, where the grill was sandwiched between a stack of cracked flat tires and a rusty wheelless wheelbarrow. Inside the small house, a threadbare beige couch and a mattress in the bedroom were the only furnishings. Ash stains branded the hardwood floor. The pit bulls curled up together in their cage in the corner. Anwar had steered some business Rob's way over the years— "making movements," he called it, like Skeet and Carl had—and whenever he did so Rob had slipped him 20 percent of what he'd made. "Kickback," Rob would say.

The look and feel of places like Anwar's, the cadence of the language spoken, the familiar topics of conversation—these elements combined to make Rob and Oswaldo feel like they hadn't, in fact, forsaken their roots. Jacinta, in their dining hall chats, constantly warned him to be careful. "You can say things to kids here and it doesn't matter, they won't mess with you. With that boy Anwar and all them, you have to watch what you say, protect yourself. It's not the same."

"Always," Rob would reply, eating at his usual spot behind her card-swiping station.

After 9/11, Rob could no longer carry a backpack of marijuana through the upgraded security of Penn Station and Grand Central. He bought a car, a low-riding, decades-old, two-door Toyota on its last legs. I couldn't imagine the vehicle having cost more than a few hundred dollars. He felt that the engine had just enough juice left to get him down to Newark and back a few times, sufficient to see him through the year. Whenever he had trouble with it, which was often, he took the car to Flowy. In the years since high school, Flowy had fashioned himself into an expert diagnostician of car engines.

Though the subject came up weightily in most of our classes, the real-world consequences of the World Trade Center remained largely unknown to us (as, in retrospect, they did to the highest levels of government). But the tragedy brought forward, with an unusual gravity, the transition we were on the verge of making. What had happened had happened in the real world. The attack had immediately, savagely altered the lives of real people, people who went to work every day, owned houses, had families, and geared their lives around something other than "expanding their minds to actualize their best selves," as Yale president Richard Levin had advised us to do at our convocation ceremony three years before. Not every Yale student came from a sheltered background, but we were all undeniably sheltered here. No matter how important an English paper or a math exam or a football game felt, the realization emerged that none of these activities with which we filled our schedules truly mattered, that soon we would leave this place with whatever GPA and other achievements we had managed to obtain, and reality awaited. Gone from our lives would be the snowball fights on quads, the food prepared daily for us, the keg stands at Sigma Alpha Epsilon, and course loads designed such that there would be no classes before noon. Very soon, our decisions would have consequences, our lives would include danger, we would experience sadness and loss and disappointment on a scale heretofore unknown. With the weight and moment of 9/11 still coursing through the culture, we felt unprepared.

We hid these fears the most effective way we knew how—by returning to the idiotic behavior that had marked our first weeks on campus. Rob was not above taking part. His stoner circle widened and gathered more frequently, sometimes lasting clear through a weeknight during which no studying was done. The car gave him more flexibility to go to Anwar's house, and sometimes on a whim to Mohegan Sun, an Indian casino an hour north. I tagged along once, and sat rigidly in the passenger seat as he drove that beater car through the densely wooded freeways of central Connecticut, pushing seventy, Outkast blaring. I'd never been to a casino, and after he gave me a two-minute tutorial on how to play craps and blackjack, I proceeded to lose $80 with alacrity and ease, at which point I removed myself from the table to observe. Rob called me a bitch, as he'd called me many times before, with affection. And I was perfectly content to spend most of the night watching him play hand after hand of blackjack and sink himself deep. His low-hanging smile belied the studiousness with which he played, contemplative about every one of his hits and splits, and more so with each $15 hand he lost. He kept throwing money on the table, always with a smile and a loose flick of the wrist. But the fingers of his left hand danced along his chips incessantly; I knew he was keeping track of every dollar in the ledger in his head. He maintained an easy dialogue with the dealer. "You had to go and give yourself an eight," he said, slapping his palm on the table after a twenty-one on the dealer's side. "Didn't you? *Didn't* you? Now why you gotta do me like that?" She was a middle-aged Asian woman, accustomed to indulging the clientele in a professional way that preserved the invisible rampart between them. Over the course of her shift at his table, Rob drew her in to the point where that barrier dissolved, and she was clearly rooting for him, almost ashamed when she drew a blackjack, beaming when Rob doubled down and won. Whenever the dealers changed, Rob gave the departing a warm goodbye and immediately began charming the next.

We'd left campus around eleven. I'd opted out of the gambling by one. Then three, four, five in the morning passed us by, and Rob played on, chain-smoking cigarettes, drinking rum and Cokes. I nursed White Russians and took a few walks around to people-watch and try the slot machines. An isolated casino in the middle of a weeknight had a weight to it, a desperation beneath the pale lights and chirpy dings of the machines. The few people there seemed to have come down from Boston or up from New York City, and they appeared to have little more to hope for in life than a decent winning streak. Upon returning to the table (my own hope being that Rob might want to leave soon), I paused to watch him from a distance of maybe twenty yards. He looked very much woven into these surreal surroundings. The friend whom I'd come to view as a kind of icon, who for three years had never once given in to the real and manufactured anxieties coursing through the rest of us, now just sat there alone, focused only on the hand in play, seized by the hope that the hand would be good enough. During fleeting moments, between haughty exchanges with the dealer and the table slapping and chip gathering, he could look serious and worn. We left at six in the morning, just in time to beat commuter traffic into New Haven. We drove mostly in silence, with Shaggy singing "It Wasn't Me" on the worn-out speakers, both of us in that woozy yet strangely sober state of having spent an entire night awake and active.

I smoked with him for the first time that semester, not long after that excursion. He'd offered many times over the years, and I'd demurred offhand, until these exchanges had become a kind of rehearsed joke.

Then one evening during November of senior year, he was rolling a joint. As typically began our back-and-forth, he raised it toward me and said with that grin, "Come on, Jeffrey, it'll chill you *out*," to which I was expected to say something like "I'm cool" or "No thanks, man."

"Okay, sure," I replied.

He blinked his eyes and hollered, "*What* the *fuck*?"

"Sure, I'll try."

Rob called to Ty, who ran into the common room. They made an event out of what followed, giving me the rite of passage that Rob had never experienced as a kid taking his first toke. The only problem was that I had never smoked anything before and didn't know how; my first attempt left my mouth tasting like ash but didn't reach my lungs.

"Nasty," I rasped through the dissociative tingle in the back of my throat.

"What about a bong?" Ty suggested.

"A bong would just about kill the kid," Rob replied, and then, to me, "Come here."

He made me sit on a stool directly across from him. He put the joint in his mouth and directed me to place my face in front of his, maybe four inches apart. "Now, just breathe in and don't stop," he said. I complied, and as I did so he pulled fast and deep off the joint and in a gentle, steady exhalation streamed the smoke back over my face. The trick was called "shotgunning," and it was effective. Immediately my lungs filled to capacity with Rob's breath, laced with THC.

"Now hold it in," Rob said. "Hold it a minute."

My track-trained and untainted respiratory system was quite power-ful, and I was happy to impress him. I was also instantaneously stoned. I'd expected to feel something like the peace Rob himself exhibited when high. Instead, I just became dizzy and began giggling at every sound I heard while a low-level paranoia fixed itself to the rear of my brain. A grin locked itself onto my face so tight that my cheeks ached for days. I was passed out not more than thirty minutes later. The next morning, while I dug at my dried-out eyes, Rob slapped me on the back and said, "You were funny as hell last night."

"Do I owe you any money?" I asked.

"For, like, two half hits?" He laughed. "Nah, it's on the house." (His tone implied that this would be the last freebie.)

"I guess I thought it would be more mellow or something," I replied.

"It's like your running. You just gotta train and you'll get there."

My running, which had consumed every afternoon and the bulk of my weekends throughout college, had gotten me little more than a re-curring hamstring pull that had long since nullified all my lofty hopes for record setting. The injury had also made me something of a bas-ket case, logging each nutrient that went into my body, obsessing about sleep, living in terror of "speed-endurance" practices, and overthink-ing races to the point where my muscles would tighten and the bad hamstring would twinge and my mind, rather than focus on the rather simple task of running forward as fast as possible, would collapse into uncertainty as my opponents ran on ahead. These stresses accounted for probably half of my waking thoughts for three years of my life. So, though my first pot experience was more or less pathetic and I wasn't impelled to retry anytime soon, loosening up a bit felt like a positive thing to do. More positive still was the experience of sharing this small, vital aspect of my friend's life.

After a time, we all seemed to calm down and focus once again—particularly the premed students staring down the barrel of the MCAT. In many ways, this test was the culmination of all the studying, lab work, and anxiety that had accompanied their chosen career path: five hours that would decide what caliber of medical schools would consider them.

These students disappeared for days at a time to study, take Kaplan courses and practice tests, and seek out any datum of information that might give them an advantage over the thousands of future doctors with whom they would be competing that day. These students resembled parents of infant triplets: bleary-eyed, beaten down, weakly managing to put a positive spin on the undertaking. Ty would score 44 out of a possible 45, placing him in the hundredth percentile nationally.

Even the science majors who were not planning on medical school tended to take the exam in order to at least retain the option, but Rob did not. When asked about what he wanted to do with his degree, he would change the subject to Rio. He didn't plan this trip so much as dream of it; he seemed to believe he could simply board a plane, bank over the ocean and land among those hills, then wing it from there. I wondered about his seeming lack of post-Yale motivation, and yet his "chillness" aligned so naturally with who he was that I never questioned it, and certainly not aloud to him. "Rob will figure it out," those of us who knew him would say to each other. "He always does." None of us—not even Oswaldo Gutierrez—knew then what we know now: that he had netted just over $100,000 selling marijuana at Yale. A small portion of this he'd already given to his mother in installments akin to the money he'd once left on the counter, small enough that she didn't question him when he told her it came from the dining hall job he'd quit long before. He'd spent $10,000 or so on school supplies and summer travel. He set aside another $30,000, also for his mother, that he could give to her when he had a real job and wouldn't have to bend believability to explain where it came from. The remaining half, "fifty large" in Rob's parlance, was to pay for Rio and float him through the next year, at which point he was confident that he would in fact "figure it out."

* * *

I'M STILL NOT sure why, but my entire academic curriculum senior year revolved around the literary "search for the father" motif. In a prestigious class taught by the literature scholar Harold Bloom, I wrote my final paper on Odysseus and Telemachus, arguing that while the son searched for the father, the father was really searching for himself. (Professor Bloom gave the paper a C-, with a single comment scrawled on page 1: "This isn't Homer, it's Hobbs!") My senior thesis on James Joyce's *Ulysses* triangulated Stephen Dedalus, his biological father, Simon Dedalus, and his surrogate father, Leopold Bloom, in an attempt to parse through the symbolic importance of blood. My final project in the creative writing tie-in to my English major was a novel, written quickly and quite poorly, about a carpenter in northern New England who, in the wake of his son's death, sets off to locate the father who abandoned him, encountering thinly veiled characters plucked from the *Odyssey* along the way. None of these projects was original in the slightest, and indeed the subjects had been explored more deftly by innumerable writers before me (meaning: my work was entirely derivative). Combined, they probably totaled 150,000 words, and on these words I worked hours each night, usually with Homer or Joyce or both open beside me.

"How do you just sit there and write shit?" Rob asked. A popular new Nelly CD was playing. Rob's musical tastes seemed to have softened over time, and in the room I'd been hearing fewer freestyle-based, full-throttle gangster rappers like Ludacris and more melodic, overproduced songs like the one we were hearing now, "Ride Wit Me."

"I don't know," I replied. "I just like words, and kind of figuring them out."

Rob knew that I aspired to be a novelist. And without having read any of the lousy short fiction I'd produced over the years, and without telling me as much, he had confidence that I'd be able to do it, certainly more confidence than any jowly, prattling English professor or jaded, overcompetitive creative writing student. The ugliness of the creative writing track evidenced itself in everything from the sample stories you had to submit for entry into the most notable authors' classes to the way every one of those professors smugly advised us during the first class to "choose a different career" and the shared understanding that if you could not speak fluidly at length about Raymond Carver's canon, then you would never succeed. On a fellowship application, under a "career plan" entry, I'd written, "Write books of a mythical nature." The selection committee had practically laughed me out of the room.

Rob's confidence was communicated with a simple look that said, *If you want to, and you don't, then that's on you.*

"How the hell can you memorize every fact in every textbook?" I asked him in reply.

"Not about memorization," he said and looked up thoughtfully. "It's like, you look at that stereo, or a clock, or whatever, and you would want to write a paragraph describing it. Me, I look at things and want to *figure it out.* Like, take it apart, see what's inside it, know how it works, learn the science behind it."

"You're like that with people, too," I said.

"What do you mean?"

"You're really curious about people's stories. Like you're always trying to 'figure everyone out.'"

"I suppose," he replied.

Later in the same conversation, he asked me why I was so obsessed with the *Odyssey.* He'd read it in high school and knew the story and themes, but he'd found the text stiff and inaccessible.

"Just all the father-son stuff," I replied. "I think about that all the time."

"How come?"

"I guess it comes from stuff with my own dad."

"He seems like a real cool pop."

While struggling to find a way to explain the grievances I had over my father (unfounded, self-gratifying grievances to be sure, being as my father was steady, generous, and devoted to his children almost beyond reason), I remembered where Rob's own father was. Skeet was mentioned so rarely in our room—maybe three times over four years—that forgetting was easy, and remembering made my search for words all the more treacherous.

"He just doesn't show or say much about what he feels. He's kind of internalized. And I care more about what he thinks of me than pretty much anyone else. So, y'know, it's something that's on my mind a lot."

"Yeah, I see that," he said, situating his textbook in his lap and pointing his face toward it again.

"Do you think about . . . that stuff?" I said. "With your dad? I mean, I know it's a lot different, but . . . ?" Immediately, I regretted these words.

"I guess," he replied. "I don't really know the man, so it's different. Mostly, I think about my ma . . ." The conversation tapered off.

Spring term brought with it a flighty, giddy feeling. Final exams still had to be dealt with—but we were *here*, we had *made it*. Now all those "lasts" were truly occurring: last snowfall, last "P is for the P in Pierson College" chants, last Spring Fling concert on Old Campus. Ty and I realized that, although Rob usually came to our home track meets, we had never seen him play water polo. He had been voted captain by his teammates both junior and senior years—a rarity on any sports team—but our knowledge of his sport remained limited to the team photo we found laying haphazardly on the coffee table one afternoon. In the picture, he stood left of center with his chest puffed out in a line of otherwise pale bodies, his face set to convey toughness.

We drove to a tournament at Middlebury College one early Sunday morning, both of us hungover from the previous night. We wandered around the pretty campus until someone was able to direct us toward the pool. We joked about the skimpy swimsuits and rubber helmets for a minute, then half slept through a game before Yale played. Seeing Rob in the water brought us out of this stupor. We were so used to him being subdued and removed—so used to him being stoned, in fact—that to see the energy he possessed in the pool reminded me of a predatory animal, like his python, Dio, once a mouse was dropped into the tank. Our eyes were locked on him, waiting to see what he would do. He did not possess the languid, long-limbed aquatic grace of Olympic swimmers; his strokes were short, choppy, inefficient. But he *moved*, and when he took the ball he placed it bobbing in the water between his arms, controlling it with his chest and head as he swam the length of the pool.

When preparing for a shot, his kicking legs held half his torso out of the water, the ball cradled in his palm still higher above his head and making rapid half rotations back and forth as he sought the right angle. We could hear the smack talk ten rows up in the bleachers: *"Nah! Nah! You ain't got shit!"* when he was defending a ball holder; *"Here it comes, bitch!"* when he was keen to score. He released these gems in a low yet resounding hiss, his teeth bared, his grin scary. That he was the only black player, from what we could tell, in the whole eight-team tournament only heightened the thrashing quality to every movement he made, every word he used to intimidate. He played with his elbows bent and often deployed toward a forehead or jaw. When he was whistled for a foul—which was often—he'd raise his arms out of the water in mystification, like a petulant NBA player. From above, Ty and I egged him on, fully absorbed in his joy, which was total.

Less joyful was the "bio" Rob gave to Elihu a few weeks before graduation. The bio was the fundamental element of the secret society tradition: in any medium you chose and over any length of time you needed, you gave your life story to the eleven classmates with whom you'd been spending two nights a week throughout senior year. You were supposed to dig deep and challenge yourself, as well as place complete trust in the listeners to keep everything confidential. The Elihu Class of '02 had been atypically diverse in a socioeconomic sense, with a disproportionate number of minority kids who'd come to Yale from poverty. Giving a bio could be stressful; one felt an inherent pressure to "tell a story," and in order to do so, construct conflict, which was harder for some than for others. When, during the winter, a girl had gone on at length about the social stresses of the Dalton School—an expensive prep school on which the TV show *Gossip Girl* was based—a poor student from Chicago had begun to seethe, to the point of interrupting her and pointing out that these were not problems, not "real" ones, anyway. The girl had become defensive; this was her bio, and an important safety net in giving it was the understanding that judgments would be suspended. But still, a kind of class warfare erupted as the group split into sides: the poor kids aligned in taking offense at having to sit through five hours' worth of "rich people problems," and the well-off kids maintaining that problems were relative and the girl should be permitted—and encouraged—to share the issues that weighed on her. Rob stayed out of the fray, as he stayed out of most of the conflicts that had occurred in the Elihu house. But on that night, he came to be regarded as the final authority on the matter, since his circumstances growing up had been the most "real" of any.

"Just let her talk," he said, sipping his brandy as if for dramatic effect. And then, to the kids who'd been hassling her, "Damn, it's like you people can't just listen without trying to start shit."

"*You people?*"

"You heard what I said. You're acting like you're all the same, so that's how I'll address you."

"That's fucked-up, Rob."

"And it's fucked-up the way you're treating her, like she's not an individual, either." Then, to the girl, "Proceed."

As Rob's bio approached, the Elihu house filled with genuine curiosity. He'd always been content to drink the free booze and smoke up the house but reluctant to engage in any of the meaningful personal debate that the secret society was intended to prompt. They figured he would keep it short and focus mainly on his mother. He might touch on racism at Yale or something controversial like that, just to see how everyone would react.

They did not expect that he would talk for four full hours about a part of him they'd previously heard nothing of: his father.

Seated at the head of a long oak table, speaking with no notes or pictures, he told them about his mother's unique filial strategy, the nights spent doing homework, the days spent wandering around the neighborhood. He told them about the fire on Pierson Street, the apartment on Chestnut, the wide orbit of men his father maintained. He told them about the trial, the prison visits, the successful appeal and its reversal. He told them about the letters he continued to send to various appellate judges every month. He painted the broad picture of a great man egregiously wronged by a system engineered against "people like him," and he walked the Elihu society through the day of August 8, 1987, as if he'd been an omniscient observer over everyone involved—the Moore sisters, the police, and the prosecutors. He spent a lot of time focusing on the murder weapon and how his father owned it because you had to carry a piece if you were "about that life." But the real murderer had broken into his father's apartment in 2E, stolen his weapon, used it to murder the Moore sisters in 2D, and then returned it to 2E. The police had then illegally removed the gun from the scene to plant on his father, so that the case could be closed quickly and spare them the trouble of having to actually do their jobs. For the entire year, Rob had placed himself above petty class conflicts that had plagued many of their discussions. On that night he made clear to his secret society that the fundamental conflict of his life was founded on precisely that belief: the white establishment would always keep the common black man down in order to cover their own asses.

Arthur Turpin had become close to Rob that year. An affluent student with an aristocratic way about him, he and Rob had passed many Thursday nights playing pool and having fun with their contrasting personas—in other words, they "fucked with each other." Arthur had always been troubled by the anger he sensed in Rob. Though he hid that anger well behind the grin and the laughter and the marijuana, Arthur felt it in the jokes Rob made to Laurel and others about their privileged upbringings, in his heavy quietude whenever socioeconomic topics came up in conversation, and in his general disdain of Yale and Yalies. Arthur saw a closed-mindedness that was, he felt, self-propagating and innately limiting. More broadly, he believed these qualities explained precisely how an intelligent guy like Rob would always make life harder on himself than it needed to be. Here he was, drinking brandy in a prestigious society in a top-ranked school, the beneficiary of so many gifts both natural and bestowed, surrounded by bright and open-minded classmates, and yet still he remained mired in, even paralyzed by, what was effectively his own racism. Of course, Arthur never broached the subject with Rob, since it was easier to screw around instead. He'd made assumptions about his friend that were treacherous to air out, the central one being the most common: you truly can't shed your roots.

On the night of Rob's bio, Arthur realized that those roots were em-

bedded far deeper than he ever could have imagined. He felt very sad
for his friend that night, listening to Rob arduously construct his own
defense of his father, the defense he believed Skeet was deprived of fifteen years ago, a defense that came with its own many loose ends. Rob
was able to intellectualize almost every argument that arose, but where
Skeet Douglas was concerned, each word of the thousands Rob spoke
came from a deeply, dangerously emotional place. In truth, even after
all the hours he'd spent in Trenton State talking to Skeet about it, Rob
seemed to have no idea where his father was or what he was doing on
that morning. Arthur found it quite obvious that until Rob was able to
place his father that day long ago, he'd have a hell of a time trying to
place himself here, now.

*   *   *

I'D BEEN CONFUSED by Rob's vague plan following graduation, and
why it seemed to center on a twenty-two-year-old Yale graduate living
with his mother in a poor neighborhood.

Then I visited him in East Orange that spring, during the reading week
that preceded final exams. I was en route to Manhattan to visit my brother,
and the side trip to East Orange was a statement of sorts: I'd realized that
though I'd offered dozens of times to take him out to dinner with my
visiting family or even take him home with me for a weekend, never once
had I proposed doing something where he came from. I didn't tell my
parents about the visit; I could just hear my mom saying, "Be careful."

Rob picked me up at the train station and acted as a tour guide. He
drove me past St. Benedict's Prep, Branch Brook Park, Schools Stadium, and ultimately to a cookout at his Aunt Debbie's apartment. What
was unnerving about Newark, as we moved west and the hospitals and
colleges and greens of downtown gave way to graffiti, grit, and loiterers,
was how cemented the poverty seemed to be, unfolding in all directions,
like the ocean going on and on, never-ending. Despite the progressive
motivations that had prompted the visit, I did feel tense as it became
apparent that I might be the only white person within three miles. And
yet, with Rob at the wheel, waving to people in the street and attaching

childhood stories to practically every corner, the neighborhood didn't feel like a slum. Its streets were dirty, run-down, very poor, and very black, but they didn't feel threatening, not sitting next to Rob. As we crossed into East Orange proper, I was attuned to the way he leaned back in the driver's seat, one arm slung out the window, skully knotted tightly, bass thumping. He was at ease.

The reception he received at the cookout—at least three dozen people packed into a small yard behind an apartment complex on Hamilton Avenue—was warm in a way I'd never experienced in my own WASP upbringing, where handshakes were followed by vague descriptions of "what's new," then dinner. Carl was there, as was Dante, and Rob's cousins Nathan and Diandra and Corey. Rob was the mayor of this potluck gathering, but he deflected any awe directed toward him. His grandmother, Frances, was in a wheelchair with tubes in her nostrils; her emphysema had been worsening throughout Rob's college years. Horace, beside her, looked very old and sullen behind a fixed smile. We stood by her wheelchair most of the afternoon as Rob asked everyone what was going on in the neighborhood, what was going on in their lives, offering small bits of advice to those having trouble at home or at work. One of his cousins mentioned that she was about to be kicked out of her apartment because she was $600 behind on rent. Rob took her aside, out of everyone's earshot, and told her he would take care of it. "I got you," he said. "Now give me a hug."

What struck me in particular was the amazement on display that not only was he graduating from Yale, but he was going to do so in four years. *"Four years!"* people kept exhaling disbelievingly, as if the typical time span for achieving a bachelor's degree was unfathomable. "My man graduating *Yale* in *four years* . . ." Jackie was the only one present who didn't seem ecstatic about Rob's pending accomplishment. She sat in a lawn chair in the back of the yard, chain-smoking menthols. She looked much older than I remembered her on orientation day, the last time I'd seen her, more gray and with a harder jaw, and she was still hard to impress—not by the effort I'd taken to come here, not by the effort Rob had taken to make it through Yale. Looking back now, it is easy to feel as if she alone knew that success and happiness in life were more elusive even than an Ivy League diploma.

Night had fallen by the time he took me back to the train station. He asked if I wanted to stop for something to eat in the Ironbound, at a Portuguese restaurant he loved. He told me how seedy Ferry Street had been not too long ago, and how its revival into a busy stretch of green and red restaurant awnings was miraculous. He used that word, "miraculous," a word I'd never heard come out of his mouth before. I said I had to get to the city to meet my brother, and I knew that Rob was heading back to East Orange to see his "boys." I also knew that he had to attend to the matter of re-upping his marijuana supply for graduation, which was going to be a boon for business. We slapped hands and I watched him aggressively pull his beater car into the traffic snarl that was Raymond Boulevard. Through the window, riding low, he looked serious all of a sudden, very grown-up.

Nobody looked grown-up on graduation day. Much like orientation three and a half years earlier, the weekend was an endless succession of ceremonies and speeches, the lawns newly seeded for the trampling pleasure of graduates and their families, most of us in some level of drunkenness at all times. To begin, elected class representatives planted a symbolic ivy vine outside one of the classroom buildings, while a sentimental, student-written poem titled "Ivy Ode" was read aloud.

On Class Day, the first of the two-day-long proceedings, we were each supposed to wear a hat that said something about ourselves. I sat next to Rob during the ceremony, and in front of us arose a three-foot replica of the Eiffel Tower from the head of a young woman, presumably of French extraction. Engineering students sported battery-powered alcohol distribution machines they'd designed. Rob, as ever, wore his skully over his cornrows. As the Class Day speaker, Governor George Pataki—on whose pool table Rob had passed out a year ago—took the stage before the twelve hundred giddy graduates and cracked his first weak joke of the afternoon, Rob hunched over to pack his white clay pipe with a pinch of marijuana and toke (these pipes had been given to us by the school, and we were supposed to break them underfoot at some point, symbolizing . . . something). Some kids around us laughed and asked for a hit; others scowled and said, "That's so disrespectful," in hissy whispers. Governor Pataki spoke gravely about 9/11, pleading that we not fall victim to ignorant intolerance. "Why did it take the worst act of terrorism to unite our country?" he asked rhetorically, fifty yards away. Later, our roommate Ty received the award for overall achievement out of the entire Class of '02.

Rob nudged my elbow and pointed to a wizard hat someone sported a few rows ahead, specked with small gold stars, like something Albus Dumbledore might wear for a Hogwarts commencement. He told me that Yale had often felt to him like the famous school for wizards: a place of Gothic spires and dark stone hallways set in another dimension, which granted access to its sorcery and secrets only to these elite few graduating with us right now.

After the ceremony, Rob took Jackie to a cocktail party for parents at the Elihu house. He was excited to show Jackie the place. He'd explained what a secret society was, but the concept had always seemed to elude her: a house set aside exclusively for a dozen college students to drink booze in and share their lives twice a week when they should have been studying. She went with him, nodded her way through the tour, exchanged polite greetings with other students and parents before her lips fell by habit into the straight horizontal line that was neither a smile nor a frown. Red wine and aged whiskey were brought around by hired servers, but she didn't drink.

After the cocktails, most students dined with their families at upscale restaurants like the Chart House and Union League Cafe, or went to Mory's for the "Cups" ritual—gigantic chalices of boozy punches were passed around a group, and whoever finished the last drop spun the chalice upside down on his or her head singing, "It's [drinker's name] who makes the world go round . . ." Rob took Jackie to Jacinta's small apartment a mile up Whalley Avenue. I'd jogged through this downtrodden area often during my time at Yale, because it lay between campus and the track facilities, and I'd always kept my head down and didn't stop. Jacinta lived there, between Whalley and Edgewood, with her teenage son. A week before, Yale's black seniors had had their own graduation ceremony. This took place at the Af-Am House, and each student asked a family member, faculty adviser, or friend to drape a scarf around his or her neck onstage. Rob and Danny Nelson had argued over who would have Jacinta bestow his scarf, and ultimately Rob had ceded her to Danny, because Danny had worked in the dining hall all four years of college. Rob's scarf was draped by the charismatic poet and sociology professor Derrick Gilbert, whose book of poetry, *HennaMan*, Rob had been obsessed with amid all his science courses. Tonight, Jacinta had a braised pork shoulder on the table. The four of them sat and ate. She and Jackie talked like old girlfriends, and throughout the evening Rob seemed tired but happy, his manner tinged with relief that these four years were over.

But they were not over, not quite yet. We still had one more ceremony the next day, when the graduating seniors from Pierson College gathered in the college quad to receive our diplomas. We filed in from the slate patio on which we'd first gathered almost four years earlier. Then, Rob had been smoking a cigarette off to the side in his Timberland boots, looking older than the rest of us. He didn't look that way anymore. Maybe in our matching navy gowns and tasseled hats, anyone would be hard-pressed to look very mature. Maybe the rest of us had caught up with him somehow, though I doubted that. Maybe we all knew him now, some very well, and so the isolationist attitude with which he'd first approached campus no longer manifested. Or maybe, most simply, he couldn't withhold a boyish smile that day.

Twenty, maybe twenty-five of his friends and family had come up for the day. Aunts and uncles, cousins, neighbors, friends—they'd all packed themselves into a procession of four-seat cars and caravanned up to New Haven. In their center were Frances and Jackie. Jackie sat beside her mother's wheelchair, both of her hands stacked upon Frances's on the armrest. The dean read each of our names from a small lectern to the right of the stage, while the master gave out diplomas in the center. When she said, "Robert DeShaun Peace. Bachelor of science in molecular biophysics and biochemistry, with distinction in the major," a cacophony of *whoop-WHOOPS* broke out from his cheering section in the rear of the tent. Rob took his time mounting the stage. With his left hand on Rob's shoulder, the master handed the diploma over with his right, and the two men lightly hugged one another, and the hooting behind us reached a crescendo to the point where the more reserved parents and students (meaning about 90 percent of those present) began turning their heads: faces calibrated to amusedly share in the joyfulness even while, in their minds, some had to be wondering why such people couldn't contain themselves a little bit more respectably. Then Rob was at the microphone on which the master had made his opening statements. He cleared his throat, a signal for his section to calm down. The heat-trapping tent grew quiet.

He glanced at a scrap of paper in his hand, pocketed it, and said, "A Yale education encompasses more than classes; it is the experience that has better prepared me for life. I would like to thank all the people who supported me in this endeavor, and I dedicate this moment to my motivation and heart, my mother."

I expected the audience, led by the New Jersey contingent, to break into cinematic applause. But for a few moments, everyone remained silent and still. The clapping and cheers, when they came, were brief. Ty shouted, *"Peace OUT!"* and we all laughed. Then Rob returned to his seat between us.

I don't recall much of the day after that, no doubt because it revolved around more drinking, more parties. People I'd barely known or openly disliked would stumble up to me and drape a bear hug over my shoulders, slurring exclamations like, "We did it!" and "We survived!" At one point I went back to our room, half cleared out at this point, just to take a breather. Rob was there, also alone, rolling a joint on our coffee table with that precious way he had. He offered me a hit. I shrugged, sure. We sat and got stoned, maybe for fifteen minutes or so. We must have talked, but about what I will never remember. Most likely, we just bullshitted without much allusion to the fact that this was it. College was over. On to the next thing, whatever that was. These moments, our last as roommates, were very calm.

I woke early the next day and, hungover, packed the last of my things. I knocked lightly on Rob's door to say goodbye; he wasn't there. Dio, his python, was coiled up in the glass tank atop the black trunk, still digesting a vermin eaten five or six days earlier. Textbooks were piled up in the corner to be sold back to the Yale Bookstore. Two duffel bags in the center of the floor were half packed with clothes. The pictures of the Burger Boyz at 34 Smith Street and Jackie at St. Benedict's graduation had been pulled down. The incense he'd burned couldn't fully mask the smell of stale marijuana; over the years, I'd grown fond of that smell, the vestiges of good times that had clung to curtains and carpeting: the smell of my friend.

I didn't wait to say goodbye to Rob. I figured that the nature of our friendship—the nature of Rob himself—didn't necessitate that final ceremony after all the ceremonies we'd already endured: the man hug, the firm-grip-thumb-lock-hand-clench-half-hug, the not-quite-tearful "Later on, man." Rob was cooler and easier than that, and he wasn't going anywhere. There would always be time, I thought.

During Yale graduation weekend in 2002, Rob wore the African scarf that he'd been given during the "Black Graduation" ceremony one week earlier.

Part IV

———————◆———————

Mr. Peace

*Ty Cantey (second from left), Rob (third from left), and I
(third from right) had a roommate reunion when they served as
groomsmen at my wedding in Brooklyn, 2005. Later in the night,
we three "Threw Dem Bows" on the dance floor.*

Chapter 9

◆

HE WAS AMAZED by what had been left behind. Expensive winter coats, racks filled with CDs, textbooks, halogen lamps, six-hundred-thread-count sheet sets that had never been unpackaged, gold and silver jewelry, stereos, Discmans, and even laptop computers: graduated seniors had simply departed without these things. And Rob—who was working the summer custodial job for the fourth straight year, cleaning up the campus between graduation in mid-May and the alumni reunions in early June—stayed to sweep it all up. He dealt with items of value first, stashing anything sellable in an industrial garbage bag that he set aside. Then came the work of hauling abandoned furniture down the stairs, sweeping up all the dust and grime and hair that had accumulated over the year, mopping and painting, reconstructing bunk beds that had been pulled apart in room after room. The various spaces he'd inhabited over the years were now empty, given a clean coat of white paint, awaiting next year. We'd all come to Yale aiming to leave a footprint; Rob knew from this work that none of us had, at least not in the dorm rooms.

He took a lot of cigarette breaks alongside the full-time maintenance employees, men he'd befriended over the years. They were generally derisive of the students, the way they felt entitled to just *leave their shit* for others to pick up. Dozens of fifty-gallon trash bags' worth of said shit lay in a mountain in a corner of the quad, next to the master's house. The

205

final task was to transport them to a Dumpster on Park Street before the last debris of our time here was hauled away.

They did sell the valuables they'd collected. Like every year, the six-person custodial team combined what they'd found into one cache of contraband. First, they sold the textbooks back to the bookstore, which paid a fraction of the cover price no matter the condition—but still, it was cash. As for the rest, each member helped unload what he could. Some used the Internet. Others pounded the pavement in their neighborhoods. Afterward, trusting one another's honesty, they divided the profits evenly. At the end of the three-week stint, Rob came away with almost $1,000. The figure paled in comparison to the money he had already saved. But still, he made enough to cover the summer's rent in New Haven. He also gave himself a graduation present in the form of a second tattoo, this one on his left biceps, of an African woman with a tall headdress seen in profile. The image matched exactly Jackie's lone body art, inked during her twenties, before Rob was a thought.

He remained on the custodial staff during the reunions in early June. A few thousand alumni from as recently as five years ago and as far back as the 1950s caught up beneath tented open bars and catered food spreads. The schedule included lectures and three-course meals and various activities like group hikes up East Rock and tours of the botanical greenhouse—but the guests (the older they were, the increasingly white and stodgy and male) mostly hung out and drank, like they'd done in college. Rob moved around the fringes of the various gatherings, emptying the trash cans and picking up the plastic cups, napkins, and spilled food. Like the very first week of school, nobody looked at him and assumed he was anything other than a janitor. Unlike the first week of school, he was one.

After the reunion cleanup was complete, he went back to work in the med school lab, where he assisted in researching the pharmacology of proteins that led to infectious disease, inflammation, and cancer. His primary focus was on the structural biology of chemokines—protein receptors secreted by cells to recruit an immune response to the site of an infection. Using X-ray crystallography, Rob spent the summer and fall isolating the CXCL12 (SDF-1alpha) and vMIP-II/vCCL2 chemokines for the GPCR CXCR4 coreceptor for HIV-1. This particular receptor also mediated metastasis in a number of cancers, as well as a mutation responsible for an immunosuppressive disease known as WHIM syndrome. The applications included stem cell transplantation and the production of medicines to halt the takeover of these afflictions. In our dorm room, we had always joked admiringly about the fact that Ty Cantey—who was now preparing for a yearlong fellowship at Cambridge, England, before undergoing a seven-year MD-PhD program at Harvard Med School—was destined to cure cancer someday. I had no idea that Rob, in the lab he'd walked to almost every day during junior and senior years, was actually helping to do it.

He lived with Raquel, in a basement apartment near Jacinta's that they called "the dungeon." The apartment was relatively small, especially for a man and a woman who were not romantically involved. The only windows were at the top of the wall, giving them a view of the calves and ankles of passersby. A gigantic hammock was strung across the high ceiling in a makeshift loft, for storage and, on occasion, amorous escapades. They kept their clothes in plastic containers and cardboard boxes. In lieu of paint that they didn't want to pay for, Raquel decorated with bohemian shawls and tapestries from her travels. Their home was not unlike a college dorm room, and their day-to-day lives were not unlike college in that they felt transient, based on their work and social lives outside the domicile. And yet, within it, they found themselves playing the roles of husband and wife. Rob came home from work and Raquel would have dinner on the table, huge spreads of Puerto Rican fare, stewed pork or chicken sweetened with plantains and agave nectar, ladled over a bed of yellow rice. Over the meal, they would talk about their days, often wearily, completing one another's sentences. Mostly, Raquel did the talking—the custodial job being too banal for Rob to bother getting into, the lab work too complicated. She was stressed about having skipped a year, the financial and social task that lay ahead, the fact that she would be finishing school alone since most of her friends had left and were already beginning their lives. Rob would calmly tell her to put her head down and do what she needed to do to get through it. He would tell her that he was her friend; she could rely on him.

Perhaps in all of his various and diverse social circles—the stoners, the scientists, the Burger Boyz—he was most comfortable in this role: sitting across from a female friend and passively permitting her to depend on him, to transfer her anxieties onto his shoulders the way his own mother rarely let him do. He was skilled at making a woman feel taken care of, and this knack had caused trouble before. Senior year, he'd been at the house Daniella Pierce shared with her boyfriend, Lamar. She was making dinner and had trouble opening a jar. She brought it to the living room, where Rob and Lamar were talking, and gave the jar to Rob. He opened it easily and assured her that she must have already loosened it up for him. They had a nice dinner—Daniella had become heavily involved in social work in the New Haven community, particularly in helping teenagers with police records finish high school, and Rob would listen to her catalog the alarming statistics for hours. After dinner, Rob left, which was when Lamar erupted at her with genuine outrage.

"What'd you give him the jar for?"

"Excuse me?" Daniella asked.

"The jar. You gave it to Rob to open it. I live here. I'm your man. *I* should have opened the jar."

"That's ridiculous," she replied, but even then she began thinking about how instinctively she had given Rob the husband's task. "You're crazy."

The intensity of the interaction—the visceral anger Rob was able to inspire in another man—amazed her. If Rob was aware of the effect he could have, he didn't show it. He did spend much of his time with women who were involved with others. He did encourage them to open up to him in ways they never would to their actual boyfriends. Sometimes he would do this in the presence of those boyfriends. He didn't seem to think twice about it, and he'd never made advances on a "married" woman. In exchange, these women braided his hair for him, watched kung fu movies with him, and cooked for him (Rob would never pass up a free meal). Generally, aside from a few episodes similar to the one with Lamar that could be brushed off as overreaction, he considered himself cool with the boyfriends. By all appearances, he remained ignorant of the fact that, over time, an increasing number of men, primarily black, began talking behind his back, calling him arrogant, calling him cheap, calling him a nigger.

"There are niggers, and there are brothers," Rob had told me once, lightly. He was referring to a song that was so peppered with the word that it made me fidget. Simply hearing the *n* word set off all sorts of alarm bells in a white guy; though Rob was grinning and clearly enjoying this teachable moment, I knew I had to be careful about everything from my responses to my expressions to my hand gestures. Under no circumstances could I say the word myself, nor could I act as though I understood anything Rob said regarding the word.

I replied with a ponderous *huh*.

"Niggers just like to start shit," he said. "They don't value human interaction, let alone human life. They're just stupid, period. They walk around, trying to act hard, trying to be bangers"—in Newark parlance, "bangers" was pronounced as two separate syllables: *bang-gers*. "That's all a nigger cares about: acting hard. Fronting."

"What about the brothers?" I asked. This word felt much safer.

"A brother's like me. He just wants to take care of his own and chill."

And during the summer and fall after graduation, that was pretty much what Rob Peace did. And even though he drove down to Newark every weekend, Jackie was not pleased.

The last four years had been the hardest of her life. She'd worked, she'd taken care of her ailing parents, she'd spent money as fast as she'd earned it on only the essentials. For the first time in her life, she'd been alone. The struggle that felt inseparable from the place and circumstances of her birth was primarily leavened by company—the big families, the stoop culture, the social gatherings outside liquor stores. But

Jackie wasn't like Skeet; she rarely ventured beyond the daily rhythms of home and work. The only leisure she allowed herself was the occasional trip to Atlantic City, where she played slots, sitting alone in a bank of strangers, pulling that crank again and again until the skin of her hand began to dry out and crack. If she couldn't find a room for less than $30, she would drive there and then drive home. Otherwise, during her relatively few free hours, she sat on the porch and smoked. Frances would be inside watching TV, hooked to her oxygen tank, and Horace would be shuffling around. Jackie would sink deep into the Adirondack chair facing the vacant lot across the street, maybe exchanging a few words with a passing neighbor while projecting her preference for silent solitude. She would think mainly of Rob, at Yale. Landing her son at such a place had been her life's primary goal, and yet the essence of that place had always escaped her. Yale, to her, was a corridor between stations, not a place with a pulse. She didn't care much about the dynamics of living there, and when Rob visited during college, he spoke of those dynamics hardly at all. Lacking the information necessary to ponder what he was doing in New Haven, she thought instead of what he would be doing when he left.

From what she could tell, after graduation he wasn't doing much. She figured that the lab work was good for him, but the only path it laid out would be toward more school, and if there was going to be more of that she didn't understand why he seemed reluctant to get his education over with and settle down. Victor, to her, set the example: he'd gone to school in order to learn to fly, and now he was doing just that in the Air Force Reserve. The only goal her son seemed to talk about was Rio. He appeared to have some vague plan of establishing a scientific career there. Jackie didn't know much about Rio, but she knew that the city was famous for parties, drugs, samba, poverty, robberies, and not science. Each time he left for New Haven, she would find a few hundred dollars in cash on the counter, the same spot he'd once left four or five dollars. She'd never asked for money. She didn't depend on it, though it certainly helped. She chose not to wonder where it came from. Because he never left more than he seemed able to afford from his lab work, this was easy to do. And yet something about these bills—maybe the haughty way he fingered them out from a roll of cash, like a real operator—worried her.

She was also worried about him leaving the house when he was home. She hadn't experienced this anxiety since he'd been a boy, and even then she hadn't worried much, because he'd usually been with his father, or with friends to look out for him. During Rob's college years, as Jackie watched from her perch on the porch, a sea change had overtaken the surrounding blocks in the form of gang violence. When Rob had left for college in 1998, there had been a few loose formations that could have been construed as gangs, mostly brought together by geographical proximity; young men had always been territorial about their neighborhoods and their drugs, and the resultant conflicts had caused most of the violence in Newark during the first two decades of Rob's life. But those threats had also been relatively easy to navigate: you knew where the boundaries were, you knew where the dealing centers were, and you steered clear—or else you made sure you knew the right people; you Newark-proofed. But when Rob graduated from Yale in 2002, there were more than a hundred gangs operating in Essex County, and these gangs, these terrible loyalties, were based on people rather than places. People were more dangerous, less predictable, less clearly demarcated. The Sex Money Murder Bloods, the Nine Trey Bloods, the G-Shine/ Gangster Killer Bloods, the Grape Street Crips, the 5-Deuce Hoover Crips, the Double II Set Bloods, the Rollin 60s Crips, the Fruit Town Brims, the Latin Kings, Ñeta, the Pagan's Motorcycle Club, MS-13— they were defined by colors, obscure symbols graffitied on walls (some of these quite artful), and rituals that had no clear cause or limits. The most powerful entity in East Orange was the Double II Sets, a group that had been "incorporated," so to speak, when a contingent of the Queen Street Bloods relocated to East Orange from Inglewood, California, in the mid-1990s (the "II" in the name referenced the "ll" of "Illtown," a nickname for East Orange). With them, they'd brought some of the practices and traditions of the West Coast Bloods, most notably a merciless treatment of disloyalty within their ranks.

The majority of gang-related homicides took place in public and were the result of retribution. But in Newark, far more than any other city in the nation, the gangs were intertwined with the drug trade in complicated ways. Twenty percent of gang violence in Newark was drug related, compared to 5 percent nationally. Gangs were known to cooperate with one another in order to string together and enforce distribution corridors, which ran like veins through the city. More than ever before, driving around these streets was a mortally dangerous endeavor, particularly if you were a black man in your early twenties with cornrows and tattoos, carrying cash and weed and desiring no affiliation with any group, and in fact carrying contempt, as Rob did, for those insecure enough to covet that affiliation. The standard warning to "watch your back" began to take on a meaning beyond the basic vigilance that a violent neighborhood necessitated; you literally had to watch your own back, because a stranger might be aiming a gun or a knife at it. At Yale, Rob's initiations had entailed singing Madonna songs in the dining hall for water polo and arm wrestling campus police for Elihu. In East Orange, initiations were completed by murdering someone, for no other reason than to prove to a tremendously cold, tremendously tight brotherhood that you possessed the hardness required to watch their backs.

*   *   *

THE BUSINESS OF dealing drugs was liquid, transient: connections appeared and then disappeared, usually due to prison sentences or attempts to avoid them. Rob's initial connect—the one given him by Flowy—had fallen off the grid at some point; most likely he'd fled town to avoid conflict with a rival, police, or both. The subsequent source of his marijuana supply had come through Carl, in exchange for small kickbacks. Carl was in his late forties now, living in an apartment in Bloomfield. He insisted on being present for any transaction Rob made with his supplier, as if the man he considered his nephew might try to cheat him somehow. So Rob would drive to Carl's apartment to pick him up, drive to the supplier's house in Ivy Hill, smell the marijuana to make sure it wasn't bunk, haggle over the price per pound—Rob had negotiated $1,800, which was on the very low end, and the supplier was constantly angling to raise the figure. Rob would go through the motions of standing his ground, speaking profanely but not threateningly while maintaining an exasperated but not derisive visage. He would act willing but not too willing to walk away. And, when the arduous transaction was complete, he would drive Carl back home, leaving him with $200.

Flowy, Tavarus, and Drew, all of whom were in Newark (like Tavarus, Drew had dropped out of college after two years), didn't understand why he dealt with Carl. Plenty of more stable people would eagerly help him obtain those pounds of weed. Even a minor drug on a minor level involved fronting: haggling with suppliers, canvassing for buyers and haggling with them, too, the presence one had to maintain in the neighborhood in order to keep business fluid. Rob had to be cool and laid back while also tough, imposing. These contradictions were necessary in order to keep the gap between operating costs and profit wide enough to make the risk worth it, and they didn't need to be compounded by rolling around with an unstable element such as Carl—who could be quick to take offense at real or imagined slights.

"He's family," Rob would mumble when asked.

"He's wack," Flowy replied.

"He's my business."

They figured that what Rob meant was that, of all the other men he could be associating with, none of them had lived in the house on Chapman Street while he was growing up, none of them had given him rides to the Essex County Jail to visit Skeet, none of them had driven the car that took his father home from prison that one and only time—an hour-long transit that Rob still carried with him. But still, his friends didn't get it. Rob's role as a dealer was already more complicated than the next guy's, because he was now a Yale graduate tagged with all the many stigmata that simple word carried in this neighborhood's underworld. Like a bird handled by humans whose flock would not accept it back, Rob now wore the unwashable scent of the Ivy League. To the extent that he could, Rob kept his Yale pedigree a secret from everyone he dealt with. If his supplier were to become aware of it, he would automatically assume Rob was trying to get one over on him, and even the suspicion was dangerous. So Rob played the role of desperate, struggling, paranoid, not-too-bright hustler once every couple weeks. And as he finally explained to his friends, he used Carl not out of loyalty or charity but as a beard to legitimize this image of himself, yet another Newark-proofing trick.

After these pickups, he would drive the stash back to New Haven, bury it in the black trunk beneath the python tank, and return to the high-definition screen in his lab to study the way proteins a few molecules wide interacted in a cancerous environment.

*   *   *

"WHAT'S IT LIKE, still being on campus after graduating?" I asked.

Rob shrugged. "Same old, I suppose. Quiet, at least."

We were walking together along the western edge of campus, to a bar. It was early August 2002, and I was visiting for the weekend. The campus was placid during these off months, populated mostly by faculty and graduate students, the quads and throughways and bars nicely untrafficked. I was there to visit a female friend who was about to enter the Yale Drama School as a playwright. I'd emailed Rob and we'd arranged to grab a drink. To me, the atmosphere felt surreal in comparison to New York City, where hundreds of my classmates and I were now beginning to make our way, flinging ourselves fervently into the entropy of city life. Knowing how eager he'd been at times to get out of Yale, I was curious about the irony of him being the one who'd stayed behind.

Rob had been dealing with rapid atmospheric transitions, far greater than the one I was pondering, for the last eight years. He didn't seem to worry about it in the slightest. And yet when he spoke of Rio, which was all he really spoke of that night, I heard a craving in his voice.

"When the sun goes down there," he said, "everyone along the beach stops what they're doing and claps. Every night." He shook his head and smiled, seeing it. I'd never known Rob to be much of a romantic, but there it was in his eyes: pure romance, not with a person but with a place. A poetry professor had once defined romance to me as "bringing two people together when every force in the universe is working to keep them apart." As Rob's still-vague plan to make it there for Carnival next spring coalesced, he seemed to feel like a part of that construction. At night before he went to bed, as he'd once done legal research on his father's behalf, he now practiced Portuguese for an hour.

We had a few drinks and talked like this, ground-level information, as was our way. Then I met up with the playwright and her friends, aspiring artists all, who talked of nothing but Big Ideas and how they would capture their essences in prose and achieve greatness that way— or at least staff writing positions on cable TV shows. In comparison to the time I'd just spent with Rob, the rest of the night was painful in its pretension.

After graduation, like many of our classmates, I'd gone home for two weeks to do nothing except be genially back-patted for my Yale diploma. Unlike many, I had no job lined up and no plans for graduate school. I'd made attempts with various organizations and charter schools to become an English teacher in New York City, mostly in Harlem and Brooklyn, but the veteran administrators had taken one look and known immediately that the urban kids would steamroll me. I stayed at my uncle's house in Summit, New Jersey, a base camp of sorts while I commuted into the city for job interviews, looking for something that would allow time to write books. Though I'd been to East Orange just weeks earlier for that cookout, I had no idea that the ritzy town in which I was crashing was less than a ten-minute drive from Rob's neighborhood; the New Jersey Transit line took me through Newark Penn Station each morning, but the proximity still didn't occur to me. Ultimately, I found a job writing a grant proposal for a broad "Life School" scheme conceived by a successful corporate event producer in the city. My brother made the connection for me, as family members were often able to do in the arena of Ivy League alumni.

Friends and teammates had already begun their finance jobs and were working upward of one hundred hours per week as data analysts. Others were beginning academic fellowships both here and abroad, or gearing up for law and medical schools. For those of us in New York, the city had a playground feeling of being unbound; an excitement fixed itself to negotiating dumpy sublets in the East Village, opening up social circles to include new and varied people, going to rock shows on Houston Street, and finding the best dive bars in which to talk giddily about how broke we all were and lament the $5 beers we were drinking. We strived to become "authentic" New Yorkers and, though we were embarking on different journeys, we clung to the idea of shared experience that buoyed us in that familiar off-to-college feeling even after college had passed us on.

Rob, in his way, did the same. For the first time, he owned a cell phone (throughout college, he'd used a beeper and exercised the device well), and he kept in close touch with everyone. Curtis was still at Morehouse on a five-year graduation plan. Tavarus was still working in real estate and had it in his head to try to flip houses, an idea that Rob took to himself, possessing as he did the start-up capital. Flowy was living with LaQuisha, still lifeguarding, landscaping, and helping friends fix their cars. Drew worked in construction. Victor had moved back in with his brother in southern New Jersey, and he'd gotten a job at Home Depot to make ends meet while hoping to eventually land a job with the FAA. Ty was in Cambridge, England, on his fellowship. Danny Nelson was getting an MBA at the University of Chicago. Daniella Pierce remained in New Haven, segueing her volunteer social work into a career. And Oswaldo Gutierrez had come home to Newark, where he was living with his family in a kind of emotional chaos that all but nullified the academic and mental progress he'd made at Yale. While his family expected him to begin contributing financially, his boyhood friends were trying to figure out what to make of him. Like Rob, he felt his psyche being racked by the relentless obligation to be of this world after the last four years had wholly removed him from it. In the meantime, he was twenty-two years old, unemployed, and in the grip of an internal maelstrom that he felt fundamentally unable to overcome. While looking for work, he helped his father's home repair business, haggling with low-income Newarkers about how much a radiator should cost with the same tricky dynamics that Rob navigated while negotiating the price of weed.

"Come to Rio with me," Rob told Oswaldo. Almost all of Oswaldo's Yale friends had been advising him to just get out of Newark, get away from his family, disengage and embark on his own life. To Rob alone, the fact that Oswaldo had to remain in his family's orbit was simply a given. Between them, Rob justified his own current living situation with the knowledge that, once he returned from Rio—once he permitted himself that vacation—he would be home for good.

"I can't dip out like that," Oswaldo replied.

"Just come for a minute."

"Ticket's over a grand."

"I'll spot you. It'll get your mind right. We'll just chill."

"No, Rob. No. Can't."

"All right, then. You need some money?"

"I do, yeah, but I'm not taking any from you."

"It's all good," Rob said, which was what he always said at some point. "How much you need? I'll take care of it."

"I'll figure it out," Oswaldo replied. "Always have."

"You need anything, you just let me know. Cool?"

"Yeah."

"You'll get through this. You're a scrawny little bitch, but you're hard, too."

And as Rob spent hours each day checking in on friends like Oswaldo, offering advice on how to achieve their short- and long-term goals, he began on his own short-term goal—which was to launder the $60,000 of cash that still languished in his black trunk.

One can launder money in two primary ways. The first option is to bring it aboveboard with the IRS, hence the business fronts and transactional razzle-dazzle that tentpoles the large-scale drug trade. This venture is expensive, not just because of the overhead costs inherent to the process but because ultimately—as is the entire point—the money becomes taxable. The second method is to do nothing, keep the money in cash, and "clean" the bills only by spending them slowly, such that the IRS would never figure out any discrepancy between cash earned and cash expended over the course of a year. Rob had no discernible reason not to opt for the latter. He made a livable income. Now that school expenses were over with, he barely spent any of his savings at all. In the great scheme of things, he hadn't made all that much money selling drugs to begin with, and Rob Peace wasn't exactly a prime target for an audit. And yet, for reasons unknown, Rob felt compelled to clean his money. Maybe he felt that, since he didn't have any employment lined up once the lab stint ended and he returned from Rio, he needed to launder his earnings in advance, while he still had a vehicle to do so. Maybe, because he planned to give much of it to his mother, he wanted to protect her. Maybe, rather than legitimize the money, he wanted to legitimize himself and feel like he was a true player with the capacity to rig the system any way he wanted: he wanted to feel in complete control of the innately uncontrollable business in which he dealt.

He used the lab where he worked, which had both university and grant funding in excess of $4 million per year. Much of the budget went toward the high-tech screening equipment and biological supplies used in their research. Just as much was used for standard lab equipment— beakers, chemicals, sterilization kits, the biochemical equivalents of toilet paper and lightbulbs. Rob began buying these items in his own name and submitting the receipts to the accounting office for cash reimbursement. These figures usually fell in the neighborhood of $500 per week but sometimes ranged up to $2,000, and one to three weeks after submitting the claim he would receive the cash, along with the reimbursement receipt that legitimized it. Because he did this slowly, carefully, over a period of nine months, neither the IRS nor the university accounting office ever took note. When a graduate assistant asked him why he had paid cash out of pocket, the inquiry came more out of confusion than suspicion: Why put yourself out in the time between expenditure and reimbursement when you could have signed a form charging it to the lab? Rob just shrugged and explained that there had been an account issue with the wholesaler and he'd needed to restock the equipment fast.

Raquel assumed that Rob was using his job to take care of the bills he had stockpiled, most likely filtering in small cash deposits along with his paychecks like most prudent people would. Had she known of the specifics, she would have surely questioned the selfishness, arrogance, and stupidity at work. If he were to be caught and subsequently present the police with all these receipts, the next thing they would do would be to question his colleagues and superiors. The cancer research lab might be accused of shoddy financial procedures; the professor who had invested so much in Rob's education would be embarrassed by any controversy. "What the fuck?" she would have asked, braving the anger that Rob unleashed in the face of anyone questioning his intelligence, his larger plans. But here was Rob at his most elusive, and he kept his roommate in the dark. In the meantime, Raquel had fallen in love and so wasn't prone to noticing any activity in and around Rob's black trunk.

Simon Rodriguez was a quiet, organized Yale graduate, working at Bayer for a year before he began med school in Manhattan. Raquel was a self-described "hot mess" with cornrows who had just been locked out of her apartment after working in a photo lab all day. She'd joined Rob at a friend's house, where everyone told her to clean up her photo equipment before Simon came home and flipped out at the mess. When he did enter, her throat closed up and her heart began pounding, and she pulled Rob aside. "I think I love him," she said.

"You want him, you go get him, girl," Rob replied, though to his knowledge a pairing of two more opposite personalities had never occurred in the world before.

To aid her pursuit, Rob proceeded to rally the others in the apart-

ment for a spontaneous Mohegan Sun trip, knowing that Simon would
never want to go. Five years later, Raquel and Simon would be married.

On Valentine's Day of 2003, after staying in New Haven for nine
months following graduation, Rob left for Rio. He had no place to stay,
no friends there, no plan. All he had was a portion of his savings set aside
for these weeks and a burning curiosity to see the place. He left most of
his things at Raquel's—he left a mess, actually—along with a few ounces
of marijuana hidden in jars of formaldehyde to "take care of her while he
was gone." The only major items he moved were Dio's tank (to Chapman Street, stoking his mother's terror) and the black trunk containing
his cash and drug paraphernalia, not wanting Raquel to be in danger on
the off-off-off-off chance that police entered the apartment. This he left
with Carl, heavily padlocked, with instructions to keep it hidden. Carl
shrugged and told him that this was no problem, and not the first time
he'd been asked to look after a container of something with no questions asked and only one order given. Presumably, the latter response
was the reason Rob had chosen his father's old friend and colleague as
the trunk's keeper.

"You stay safe now," Jackie said in parting to her son. They were
standing on the front porch by the two Adirondack chairs. She still had
no idea why he was going to South America, only that he could never be
talked out of it. She didn't know when he was coming back, either; the
ticket was one-way.

"Always," he replied.

"I hear they have people down there that cut your pocket open with a
razor, and your wallet just drops out, and you never feel a thing. So, you
keep your wallet in your front pocket, with your hand on it."

"C'mon, Ma, I grew up in the hood."

"Okay, then. Whatever you say."

"You're my heart, Ma."

Tavarus dropped him off at Newark International Airport. "When I
get back," Rob told him, "we'll start looking at houses. We'll do it. We'll
make it happen." Tavarus began counting the days.

*   *   *

THERE IT WAS, Copacabana. The white sand rolled out on either side, and the green water before him stretched a few thousand miles to Antarctica, which at the moment sent a cool breeze north over the city. Sugarloaf Mountain thrust up sharply in the distance to his left, and the Cristo Redentor statue loomed open-armed behind and far above him. Across the water to the west, the Vidigal favela (favelas are the Brazilian version of slums) cut into the rain forest, where the densely stacked tin roofs and narrow alleyways ascended the hills and the squalor contained therein somehow appeared gorgeous from this long angle. He stood and watched the people. Thousands of them covered the hundred yards of sand between the city and the beach, beautiful people descended from a combination of European immigrants, Amerindian indigenous people, and enslaved Africans, all that blood and culture mixed and evolved into a city of people who seemed genetically engineered to relax and enjoy the scenery. Rob had no doubt imagined this very picture on the flight here, and the picture proved strikingly accurate as he waited, duffel bag slung over his shoulder and with no place to stay, for his first Rio sunset. The orb touched down over Vidigal, and Rob found that what he'd heard was true: people did applaud.

For the first time he could remember, he had nothing to do and no one to worry about.

He found a room in the South Zone, where the good beaches and most of the parties were. For $400 a month—less than the basement apartment in New Haven, less even than Tavarus was paying for his dilapidated one-bedroom in East Orange—he had a decent-size studio with French doors that opened directly over Ipanema Beach, rippling white curtains that parted onto a semicircle of marbled balcony perched above sand the color of pearls. He would wake up, drink coffee beachside while reading the news in Portuguese, and then walk along the ocean, sometimes for hours, past the entire length of the city. Then he would have a few drinks, also beachside, and people-watch—primarily the women, whose thongs he learned were famous worldwide for a reason. Then he would walk some more, on the hard sand down by the water, warm waves lapping over his ankles. And the sun would arc across the sky, and at some point he would find a spot of dry sand and smoke a blunt, sharing with any passerby who asked, knowing that this was part of the culture here—nobody cared, they just let you be—and he would wait for sunset so that he could stand up and clap his hands with everyone else. He'd swim while it was still light enough, straight out for half a mile with his strong choppy strokes, his eyes open and pointed into the depthless green, weaving through fishing boats and yachts, until he stopped to turn around and tread water for a moment, gazing at the city from afar as the dusky light thinned and the shoreline began to glow with multicolored pinpoints of electricity before plunging his head again into the now-dark water and swimming back toward civilization. He didn't stand out for being a nerd in a pink school uniform here, as he had in East Orange. He didn't stand out for being black and wearing a skully, as he had at Yale. He didn't have to keep track of bills exiting and entering his wallet (kept in the front right pocket), as he had always. He was just a man on vacation, cutting a broad, muscular silhouette against the southern horizon as he walked along the beach. Once cleaned off, he struck out into Rio each night, on foot or by bus, to drink and smoke at whatever party looked the most pleasing in passing, and within a week he had made friends—some tourists passing through, some transplants from America or Europe, most of them lifelong residents from all the various neighborhoods, each of which he would explore over the coming weeks.

Rio was almost evenly split between Cariocas (the light-skinned descendants of European settlers) and Pardos (the brown-skinned descendants of native Brazilians and African slaves). Like Newark, the city had experienced a massive influx of rural minorities looking for industrial work during the 1950s. Like Newark, a large number of these minorities had been segregated into the favelas. Like Newark, the city had attempted to incorporate these slums into public housing projects, which—like Newark—had only exacerbated racial tensions and violence. Like Newark, the decline of the manufacturing sector had cast these outlying neighborhoods into permanent poverty that became a breeding ground for drug traffic. Unlike Newark, the various socioeconomic groups within the city intermingled fluidly in public spaces, and a person like Rob could travel almost anywhere he wanted without fear of confrontation, without having to watch his back.

A friend from Yale, now on spring break from the Teach for America program, happened to be traveling through South America with his girlfriend and came to crash with Rob. The girl watched the two men ride horses along Leblon Beach, their silhouettes passing to and fro across the sunset. She'd known Rob at Yale, had been curious about him but never intimate. The fact that almost a year after graduation found this man—whom she'd always thought to be an irritable, cynical boy from the hood—riding a horse along a South American beach, literally shouting, "Yahoooo!" again and again, was mind-boggling to her. The next day, Rob took them in the cable car to the peak of Sugarloaf Mountain, where they had a view of the unique sprawl of the city, like fingers poking into the impenetrable jungle. They followed the excursion with samba dancing at a club.

A week later, Curtis flew down from Atlanta. He hadn't needed much cajoling to do so; the serenity in Rob's voice that rose above the static of the international call had been sufficient. On his first day, they hiked up Corcovado, at the top of which the soapstone Cristo Redentor statue, that worldwide symbol of peace, stood a hundred feet tall. The steps were covered with brightly colored mosaic tiles, a hypnotic collage of religious and cultural imagery. The tourists constantly stopping to bend down and look more closely created a logjam. Curtis was out of shape and trying to push his way to the top, wondering why they hadn't just taken the elevator.

"Yo, Paolo!" Rob suddenly stepped out of the crowd, over the precarious railing and onto the slope, where a man who might have been a hundred years old was on his hands and knees, regrouting a cluster of chipped tiles. They embraced and began speaking in rapid Portuguese. Curtis gradually gleaned that Paolo was not simply a custodial employee of the city tourism department. He'd actually built the stairs himself, with his father, sixty years earlier. Now he lived with his wife in a one-room cabin near the base of the steps, and every day he worked to maintain the stairway. Later, Rob and Curtis ate dinner in that cabin, spicy stewed pork served over rice. Rob and Paolo kept a running conversation in Portuguese that Curtis couldn't understand as Rob finished bowl after bowl of stew.

"What were you talking about the whole night?" Curtis asked when they left.

"Nothing much," Rob replied. "Just asking questions about his life."

"He fixes stairs. How many questions can there be?"

Rob laughed. "Over a million people a year walk up those stairs. And he built that shit. The man has seen a lot of things, met a lot of people." There were notes in Rob's voice that approached envy of the simplicity of it all. "Also, I needed to get that recipe."

He made the recipe a few nights later, for two women they had met, Kaliana and Iris. They were curvy—too much so, in Curtis's estimation, but Rob thought they were just about the most beautiful women he'd ever met. He told Curtis to pick one; which girl didn't matter to him. Rob ended up sitting next to Kaliana. As he set dinner down on the table on his balcony, Kaliana noted, wide-eyed, that a man had never served her before. In Brazil, even in the modern city, the woman served the man. By the time the entrée was set down, Curtis realized that these girls would probably marry them tonight if asked. And he didn't put it past Rob to ask, so entranced was his friend—not necessarily by Kaliana herself but by the lifestyle she represented. Both girls spoke some English, but Rob preferred to talk in their language, slowing his cadence, enjoying it when she laughed at him for flubbing a tense. Curtis, left on his own, conversed awkwardly with Iris. He hadn't seen Rob much over the last four and a half years, just Thanksgivings and a few weeks during the summers, reunions that had thinned as the years had gone on. Observing him now, having somehow forged an existence in this city in the Southern Hemisphere where winter was summer, Curtis suddenly understood what the word "peace" meant to Rob Peace. The four of them went out that night. Rob drifted away with Kaliana, saying he'd check back in tomorrow. Curtis didn't see him for two days.

When he did come back to the studio in Ipanema, he hadn't gotten married, but he did want Curtis to come up into the Rocinha favela with him.

"Nah," Curtis said. "As if we don't get enough ghetto back home—you want to drag me into the hood on my vacation? Don't think so."

"It's cool people," Rob said. "It's real. And Rocinha isn't even a bad one. There are tourism buses that go up there."

"Sightseeing in the favela?" Curtis asked.

"Yeah. It's called 'slum tourism.' Fucked up, ain't it?"

"How do you know people over there anyway?"

Rob shrugged. "I'm good at meeting people."

Curtis still didn't go. He had one day left and wanted to spend it on the beach. Rob came home that night with Kaliana and more marijuana than even Rob could smoke during the month further he was planning to stay—even during Carnival, which Rob was keen to spend completely stoned around the clock for a week. The quantity made Curtis wonder if Rob was dealing here, if he was selling drugs in a place and culture he didn't fully know, governed by a legal system with far fewer safety nets than even Newark had.

But he didn't ask, not wanting to spend his last day here in the precarious position of trying to tell Rob to be careful. Curtis had one of the best nights of his life.

Carnival was ten million people, dressed in very little, dancing in the streets as *micareta* bands played from moving truck tops. It was a never-ending buffet of spicy food, fruity drinks, and masked faces perched on dancing bodies. It was hair, glitter, flesh, and all of it in constant motion. It was a choreographed parade of costumes, a chiaroscuro of color worthy of Kandinsky. The sheer scope of the party, and the avidness with which the people—musicians, dancers, cooks, tourists, rich, poor, young, old, Carioca, Pardo—descended onto the streets was beyond anything Rob had ever hoped to experience. As a child, books had been his passageway into foreign, sometimes utopian worlds. Carnival wasn't just an incarnation of that passageway in reality; it was everything that lay on the other side, where the only thing that mattered was the moment, and millions of people were able to inhabit that moment with ease and, predominantly, with bliss. People back in the States talked about Woodstock this way, or Burning Man, or the Kentucky Derby, or Halloween in Greenwich Village. But none of them had ever been to Carnival. Rob had now, and he didn't want to go home.

*   *   *

THE PLANE BANKED through the overcast April sky, dropped through a layer of low-hanging clouds, and Newark materialized below. From the height of a few thousand feet, the city didn't appear to lie very far from the Empire State Building and the Statue of Liberty, the narrow column of Manhattan. The canvas appeared as one continuum of hyperdeveloped land, gray and veined with freeways. From this height, everything seemed to move slowly.

His plane landed at dusk, and he trudged through Newark International with the other travelers—thousands of people setting out on or returning from trips that looked nothing like the one Rob had just completed. Flowy picked him up at the airport. By the time they cleared the terminals, night had fallen. Rob told Flowy where to take him.

"You don't want to stop at your ma's first?"

Rob shook his head. As they entered the Oranges, he must have wondered what had happened to all the color, the human fluidity, the panoramic views that were still vivid in his mind. Ten minutes later, they parked at Carl's building. A few men loitered outside the front entrance, beneath a flickering, buzzy light.

Rob asked Flowy to wait for him, just a couple minutes, and he walked past the men, inside to Carl's apartment. His uncle, by heart if not by blood, opened the door. He was edgy as he asked about Rio and why Rob had come home earlier than he'd planned. Rob didn't answer, didn't say that this edginess *was* the reason. Rob had sensed it in Carl's voice a few days earlier when he'd called to check in, and he'd known what it meant. He'd bought his return ticket immediately. His money was more important than a few more weeks in Rio.

"You want a drink? A smoke?" Carl asked.

"Just want my trunk," Rob said.

Carl led him to the closet, where the black trunk was wedged in the very back and covered with clothes. Carl stood on the far side of the bedroom as Rob pulled the trunk out. He saw immediately that the lock had been pried off and sloppily reattached. During the few seconds needed to pull the trunk out of the closet, he experienced helplessness, rage, regret, and most of all the despair of his own idiocy. Opening the trunk must have seemed like a formality, because he already knew that his money was no longer inside. He did open it, and his eyes confirmed that not only his savings but the time he'd put into earning it had vanished: four years' worth of Metro-North train rides, bulk drug transactions in shady inner-city homes, putting aside schoolwork so that a dozen kids a night could cycle through his room, the close calls and strained friendships. Vanished, too, was the year ahead that the money had been set aside to buy him, a year he'd intended to devote to Jackie.

And Rob was the one who had decided to keep it in cash rather than a checking account. Rob was the one who'd needed to leave the country for so long. Rob was the one who'd left the trunk with a man capable of opening it. Rob was the one at fault here.

Carl was behind him, mumbling something about debts and things being hard and his intent to pay the money back. Rob didn't listen. His clenched fists loosened, though he refused to turn and face the man. He leaned over and lifted the trunk. Because the lock was broken and the lid loose, he had to carry it upright in front of his chest, using both arms. The empty pipes and bongs that remained inside—some of them ornate and carrying sentimental value for him—clattered around hollowly. At this point, he didn't care that there were men outside who were not above jumping somebody carrying a trunk like this. They could take it from him if they wanted. He must have still been hearing Carl's voice, talking about the past, his needs, what he felt he was owed for his role in Rob's life. Rob's mind was most likely already inhabiting the future, precarious now, holding none of the freedom he'd promised himself.

Chapter 10

———————◆———————

H AVE YOU SEEN that movie with Tom Cruise, *The Firm*?" Coach
Ridley asked, and Rob nodded. "It's kind of like that."

"What do you mean?"

"Once you get in, it's hard to get out."

Beneath the light film reference, Coach Ridley's tone was serious.
Being a high school teacher anywhere involved a certain amount of
wear and tear, not to mention a low salary. But being a teacher at St.
Benedict's was a way of life, and a draining one. Ridley could tell that
Rob was approaching the prospect of joining the St. Benedict's faculty
as a stopgap more than a career, a means to float himself for a time.
From a practical standpoint, Ridley felt that Rob, with his BSc from
Yale, could find an employment bridge that paid better and demanded
less, and that offered him more flexibility in figuring out his next step.
As they spoke, Rob kept nodding and looking around his former coach's
cluttered office—textbooks, water polo trophies, loose-leaf papers of in-
determinate purpose, the stuff that made up a teacher's life—and the
teacher sensed the gears within his skull not turning so much as grind-
ing noisily together.

The summer of 2003 had been the most uncertain of Rob's life, with
no job, no schoolwork, and suddenly no money. Of all his evolving
dreams and goals, the one constant had always centered on his mother,

taking care of her, giving back what she'd given him. Now he was living in her house again, eating her food, seeing her out the door in the morning and waiting for her to come home at night. He must have felt like one of his uncles or cousins, who'd struck out on their own, failed in some way, and been forced to return home to Chapman Street. Most grad school applications had been due in the spring; he'd missed them while in Rio.

He felt perhaps the most unkeeled when he visited his father in Trenton. In Brazil, he'd made mental notes of everything he was going to tell his father: the women, the favelas, Paolo's cabin, Carnival, the thong bikinis, and any other experience that might nourish the prisoner in some way. Unlike Yale, whose world was completely inaccessible to a man convicted of murder, Rio was a place that Skeet might be able to close his eyes in his prison cell and want to be, and Rob had aimed to give to his father this gift, to let them walk together along those beaches. But now he couldn't, not after what the trip had cost him. And so the tenor of their visits remained as they had been before he'd left. The Rio trip proved to be a reaffirmation of the nature of Rob's family and neighborhood rather than the transformation of his interior that he'd intended it to be. But still he wanted to go back. He just needed to work first.

Work: he dwelled on the word and its meaning as he made his rounds that summer—rounds that took him by Flowy's, Tavarus's, Drew's, and Curtis's. All of them were working: respectively, landscaping, real estate, construction, and marketing. All of them had stable living situations, girlfriends, paychecks. Rob, who had worked harder than any of them over the last eight years, had none of these stabilities. For the first time, his friends were the ones giving him advice, hooking him up with suppliers so he could hustle a little bit, letting him crash on their couches, brainstorming job possibilities. They were carrying him, in a sense, as they collectively struggled to figure out how Rob might get by the way they were all getting by. "Getting by" wasn't something they'd ever thought Rob Peace might need their help doing.

His rounds also took him frequently to St. Benedict's. The school was quiet during the summer, but teachers were there running tutorials to keep the students busy and safe while the faculty prepared for the year to come. Teachers like Friar Leahy and Coach Ridley would ask him about Yale, his lab work, Rio, and Rob could feel like an achiever again. His old high school remained one of the few places where that feeling was authentic.

Dexter Lopina had been Rob's classmate there, and one of the three students perennially jockeying for the 4.0 GPA. After graduation, Dexter had gone to Essex County Technical Institute for a degree in computer science, their college years having coincided with the expansion of the Internet into all facets of American life. He could have gone to an Ivy League school like Rob had, but Dexter had been practical in mapping his life: he loved computers, and he'd set himself up for a career working with them—such as his current job as the head of IT at St. Benedict's. Dexter remembered high school, when he would arrive at St. Benedict's around seven thirty most mornings and find Rob asleep in one of the classrooms, power-napping between lifeguarding and morning convocation. He remembered those minutes of sleep seeming to symbolize some burden that Rob carried quietly and alone, and he sensed that burden having grown in the years since. They went out to lunch at the Burger King on the corner, where Rob grumbled about needing a job. Dexter tried and failed to find vestiges of his old classmate. Across the table in the fast-food restaurant he just saw a young man struggling. Casually, he said, "Hell, why don't you just teach at St. B's? It'd be fun."

The idea wasn't as spontaneous as Dexter presented it. In fact, Friar Leahy had been thinking about this for some time—he may have even planted the notion in Dexter's head. He'd been tracking Rob closely during his various visits to the school since college graduation. Like Dexter, he'd been attuned to the weight that seemed to be bearing down on the young man. But unlike Dexter, he wasn't surprised that the former group leader and Presidential Award winner had run up against such a wall in his life. The situation reminded him of one of his first students, Class of '74, the year the school reopened. The very bright

African American student had gone to Harvard and won a Rhodes Scholarship. Then he'd returned to Newark during one of the most accelerated spans of the city's deterioration. Overeducated and under-skilled for most jobs available, he hadn't been able to find work. The man had cracked up under the pressure of living in two worlds—being surrounded by friends from a hardscrabble youth and yet set apart by his elite education. Eventually, he'd killed himself.

Friar Leahy believed Rob to be far too confident and mentally sound to be driven toward suicide, but he also knew he might benefit from returning to the place where his potential had once blossomed. In August, he offered Rob a job teaching biology to freshmen and sophomores.

"It could be good for a minute," Rob said, almost resignedly. He and Curtis were sitting on the hood of Curtis's car, smoking a joint amid the cherry blossom groves of Branch Brook Park. He approached the decision scientifically, reducing it to pros and cons. Pros: it was (barely) a living wage, a place and people he knew well, he would be very good at it, the job would look decent on a résumé, he'd have plenty of time off to travel and figure out his life. Cons: it was (barely) a living wage, the kids would annoy the hell out of him, the work would probably be more taxing than he thought, teaching at this level wasn't what he wanted to do.

"How much they pay?" Curtis asked.

"Twenty-seven five."

Curtis nodded. He was making $40,000 a year in an entry-level position at a marketing firm, and he saw something fundamentally wrong with a world in which Rob Peace was earning 30 percent less. "You'll have fun," he said finally, "but just don't, like . . ."

"Don't what?" Rob asked.

"Don't get stuck there."

*   *   *

A DOZEN OR SO people hung out in a small living room, open bottles of cheap liquor and dollar store juices on the coffee table, music playing,

TV on, marijuana haze thick. Rob was talking to a girl on the couch, probably telling her what Rio was like. He didn't know many others at the party; he'd just tagged along with Tavarus and Flowy near the end of the summer.

"You the dude went to Yale?"

Rob looked behind him. He'd never seen the guy before. "Yeah," was all he said.

"So what're you doing in my house?"

"What's it look like? Chilling." Rob grinned. And the guy didn't like the way the grin looked.

"Go 'slumming' somewhere else," he said.

"I'm not leaving," Rob replied. And then, "What?"

The room did what all rooms, whether at Yale or in East Orange, did when two men prepared to fight: it stopped, and people backed up to clear space, their faces exhibiting more excitement than concern. And Rob must have been gauging those faces, looking for familiar ones and finding none (Flowy and Tavarus were in the backyard), trying to figure which ones would back his opponent and finding many.

"C'mon," Rob said. "If you want to start shit for no reason, then start."

Then they were out on the front porch, arms locked together in close quarters, exchanging short jabs in order to prevent uppercuts and haymakers, calling each other "bitch," "motherfucker," "nigger." The fight was real, one that drew blood—which, as Flowy and Tavarus rushed forward from the crowd, they considered the stupidest thing their friend could possibly have allowed to happen. You never knew who was carrying a gun or a blade. And even if they weren't carrying now, they probably would be tomorrow. Finding out where someone lived was easy enough to do.

They broke up the fight as cleanly as they could. Flowy knew the guy and talked him down while Tavarus hustled Rob onto the street, toward their car.

"You can't do that," Tavarus said.

Rob was breathing heavily, the muscles of his face tight and hot, rushing with blood. "What the hell am I supposed to do?"

"Chill. Walk away."

"Why?"

"Because what if us two aren't there?"

Rob still liked to walk around the neighborhood, he liked hanging on stoops beneath the oppressive summer heat, and he liked house parties at his friends'. But he had to be careful now about what he said. For four years at Yale, he'd sat at the center of his circle with free rein to utter whatever was on his mind. He was well known for calling people out on their "bullshit." But he'd been able to exercise that tendency with the concrete awareness that his words had no consequences, not real ones. Maybe someone's feelings would get hurt; maybe there'd be an argument. Even so, nobody at Yale would ever come at him, no one carried lethal weapons, no one constructed the particular walls around his pride that, if penetrated, might impel him to want to inflict severe physical harm. The situation was different in Newark—more so now than ever, since the gang explosion had begun. Offend the wrong person with a word or an expression, and Rob risked having a loyal militia patrolling the streets of East Orange, armed, with no compunction about putting a bullet in someone.

Whenever that word, "Yale," was uttered, even in the lightest way possible, Rob did what he could to undermine its connotation. An exchange might begin with someone saying, "I still don't believe a punkass like you went to no *Yale*; you're just *lying!*" and Rob would shake his head with a doleful semismile and say, "Yeah. I did that shit." Then later, he would politely ask whoever had invoked the university never to do so again. He didn't need or want that Yale label on his leather jacket.

Across the Hudson River in Manhattan, his former classmates were wearing the same label like a badge. We went out in groups, herding through the East Village and SoHo the way we once had through the quads of New Haven. We went to mixers at the Yale Club on Thursday nights, hobnobbing with other alumni over bowls of gourmet potato chips and heated silver trays of pigs in blankets. We had parties on walk-up rooftops and gazed at the uptown skyline, feeling like those towers had been built not for commerce alone but also for us and our dreams.

The summer before Rob began teaching at St. Benedict's, I returned from two months living in Tanzania, where I worked writing grant proposals for an environmental nonprofit. In small villages dotting an arc of mountain cloud forests that rose dramatically from the Maasai Steppe, I'd helped people build wells with money my writing had secured. I'd hiked through a forest in northern Mozambique where cannibals were known to live. One afternoon I'd almost been trampled by an elephant, and the following evening, while urinating in an outhouse, a black mamba had slithered lazily between my feet. I'd snorkeled alone in great white–infested waters a mile from Zanzibar's shore. I'd lived in a small house, built by hand, on the edge of a mountaintop, and each morning a carpet of clouds condensed hundreds of feet below the front door and ascended the cliff face, passing over me in a thick mist, then giving way to a mesmerizing view of the savannah. When I returned to New York, I couldn't wait to tell Rob, tell him that I'd done something he would genuinely admire. I'd tried emailing his Hotmail account from the rare functional Internet kiosk in Dar es Salaam, but my message had been returned by MAILER DAEMON, saying that the address no longer existed.

The cell phone number I had didn't work, either. I contacted as many mutual friends as I could think of, but no one knew how to get in touch with Rob Peace. How strange it was that, in the minds of these friends (admittedly not his closest at Yale), Rob had already become a kind of fond but removed afterthought: "Oh, yeah, Rob Peace, no, I haven't heard from him since college, I wonder how that dude's doing . . ." Finally I thought to ask my mother if that contact sheet, the one we'd received before freshman year, still existed. She found it at the bottom of a drawer in my old desk at home, and I called the house on Chapman Street. No one answered the first few times I tried, and there didn't seem to be an answering machine. I began letting go of the effort, distracted by the nonprofit work, the novel I was working on, the girls I was pining for. Not until late in the fall did our roommate Ty, now in his first year at Harvard Med School after completing his fellowship in Cambridge, email me a cell number.

"Hey, Rob," I said. And when it took him a moment to place my voice, "It's Jeff."

He mumbled, "Hey, whassup, Da Jeffrey?"

"Just wanted to see how it's going."

"It's going."

"What are you . . . up to?"

"Just started teaching."

"Like, in grad school, or . . . ?"

"Nah. High school. St. Benedict's."

"How is that?"

"It's cool. I want to kill these little shits sometimes, but it's cool."

He was in the middle of his workday and jumped off quickly, before I even thought to mention Africa. I hung up and sat in my two-hundred-square-foot studio in Little Italy (my salary from the nonprofit was a free rent-controlled apartment in the chic neighborhood), and I fell into a brief but unsettling state of melancholy. The truth was he hadn't seemed all that interested in hearing from me, which implied that, just as Rob had seemed to be fading from friends' minds, so were we from his.

*   *   *

ON A NIGHT IN August 2003, not long before we'd spoken, one of Rob's bulk suppliers had pulled a gun on him, after Rob had threatened to walk away in the midst of a failed negotiation. The threat was fairly standard; the gun was not. Rob didn't know if the weapon was loaded, and he later claimed to be certain that its bearer had no intention of actually pulling the trigger. But triggers did get pulled—they were pulled all the time here. They'd been pulled on former classmates from Oakdale, Mt. Carmel, and St. Benedict's. They'd been pulled on friends of both his mother and father. One had been pulled on Charlene and Estella

Moore. The feeling of having the barrel of a revolver trained on you at close range was a purely visceral one, he confided in Oswaldo Gutierrez just before the first day of school. All the knowledge in his brain of chemokines and crystallography, all the triumphs and disappointments of his life had been rendered worthless, and his consciousness had narrowed to a very fine point of focus, no wider than the muzzle of a .22 caliber revolver. He paid the extra couple hundred dollars that the supplier demanded of him. Then he began his high school teaching career, and he got out of the game.

The incident with the revolver, along with the loss of his savings, had provided bookends to the summer of 2003. During the months between, the business of hustling had cost him more in anxiety than it had returned in cash. Dealing had been too cushy at Yale; he'd been spoiled there by classmates who came to him and would pay what he asked. In Newark, driving around dangerous streets in the middle of the night to haggle over $5 and $10 with desperate men and women (the women, he felt, were the hardest and saddest to deal with), the work seemed to epitomize the "wear and tear" Wayne Ridley had mentioned in the context of teaching high school. At its foundation was the exposure to the people who lived and died by this commerce—not just the dealers and suppliers, but the users as well.

Rob was self-aware enough to understand his own relationship with marijuana, which wasn't complicated to him. He knew the science behind it. He knew what it cost him. Though he was addicted to it by all definitions regarding frequency of use, he was intelligent enough to control that addiction. "High functioning," he called himself. But seeing regularly the people who had an even greater reliance on the drug, yet without the ability to understand what that reliance meant, spawned pity in him. Outwardly, this pity manifested itself as scorn. "Motherfuckers be *lazy*," he would say to Flowy, Tavarus, and Curtis. But within his consciousness, his friends believed him to feel extraordinarily sensitive toward this widespread plight in the city in which he'd grown up, and perhaps even guilty in knowing that, had he not been born with his particular brain and his particular mother, he wouldn't be any different from these people. And maybe that was why he stopped providing them with weed.

Those who knew him well couldn't believe it when he gave up dealing, a decision that went far beyond risk or morality, far beyond the moment of finding himself on the wrong end of a gun. These friends were happy for him and this strong movement he'd made toward reactivating the lifestyle that had gotten him into Yale the hard way.

Perhaps as a part of that movement, once the school year was under way, Rob ultimately forgave Carl. For months, he'd been avoiding the man, telling Jackie to keep him away from the house (though never telling her why), staying away himself when Carl was there. And then, suddenly, his rage seemed to disappear. He entered the parlor one evening to find Carl sitting on the sofa, and he nodded and said, "What's up?"

Carl replied, "Same old."

Then the two men sat down to dinner with Jackie, Horace, and Frances.

Later, Rob told Curtis, "The man's like a dog. You can't blame a dog for eating up a steak if you leave the steak on the floor."

*   *   *

THE GROUP WAS called Unknown Sons, named that by the students who participated. Nine kids had shown up today. Rob didn't run the meetings—that was done by one of the professional counselors on staff at St. Benedict's. But he often attended, usually just to observe. Every member of the group came from a fractured family, and though each brought experiences specific to him, sharing those experiences helped ease the feeling of aloneness that invariably attached itself to losing a parent.

A student was talking about his mother's drinking and how his attempts to get her to stop—pleading with her, shaming her, hiding bottles—only made her angry, which caused her to drink more.

"You're trying to fix her," Rob spoke out and felt the weight of nine troubled souls watching and listening.

"Well, yeah," the boy replied. "Get her to cut that stuff, anyway."

"You can't fix the person causing the problem. You can't worry about other people. Only one you can worry about is you." The boy nodded. "And sit up straight, while you're at it."

"Yes, Mr. Peace." The boy sat up at his desk.

Morning convocation, classes, lunch, classes, practice: for eleven hours a day, Rob's life played to the very same rhythm that had existed before he'd gone off to college. And this rhythm was a pleasing one.

He was a good teacher—not great, necessarily, but very good, and with an innate ability to connect with his students on the level at which their minds operated. Rob had always approached his schoolwork with a cumulative mentality: stacking one new understanding upon the other until the full picture was imprinted in his memory. Memorization had never been the goal for him, as it had been for many other premeds; understanding had always been the goal. As such, teaching introductory biology to underclassmen required almost no effort. He used neither textbooks nor notecards in his lectures. He made a clear distinction between students who truly weren't able to grasp the basics of photosynthesis or genetics, and those who were capable but unengaged. On those in the latter group, he came down hard.

"You're lazy, aren't you?" he would ask.

"Nah, just bored," would be the response.

"You're bored in my class?"—with one of his *psha* sounds—"Here's a hall pass. Go somewhere else more stimulating. Good luck on the test next week."

Wide-eyed, disbelieving: "Thanks, Mr. Peace."

And when the student received a poor grade, Rob would have him stay after class and say, "Now let's get to work."

"Yes, Mr. Peace."

He commanded respect by being the man he was: the tough and hard-talking owner of the Presidential Award and the Yale diploma. At the same time, as he did outside school, he kept his rare pedigree under wraps to the extent that he was able. He easily could have approached his role as teacher along the lines of, *Look at what I've accomplished, here's how I did it, now emulate.* He chose instead to get down in the muck with his students, drill them with good study habits, embarrass them when they copped attitude, and utilize their pride as the primary motivator of their lives, as it had been his. He didn't spout lectures about actions and consequences, avoiding the kind of life they didn't want to have. He focused on the life they *did* want to have. His attitude toward his students' work habits was the same, in a way, as it had been toward me and my writing aspirations: "If you want to, and you don't, then that's on you."

Jarring to him was how sensitive, or soft, the students collectively seemed to be, as well as how aggressively they talked back to authority figures. Rob recalled being slapped by seniors when his shirt was untucked, profanely berated by teachers and coaches on the rare instances when he failed to put forth a full effort. He recalled those thousands of laps the swimming and water polo teams endured without question. He recalled an unspoken, almost solemn understanding among his class that what they were doing in this building was vital and these punishments were a necessary part of the journey. He recalled a pervading silence—in the classrooms, in the library, in the hallways aside from the freshmen singing school songs—that spoke to the fact that what was happening here went beyond the anxiety of college acceptance letters and approached the realm of life and death.

He did not recall parents coming to the school and angrily demanding a sit-down with Friar Leahy following a relatively minor disciplinary action, which happened to Rob just a month into the job. A sophomore had disrespected him in class. The incident was nothing major: the kid had been talking in the back during Rob's lecture, and Rob had called him out on it, and he'd mouthed off, and Rob had done the same thing he did whenever anyone talked back to him, Yalie or family or hustler. He'd confronted the situation directly.

"You think you're the Man now, don't you?"

"No. Just don't need you all up in my face."

"You think I'm in your face?"

"Yeah."

"No," Rob said. "If I was in your face, you'd be running. I'm just asking you, what benefit do you get out of interrupting my class?"

"I don't know. I had something to say and I said it."

"Tell me, what was it?" The boy looked away from him, blood beginning to color his expression. "Tell me and I'll get out of your face."

"It was nothing."

"Nothing, huh? Sounds pretty damn important. Now tell me something else. Tell me what you've done for someone today."

"What?"

"Name something you've done for someone else today."

"I don't know."

"Exactly. You haven't done anything for anybody. So shut the fuck up."

The next morning, in Friar Leahy's office, the boy's mother made a loud fuss about the humiliation of her son and how this was not what she paid tuition for, etc. She wanted an apology. Rob gave her what she wanted, but the fact that he'd done so ate at him for weeks afterward. He hadn't been in the wrong, he was sure of that, and he couldn't remember a single prior instance in his life when he'd given a false apology— except maybe to the master and the dean when they'd confronted him about dealing at Yale.

Once water polo season began, the pool was no different: kids begged out of workouts, half-assed their laps, pushed their feet off the bottom midway, pointing defiant eyes at Rob as he told them to get their fucking heads in the water.

Coach Ridley laughed when Rob vented about it, and he reminded his former player about a certain freshman who could barely swim, who had ditched practice for a week: "Something about a sprained back and sneezing while pulling a milk carton from the fridge?"

Rob said, "That actually happened. A hundred percent legit."

"Just remember," Coach Ridley told him, "these kids aren't that much younger than you, and you and your boys were a bunch of punks, too. It's part of the job. Don't let it get to you or you'll go nuts."

The uniforms had changed. Kids couldn't wear red, blue, or yellow due to the recent flourishing of gang culture in the city. They wore white and gray instead. The kids, in Rob's mind, might have gone soft, but the neighborhood around them had become harder in the years since he'd left. In the weight room, on bus rides, in tutoring sessions, he talked to them about Newark-proofing themselves, living in the hood and respecting the hood without becoming a part of the hood. When he'd been a student, the school had addressed these pressures through discipline and activity but without pointing directly to the anxiety of poverty and violence. But parents were less willing to hand their children over to the school and its philosophies now, and so the teachers were not permitted the same level of influence over the students' time. Rob sought to influence their minds instead. Again and again he told them, "Don't mess with drugs. Don't mess with people who mess with drugs. Don't get involved. It's not a game you want to be playing." While hypocritically failing to acknowledge his own history, a certain world wisdom evidenced itself in the words that rendered this lesson—which would have been rote coming from most other teachers—worth listening to when it came from Mr. Peace.

*   *   *

THE PROPERTY ON Greenwood Avenue, less than a mile from Chapman Street, looked the same as those around it, if moderately worse for wear. The cracked paint was olive green with pale blue details. The three floors were sectored into separate apartments, with a front porch and backyard. A few of the windows were boarded up, and water stains veined the ceilings of the first and second floors. The neighborhood was not good by any stretch, but he could walk in and out of his door without worrying too much about who might be watching.

Ten thousand dollars down on a $90,000 house, with a fifteen-year fixed 5 percent interest rate, came out to roughly $700 per month in mortgage payments, plus insurance, plus taxes. He did the math, weighed the costs against his desire to own property, and bought a house.

Jackie did not understand this decision. Her son was twenty-four and unmarried, making as much as she'd ever made and in a more respectable profession but still not very much at all. If you had money, you spent it on your family. And the family needed it. Frances was too sick with emphysema to rise more than once a day from her bed in the first-floor living room (Rob gave $300 per month toward her medical costs, about 15 percent of his salary). And Horace sat hunched over in an easy chair beside his wife as each day passed and turned into the following, resigned to his worn body and dulled mind. Meanwhile, Jackie—now fifty-five years old—looked at him and saw what would happen to her, and not even too long from now.

She cherished so very much having Rob home—a strong male figure who could take care of the minutiae that, while he'd been away, had accelerated this aging process in her. And Rob doted over his grandparents, running out to fetch whatever they needed or wanted: tea, eggs, whiskey. They were people who had fought, and fought strongly, to raise a family and keep the house secure. He respected what they'd done above all things. The house on Chapman Street had taken on an elevated meaning when he'd come home from Rio. The house simply was; it had been here, lived in by the Peace family, for twenty years before he was born, and it had been here for twenty-four years since, and it would be here twenty years from now. No matter what he learned or where he went, these walls would always stand erect on this plot of land as a port of call for all those bearing his surname as well as some, such as Carl, who did not. The house was run-down and sparsely furnished, as it always had been, but it was also the most permanent and dependable entity he had ever known.

So why, Jackie wondered, was he so compelled to leave it?

"I just don't understand," she told him, shaking her head, smoking her menthol. "It's just money you don't need to spend."

"It's not spending money," Rob replied. "It's an investment."

"You can't think of any better investment than a busted-up house?"

"I'll rent out the upper and lower units. That'll cover the mortgage and taxes."

"Good luck collecting rent on time from anyone who wants to live on Greenwood."

"Oswaldo's going to help me make it nice. Then, down the road, I'll sell it. Make a profit."

"Don't you know how *expensive* it is to fix up a house? Those contractors are cheats, all of them."

"Ma, please." He'd explained this before a few times, and listened to her reservations just as many. She'd been quiet about his Rio vacation, though she hadn't understood it. Now that he was teaching, she didn't mind so much that he seemed to have no plans to go back to school anytime soon. Her son had always possessed a natural capacity to influence people, and a place like St. Benedict's seemed to her an ideal place for him to use that gift. But as for the house on Greenwood, she had trouble standing idly by and watching her son make a mistake.

She'd known something like this would happen. Subconsciously, she'd known from the moment she'd taken him to Yale the first time: that her son would come home from this place and she would have no power to mother him anymore, because he would presume to know everything, just as the toddler incarnation of him, "the Professor," had. Jackie wasn't as smart as her son. What she did have that he lacked were years—she had experience. While he certainly had more than most other American men his age, he didn't have as much as Jackie, not by a wide margin. All she wanted to do—all any parent wanted to do—was use this commodity to help her child in life. Experience had taught her that buying a fixer-upper in a lousy neighborhood for very little money down and a high interest rate was a terrible idea.

But Rob was like his father when he had his mind made up, and she didn't have the stamina to keep battling him.

Tavarus, with his real estate know-how, had first brought the idea of home ownership to Rob. He'd done the title research. He'd explained the math associated with flipping properties—a process he'd become enamored of when he'd seen a young, hippie-looking white man gutting the house next door to his apartment, who had explained how he would profit $30K in six months' time. He'd helped Rob compile the necessary information to secure the particular loan with so little money down and minimal financial review (a loan that, five years later, would be known nationwide as "subprime"). They thought that if this one worked out and turned a profit, they could repeat the process with two properties, and four after that, and on and on.

Oswaldo Gutierrez, who a year and a half after Yale graduation was still working for his father's home repair business, took a look at the place a few days after Rob officially moved in. He took in the disintegrating plaster in the bathrooms, the shorted-out electric system, the boiler that must have been half a century old, the lopsided foundation and leaky pipes, and then he looked at his friend's face—with its boyish, almost beaming pride—and he could not integrate the two in his mind. Simply bringing this house up to code would cost in the low to mid five figures. Making the place into what Rob seemed to envision would cost in the mid to high five figures. And the owner was a first-year high school teacher with no savings.

"I'm proud of you," Oswaldo said, thinking a hundred other things. "I've never known a twenty-four-year-old homeowner."

"Feels good," Rob replied.

"If you want to start renting soon, you should start with the boiler."

Together, they went to work. Oswaldo didn't have the heart to say aloud how hopeless the endeavor actually looked to him. In no world could lead be turned into gold, and certainly not in East Orange. In the end, he had fun; meeting up with Rob at the house on Saturdays and Sundays to haul junky furniture up and down stairs the way Rob and I had at the beginning of each school year became one of the few aspects of his life he could look forward to. Dealing with Rob's dream—doomed though he felt it to be—gave Oswaldo a reprieve from the folding inward of his own dream of becoming a doctor. He'd been too busy dealing with his grave emotional problems while at Yale, and then with his equally grave family problems after graduation, to even keep track of application deadlines, scholarships, loans, the economics of a poor family and an expensive education. That was his own fault, he knew. A more put-together person could have sorted through and accomplished everything. But still, the long-held pursuit had whisked past him so quietly, and he found something wrong with the reality that when he'd been in high school, everyone around him had been geared toward helping him achieve his goal of going to college: teachers, counselors, classmates. But now, five years later and with the next step carrying even greater life implications, there was no one to tell him what to do. Instead, the people around him seemed to do nothing but ask things of him—and suddenly Rob, for practically the first time ever, was doing the same.

* * *

"GIVE ME THE damn ball!"

Hrvoje Dundovic scanned the long rectangle of water before him, a froth of bobbing heads and waving arms. As had been the case in high school, identifying Rob amid the bodies was easy. During a water polo game, Rob was always either grinning or leering, and his bared white teeth stood out like a beacon. Hrvoje swiveled his palm behind the ball and lasered it to Rob, who thrashed toward the goal, then reared up suddenly and placed a lob—the softness of which belied the sharp jerk of Rob's arm, like a change-up pitch—into the top left corner of the net.

Hrvoje and Rob had kept in touch ever since coming across one another at a water polo tournament, sophomore year of college. Hrvoje had played for the University of Vermont. He'd been warming up for a game when he'd heard that low, amiable voice that had once asked him about prog rock music. "What up, Herve?" The shortening of the name had once been a shared joke, a reference to all the teachers and students who'd never learned how to pronounce it correctly. Rob was squatting at the pool's edge. Hrvoje freestyled over and they caught up briefly. They'd been in touch every few weeks in the years since. Now they played together in an informal pickup water polo league at Rutgers

University, just north of Trenton: a long haul for a short game, but also as good a means as any to step away from life for a few hours.

Hrvoje always asked if they could carpool there and back, a forty-five-minute drive each way. Rob never did, because before each game he went to Trenton State to visit his father.

Skeet had gained weight, mostly upper-body muscle from lifting weights. But a new padding had layered over his neck and face that looked unhealthy, an effect exacerbated by his increasingly slumped shoulders. Rob had been swimming with the St. Benedict's team a few days a week and had lost a few pounds of lingering "Rio weight." The hours each day he spent at the head of his classroom had also straightened his posture, such that when he stood now he reached his full height of five eleven (at Yale, trudging around in his skully, he'd looked more like five nine). The two men suddenly appeared less alike physically, but their primary interest together remained the same: freeing Skeet from prison. Since the overturned appeal in June 1999, they had tried to launch various new offensives. Rob had met with potential attorneys sporadically throughout college and over the last year; he'd encountered the very same problem that Jackie's coworker had first warned her about on the day she'd received word of Skeet's arrest: good lawyers cost too much, and bad lawyers wouldn't be able to do the job.

Arguing Skeet's release no longer centered on whether he'd actually killed the Moore sisters but rather on the legal structure—the chemistry of identifying and isolating inefficiencies in a closed system. During the postconviction relief hearings in 1999, Skeet's representatives had argued that due to a system failure on the part of the courts, Skeet had been deprived of the ability to adequately prove his innocence during trial. The ins and outs of that argument had been obscure at times, but fundamentally they'd still been trying to prove that Skeet had been innocent of the crime for which he'd been convicted.

Now, in 2004, their task was to prove that the eventual reversal of his postconviction relief had been a flawed decision, that the district court had "failed to apply the correct standard of review pursuant to the terms of the Antiterrorism and Effective Death Penalty Act (AEDPA)." To do so, they relied on the small type rather than the broad issues; each new strategy seemed to take the father and the son farther and farther away from the actual, tragic events of that August morning in 1987 and the sprawling ramifications thereof. Rob still spent time in the Essex County law library downtown, going there straight from school on days the water polo team didn't have practice to slip in an hour of research. He was parsing through past murder cases and appeals, looking for precedents, or, in Latin, stare decisis, "to stand by things decided." Because the primary relevant cases had already been exhausted during previous efforts, applicable precedents were very hard to find in those brown-spined legal texts with faded gold lettering. But with painstaking effort and extraordinary attention to detail, Rob gathered factoids that might one day help them. He noticed that, at one point when presenting the overturning of Skeet's appeal in June 1999, the judge had misquoted a certain standard of review, and that misstatement was similar to one that had occurred in an earlier case, which had resulted in a mistrial. Rob recorded data such as this in his black-and-white composition books, each new thread of legal jargon its own small conquest.

For almost fifteen years now, Skeet had been a model inmate. His record showed no disciplinary red flags—which was miraculous, as perpetrators of violence against women were often singled out, "marked" by other inmates. His periodic psychological evaluations were stellar; he was sensible and sane and popular in his cell block. He made people laugh but was careful not to derive that laughter at the expense of others. He had a job on the custodial crew, the highest level of labor available to murder one criminals. He was active in a church group. Most of the guards regarded him well, because he carried a particular pride that enabled him to stride around the concrete prison yard, talking loudly, making jokes, maintaining a running commentary on the daily goings-on—but without pissing off those perennially looking for a reason to be pissed off. By all accounts, Skeet was cool with everybody.

A crucial aspect of staying that way was to speak very little about his son. Everyone knew that Rob's visits were vital to him; those who had been in prison for as long as Skeet were familiar with the way family visits tended to taper off over time, as their absences from the lives of their loved ones became entrenched. Parents could be relied on to come. Spouses sometimes could and sometimes couldn't, depending on the spouse. Children, especially those who had been young at the time of incarceration, tended to drift away the fastest. The fact that Skeet's boy still came, and had been coming religiously since age ten, was inspiring to the others. Above all else, Rob's loyal showings proved that Skeet hadn't been lying when he'd told others that he'd been a great father. But Skeet's fellow inmates knew nothing at all of who this son was. When it came to Yale in particular, the dynamic for Skeet on the inside was the same as it was for his son on the outside: if Skeet went around Trenton State Prison talking about his son in the Ivy League, most would call him a liar. Some would call him uppity. And a very few would be impelled to do something about it. But Skeet was proud of his son—and guilty for the time and emotion his own situation drained from him. He spoke of these feelings only during church meetings, and never extensively. In contrast, on the cell block, he would return from time with Rob and sink into his hard cot and lace his fingers behind his head and stare at the gray ceiling, in silence. At the same time, Rob would most likely have been driving back into Newark, to his home on Greenwood Avenue that, months after he'd bought it, weeks after he'd planned for the renovations to be complete, with thousands of dollars invested, remained a shell, a mirage of something better.

Skeet kept a button in a small wooden keepsake box. The button was the size of the circle created by touching his thumb and index finger together, blue and white, with the Yale bulldog logo in the center. Jackie had sent it to him after Rob's acceptance. He kept the trinket tucked in the bottom of the box, beneath pictures of Rob, letters Rob had written, a postcard from Rio, and a mix tape Rob had recorded in junior high.

In the winter of 2005, halfway through Rob's second year of teaching at St. Benedict's, Skeet became conscious of a new shift in his son:

Rob began asking him for advice. He had tenants on Greenwood now, and—as Jackie had warned him—extracting rent was a part-time job in itself, tiresome with false threats on both sides, providing only enough to cover the ever-present costs of the property, no more. The teaching job was secure and mentally easy, but—as Wayne Ridley had warned him—emotionally taxing. Each day left him with little reserve energy, just enough to want to smoke up and go to sleep. He had girl problems. He had money problems. He had problems with Jackie. Skeet confided to his friends in the Christian discussion group that, as a father, all he wanted to do was help his kid. But as a prisoner, he did not have the capacity to offer advice regarding the world outside these brick walls and turrets. The only thing he could confidently tell his son was to prioritize Jackie above all else. His mother was a great woman, he would say.

Skeet had been feeling weak lately—nothing new, considering the D-grade food they ate, the lack of exercise and sunlight. A different kind of fatigue began overtaking him that winter, which felt terminal, trickling down through his body from his head. He didn't visit the prison doctor, though, because the medical ward was depressing and thick with others' diseases. And perhaps he didn't truly want to know what was happening to him.

* * *

THE PENN RELAYS at Franklin Field in Philadelphia were like a national party, with races instead of a DJ at its center. Tens of thousands of people came to watch runners ranging from below-average high school athletes to Olympic medalists compete. The crowded corridors of the stadium resembled an industrial cattle ranch. I'd been coming to the relays since I was a kid, with my father. I'd run at them for eight years through high school and college. In April 2005, I brought my fiancée down from New York to meet up with old teammates and coaches.

I'd met Rebecca one year earlier, through a friend, in a bar on the Lower East Side. Six weeks later—six weeks of walking around the city in a state of intoxication together, talking until three and four in the

morning each night, feeling so in love that we sometimes forgot to eat—
we'd been sitting on a sidewalk bench drinking margaritas from paper
cups, and I'd blurted out, "So will you marry me?" (the concept having
occurred to me only a half second earlier).

My parents and siblings had barely spoken to me since—because
we'd known each other for less than two months, because I'd just
turned twenty-four years old, because I was an aspiring (or "wannabe")
novelist who walked dogs to supplement nonprofit sector wages. I'd always been the quiet one, considerate in my actions and conservative
in my decisions. That I could be ignorant and disrespectful enough to
make the most important decision in my life spontaneously, without
their wise and experience-based input, without a single thought as to
the implications of that decision—this was beyond the comprehension
of anyone who loved me, and it tore my allegiance between a woman
I'd known for weeks and the family I'd known all my life. No one was
wrong, necessarily, and my parents were acting purely out of love and
an understanding of long-term life that I did not possess. But still, a
year's worth of holidays were rendered tense and fraught. Exchanges
with family members became strictly informational. Discussions on the
matter with Rebecca often became fights, and more than one night had
found her weeping facedown into the bed while I walked alone with my
dog around the city in the early-morning hours, with no idea how to
make things good again.

Such was our state when Rebecca and I trained down to the Penn
Relays. I held tight to her hand as we navigated the maelstrom of human
bodies toward the end zone bleachers where Ty Cantey and a few other
former teammates were supposed to be. We found them, caught up,
swapped a few college stories that seemed to bring forward just how
young and stupid we all were—just how naïve I was to be engineering
my life around whimsy.

Then Rob was sitting on the bleacher right above and behind us,
with an arm locked around my and Ty's necks. "Whass*uuuuup*?" he said,
imitating a popular Budweiser commercial at the time.

I hadn't seen Rob in two years, since that night in New Haven. He was slightly heavier than he'd been then, but his laugh was the same, his rapid-fire knuckle cracks were the same, his grin was the same.

I introduced Rebecca, and Ty interjected, "Da Jeff is getting fucking married to this girl."

Rob thought it was a joke. Then he leaned back, examined me as if in appraisal. He slapped his palm against my back hard enough that I had to grab the seat to keep from toppling forward. "Damn, son," he said. "That's a strong move."

The wind swirled around the stadium as the four of us sat and talked about where we were. Ty was two years into a seven-year MD-PhD program at Harvard, and he seemed worn out. The only way he knew how to study was very, very hard, all night, multiple times a week. He'd been studying this way for six years and racking up debt daily along the way. Between Yale and Harvard, he now carried more than $300,000 in student loans. On that day, he hinted at the reality that the research career he'd once aspired to would not go very far in repaying that amount, and he was considering cutting short the PhD component in order to specialize in a more profitable field of medicine, like orthopedics or dermatology.

I couldn't believe that word, "dermatology," had exited my friend's mouth. That Ty Cantey—who had won the graduation award at Yale for overall achievement in the entire senior class, and who had seemed destined to add a Nobel someday—was considering a life spent treating zits and giving Botox injections felt sobering. Yet Ty seemed as slaphappy as ever, and we remembered a night when his girlfriend—"the Predator"—had gotten so angry with him that she'd clawed his arm, drawing blood, and he'd shut her out of the apartment. Throughout, Rob had been rolling around on the couch, gut laughing harder than I'd ever seen. "She made you her bitch!" he'd squealed over and over, through tears, and he said it again now while Ty blushed, unable to deny it.

In the context of old friends, Rebecca's presence made me feel more grown-up and presentable to them—certainly more so than the nonprofit job, or the unpublished novel that I spent most of my days and all of my nights editing and reediting. Rebecca and I had our own narrative in the fast engagement, the family pressure that only strengthened our bond, the wide-open future in which we would surely succeed. This narrative was silly if not stupid, but we remained in that punch-drunk stage of love, oblivious of how annoying we might have been to others, and so we blithely rendered the romance to Ty and Rob. Not present in their reactions was the skepticism we'd been receiving from almost everyone else in our orbit regarding the choice we had made. Ty was already talking about the bachelor party. Rob nodded along quietly, not jumping up and down but very present, very *there*, the way he'd always been for us in college, emitting a kind of wisdom even when he wasn't speaking any words.

Later, Rebecca and Rob sat together, apart from Ty and me as we watched the races and marveled at split times.

"You picked a good one," he told her, gesturing toward me.

"I know," she said.

"No," he said, looking directly into her eyes, face beyond serious, nearly grave. "For real. He's my boy. He's one of the good ones."

Near the end of the afternoon, Rob and I made a food run to the vending area, and he said the same to me: "That's a good woman; you're a lucky man." I asked if he recalled my college heartbreak sophomore year, and the night he'd spent trying to "get me right." He grinned and shook his head, surely recalling my pathetic state. "Yeah, well, look at you now, brother. Things always come around."

Rebecca, more than me or Ty, understood Rob's language. She'd grown up as one of the few white girls on her block in Fort Greene, Brooklyn, known during her youth in the late '70s as "Bang-bang-shoot-'em-up-Fort-Greene." Her parents were both social workers and community activists who had never made more than $50,000 between them. They spent some evenings trying to shoo the johns from local bars. The thick wrought-iron cages set over the doors and windows of their home didn't always prevent burglaries, as intruders found a passage in through the roof. Rebecca had been mugged at gunpoint with her mother while walking the block between the C train and their front door. Her father, who was legally blind, wore a bridge in his mouth, because half of his teeth had been knocked out by a mugger in Fort Greene Park in the middle of the day (though, due to the tide of gentrification that would never be possible in East Orange, her parents' home, purchased for $5,000 down in 1970, was now worth upward of $2 million). From Rob, she sensed the weight of similar experiences, and she knew that those experiences lent a grace to even the simplest of sentiments. When he told her that I was his boy, he meant it. In a way that was less fleeting than the day itself, his words solidified the decision she had made. If a guy like Rob Peace saw value in the man she was going to marry, then she knew it must be there. Because Rob wouldn't humor her about something as real as friendship.

* * *

WE WERE AMERICANS in our midtwenties, finding apartments and homes, meeting our future spouses, picking (or sometimes falling into) our future careers. We were creating our social circles and the hobbies around which those circles would revolve. We were becoming adults, or at least people who could present as such. This coming of age, in our particular generation, was warped, because of the accelerated pace at which the world seemed to be changing. We hadn't had cell phones or email in high school; our lives depended on them now. We began to manage relationships exclusively through text messages. In no moment of the day were we unavailable to anyone interested in our time. We shopped differently, read the news differently (or not at all), made plans differently. A cultish aspect had overtaken pop culture, with Apple products, the synthetic takeover of music, *Sex and the City* theme parties. Meanwhile, the country was in two wars that we—and by "we" I mean the people I knew in Manhattan, most of whom hadn't been present on 9/11—felt only abstractly connected to. With the world and its goings-on constantly blasting through our computer screens, relevance was the thing we craved, whether it was obtained in the media spotlight or with the accumulation of wealth or in being counter-everything or finding an apartment in a cool neighborhood. For a socially phobic and culturally antiquated guy like me, I was content to watch from the outer edges.

Observing people I'd gone to college with, tracking the personality changes that had occurred between the blotto days preceding graduation and now, was both nourishing and unsettling. A girl who had been renowned on campus for her hard drinking and, shall we say, liberal attitude toward sexual relationships, was now a straitlaced lawyer for a prestigious firm, engaged to a successful banker a decade older than she. A charismatic and admired football star was now working 120-hour weeks at Lehman Brothers, with a growing paunch and personality dulled by all the numbing data he spent those hours analyzing. The senior class president, who had seemed built for a powerhouse political career, had become an Episcopal minister in a small rural town. As so many of us had done in college, we were still reinventing ourselves.

Everyone paused in the weeks after Lyric Benson died. She had been a classmate in Pierson College, beautiful, with an unbridled energy. She was the girl who, on one of the first nights of school, performed a belly dance over a very stoned Rob. An actress in college, she'd begun building a film career quickly afterward, with an Amex commercial and a guest appearance on *Law & Order*. In small, meaningful steps, she was heading toward her dream. However, as she did so, she dragged an anchor from college. During senior year, she'd begun dating an older man who lived in New Haven. He was in his midthirties, handsome in a worn-out way. He sported a long ponytail and fitted suits and became a staple at college parties. A rumor circulated that he worked for the CIA, or had been an Army Ranger, or both. To her female friends, he was mature and alluringly mysterious. To her male friends, he seemed like a pathetic predator of younger women and a liar (also, we were jealous). Either way, people were sure that the romance would run its course quickly, and Lyric would grow wiser. We were all growing wiser.

In the spring of 2003, he shot her in the face, fatally, at point-blank range. The murder occurred in the vestibule of her Chinatown walk-up building, in front of her mother, as recompense for ending their engagement after he'd begun exhibiting obsessive behavior. Then he'd killed himself. Her picture had been on the cover of the *New York Post* among other publications. The pure grisliness of the murder-suicide enthralled the whole city for half a day. Among those who knew her well, the tragedy was paired with a terrible set of emotions—loss, regret, and the guilt of knowing that if they'd been experienced enough to have foreseen such an ending back in college (though, granted, no one could have foreseen *this* ending), they could have guided her away from him sooner, and she would still be alive. The proximity to this kind of violence, this permanently engraved cause and effect, had been previously unknown to almost all of us—Rob Peace being one of the few who had knowledge of murder, premature death, the feeling that coursed through that particular brand of funeral. Lyric's death reminded us that having a Yale degree on our résumés could open many doors, but it couldn't protect us from life, which didn't much care about résumés.

Amid all the change and drama surrounding the Class of '02, Rob's life in 2005, in the midpoint of his twenties, was defined by how little things changed. His friends and family were trying to get through one day and then the next, as they always had. The hustlers along Center Street still leaned against the same walls and tried to start the same shit with young children in their school uniforms. Old friends of his father still told the same Skeet stories while leaning out from their front stoops. Sharpe James was still the mayor, though increasingly embattled, with a face weathered by his time in office and a challenge by the young, charismatic, and Yale-educated Cory Booker. Jackie still worked the same schedule at the same nursing home for the same pay. And Rob was still walking into the same building each morning that he'd walked into during high school, passing beneath the sign that read WHATEVER HURTS MY BROTHER HURTS ME.

The primary change Rob had been dealing with since he began teaching had to do with his grandfather Horace. Though he wasn't technically diagnosed, he clearly suffered from dementia, or some comparable waning of the mind. He watched TV most of the time, but if left alone he got antsy. The previous summer, in 2004, he'd left the house, gotten in the car, and driven off as if going out to buy bourbon. Eight fraught hours later, he'd calmly called Jackie from South Carolina, where he'd driven to "visit family," even though the Peace family didn't have people in South Carolina. Rob had flown down to drive him back. Afterward, Rob did even more than he already was to take the burden of the elder generation off his mother, an effort born of the guilt he felt for the hours she'd worked, the education those hours had given to him. As a boy, he'd compensated by taking care of household chores. As a young man, he'd contributed money from his "campus jobs." Now, in addition to the same chores and fiscal contributions, he did his best to care for Frances and Horace, whether that meant sitting with them in the living room watching reruns of the sitcom *227*, or shuttling Frances to endless doctor's appointments to treat her emphysema, or telling stories about Rio (censored versions, no doubt). Horace passed away, peacefully, in 2005.

At this time, Rob had a college degree. He owned a car and a house. He traveled as much as he could during breaks from school. He helped his family and friends as capably as his means allowed. In most contexts, he was living a successful life already, and because of who he was, he still had potential for so much more success.

But his time at Yale, in the eyes of those close to him, had altered the meaning of the word "success." And he needed to make changes, belated though they might be, if he was going to get closer to whatever that word had come to signify in his mind.

Later that summer after the Penn Relays and after Horace had passed, Skeet collapsed in the prison yard. His blood was drawn in the prison medical ward and sent to a state lab for testing. And when the results came back, Skeet found out exactly what had been making him so tired.

Chapter 11

———————◆———————

S TEAMING MOUNDS OF beef and pork, lathered in oil and sugar, rose above the brims of the platters between us. A large pitcher of sangria was already halfway emptied. On the Friday afternoon before my wedding, I'd taken a break from the manual labor of preparation for the reception, at Rebecca's parents' brownstone, to take the Path train to Newark for lunch with Rob. I'd enlisted him as a groomsman. He hadn't been able to make it to the bachelor party a few weeks earlier, and I was glad about that: the event had been suitably lame. But that Friday, Rob left St. Benedict's during lunch to pick me up at Penn Station and take me to an all-you-can-eat special at Fernandes, in the Ironbound, his favorite *rodízio* restaurant. He went there often and had an established routine: eat, take a cigarette break, drink, cigarette break, eat and drink, cigarette break, eat, cigarette break, drink. He said that not eating and drinking simultaneously allowed the stomach to expand more comfortably and accommodate more food. I had never seen a performance like it. The meal lasted for over two hours.

My family situation had improved: everyone was coming to the wedding, and my parents were throwing the rehearsal dinner that night. But an edginess still surrounded the event, if only because very few people in my orbit seemed to have any faith in this marriage lasting.

I mentioned these tribulations as briefly as possible to Rob during one of the "drink" phases of the meal. In college and after, he'd always seemed to live in a world above the one in which my own various troubles existed. Though always willing and capable of giving advice, he did so with a remoteness that colored whatever he said as wise. Today was no different. He said, "People bring their own shit to the way they see things. If they don't believe what you're doing is right, that's their choice. But the choice has more to do with them than with you. Don't worry about it. You made your own choice."

I'd trekked here this afternoon hoping to be centered by him and his Robness, and he didn't disappoint. Mostly, he told me about Rio and his plans to go back. The wistfulness in his voice was absolute, trumping anything he said about being a teacher, coach, or homeowner.

"I guess, with all the vacation time, it shouldn't be too hard for you to get there," I said.

He laughed. "That's the thing about it—you get all this time, but there's no dough. Vacation? I spend those weeks working."

"Working what?" I asked.

He shrugged. "You know. This and that. Whatever I can pick up."

I had sold my first novel just a few weeks before, for enough of an advance to provide security for roughly a year. People usually reacted to this news in one of three ways: with exaggerated elation, expounding on the achievement (from friends); with a ho-hum, "Oh, that's good news" (from my family, followed by a pessimistic, "So do you have to give that money back if the book doesn't sell well?"); or with low-key compliments veiling competitive contempt (from other writers: "I guess the whole 'young guy in New York' thing is back in vogue . . ."). Rob's reaction was one I'd never heard before. "Let me know when that comes out; I'll pick up a copy," he said without surprise or manufactured congratulations, but simply as an extension of the steady confidence he had in the fact that I, or anyone, could accomplish our dreams if we stayed the course long enough. Not sure how Rob would feel about his ex-roommate writing a book about a gay man who sociopathically seduces both halves of a married couple, all of them Manhattan-based Yale alumni, I just shrugged and said, "Will do."

The following night, an accident on the BQE caused a traffic snarl that plugged every western passageway into Brooklyn; Rob was stuck in the Brooklyn-Battery Tunnel during the ceremony but made it to the reception. He brought a date whom he hadn't mentioned the day before, Katrina. She was very beautiful, with short dreadlocks and a sparkly smile. Along with Ty, another track teammate named Phil, and the family who lived next door to my in-laws, they were the only black people there. Hurricane Katrina had just struck New Orleans weeks earlier, and she spent much of the night humoring guests who bombarded her with comments like, "That's an unlucky name these days!" Between pictures, trying to make sure my family were enjoying themselves, toasts, and conversations with eccentric uncles from both sides of the aisle, the night passed quickly. Whenever I did manage to escape, Rob and Katrina were always close by. He remained, as ever, an easy retreat, one with whom there was no pressure to perform. He brought me a lot of drinks, knowing that the path to the bar was fraught for the groom. Ty requested a Ludacris song from the DJ, and we did the "Throw Dem Bows" dance they'd taught me in college, three or four of us alone in the center of the tiny dance floor in the parlor, for a few moments traveling back to simpler times. He and Katrina left quietly, with a pat on my shoulder and a nod. He slipped me an envelope containing a fifty-dollar bill, no note, as a wedding present.

"Gonna go get some ass," he said. "I'll see you, Da Jeffrey."

"Soon, right?" I replied.

"Trust," he said.

I watched them walk up South Portland Avenue, Katrina's forearm slipped through the crook of his elbow, his shoulders hunched, his footsteps heavy beneath the midnight streetlights.

Rebecca and I left for Los Angeles the next day, where we were moving (temporarily, I thought) because of her job working for a small film company.

That was the last time I ever saw my friend.

*   *   *

"WHAT ARE YOU doing, man?" This was Big Steve Raymond, Victor's older brother. They were hanging out in Rob's unit on the second floor of his house, barely furnished, still a work in progress. Rob was cutting a half pound of weed into dime bags, fielding calls on his cell phone, pounding coffee as he prepared to head out for a night of deliveries. His hiatus from dealing had lasted for about a year and a half, at which point financial pressures—no doubt arising from home ownership and renovations—had impelled him to resume his old profession, that too-easy equalizer. He'd done this quietly at first, and then less so.

"What you mean?"

"I mean, come on, man, what the fuck? You don't need to be doing this . . ."

Rob laughed gently. "It ain't for shits and giggles."

Big Steve let the matter drop; he felt almost embarrassed offering his opinions to Rob. Though he was six years older, and he and Victor had survived more than their share of hardship, Rob was still the smart one, the Yale grad. Steve had dropped out of college freshman year, when his parents had passed away, and since then had been working primarily as a night security guard downstate in Browns Mills, New Jersey. He'd never done more than tread water, but not drowning felt like success. He and Victor lived together now; Victor was still working as a salesman for Home Depot, nervous because the FAA, due to the quick burnout of air traffic controllers, rarely hired anyone older than twenty-eight. Steve's chest felt heavy watching Rob dealing drugs again, and dealing on a low level that left him a weary shell most days. Whenever he raised the matter, however, Rob would cut him short with these vague declarations about "doing what I gotta do."

At Yale, most everyone (except Oswaldo Gutierrez) refrained from telling Rob what to do, because of the way he'd grown up in Newark. In Newark, most everyone (except Oswaldo Gutierrez) refrained from telling Rob what to do, because of the way he'd gone to Yale.

Oswaldo's advice was the same that, a few years ago, he himself had refused to hear from others: "Get the fuck out of Newark. Get the fuck away from people who won't get the fuck out of Newark."

He couched no vitriol in these declarations; Oswaldo just stated the reality of things as he knew them. Three years after graduation had found him working in a taco shop, getting high all the time to metabolize the fact that he was working in a taco shop, recklessly exposing himself to danger—such as the night he and Rob had been smoking in Orange Park, and one of their friends had mouthed off to a couple of Bloods trolling the park; guns had been drawn, and Oswaldo and Rob took shelter with "Auntie," Victor and Big Steve's aunt, in her nearby apartment. Oswaldo had suffered another nervous breakdown, but unlike in college, there hadn't been a renowned psych ward into which he could comfortably check himself. So he'd driven to New Haven, just to get away, crashing with Anwar and other townie friends. He went to Yale's Career Services and told a counselor there that if they didn't help him figure out what to do, he'd most likely be dead in a year. With guidance, he was admitted to the Perelman School of Medicine at the University of Pennsylvania the following fall, 2005. Now he was one year into a graduate degree in psychiatry, and he urged Rob whenever they spoke to follow in his footsteps—frustrated again and again by his friend's ingrained belief that following in anyone's footsteps would somehow betray who he was. Oswaldo thought that was nothing more than a cliché but resigned himself to the fact that getting too involved in such intractable, street-bred personality walls such as Rob's was exactly the kind of thing that had caused his mind to spiral dangerously away twice in his life.

Why wouldn't Rob just listen? Even as Oswaldo intentionally began to disengage, the question nagged him, and in certain moments, studying alone in the library toward his degree, haunted him. Rob should have been studying alone in the library, too—not hanging out with all those friends in the hood.

Which was the answer to his question. Rob wouldn't listen because of his friends, from Oakdale and Mt. Carmel, from football games, from the stoops of East Orange, from St. Benedict's, from his various dealing networks. These people were all grown now. Some, like Shannon Heggins, a junior high school girlfriend of Rob's, had children with fathers who'd already split. Some, like Curtis, had decent jobs and were doing just fine. Some, like Flowy, were living more precariously. Some, like Tavarus—who'd just been arrested for possession with intent to distribute, the mark on his record akin to having a 0.7 GPA in high school but much harder to fix—had already fallen below the line. And Rob strived to be the Man among these peers. If someone needed money for rent or for kids' clothes, Rob thumbed it over. If someone's car broke down and he needed a ride, Rob picked him up. If someone was bored and wanted company, Rob rolled through. These efforts went both ways. Once, when Rob's tire blew out at one in the morning on the Merritt Parkway en route to visit Daniella Pierce—still working in New Haven on urban education policy reform as it pertained to ex-felons—he called Flowy, who immediately hopped in his own car to bring him a spare and work the jack (Rob, for all his knowledge, was helpless when it came to cars), an hour's drive each way, with tolls. When he had trouble pulling rent from his tenants on Greenwood Avenue, Drew came by to intimidate a payment out of them. Victor and Big Steve had taken Dio off Jackie's hands when he'd first gone to Rio, and they'd ended up keeping him for three years as the pet had grown from a short stack of coils into a thick, formidable reptile capable of popping the metal lid off his own tank. (Victor ultimately gave Dio to a local pet store owner, who most likely found him too big to sell; I sometimes wonder if the snake was released, and is now still making slow S-curves through the Pine Barrens, prowling for mice and squirrels.)

Friendship, in this community, was simple: it meant being there. Friendship necessitated no pride, no projection of having your shit together if you didn't, no passivity, no judgment—and especially no fronting, which had characterized so many relationships at Yale. Friendship here was the most dependable means by which they were going to get through their various lives. Because of the value Rob placed on relationships, he could reply, "Chill, I'm on it," whenever Oswaldo hammered on the fact that Rob was better than where he'd grown up, and that a very big life lay in store for him if he would only take the first steps toward it. Because no longer would that life step toward him the way Charles Cawley had in the St. Benedict's gymnasium.

Oswaldo also understood that Rob fronted more than anyone else Oswaldo had ever known. As in high school, when Rob had veiled his personal hardships with intelligence and leadership, he now veiled them with a generosity that was incredibly costly, in both dollars and emotional drain.

The emotional drain intensified when, on a prison visit in the fall of 2005—not long after my wedding—his father told him that he had cancer in his brain.

*   *   *

RAQUEL HAD GRADUATED from Yale a year behind us, in '03. Simon, her future husband, was still at a prestigious med school in Manhattan studying cardiology, and she moved to the city that summer, just after Lyric Benson's murder. She lived with Simon on the second floor of a building his parents had just bought on 119th Street and First Avenue, in Spanish Harlem. Their home was a run-down unit above a street that not five years prior had been a drug-dealing hot zone (renovations began immediately, and the house was practically gutted around them). She worked for a nonprofit documentary film company and freelanced in the TV industry. Because much of her work involved shooting B-roll film in nightclubs for shows like HBO's *Taxicab Confessions* as well as attending wrap and premiere parties—and also because she'd been using drugs like Ecstasy since she was fourteen—amping up her nightlife seemed like part and parcel of her chosen career. These self-destructive habits were accelerated by a number of factors she couldn't control: Simon's long hours, being responsible by remote for the less self-sufficient members of her extended family in Miami, meeting her father for the first time in a dingy motel room in Little Havana and encountering a stranger who didn't much care for her, and the fact that drug use was common among so many of her friends, from both childhood and Yale. She carried on, sometimes heading straight from a nightclub to work in the morning. Simon was very straight, very driven, and very loyal. Between twelve-hour shifts at the hospital, he trained seriously in Shaolin kung fu, kendo, and qigong while Raquel's life, increasingly, revolved around partying.

Throughout these years, Rob stopped by often, bringing weed and a fleeting hour of good company with him. He had a knack for appearing when she most needed his face and voice to recenter herself. He'd come by late, usually after midnight, when he had deliveries to make in Harlem. Quietly, Rob had been branching out his network geographically, for reasons having to do with safety more than money; he didn't want to become too conspicuous in the small world of East Orange, where the Double II Set Bloods ruled much of the commerce and didn't look kindly on competition. Raquel was an outstanding cook, and as when they'd lived together in New Haven, she always had food waiting, along with a bottle of Hennessy in the cupboard reserved for him. Rob would eat a lot, and then drink—also a lot. If Simon was at the hospital, they would share a joint or a bowl or a blunt. Rob would invariably come in with a scowl, complaining with exhaustive sighs about the bureaucracy at school, about his tenants, about tolls and traffic on the George Washington Bridge. But the food, alcohol, and THC would calm him until he reached a place of easy laughter pouring through that grin, that old grin that she and everyone else remembered from college. When he reached that place, he would talk of travel.

Rob's cousin Nathan worked for Continental Airlines. Included among airline employee perks was a certain allotment of "buddy passes," certificates allowing select friends and family to travel on standby, at cost, anywhere in the world. Nathan gave one to Rob, and he used it to visit Rio twice more during summer breaks. But he'd begun looking for destinations far beyond Brazil. A college classmate was teaching English as a second language in South Korea. He wanted to go there.

Hrvoje Dundovic had been talking wistfully of returning to Pula, Croatia, during their water polo games. He wanted to go there. He had aunts, uncles, and cousins in Ohio, Florida, and Georgia. He wanted to visit all of them. He'd constructed a second community in Rio de Janeiro. He wanted to live there part-time, and maybe teach at the Federal University, once he got his degree. At least, he said he did.

"What is stopping you from doing any or all of those things?" she asked, having herself found a way to travel during college.

He gave a gentle glare from beneath his hard brow and rubbed his thumb back and forth across his fingers.

"Oh, shut the fuck up," she said, laughing. "Woe is Rob Peace! Woe is Rob Peace! You went to *Yale*. If you can't figure out how to do what you want to do, that's your own damn fault."

"Yeah," he replied. "Yeah, I know."

When he left, he spent the early-morning hours driving around Harlem, the Bronx, and Brooklyn, where most of his non-Newark clients lived. He'd pick up $10 here, $30 there, maybe returning to his apartment on Greenwood around five or six with $100 to $200 profit after overhead and eighty miles logged on the odometer. Then he'd power-nap until seven and get ready to go to school. After a day of teaching and coaching, he usually stopped by Chapman Street for dinner with Frances and Jackie, if she wasn't working the night shift. Back on Greenwood Avenue late at night, when he wasn't dealing, Rob continued working on his father's behalf.

He wasn't trying to engineer another appeal at this point; he was simply trying to gain his father access to medical treatment outside the prison medical ward. All he could do was write letters that emphasized his father's good behavior, listed the jobs and meeting groups with which Skeet was involved, and—increasingly as Skeet's illness progressed through the winter of 2006—pleaded as a son on behalf of his dying father.

. . . I am twenty-five years old. I graduated from Yale University in 2002 with a degree in molecular biochemistry and biophysics. I now teach biology at the St. Benedict's Preparatory School in Newark, NJ. I plan to go to graduate school next year to continue my education and become a college professor. Though I was just seven years old when my father was incarcerated, none of my achievements would have been possible without him. This is not because he did homework with me when I was little. Even after he went to jail he called me. He told me to study hard and take advantage. It wasn't just his words that helped me. It was the way he carried himself in prison. He kept his dignity. He did not cause trouble. He did not show any weakness during the many times I visited him. He inspired me to be who I am and who I'm going to be. Clearly, my father's disease cannot be properly treated in the penitentiary medical ward. I studied the chemistry of cancer at Yale Medical School during my time as an undergraduate. I know exactly how it works and what it does. My father needs clinical treatment right now. In light of his record, I do not understand why this cannot be made available to him . . .

But Rob was fighting a battle that would not be won. Statewide, the correctional facilities went on complete lockdown beginning in the early spring of 2006, due to an intercepted letter sent by a Bloods leader named Lester Alford. In the letter, Alford had stated that over a dozen weapons had been stashed in four prisons, including New Jersey State (formerly Trenton State), and a coordinated uprising was planned that would culminate in the assassination of Mayor-Elect Cory Booker. While the authorities checked into the validity of the letter—most believed it to be dubious, since the language was not coded the way most gang correspondence was—all inmate-release programs (furloughs, conjugal visits, work-release, and medical) were suspended indefinitely. All Rob could do was visit the prison as often as possible and look through the Plexiglas at his father, a man who had always been broad and thick—like his son—and had become more so through sixteen years of weight lifting in the prison yard, and now began to waste away as if some invisible spirit were penetrating the prison walls each night to peel away layers from both his mind and his body.

* * *

FRIAR LEAHY SENSED the turbulence. Rob was perhaps more adept now than he'd been even in high school at concealing whatever struggles he was going through. He went through his days as he always had: giving lectures on simple cell structure, bringing the hammer down on sassy students, teaching the geometry of shot angles in the pool. Friar Leahy knew about Rob's father, as Rob had formally asked permission to leave school early once or twice a week to get down to Trenton before visiting hours ended. But whatever weighed on him now was heavier even than Skeet's declining health. Whether his father's illness precipitated a larger existential question of what he was supposed to be doing or whether the two existed on wholly separate planes of consciousness, Friar Leahy didn't know. What he did know—what Coach Ridley had known during their first conversation about becoming a teacher—was that Rob was not destined to work at a high school. He also knew that Rob Peace was strong enough, resilient enough, and smart enough to figure out what he was destined to do. At least he hoped that to be the case, because he knew that Rob would neither ask for counsel nor receive it if given.

The water polo team was not strong, but they still traveled to tournaments every weekend. He and Coach Ridley would take turns driving the vans. When Rob wasn't driving, he sat in the back, with players such as Truman Fox. Truman was a quiet kid, white with blond hair, relatively affluent. He was also lazy, one of those who tiptoed along the bottom during laps and found creative ways to dip out of the weight room. Rob—"Coach Peace" to Truman—singled him out, though not as harshly as some of the others. He treated the boy almost like a science project.

"Why are you here?" Rob asked.

"Because we have to play a sport; it's required," Truman replied.

"Okay, so play it, don't just fuck around."

"I'm not fucking around."

"You're not making it hard."

Truman didn't know what that meant.

"If you go into something, you better make it hard. Otherwise what's the point?"

Truman still found his words elusive, yet intimidating. Rob was wearing one of his dark glowers, signaling exasperation.

"Look, anything you do, if it isn't hard, it isn't doing anything for you. So you're better off not doing it. Use your time somewhere else."

That Saturday, when Rob opened up the weight room for a voluntary session, Truman was there. After that, their van ride conversations strayed away from the sport of water polo and the reasons for playing it. Rob would look out the window at the dense foliage sweeping past on the interstates of New England and Pennsylvania, and he'd ask Truman about his family, his upbringing, what he wanted to be when he grew up. He talked about what he believed defined a Real Man: someone who had honor, curiosity, respect for women, and took responsibility for his people. The talk was real, and Truman remained surprised that Rob was willing to engage with him this way, being as they'd come from such different backgrounds. Not apparent in these moments was the hard, glaring façade Rob often brought to the classroom and the pool; he looked soft, even gentle. The fact that Coach Peace went out of his way to be friends with him was powerful, and Truman held on to that power tightly both at school and at home. He felt that if Rob saw a spark in him, even if Truman himself did not, then it was his own responsibility to stoke it (Truman would ultimately play water polo in college). He didn't know that on a normal day after practice, while he and his teammates were changing back into dry clothes, his coach was mentally preparing to spend the night selling drugs.

* * *

Procuring enough marijuana to distribute was not difficult, but procuring quality marijuana was. At Yale, the quality had barely mattered; college kids would smoke anything, and most of them didn't know the difference. In the city, although many drug users would smoke anything, they had more options and less disposable wealth. To remain the go-to guy in his small network of buyers, Rob had to be available when the calls came, and he had to provide a product that was reliable in the high it engendered. There were two primary types of high. "Body stone"—also known as "couch lock," the typical effect of smoking the *indica* strain of the cannabis plant—was characterized by a very intense lethargy, a difficulty with and indifference to practical tasks, and a desire for meditative solitude. "Head high"—from the *sativa* strain—was more energetic, typified by stoned people talking and laughing with enhanced visual and auditory senses, prone to psychedelic experiences and, sometimes, bouts of paranoia. Rob wasn't particularly fond of either; when stoned, he preferred to be somewhere in between: able to accomplish tasks and operate in the world, but to do so in an unbothered state, free from the gravity pulling him in all directions. As he struggled with his mother's needs and his father's illness and his own stasis, he sought to engineer the high that suited him.

In the basement of 34 Smith Street, where Curtis lived alone now, Rob invented his own personal strain of marijuana, an indica-sativa hybrid known widely as Sour Diesel. The Burger Boyz had once packed themselves into this space to do their homework over sodas and Mrs. Gamble's cooking. Now Rob spent nights there alone constructing a hydroponic system of planters beneath LED lights, which consumed more than three-fourths of the floor space. His parent plants were sent from the Emerald Triangle in California, heavily wrapped in dozens of layers of cellophane to contain the scent, then packaged in kitchen appliance boxes—toasters, blenders, microwaves, appearing as an eBay purchase. Patiently, through the same process of trial and error that had defined his years in the lab, he used simple biology to fuse various genotypes in the seedling stage, and over the course of months in early 2006, he perfected his strain. The basement wasn't big enough for mass production, but it spawned sufficient product to cut his Sour Diesel with the less particular buds he bought from his connects. To intensify the

high—and raise profits—he used the low boiling point of butane to dis-
till hash oil from the typically discarded stalks and leaves, which he then
dripped into the smokable buds. This work was repetitive, laborious,
and dangerous (not just because of the police patrolling the neighborhood, but also because butane fumes are poisonous, and he had to wear
a gas mask while he worked). But, during the winter of 2006, this was
how Rob spent the bulk of his free time: alone in the basement making
designer marijuana.

"Why?" Again and again, his friends asked him this question, with
humor more often than not. At the time, Rob's day-to-day seemed like
a sitcom to them: Yale grad high school teacher running a marijuana lab
out of his best friend's basement in Illtown.

Rob would just shrug and give one of his that's-my-own-damn-
business looks, and his friends would answer their own question: he
needed the money, and this was something he knew how to do.

But over time, as his fatigue grew—the energy-suction of tending to
his students at school and his family at home, paired with the stress of
operating an illegal enterprise in a gang-dominated arena, plus barely
sleeping in general—they began to see that Rob's condition went deeper.
In that basement, Rob felt in control. He had created something, and his
work was bringing in money, and that dynamic gave him pride.

*   *   *

HE FOUND A LAWYER in Toms River who, after reviewing the vast history of documents Rob organized, visiting Skeet, and naming a retainer
that Rob could afford after a winter of intensive drug dealing, agreed
to file one last appeal. In place of courtroom hearings, the argument
consisted of a six-page brief, written and filed with a much larger com-
pilation of supporting documents, asserting that Skeet's postconviction
relief had been overturned by an "improper standard of review."

Skeet was living in the prison infirmary, weak, and heavily sedated;
the prison medical ward didn't stock much in the way of cancer treatments, but it had plenty of pain medication. For the first time since

Skeet's reprieve during Rob's senior year of high school, Rob was able to visit without the Plexiglas between them: to look into his father's eyes without a coating of dust, to breathe the same air while they spoke without telephone receivers, to hold his father's hand. The summer was hot and muggy despite the air-conditioning, which was one of the few benefits of living in the infirmary. Rob made no effort to travel that summer. He had been coming to the prison up to five times a week, though rarely with anything to report about the appeal: the forms had been filed; the State had countered; the judge was reviewing. They both knew that however the appeal turned out, Skeet did not have long to live.

Brain cancer, in comparison with other terminal forms that impacted bones or vital organs, usually involved less physical pain. His tumor had not ravaged his body aside from the dramatic weight loss, and steroid treatments had helped alleviate that effect. The building pressure within his skull caused intense headaches and nausea, but another regimen of drugs eased the physical sickness to a manageable degree. His face appeared increasingly swollen, a symptom Skeet seemed to bear well. Mostly, he was just very, very drowsy, and the intensity of his fatigue began to mark his life's inexorable waning. His mental faculties flickered on and off; some visits he would exhibit that old charismatic ferocity, while others he was impossibly far away and mouthing inaudible words known only to him. On those days, Rob would sit silently beside him for the entirety of their time. That Skeet's illness decayed his mind over his body might have been a comfort to Rob; he might have witnessed or projected some semblance of well-being onto his dying father that manifested, mostly, in long periods of sleep. Just as likely, Rob might have taken a vicious offense at this last, cruel turn in his father's fate: very few people in Rob's life had cherished their brains more than Skeet, and that was precisely where the disease had fortified itself. Meanwhile, up and down the ward, prisoners lay in cots separated by yellowed curtains, their existence announced by the steady chorus of complaints regarding their various discomforts, mostly due to infectious diseases and the deficiency of their treatments.

On August 16, 2006, Rob learned that the final appeal had been denied. The judge decided that "the District Court applied the correct standard of review in determining that the Appellate Division's decision was not contrary to, or did not involve, an unreasonable application of clearly established Federal law, as determined by the Supreme Court of the United States."

On August 22, Skeet slipped into an unconscious state, the final event for most patients with his condition. Some took days or even weeks to pass away. But Skeet's respiratory system failed that same night, and he asphyxiated quietly, alone, in his sleep, a month shy of his sixtieth birthday.

*   *   *

ROB HANDLED THE funeral arrangements. Very few people attended the service in East Orange. Skeet's old friends in the neighborhood still told stories about him, but not many had stayed in touch with the hero of these stories. Almost no one in Rob's life even knew what had happened. In Rosedale Cemetery less than two miles northeast of Chapman Street, he stood with Jackie at the foot of the plot while the coffin went down. His head was bowed and his body provided a column against which his mother could lean as her mind revisited the decisions that were now being laid to rest along with Skeet Douglas's body. They each dropped a lily into the grave, and they left as the dirt was being packed in.

Rob didn't buy a tombstone. Like Skeet's legal options throughout the nineteen years that had passed since his arrest, a proper stone was too expensive, and an affordable stone wouldn't do the job required. The plot was marked by a thin strip of brown concrete with a metallic disc bearing the number 54, and a small depression in the ground, six inches deep and nine in diameter, an earthen flower receptacle.

Later that day, Rob and Victor went to Orange Park to smoke, a cathartic ritual dating back to Mt. Carmel. Rob said, "I lost my father three times. First when he went to jail. Second when he went back to jail. And now he's in the ground." Rob looked up and turned his head toward his oldest friend. "Thank you."

"For what?"

"Coming to the funeral. Means a lot."

Unlike the moment in this same spot eight years ago when they were talking about the uncertainty of college, or the moment shortly after that when Mr. Cawley gave Rob the paper napkin that removed the uncertainty, he did not cry.

* * *

HE'D NEVER FAILED a test before, and he was pissed.

"The questions they asked, it was, like, the most obscure shit imaginable," he told Tavarus, who considered that listening to Rob Peace bitch about an exam was one of the least likely scenarios he could have ever imagined.

"Go back, take it again," Tavarus replied.

"I don't have time for this shit!" Rob yelled, activated despite the setback.

Peace Realty. The new goal coalesced in the wake of Skeet's passing, as the '06–'07 school year began. After two-plus years of home ownership, he'd finally renovated the house on Greenwood to a decent state. By living with Jackie on Chapman and renting out all three units on Greenwood, he was actually turning a profit of $1,000 a month, though that number fluctuated depending on repairs. The process of making Greenwood work had been clumsy, protracted, and too much hassle for what he earned. In some ways, the clumsiness was what compelled Rob to become more involved in the real estate market, as trial and error more often than not led to success. And he wanted very badly to be successful in real estate.

Whereas the relative success of teaching was almost abstract in that it was contained within those most self-contained of creatures (teenage boys), he saw something pleasantly simple about the real estate cycle: locate an undervalued property, buy it and renovate, find the right homeowner, and come away with $20,000 or $30,000 cash in pocket. Success in real estate required skills that Rob believed were some of his strongest: the work ethic to locate those homes, the social skills to negotiate with people ranging from rich lenders to working-class contractors to poor renters, and the desire to make money in crafty but fundamentally honest ways. And, at least in Rob's idealized vision, he would be making a positive mark in the world. Because a house meant shelter. It meant heat. It meant security. Above all, it meant family.

Some friends who knew about Skeet's passing felt that something equally powerful drove him: Rob had lost not only his father but also the goal of releasing his father in which he'd invested so much work since high school. He'd achieved almost every objective he'd ever laid out for himself: swimming, college, Rio. But this one, probably his most valued, had beaten him. As he laid out this new goal for himself, those around him saw emotional progress, and perhaps recovery.

He knew from his high school stint working in title research that many people who pursued profits in real estate did so in less than intelligent ways, due either to ignorance, dishonesty, or the pressure of time. Rob desired to be neither ignorant nor dishonest, and he didn't plan on rushing. But before he could do anything, he needed to pass the Realtor's exam. While flipping houses did not require a Realtor's license, he wanted one in order to access the Multiple Listings Service that contained the most up-to-date information on current properties. Without that access, he would be working from behind the competition. He passed the exam on his third attempt, in January 2007, and he partied the entire weekend with the energy that had characterized graduation weekend at Yale. The malaise that had gripped him for the past two years seemed to have lifted; the man drinking vodka shots and cracking jokes and rallying for a trip to the strip club resembled the kid the Burger Boyz had known in high school, the kid who had carried them all. From beneath the festivities arose a new determination, an orderly alignment of the future he now envisioned.

He would finish out this school year, his fourth.

He would continue living on Chapman Street and hustling at night.

He would save money with the same frugality and vigor he had since he was a kid.

At year's end, he would start investing that money in houses, beginning with three or four inexpensive urban properties similar to Greenwood, the cumulative rent of which would theoretically provide him with an income of roughly $3,000 to $4,000 per month, in addition to his drug earnings, which he planned to ramp down on the same time frame.

Once fixed up, he would flip all the houses except for Greenwood and come out with $100,000 to $150,000 profit.

Half of this he would invest in more real estate.

The other half he would use to support Jackie and begin graduate school.

As soon as the math worked out, he would stop selling drugs completely.

At least, this was how the next few years coalesced in his mind.

He went through this itemized list with Curtis and Tavarus over and over. Curtis's stepfather was an accountant, and he would help with the incorporation of a company—not technically necessary but useful in terms of credibility. Oswaldo was in medical school at Penn, but his father was around to work on renovations at a low rate. Tavarus would perform all the title research. Wherever a connection could be made to family or friends, Rob made it.

As he wrote and rewrote the hard numerical figures in a composition notebook—his handwriting, as ever, impeccable and slightly effeminate—he drew the vision further and further outward into the future, where his thinking became less analytical, increasingly idealized. Once Peace Realty had built up a reputation for savvy and efficiency, he would move into the commercial market, buy vacant storefronts along South Orange Avenue, and install real businesses, the kind that represented a neighborhood in ascendance rather than stasis or decline: delis and coffee shops and clothing stores instead of funeral homes and weave salons and check-cashing centers. The capital for such an undertaking would come from white men in suits who worked downtown, knew the mayor personally, believed in revitalization, and respected someone like Rob who had the education and street-level knowledge to accomplish it.

Night after night that fall, as the weather drove backyard barbeques at 34 Smith Street inside for round-table conversations in the kitchen, the Burger Boyz talked about what they would achieve. They didn't reference the luck that seemed vital to anyone in East Orange raising his station; they'd each run through enough bad luck for fifty young men, and their optimism was total, driven by the fact that Rob was operating at their center once again.

Friar Leahy, in the offices and hallways of St. Benedict's, saw something different. He saw a man who was burnt out, a man who was conflicted, a man who was refusing to come to terms with the loss of a father. Rob had never spoken much, neither in Unknown Sons gatherings nor faculty meetings. But he'd always listened, had always processed the obligations of being a schoolteacher quietly, studiously. He'd always put forth the effort required to perform his job well. At the end of the '05–'06 school year, the students had given him the Teacher of the Year award. Not so as the '06–'07 school year wore on: when called on to speak up on matters ranging from the annual budget to cutlery being stolen from the cafeteria, he'd come out of his thoughts reluctantly and say, "What? Sorry, zoned out." Sometimes there would be contempt in his voice akin to a disengaged teenager being called out in the classroom, a note of *Tell me why this is worth my time?* During classes, his patience and air of peership frayed; a typical confrontation with a student who'd cracked a joke during Rob's lecture had ascended into an uncontrolled shouting match (as was custom now, the parents complained, and Rob was called in for another reluctant apology). During practice and tournaments, he let kids slack off, as if lacking the energy to dog them.

In the context of this high school in this city, disengagement was always the first sign of problems at home.

Friar Leahy sensed that the former Presidential Award winner's tenure as a schoolteacher was reaching its natural end. In keeping with the school's method of dealing with its students' personal lives, he did not confront Rob directly about any particular problems he might have been having. Instead, in the winter of 2007, he mentioned the Appalachian Trail hike coming up in the summer, which Rob had helped lead for the last three years.

"I'm just thinking ahead and wanted to make sure you were on board this year." Rob looked away, toward a state championship soccer trophy in Leahy's office.

"I might be traveling this summer," Rob said.

"Where to?"

"Hopefully Rio. But also Ohio, to see family."

"Okay, that's totally fine," Friar Leahy replied. "The boys will miss having you."

"Yeah," Rob said. "And also, I'm thinking about graduate school, for chemistry. I'm thinking about doing that next year."

"I think that's a very wise move," Leahy said without hesitation. "So you want to keep teaching on the next level?"

Rob shrugged. "Maybe. Right now, just starting to think about the applications."

"Anything I can do to help, you tell me. Got it?"

"Thanks, Father Ed."

*   *   *

ON JULY 1, 2006, Cory Booker officially took office as the new mayor of Newark. He'd gained fame in the late '90s as a city councilman who would sleep in a tent at city housing projects, hold hunger strikes and live on food stamps, patrol bad neighborhoods himself and physically confront the dealers holding down their corners. His victory was the first regime change in two decades, and it happened only after six years of near-bloody battling between the young, charismatic, light-skinned, Stanford-Yale-Oxford-educated upstart and the old, grizzled, but equally charismatic incumbent. The tension between Cory Booker and Sharpe James had been national news for most of the '00s. The 2002 election, which Booker lost, was documented in the Oscar-nominated *Streetfight*, which between talking head interviews showed intense footage of the predominantly poor, black constituents who ardently supported James's altercating with the working-class whites and Puerto Ricans who fought for Booker and his eloquent calls for public service and revitalization. The documentary was a near-perfect picture of a specific place and time: the declining city at risk of being left behind, the shoulder-height view of the vast number of problems in play, and the presentation of two equal and opposing paths forward whose backers were split almost definitively along socioeconomic lines. The 2002 election had been beyond combative; a riot nearly broke out when Booker showed up at a street basketball tournament that Sharpe James was already attending, and James called Booker "a Republican who took money from the KKK and the Taliban . . . who's collaborating with the Jews to take over Newark." When James—who was constantly being investigated for various alleged corruptions—won the election by a margin of 53 percent to 47 percent, his victory seemed to cement Newark's representation of "permanent poverty," a culture of violence and corruption (at least if you subscribed to the *New York Times*).

Mayor James pulled out of the 2006 election and anointed the deputy mayor, Ronald Rice, as his successor. Booker, backed by the majority of corporate interests in the city, outspent Rice twenty-five to one and won the election with 72 percent of the vote. (Two years later, Sharpe James was convicted on five counts of fraud for conspiring to rig the sale of nine city lots to his mistress, who quickly resold them for hundreds of thousands of dollars in profit.) The new mayor's campaign pledge to beef up the police department in order to make Newark the national leader in crime reduction was what inspired the Bloods' assassination attempt, which in turn had denied Skeet Douglas the possibility of external cancer treatment.

Booker came into office with an ambitious "100-day" plan to increase police forces, end background checks for many city jobs so that former offenders could find employment, improve city services, and expand summer youth programs. Though Newark city government did not extend to the Oranges, his rise suggested a shift in the direction of the city. Even those who had voted for the "other guy" were curious, and perhaps even hopeful, about what the future might bring.

"That's your boy," Rob's friends would say, messing with him. "Went to Yale and everything."

Even in this context, Rob was uncomfortable being associated with Yale, let alone the charming, some might say slick politician who hadn't even grown up in Newark himself. "We'll see what he does," Rob said. "He's been talking a long time. Let's see how he does now that he's in it for real." And his expression said, resignedly, *I don't have high hopes. Now let's talk about something that matters.*

* * *

"Yo, GET UP HERE!"

Rob was in the basement at Smith Street around midnight, gas mask on, filtering hash oil through the tiny perforations at the end of his sieve. Around him, the hydroponic planters formed three sides of a rectangle. The auto-timed LED lights above the sprouting plants blasted white light, screwing up Rob's internal clock even more than his odd hours already had.

He went upstairs, where Curtis and Tavarus were peering out the front window.

"Boobie's back," Curtis said with rare concern. Rob looked casually through the crack of the curtain. A sedan was parked directly in front of the house, engine idling. A glowing ember was visible through the windows, being passed among multiple silhouettes.

"Yeah," Rob said, "that's his ride."

He'd been hearing noise from his connects that Boobie, a forceful member of the Double II Sets, had a beef with Rob—because by now word had slipped that his Sour Diesel was "off the hook" (meaning something so new and fresh that it could be taken straight off the hanger at a clothing store). Word had also gotten out that Rob had been dealing to some of Boobie's people. He wasn't poaching clients; he'd just become the guy they called if Boobie couldn't be reached. Generally, this was not considered encroachment.

"That stupid motherfucker," Rob said, seeming more exasperated than afraid.

"Should we call the police?" Curtis asked.

"Are you crazy?" Rob replied as he gestured with his eyes to the basement below.

"Let's just head out the back," Tavarus said. The house occupied a double lot, with a rear driveway that exited onto Telford Street, one block east of Smith. "Head to Flowy's."

"They probably have a car on Telford, too." Rob sighed and put on his old leather jacket. "I'll go take care of it. I mean, these fucking stupid people, I just can't stand stupid people . . ."

Before his friends could stop him, Rob was outside knocking on the driver's-side window of the car. The window lowered halfway. Curtis and Tavarus watched. The street was deserted.

Rob was bent over, his head just outside the opening in the window. His hands made wide gestures on either side of his body. The head inside the car, presumably Boobie's, was shaking from side to side, then nodding up and down. They heard garbled voices. Rob's remained genial. Then Boobie laughed.

The window lowered all the way, and Boobie's arm extended toward Rob. The only reason Curtis and Tavarus knew there was not a loaded gun fixed to the end of that arm was that Rob took it in his own, forearms forming an inverted V with the hands locked at the thumbs. Their other hands gripped one another's shoulders. Rob took a hit from the joint inside the car, and the vehicle pulled out as he turned back to the house.

"*Damn*, it's freezing out," he muttered when he came inside.

"What was that?" Curtis asked.

"It's all good," Rob said. He strolled back through the kitchen and made himself a screwdriver from the 1.5-liter bottle of Smirnoff on top of the refrigerator. Then he grabbed the gas mask, put it on, and went back downstairs.

*   *   *

THE FOLLOWING SPRING was his last at St. Benedict's, and the feeling was similar to that which had marked our final semester in college: a mixture of nostalgia for the past and excitement about the future as he performed the tasks he'd performed each day for four years, tasks he would never perform again. He went on his last water polo tournament weekend and stayed up in the motel room he shared with Coach Ridley, watching action movies and putting off the moment when one of them had to check on the players' rooms. He taught his last classes on Darwinian evolution, recessive genes, and cellular structures of plants. He sat through his last faculty meetings and pulled his last students aside in the hallways to drill the importance of discipline. He attended his last senior banquet, listened to the last Presidential Award winner give a speech to parents, teachers, and guests. As in most years, Charles Cawley was one of those guests.

Rob had seen Mr. Cawley a few times during his teaching career, usually at homecoming and the senior banquet. They had always made a point of speaking with one another, but these had been increasingly distant, at points awkward, conversations as Rob had become more and more aloof. After the speech at the 2007 banquet, Mr. Cawley approached Rob's table, as he had done Rob's senior year nine years earlier. Rob stood up, shook his hand, and said, "Hey, Mr. Cawley, how's it going?"

"How's it going with you?" Mr. Cawley replied.

"Getting by."

"Friar Ed told me that your father passed. I'm sorry."

"Thank you, sir."

"And I understand you're leaving the school?"

"Yes."

"And what are your plans?"

"Grad school."

"Oh, which one? I'm curious."

"Not sure yet. Still working on it."

Mr. Cawley looked into Rob's eyes and understood that the young

man was saying this only because he was supposed to. He saw something more in those eyes: anger. The emotion wasn't nakedly apparent,
but Mr. Cawley was a professional at reading the subtleties of people.
The elderly and wildly successful credit card magnate believed that certain human frailties could actually help fuel success. Insecurity drove
billionaire entrepreneurs. Emotional instability made for superb art.
The need for attention built great political leaders. But anger, in his experience, led only to inertia. He remembered when he'd offered to pay
Rob's tuition at this very event, in this very gymnasium—an offer he'd
never made to any student before or since. As a financial master, Mr.
Cawley looked at the world in terms of investments, of risk and reward.
In 1998, the "investment" in Rob had struck him on paper as one of
the lowest-risk and the highest-return; he saw no possible downside in
giving this rare boy the slight push (Yale's four-year tuition of $140,000
being slight for a bank CEO worth nine figures) he needed to reach
the pinnacle for which he was already headed. Almost a decade later,
as Rob broke off eye contact to gaze down at the floor as if there were
a pit between them, Mr. Cawley understood that a life wasn't lived on
paper. He was not disappointed so much as confused, and he opted not
to inquire further into what exactly had happened to Rob's psyche between Yale graduation and now. He wanted to spare himself the sting
of his own poor judgment. This conversation was the last he ever had
with Rob.

The fact was that Rob hadn't filled out any grad school applications.
He'd been too busy over the last few months poring over real estate information, and all the study had led him to the conclusion that Newark
and the Oranges were not the places to invest in property right now.
Cory Booker's ambitions, predictably, were expensive, and the mayor
had already installed an 8.3 percent hike on property taxes to help pay for
them, the largest such increase in the city's history. From his experience
managing the Greenwood property, he knew that finding tenants with
the credit to make security deposits was hard enough, and extracting
rent from them on time was harder still. Even so, the average property

value remained in the high five figures to low sixes, inflated by their proximity to so many well-off neighborhoods just beyond. Profit margins were thin, and effort expenditure was high. Lenders were hard to deal with, suspicious and often crooked. Jackie had been right: buying property in the neighborhood where he'd grown up was a bad idea. So he looked elsewhere, and he landed on Ohio.

A few of his aunts and uncles lived in and around Cleveland. Rob had visited many times, and he'd seen an opportunity: modest houses on decent plots in diverse working-class neighborhoods where the economy was driven by historically stable manufacturing companies. Newark had been just like that, once, before Rob's time. He'd been making weekend trips to the area to do title research in the records offices, make connections among the lending community, and prospect houses in person. Home values in many of these exurb communities fell as low as the mid five figures. The people who wanted to live there tended to have stable jobs and families. Money was still easy enough to come by. As a starting point for Peace Realty, the location made sense.

But all the traveling had been expensive, and would become more so once he actually established a presence. Rob was naturally frugal; he always had been. He hated paying $300 for a ninety-minute flight, hated renting cars, hated paying more than $100 a night for dingy hotel rooms. Above all, he hated the fact that nine months after having established Peace Realty as his next career move, he hadn't actually accomplished anything—and so he would need a paying job to float him in the interim between leaving St. Benedict's and profiting off his first group of properties.

Rob did end up going on the Appalachian Trail hike early that summer. He took the position in the back of the line to prod the stragglers. He helped with tent setup, cooked beans and rice over campfires, and led circular conversations about goal setting as the logs broke down. Mostly he walked alone through the quiet forest, appearing pensive and often unapproachable. The hike itself was uneventful, one of the easiest they'd ever had. When the bus picked them up at the Delaware Water

Gap, Rob was given a send-off in the form of an ovation and a school T-shirt.

An hour later, the group disembarked on Martin Luther King Jr. Boulevard in downtown Newark, filthy and weary, and the students scattered toward their parents' waiting cars, and the teachers went to the parking garage to head home to their families. Rob lingered in and around the school for a few more hours. He went to the science offices to make sure his stuff was all cleared out. He went to the pool to check his coach's locker and take a shower after ten days on the trail. Then he went, almost immediately, to his new job at the Newark International Airport.

From left to right: Rob Peace, Curtis Gamble, Shariff Upton (one of Rob's high school water polo coaches), Drew Jemison, and Julius "Flowy" Starkes. At house parties like this one in East Orange, the Burger Boyz could travel back to simpler times in high school.

Part V

---◆---

Baggage

Rob visiting Pula, Croatia, for the second time.

Chapter 12

———————◆———————

T HE SKIN OF his face and forearms had darkened to an inky hue.
The sun bore down directly overhead, its heat absorbed by the
asphalt underfoot to the point where the rubber soles of his work boots
softened and began adhering to the ground. At its peak, the temperature
on the tarmac could reach upward of 120°, and the heat became locked
between the blacktop and the haze of thick exhaust fumes firing out
of the jet engines as they endlessly jockeyed around him. Rob's bright
orange vest called to mind his father's prison uniform during those first
three years at Essex County. During the most heavily trafficked hours,
he wore noise-canceling earmuffs, but he preferred not to. In the tall
windows of the terminal one story above, he could see the travelers
waiting for their planes, listening to music or pecking on laptops, young
children with faces pressed against the glass in awe of the massive vehicles that would carry them into the sky. Below the terminal, on ground
level, Rob hefted their distended suitcases, their golf clubs and strollers
and duffels, into the cargo hold.

"Yo, Peace."

"Whassup, Peace?"

"Need you over here, Peace."

His coworkers were almost all men, typically broad men with hoarse
voices who had been doing this work a long time. They had their systems

and their silent language; they knew how to move the bags fast enough
to satisfy the gate attendants upstairs but slowly enough so as not to faint
from exhaustion. A careful efficiency governed their work, a weighing
of the most important commodity in the airport, time, against the most
important commodity of the laborers, stamina. Rob fit in seamlessly,
almost anonymously. He didn't complain—in fact, he rarely spoke at
all on the job. During breaks, he typically read alone in the employee
lounge, or took a cigarette to the subterranean parking lot outside the
terminal set aside for staff smokers. While working, he was strong and
tireless, not susceptible to the general stress that trickled down from
the dispatchers constantly barking from the control tower. Most people
rattled easily at first due to the unceasing chorus of *hurry it up, hurry it up,
hurry it the FUCK up.* Others became mean and irritable. Peace, which
was the name by which he was known, struck others as being very chill;
he was simply there, on time, making sure the work got done but never
putting his personality forward beyond the work. He was the kind of
guy you wanted in this arena, especially in the heat of the 2007 summer:
muggy, stagnant, unrelenting.

"You didn't go to college so you could carry people's luggage," Jackie
said, not sniping necessarily but simply telling him the truth. "You don't
even need a high school diploma to do this job."

Hearing her say this over and over—her jaw set and thrust forward,
her tone objectively observant—was the reason he found himself coming around Chapman Street less and less often since Continental had
hired him. At first he'd replied aggressively with various versions of,
"I'm the one trying to make ends meet around here, and that wasn't
going to happen on a teacher's salary." And these exchanges became
real arguments, the kind that flushed their faces with blood and urged
them harder and deeper into one another's weakest points. Her debating
points were logical and immediate: he was a Yale graduate, a scientist, a
teacher, one who had benefited from the sacrifices of others, so what the
hell was he doing working the lowest-level job in the entire airport? His
were more abstract: he had a plan that one day would make sense to her,

and in the meantime he was a grown man who had the right to make his own decisions—decisions, he was quick to remind her, that had historically turned out well. Then there were the wages, the benefits, the liberation of his mind that the manual labor allowed. In essence, he'd swapped mental wear and tear for physical. When he was a kid, before St. Benedict's or Yale, an airline job would have been seen as a solid career path, as it was for his cousin Nathan. In his evolving view, the fact that he'd gone to those schools and accomplished those things didn't need to complicate what life had once been about: the simplicity of providing for oneself, without expectations. At a certain point, he couldn't explain these feelings to his mother; they came off as defensive, which was a platform Rob hated to stand on.

When her son left, Jackie would sit on the front porch, stewing and chain-smoking in the dusky summer light. Her frustration had little to do with disappointment but rather with fear. She was afraid for her headstrong son, because no matter how articulately Rob spun his circumstances, she knew what almost forty years of manual labor felt like (terrible) and what it earned you (very little). Her son seemed to be belatedly rebelling against all his celebrated accomplishments—as well as the responsibilities inherent in them, the obligation to his own talent. In that rebellion, she saw a young man who was confused and upset that his life wasn't stacking up to be what he and everyone around him had always assumed it would. In short, she saw weakness. Rob's extreme and not always coherent argumentativeness, which deployed in force whenever she brought the subject up, supported her view. His whole life he'd listened to her, whether she was complaining about work or pressing through the tricky economics of paying for high school; by listening in his gentle way, he'd made things okay. He'd been her sounding board, her life partner, her heart. Now, at age twenty-seven, when he should have been thinking about starting his own family, he was sassing her like a child. Whatever future he saw for himself right now, however vividly he saw that future, its images lay beyond the reach of her bewildered eyes, even if those eyes were literally and figuratively shortsighted.

Jackie was almost sixty years old. Though she had never known about Rob's second job, she might have found some solace in the fact that, as he'd done during his last career shift at St. Benedict's, he'd stopped selling drugs for the moment.

In addition to being able to give out buddy passes, Continental employees themselves flew for free on standby—a fundamental component of Rob's short-term plan. He had gotten the job through Nathan, who worked in the control tower as a kind of runway manager, tracking incoming planes and moving the tarmac workers around from gate to gate to accommodate them. Nathan and Rob had recently traveled to Amsterdam together. During that week of excess, Rob had learned that as long as employees logged their monthly quota of 160 hours worked, they could go anywhere at any time. No longer did Rob have to wait for national holidays to make his sorties to Cleveland and Orlando to prospect properties; no longer did he have to hustle in order to afford the tickets. The airline had thousands of employees at Newark International, and the supervisors were generally bottom-line types. The attitude was: get your work done, doesn't matter how. Weeknight shifts were preferred, because there was less runway traffic and the air was cooler, so it was relatively easy for Rob to trade nights for days and weekends, transactions he treated like any other form of dealing. He front-loaded his months with double and even triple shifts so that he could clear space to travel, and to further the cause of Peace Realty.

By the end of his first summer working for Continental, he had narrowed his target neighborhoods down to three in Cleveland and two in south Florida. A $10,000 down payment on a property there would require a monthly mortgage payment of roughly $400. If he could pin down four houses, he would be paying a total of $1,600 each month, which was only marginally more than the house on Greenwood Avenue was bringing in. The challenge was to find properties in relatively good condition so that the renovations wouldn't put him underwater. "I don't need to be replacing no more damn boilers," he said to Tavarus. He'd known that these stipulations would be harder than they sounded, but he didn't know how hard they would actually be.

Most of the available properties Rob could afford had suffered some form of neglect. Even for a middle-class family with steady factory income in Ohio, avoiding maintenance costs was always easier than addressing them. And by the time the family had saved up enough to pay for a major repair, they were probably in a position to move to a better neighborhood anyway. What they left behind were shorted-out lumps of electrical wires stapled into the crawl spaces, rot, rodent and insect infestations, cracked foundations, asbestos and radon and mold, water damage. Rob would spend four-day weekends going from house to house, crouching in the crawl spaces with a flashlight to look at water pipes and gas lines, swearing at the rats. At night, he would mutter on the phone to friends, "How is it possible that not a single fucking person in America knows how to respect a goddamn house?" And on the rare occasion when he did find an ideal property, he would lose it to the competition—real estate prospectors with the exact same idea, who had the benefit of operating locally and with far more liquid cash to invest. At the end of these trips, he would disembark at Newark International, pull his small rolling suitcase through the terminals, and try to ignore the families of hyped-up children leaving for summer vacation, the businessmen in suits walking very fast while thumbing their cell phones, the students with gigantic canvas duffels heading off to college. Often, he would just go straight to work, with two weeks of sixteen-hour days ahead of him to make up for the fruitless ventures.

"It's frustrating as hell," he said in the kitchen at 34 Smith Street in early September. He'd just come home from the airport. Flowy, Curtis, and Tavarus were there, smoking, having their first drinks of the evening over aluminum containers of chicken wings. The first thing Rob did was crack his joints the full length of his body while his friends cringed. *Rat-tat-tat-tat*, endlessly, impossibly, grossly realigning his diarthrodial joints. Then he poured himself a tall vodka with cranberry juice, sat at the table, and took his boots off.

"Well, shit, you thought it would be easy building an empire?" Flowy asked.

Rob shook his head and exhaled. "Just didn't think it would take this long."

Rob hadn't discussed the move to Continental with his friends. He hadn't discussed many decisions at all since he'd taken the St. Benedict's job four years ago.

"Anyway, fuck it," he said, meaning, *Let's talk about something else.*

Tavarus had a son now, named Christopher, who was a year old. The mother was his girlfriend, Darlene. Their living situation was precarious at the moment, crammed into a small one-bedroom in the North Ward of Newark. The baby had been accidental, and they had no plans to get married, but they were both working and seemed happy, above the line of self-sufficiency for the moment. When their own personal topics became grim or redundant, the friends talked about that: the first child born among the Burger Boyz, and a boy no less.

Flowy had been with his girlfriend, LaQuisha, for six years, but they'd been careful about contraception. His foremost reasoning for choosing St. Benedict's had been to avoid getting someone pregnant; childbirth and education were more or less mutually exclusive in the neighborhood where he'd grown up. Now that his education was over, Flowy thought of fatherhood in terms of leaving the hood. He'd seen babies become anchors among many of his friends; the new costs paired with the necessity for proximate family child care rendered moving even a few miles away impossible. Tavarus's situation served as a prime example. Flowy didn't know how he was going to move, but he talked about it often, the dream of getting out of Essex County and settling down someplace where there was space, trees, and no gangs. The problem was that in places like that there were no jobs, at least not for him. There were enough indoor and outdoor pools in Newark for him to be lifeguarding most of the time, and the job required more than CPR training. He also had to keep gang fights from breaking out using skills he'd developed growing up. Where neighborhoods were more spread out and the pools belonged to country clubs, this particular job qualification didn't help him, nor did the dozen-plus tattoos he now wore, many of them the result of "tattoo parties" he sometimes hosted: Matthew 20:7, Psalms 23, and numerous tributes to friends he'd lost.

Curtis's marketing job was secure but promised no upward mobility, and being beholden to corporate types had been grating on him for two years now. In high school and college, he'd been the dynamic center of his social circles, the person others looked to when they wanted to know where to go. He'd been always in motion, planning the nights, planning the weekends, planning the future. Now he worked on a team of public relations people servicing energy companies, which seemed pointless to him, since energy was an inelastic demand and thus had no real need to be promoted. He'd lived in a condo in South Orange for a few years but had ultimately moved back to Smith Street when his mother had moved away; after more than thirty years there, the neighborhood had come to feel too dangerous for her. The house was fully owned, and the economics made enough sense to justify the more precarious environment. He didn't know what his next job should be, just that he was gaining weight, both physically and mentally, in his current job.

They talked in and around these subjects, but mostly they talked about other things—such as their high school years and how theirs had been the best class in the history of St. Benedict's.

They had a good night; each of them felt his various pressures easing off, as always happened when they were sitting at this table in this house: their shared stories, their verbal shorthand, the nonjudgment that was the rule, and the feeling of total seclusion from whatever was going on outside these walls. Though they had congregated at this table less often as the years rolled by, the feeling it gave was vital, knowing that on a random weeknight like this, one or all of them would always be here to download.

The blunt came around to Rob and he passed.

"You're really still worried about that?" Curtis asked. He was referring to the random urine tests at Continental. Rob hadn't smoked since before he started working at the airline, and that helped explain why he'd been so uncharacteristically short-tempered; he'd given up his most effective outlet for stress, could no longer release it from his chest alongside artful plumes of smoke. "C'mon, man, no one's gonna test you. It's just to keep you scared."

"They've tested people," Rob said. "It's real. We're talking about *airplanes.* Big ones. Lots of them. You think they fuck around with that?"

Actually, his friends had been floored when Rob quit smoking marijuana, even more so than they were when he stopped dealing. Rob Peace, who had smoked practically every day since high school, had quit cold turkey. And he'd done so almost imperceptibly, just passing joints and blunts and bowls along when they came to him, saying quietly, "I'm good," or, "I already had," or, "Heading to my ma's house in a few." This meant that he was beyond serious about real estate, and the job that allowed him to pursue it. This was not a whim or a stopgap; this was what he wanted to do. Even when he sounded as he had tonight, pissed off and slightly helpless about repeated setbacks, they didn't worry. For as long as they'd known him, Rob Peace had always achieved what he'd wanted.

In the fall of 2007, just as Rob began to feel that he'd gotten a sense of the hidden intricacies of the real estate market—that when the right property came up, he'd have the wherewithal to get in first with confidence—the housing bubble burst in earnest. Plummeting prices and the mass offloading of property should have been a stroke of luck in the arena in which Rob was trying to operate. In theory, he would be able to grab up the properties even cheaper than they already were, and then wait for the rebound. But along with the fall in prices came the breakdown of the subprime lenders market. And Rob, whose whole business plan hinged on being a good subprime lending candidate himself, learned gradually over the course of the fall that even if he were to find one or more properties that fit his designs, there wouldn't be any money available to him. For the foreseeable future, the holdings of Peace Realty would be limited to one property at 122 Greenwood Avenue. And Rob would be using his free flight benefits less for business and more to travel the world.

* * *

WE TALKED TWO or three times that year. These conversations were typically brief; my soft-spoken, halting voice did not lend itself to cell phones. "Damn, why can't you speak up?" he said more than once.

"I'm trying," I replied. "Can you hear me now?"

He laughed. "You sound like a mouse, same as you did in college."

He talked about all the traveling he'd been doing—Rio again, South Korea, and an aim to visit Croatia soon—but he never told me that the reason he was able to do this was that he worked in the luggage department of an airline. I told him about the release of my novel the previous spring, right around Rob's departure from St. Benedict's.

"Yeah, yeah," he said. "I heard that some magazine was comparing you to *The Great Gatsby* or some shit?"

"That might have been a stretch," I said.

"Look at you, Da Jeffrey, my boy, all famous now."

I just laughed, and as he'd withheld the specific nature of his employment from me, so, too, did I avoid informing him that this novel had sold only a few thousand copies, that my second novel had failed to sell to a publisher on the first go-round, and that, while working insecurely on a third, I was copyediting self-published self-help books in order to pay our rent in Los Angeles. I didn't tell him anything about my life that would suggest I was doing anything other than what I'd always aspired to do. As far as either of us knew at the end of these calls, we were both all good, and always had been.

I asked about Katrina, the girl he'd brought to my wedding. The *psssshhh* sound he made told me what direction that had gone in.

He asked about Rebecca, and I said she was fine.

"She knocked up yet?"

"No. But we're psyched to start a family, we're trying." We'd been trying for two years, in fact, and Rebecca had had three miscarriages. I didn't feel comfortable revealing those troubles, either.

He laughed. "Good luck with all that. Trying's the fun part, from what I've heard."

We ventured no further. The distance between us and the maleness of our friendship precluded revealing anything that truly mattered, and at the time I was too naïve to know that if you were friends with someone—truly friends—then you told him what was going on ("It's called 'catching up,'" my wife informed me when I asked how it was possible for her to yap with her girlfriends for as long as she did and share every innocuous detail of her life). Instead, I thought that by concisely presenting the most easygoing and put-together version of myself, I was being "all good."

Really, I was just fronting. And Rob was doing the same.

*   *   *

"'I'm *starting* TO fucking hate you' . . . Nah, nah, I didn't say that, I didn't say, 'I fucking hate you'—I said, 'I'm *starting* to fucking hate you.'"

Victor and Big Steve looked at each other for a moment, then both of them began hysterically laughing. Rob pinched the phone between his cheek and shoulder in order to raise his arms and give them a helpless, exasperated look, and he mouthed, *I can't believe this bitch.* They were in the small house Victor and Steve shared in Browns Mills, a little over an hour south of Newark. Rob had come to spend the night. Then a girlfriend of his, whom he referred to only as "Philly" (where she lived), called and hassled him about not telling her where he was. The conversation had escalated, as his conversations with women often did. "Female shit," which was what he called pretty much everything women did or said, was one of the few things he had no patience for.

"Thug love," Victor said after Rob finally got off. "That's what I'm going to start calling you." And indeed, that night Victor changed Rob's contact name in his cell phone from "Shawn" to "Thug Love."

His close friends had always been flummoxed by Rob's approach to romantic relationships. He loved women, and he had little trouble getting them to love him. His tell-it-like-it-is approach to humor, for whatever reason, was attractive. ("You're just mad cuz I'm prettier than you," he'd once said to a girl giving him attitude outside an East Orange bar; a few minutes later, he came away with her number.) But once a relationship started, all he did was complain and provoke. He would say he was going to be somewhere, and then he would be somewhere else, and when the irritated call came, he would feign ignorance and improvise creative new ways to make the problem her own fault. Rarely did his friends meet the women with whom he was involved; to parties, he would bring other girls—often unattractive ones, what his friends termed "busted"—whom he cared nothing about. Not many nights passed without a phone call that he would take into the next room while Curtis, Victor, Drew—whatever guys he preferred to hang out with over his girlfriends—overheard him progress through the beats of the same self-wrought arguments, almost as if following a script. Typically, these had to do with time, his lack of it, his inability to respect it. When the relationships ended, as they invariably did, his friends would crack that the girl in question had "been Robbed." Victor traced this pattern back to Zina, his freshman-year girlfriend at Yale. Before she'd broken his heart, Rob had always been shy and hesitant around girls. Afterward, almost instantly, he'd become bold, crass, and too often mean.

"Why do you do this to yourself, man?" Curtis asked him after a particularly vitriolic phone spat with a woman Rob called "Lawyer Girl." "I mean, *damn.*"

"When we're together, it's cool, but when we're not together, she goes crazy."

"So bring her over here sometime."

"Nah, you do *not* want to see what this looks like in person."

Curtis laughed; never did his best friend seem so helpless, so not in control, as he did when a girlfriend called to chew him out. But he was also concerned. He didn't know anyone else who was better equipped to care for women. Rob had his mother and grandmother, of course, whom he doted on religiously even when they'd been fighting about his airline job. He checked in on Raquel Diaz and Daniella Pierce often and listened to their problems with attentive thought if not always with patience. Shannon Heggins, his junior high girlfriend who was now raising a daughter alone, relied on him to bring dinner to her apartment multiple times a week. He had cousins, neighbors, former classmates, so many others whom he took care of devoutly. The fact that Rob could spend so many of his waking hours—the majority, it some- times seemed—tending to the women in his life, and yet he couldn't get through one phone call with a serious girlfriend that didn't bring him to profane heights of frustration, was bewildering. Both his male and female friends egged him on in this regard; they found no end of amusement in seeing Rob Peace, the Man, reduced to a stammering, flailing, one-dimensional sitcom character. And yet they also believed this repetitive playacting embodied a greater struggle inside him, one he refused to discuss. The fact was, he seemed positively determined to stave off anything resembling a functional personal relationship until he reached a place where he could take care of Jackie. And in the fall of 2008, with the housing market stalled and Rob's savings drained once again, that place lay farther and farther away.

"The only thing that will save you," Raquel had told him in her apart- ment one night, "is a good woman."

Rob sipped his Hennessy and smiled, though not the grin she ex- pected, the one that both absorbed and deflected. This smile was fainter, almost wistful. "Girl," he said, "at this point, I wouldn't know what to do with a good woman even if I found one."

Raquel's belly was round and her skin glowed. Six months earlier, a two-day bender had found her in the bathroom of a friend's apartment on the Upper West Side, peering into a mirror as blood crept from both her nostrils. Her friends were all asleep, and she had scraped up the dregs of the party powder, trying to figure out how she might cram another spoonful of cocaine up past the source of the bleeding, thinking, *If you're going to do this, then you have to watch yourself do this*. She did watch herself, then stemmed the blood flow with toilet paper and continued. At four or five that morning, in a cab on the way back to East 119th Street, it oc- curred to her through the haze that she could conceivably have died at some point during the last forty-eight hours. Simon was sitting calmly on their futon. By now the home renovations were finished, and their apartment was modern and roomy. He hadn't heard from her the whole time she'd been out. She started weeping in front of him, certain that he was about to tell her to leave both the room and his life. Instead, he said in his calm, steady, devoted voice that contained a love she suddenly knew how to receive, "Where've you been, baby? I missed you."

"I'm sorry," she replied. "I have to slow down. I have to change. I have to stop."

"Don't be sorry. I'm glad you're home."

She nodded, wiping constantly at her numbed nose, and sat beside him. Simon had never been a physically emotive man, but now he put his arm around her and savored the press of her head against his shoulder.

Ten days later, she learned that she was seven weeks' pregnant. In November 2007, she gave birth to Felix Rodriguez, a healthy ten-pound boy. Ten days after that, Raquel and Simon were married at City Hall.

In the meantime, Rob had become involved with Inayra Sideros, her aunt.

Ina was only a year older than Raquel, whose mother's and grandmother's pregnancies had overlapped by a month. She had penetrating eyes and olive skin. Her thick, dark dreadlocks fell below her waist. Rob had met her in 2003, when she'd come to New York to visit Raquel. He'd keyed in on her immediately, but not with any of his worn-out lines. Raquel had noticed the spark, and in the same way that Rob had subtly arranged her own first night with Simon, she returned the favor in kind by asking Rob to show Ina around New York. He'd taken her to a restaurant in Manhattan, then to a few parties in Newark. He employed the same gentle mannerisms with which he treated his platonic female friendships, and that's how they related to each other for the first four years of their relationship: friends, what Rob was best at being. During that time, he'd been teaching at St. Benedict's while she worked as an office assistant at a plastic surgery practice in Miami, and they kept in touch over the phone. Now that he worked for Continental and an airplane was akin to a taxi, he traveled down to see her all the time beginning in the fall of 2007.

He would call her on a Friday evening, just off his shift at the airport, and say, "I'm thinking of rolling by—you around to chill?" Three or four hours later, after walking off a flight, he'd show up at her door and, once she let him in, head straight to her couch, sinking in deep, with a protracted exhale. They spent a lot of time in silence, each enjoying the proximity of the other. His dreadlocks fell a quarter of the way down his back now, and they would compare the density of the hair, the consistency of the braids. Sometimes they would drive to South Beach for a party, or simply to sit in the sand and watch the light from all the beachfront hotel towers play off the dark water. The visual reminded him of Rio, which he spoke of all the time: his friends down there, the attitudes, the career opportunities he would have if he were to make a permanent move. When Ina had met him, he'd been a teacher recently graduated from Yale. Now that his résumé seemed less compatible, Ina had been prepared for him to become something of a basket case, a lost and angry soul burdened by his upbringing and quick to blame it for any and all problems he had. She knew plenty of tiresome guys like that in the barrios of Dade County, and she wasn't eager to import another one from Newark. But the man she came to know intimately didn't meet this expectation. He talked about those aspects of his life—the poverty, the single parent, the dangers and influences of the streets—but he did so casually, laughing often along the way. These elements of his youth were certainly a part of him, but as a birthmark rather than a scar. To her, he just seemed like a good guy who was trying to figure it all out and having a little trouble along the way; he seemed thoughtful, confident, and above all hopeful. Ina had her own struggles with having grown up poor and surrounded by people who seemed intent on remaining that way, and when Rob spoke about where they were now and where they could be in the future, some of his optimism seemed to waft out of him along with the streams of marijuana smoke, and then drift gently downward onto her.

"You're cool, girl," he said, lying beside her, no Thug Love present in this moment.

She inhaled his scent and replied in kind, thinking about a life with this man. He'd spoken about graduate school and various academic career paths—spoken around them, mostly. "Teaching's easy for me," he said, "because I just know the shit." She visualized him giving a lecture in front of a college auditorium filled with rapt twenty-year-old science nerds. Often, the image would make her laugh gently, and Rob would say, "What the fuck?" and she would reply, "Nothing, nothing." The life he had in store seemed to her a good one, and she hoped to be a part of it.

And yet, as they became more intimate, he gradually became more elusive. He'd say he was boarding a plane and then fail to show up. He wouldn't return her calls, sometimes for weeks. By the winter of 2008, he was spending more time in Miami than ever but seeing less of her. The situation did not lead to the fierce confrontations to which Rob was accustomed, and which he at times seemed intent on baiting from her. Though "Aunt" Ina was twenty-nine years old, she was mature; her maturity was what had drawn him to her, the way her attitude transcended her age, and she could smoke weed and party but still seem to float above the life-stalling whimsy that marked most days. She and Rob had talked hypothetically about being together, how easy that would be. But they'd made no promises, and she refused to become possessive. Her concern for him trumped any ownership she was inclined to feel, and she had enough experience to know that voicing concern to a man like Rob invited nothing but anger in return.

Rob had his own friends in Miami now. Some of them she knew, some she knew of, some she didn't want to know. They were hustlers of the particular variety bred in Miami, where marine passageways to Cuba and Mexico made the business as cold-blooded and fraught—and opportunistic—as anywhere else in the country. She'd grown up directly adjacent to this commerce. Simply by virtue of geography she'd known men who had turned up savagely gutted in hotel rooms and Everglades swamps. She knew other men, some of them related to her by blood, serving long prison sentences. In a city like Miami, where that brand of easy money was always so tantalizingly close, the obstacles to living an honest life were hard to overcome. Ina had not been above dealing marijuana herself from time to time, in a courier capacity, which was basically what Rob became that winter: a courier of bulk marijuana, using his flight privileges the way locals used cars.

The transits usually began with a trip to Overtown or Liberty City, where weed was plentiful and so, according to the laws of economics, cheap. He'd pick up two tightly wrapped cellophane cylinders of weed, no more than a pound each. These he would surround with a layer of lavender and other pungent herbs, also tightly wrapped, and then bind them in gift-wrapping paper, complete with a bow that he would coil prettily with the swipe of a scissors blade. He would stuff these parcels into his high-top Timberland boots, the same style as those he'd worn at Mt. Carmel and made illegal at St. Benedict's, and plug them with wads of dirty socks. At the airport, where he'd acquainted himself with many of the security workers through his frequent trips, he would make sure he was traveling during a friend's shift at the scanner station (because he flew standby, he could time his flights freely). He would chat these people up on his way through and complain about how he had to cut his trip short because of some bullshit at Newark International—bitching about airline bureaucracy being everyone's favorite topic. And he would pass through and board his plane. In Newark, he'd drop off the packages with one of his old connects and pocket the difference, typically in the range of $500 for the two pounds and maybe two hours of actual "work." The risks had never been higher, now that they included the FAA and DEA. He assumed these risks casually.

"What the hell are you doing?" Ina asked, watching him wrap the drugs in green and gold wrapping paper dotted with pictures of streamers and pointed hats.

"Gotta get my money right," was all he said, and he smiled at her, and the smile was dangerous, unconcerned and affable, the kind of smile that had landed ex-boyfriends of hers in jail.

"Explain to me how this is worth it."

"Let's just not talk about 'worth it.' Okay?"

She knew about Jackie, about Frances, even about his father. Indeed, she'd spent a night drinking with Rob in Newark the day after Skeet's funeral and had been indelibly touched by his grace in the wake of tragedy. She didn't bother bringing them up, inviting him to justify his actions with the mathematics of his family. She already knew how skilled he was at performing this equation. Like most people in his orbit, she had never won a debate with him. She had her own baggage that she'd been dealing with for years and that Rob had helped her deal with through dozens of hours of talk. What she knew, and what she couldn't believe Rob didn't know, was that problems such as theirs, problems that traced back generations and involved far more than money (though money was often their emblem), would never be solved with $500 every two weeks.

But Rob, whom she loved, had a plan. He always had a plan—a plan for the day, a plan for the year, a plan for his life. He rendered these plans simply, using ground-level details, and he tied his decisions to them tightly. When he talked through the path he planned to take from this moment to graduate school, with the flailing real estate market in between, his plans almost—*almost*—made sense. But the risks he took for the profit he made, from a big-picture standpoint, seemed only obliquely related to those plans. And Ina gradually understood that Rob didn't seem capable of seeing the big picture, the way he had when they'd first met. He trafficked almost exclusively in the day-to-day: this shift at work, this flight, this city, this transaction, this chunk of money. No matter how skillfully he was able to string these moments together and stretch them into future years, he nevertheless struck her as inextricably lodged within the minute in which he was living.

And never more so than when he asked for her help in a new venture, which involved guns.

*　　*　　*

DARLENE, TAVARUS'S GIRLFRIEND, unwrapped Rob's gift for their son's second birthday in March 2008. Christopher was light skinned and thick haired and wiry like his dad. Rob, who had been named Christopher's godfather, gave him a full-size dirt bike.

Tavarus laughed. "It's a little big for the little man."

"He'll grow into it. Do you know how many hours it took me to put that thing together?"

"Thank you," said Darlene, and she made a little show of propping the boy up on the bike seat, his feet dangling six inches above the pedals.

They were in the backyard of 34 Smith Street. Rob had three seasoned pork loins roasting on the grill at low heat, his specialty, a dish he'd brought home from Rio. A tall clear plastic tank of vodka punch perched on the fold-out table beside the grill, to which Rob had helped himself many times. About two dozen people were milling around the driveway, beside the vegetable garden Curtis planted each year, wishing Christopher a "happy born day." Neighbors popped in and out, young teenagers who had been not much older than Christopher when the Burger Boyz had first begun congregating here to study and hang out. Then, these kids had been little energy bundles running away from their mothers down the street, laughing gleefully while the women sprinted after them shouting, *"Get back here right now—you don't DO this to your mama!"* Now they were almost young men, wearing ribbed tank tops and skullies and tripped-out footwear. Some of them dressed in red, the color of the Double II Sets. The elderly ladies who'd watched Rob play street football behind their fans seemed not to have aged at all in the past fifteen years. Music blared: Young Jeezy and 2 Chainz and Drake. *"Fuckin'* songs," one of the children called them, due to the explicit lyrics, prompting laughter all around. *"Fuckin'* is *not* nice."

Everyone was happy to have Rob there, because he often missed events like these, the celebrations that marked the passage of time. Sometimes he would disappear for two or three weeks straight, telling no one where he was going, and the lives of his friends would adjust to his absence, reducing him to the occasional, "I wonder what he's doing right now?" and the invariable response, which fell along the lines of, "Getting head on a beach somewhere while smoking a big fat blunt, no doubt." Then he would suddenly reappear, walking in the front door of Smith Street and heading straight for the Smirnoff on top of the refrigerator. He'd make himself a drink, sit, and launch back into the last conversation he'd had before he'd taken off, about music or the neighborhood or a girl. He'd been to Seoul, Amsterdam, Berlin, Madrid, Tokyo, Croatia, and places they couldn't remember. He was always at his most peaceful before leaving on one of these sojourns, always at his most restless and uneasy upon his return. He'd put off graduate school applications for another year and now was talking about the fall of 2009 as a start date. Real estate remained his go-to topic when talk turned to the future, but very few of his travels had anything to do with Peace Realty. No one understood why he was screwing things up with Ina; she had visited more than once, partied here on Smith Street, and was the coolest girl Rob had ever met.

A month after Christopher's birthday party, Rob woke up naked in a one-room corrugated aluminum lean-to high in one of Rio's favelas. His wallet and clothes were gone. He had no memory of the night before; it had begun with a woman, and his recollection ended with hopping on a bus with her. His head ached, but he thought clearly enough to check his abdomen for sutures to make sure his kidneys were where they should be; black market organ transplants were big business in Brazil. He found clothes and made his way down the maze of narrow alleyways to the city proper, thankful that he hadn't been carrying his passport that night. It was April. He would turn twenty-eight in two months.

When he came home a few days later, having cut his trip short, he said to Jackie, "Ma, I am going to get it right, I am going to take care of you."

To her, these words seemed like a plea more than a promise, and to himself more than to her.

"I don't need you to," she replied. "I never have. Don't you go worrying about me. Take care of yourself. I just want you happy foremost, and I want you around if it works that way. I want you settled."

Jackie was fine. She supervised the kitchen now. She had her own office at the nursing home. She was off her feet. She had TV shows she liked to watch in the evenings. She had a pension and was set to retire in three or four years. After that, she had her own plans, just like her son: she wanted to travel and see for herself a couple of the places Rob was always going on about. She was confused by all this talk of buying her a house. She'd lived at 181 Chapman Street for almost fifty years. She'd been poor for the same amount of time. That was the life she knew, and she was more or less content with it. She didn't understand how her strong, bright boy could bring himself such discouragement trying to change what she had; she didn't understand why he couldn't hear her on the rare instances she'd tried to explain it to him.

Jackie hadn't been present at the Unknown Sons meeting when Rob had told a student that he couldn't worry about fixing other people, he could only worry about himself. If she had been, maybe she would have repeated those words to him now.

"Go back to school," was all she could say, in her soft, understated manner. "That's what I want to see. That's where you've always done your best."

Chapter 13

◆

"I CAN SELL ANYTHING."

Rob's face was low to the wooden table, across from Hrvoje. His eyes projected a rare intensity, as he considered his visits to Pula, Croatia, some of the most relaxing weeks of his life. They'd spent most of the day on Hrvoje's father's small skiff, just cruising along the rocky coast of the Istrian peninsula. Tall, jagged stone cliff faces dropped into the aquamarine water and cast dramatic shadows beneath them. The temperature was in the mid-70s, and the clouds were wispy and dissipating. Hrvoje steered while Rob, wearing shorts, a white T-shirt, and flip-flops, rode in the bow, leaning forward like a kid trying to get ahead of the craft, his loosely bound dreadlocks fanning across his upper back. Hrvoje had grown up here, where the beauty of his coastal hometown belied the violence surging across the rest of his country as well as the collapse of its currency, the combination of which had impelled his relocation to Newark. He'd motored past these cliffs hundreds of times; their majesty had not dulled, and there was something vital in watching Rob Peace watch the scenery, drinking it through his eyes like an elixir, the muscles of his arms and back gradually loosening, his expression serene.

Tonight, at an old-fashioned bar near the city center, his expression was very different: ominous and astray.

Hrvoje knew about the drugs; he always had. But Rob was talking about something else, something Hrvoje had a feeling he didn't want to know about. He'd simply asked what Rob's next step was, assuming he wasn't going to work on the tarmac for the rest of his life. He'd expected more murmured, probably empty talk of graduate school. The place Rob went to, the sinister energy in his eyes, caught Hrvoje off guard. Since their first interaction talking about prog rock, he had rarely felt uncomfortable around his friend.

He said, "Rob, what are you *doing*?"

"Just some movements going on, to get me to the next thing."

"No," Hrvoje replied. "I don't want to know about it. I'm saying, you don't have to *do* any of this stuff. Don't you get that?"

Rob smiled and shook his head. He leaned back, drank from his beer stein, and reverted to his usual, disarming self. "Anyway . . ."

Hrvoje lived with his wife, Marina, in an apartment in Union, about forty-five minutes west of East Orange. He was ambivalent about living in New Jersey and pined for his home country, but he had a good job with a Croat-based shipping company that sent him home often enough. Every now and then as the years went by, he would trek to the hood to hang out with the Burger Boyz on Smith Street. He knew that even driving the half mile back to the I-280 after midnight was not smart, but he also knew from experience how to sustain the right kind of awareness. Seeing old friends and laughing about high school was worth the risk. More often, Rob would visit him in Union, always seeming glad to get out of his neighborhood for a night. He'd sit at their kitchen table with Marina and drink grappa and ask about their homeland before ultimately passing out on their couch. From these many nights had sprung the idea of tagging along on one of Hrvoje's trips home.

Unlike the ethnic buffet of Rio, Croatia didn't have a minority population to speak of. Rob could go entire trips without encountering anyone of color. Partly because of that, he became something of a celebrity in Pula, a town of sixty thousand complete with ancient stadium ruins in its center. The culture was embedded in every natural and architectural surface, and when residents saw a person like Rob Peace wandering around aimlessly, they didn't want to call the police—they wanted to talk to him, share their stories, hear his. To him, the place had no negativity, no fear or suspicion or territoriality, and hardly any crime. People were generally happy and curious and self-sufficient. Considering the recent history of the country, Rob was in awe of the energy that characterized Pula, the absence of hostility.

The draw heightened when he met Lana Kasun. She was just shy of six feet tall, with a perfect angular face, tan skin, and sun-streaked blond hair. She was Marina's cousin, a fashion model in Croatia, and also, soon enough, what could be loosely termed as Rob's girlfriend. Days with her were easy, because of the slight language barrier, and because she was an independent spirit, free from the manic, possessive qualities he saw in so many women back home. She treated the world, and Rob, in a spritely way, day-to-day-centric, and with minimal knowledge of where he came from for these visits. In heels, she towered over him, and at the taverns she would do little pirouettes and then fall into his lap with her long, languid arms laced around his neck. Nobody had ever been able to drink Rob under the table, but Lana could at least keep up.

A week into his first visit, he told Hrvoje that he would move here someday and began talking about some scheme he'd conceived of to sell ice makers here, since no one seemed to have them.

*   *   *

"NO, ROB," INA SAID. "Fuck no."

For over a year, he and Ina had been going to a local gun range in her neighborhood in Biscayne. They would wear the earmuffs and line up in adjacent slots to have accuracy contests. They would whoop and taunt one another throughout the shooting practice, the sharp scent of gunpowder filling their nostrils. In the fall of 2008, Rob convinced her to obtain a legal gun license. She didn't understand why; guns and legality were not often linked in her neighborhood, and she had no desire to own one anyway.

"Who knows when you might need it?" he'd replied. "Gets heavy where you live, and you don't have an alarm. I worry."

"Don't worry about me." Still, he'd made some kind of sense, and she'd gone ahead and gotten a license, with no intention of actually buying a gun.

Then, very casually a few weeks later, Rob made a proposition: he'd give her the money to buy a few handguns in the $300 range, and she would then file a claim saying the guns had been stolen. In the meantime, he would sell them on the black market in Newark for double the price.

A strange alchemy of confusion and anger coalesced within her, seeing how he had manipulated her over the last few months, edging her toward qualifying for gun ownership in the form of fun and protection, interspersing this with increasingly grave stories about his grandmother's health expenses, and then putting her in the position of having to choose between his need for money and her own historically malleable morality.

Over the past two years, she'd helped him network drug contacts around Miami. She hadn't been involved in any commerce beyond those introductions, and she hadn't thought twice about it. Marijuana was easy to compartmentalize as harmless, safer in many ways than cigarettes, an organic substance that offered a peaceful escape to a lot of people who depended on just that. Rob could be shady about that aspect of his life, and she'd come to feel that dealing was more of an addiction, or at least a habit, than the actual consumption of the drug. But he'd always protected her from what he did and had never seemed in over his head; he'd never put himself in a position from which he couldn't also extricate himself.

Guns were on the extreme opposite side of the spectrum. Guns were cold, hard objects whose sole purpose was lethality. Without the threat of death, a gun was useless. So she told him no and, additionally, to get the fuck away from her. He did not respond with anger, as she half expected. He didn't attempt to reason her around to his perspective. He just nodded and said, "It's all good," and they resumed their day.

For the next few Miami visits, she remained wary around him. She didn't want to ask whether he'd found someone else to buy guns for him, but she desperately wanted him to confirm that he hadn't, that her reaction had driven some increasingly needed good sense into him. She called a few of his friends in Newark and angled in loosely on the subject. No one had heard anything about gun dealing on his part. But that didn't necessarily mean anything; Rob was good at nothing if not keeping his life compartmentalized.

She had known him for six years now and was familiar with all of his triumphs and setbacks and dreams. She was also familiar with the fact that very few people in the world had the options that he had. She'd certainly known people, like her niece Raquel, who had come from difficult circumstances and gotten out of them spectacularly. In most cases, a definitively benign force had been present to enable the rise. Raquel's mother had driven her fiercely to do well in school, such that high academic prowess had been the only option. Others had come upon money by luck, or had relatives acting as patrons. Rob had had none of those things. All he'd had was a home, and a harried home at that, paired with his own drive. What he'd achieved, he'd achieved almost exclusively on his own. And now he was throwing it all away on his own, too; he was focusing that unstoppable drive on the very thing that could ultimately stop him.

Her heart ached over the fact that Rob's life had come to this, and that he—the smartest and most expansive person she knew—failed to see the wrongness therein. The sheer stupidity that she was watching bloom in these increments took root in Ina's head throughout that fall of 2008 and led to much self-reflection—and ultimately to an option she'd always considered but never taken seriously.

That fall, Ina cut off her dreadlocks and enlisted in the navy. With her education, enlisting felt like the single permanent exit from the cycle of crime and immobility to which her relationships seemed inextricably linked, a link that was clarified by Rob's desperate and dangerous behavior. The fact that her friend and sometime lover was trying to smuggle firearms made the decision an easy one.

"There are three ways out of the world we grew up in," Raquel told her aunt in an attempt to lessen the drama surrounding her decision. "I went domestic. You're going military."

"What's the third?" Ina asked.

"The third is Rob's way," Raquel replied.

When Rob saw Ina for the last time, in early January 2009, she was wearing her uniform under her combed shoulder-length hair. He whistled. "You look good all decked out."

"Don't make fun of me. This is hard. You know how much I cried seeing my hair on the floor?"

"I'm not making fun. I'm proud of you." She could see that he was sincere.

"I just want to change my life."

"You're doing what you got to. I understand completely."

He gave her a strong hug before he left, first to make a pickup in Liberty City, then to get on a plane back to Newark. Three months later, after boot camp was complete, Ina went to Afghanistan.

Before she left, she said to Rob over the phone, "You know what? I pray for you. I pray that you'll be okay." She'd built up courage to voice these words.

"No, I pray for you," he replied.

"I'll be fine."

At roughly the same time that Ina shipped overseas, in the spring of 2009, Rob was promoted at Continental, from luggage to the super tug crew, driving the small but powerful vehicles—really just engines with two seats carved out—that towed the planes between gates and runways. Senior managers at the airline had approached him a few times about moving to a better-paying and upwardly mobile administrative position where his résumé could be applied to better use; he'd always declined. Admin meant a desk. A desk meant a chair. A chair meant the end of his travels. But the super tugs appealed; the work was more stressful, but it paid better and big chunks of each shift were spent idling on the runway with his head buried in a book, waiting for clearance from dispatchers.

Aside from Jackie, no one had asked Rob any serious questions about what exactly he was doing. If friends or family made an attempt, he would cut them off with opaque allusions to a larger plan, or even with a look that seemed to say, *I'm the one who went to Yale, so trust me, I know what I'm doing.* But his cousin Nathan, even though he'd helped Rob procure his original job at Continental, confronted him after the promotion. "Shawn," he said, "if you keep going on like this, you're going to be working for me the rest of your life. And there's something wrong with that." Rob just shrugged.

During one work shift, he was paired with Julio Vega, the captain of the thirty-person tug crew. Rob was famous now for the effort he invested in traveling; in twelve years working at the airline, Julio figured he had traveled maybe a quarter of the amount that Rob had in his first twelve months. But other than that, he remained largely an unknown. He was fun to ride the super tug with, because of his jokes, but his presence brought a weight into the cramped vehicles, an uncomfortable reserve that made you feel like you'd better watch what you say. That quality could make eight hours feel like an awfully long time. Julio was reading a how-to book about financial planning. He glanced over at Rob's book, tucked discreetly on the far side of his lap. He saw a page filled with what looked like math problems, but with letters and rune-like symbols where numbers should have been, alongside complicated geometric shapes.

"What the hell are you reading?" Julio asked.

"P-chem," Rob mumbled, turning the book away. "Physical chemistry."

"Why?"

"Just trying to stay up to speed, you know."

"Peace, who the fuck are you?"

Before the dispatcher told them to move again, Julio learned where Rob had gone to college and that he'd been a science teacher. Rob told him to keep that on the down low, but Julio couldn't help propagating the news—it was too damn strange, funny even. A low-key movement began to start calling him the "Professor," like his preschool teachers once had. The glare Rob gave in response cut the effort off at the head

with the surety of a guillotine. Then they called him Peace again and let
him read his books without hazing.

"I don't get it, if I'd gone to Yale, I'd be fucking *proud* of it. I'd be telling *everyone.*" Rob and Lisa Wingo were in the smoking section of the
garage, both freezing. Lisa worked at the check-in gates. She was five
one and stout, and she spoke fast and constantly. When she wasn't talking, she was laughing. They'd become friends when Rob had said, "You
don't shut the fuck up much, do you?"

"I'm a single mother of a girl in middle school. If I shut the fuck up,
she'll start talking and I'll never get a word in again."

When their shifts coincided, they'd have a drink afterward at a bar
near the airport called Terminal One. He came by her apartment in
Elizabeth fairly often and helped her daughter, Dawn, with homework.
The girl was as sassy as they came, but when Rob was around, she would
just stare fawningly at him while he guided her through fifth-grade
reading lists and simple division. Like his father, Rob insisted on proper,
legible handwriting. After bedtime, Rob would stay and drink and watch
TV and usually sleep on the couch. He called Lisa "Oompa Loompa"
for her particular shape; she called him "Predator" for his dreadlocks
(the same name he'd divined for Ty's girlfriend in college). He brought
food, checked in often on the phone, and in many ways filled the gaping
absence left by her daughter's father. Rumors began among the smokers
that they were dating. "I could never date that man," Lisa replied. "We
both like to needle each other too much. But someone should—he sure
as hell is nice to have around."

More than a few workers at the airport talked behind Rob's back, with
a thick sense of schadenfreude, about the fact that a Yale grad had no
business doing what he did, that he was taking a good job from someone
who actually needed it, that his aloof demeanor was tied to the smug-
ness of thinking he was better than everyone else, that he must be some
kind of fuckup to have ended up where he was. Lisa knew that Rob was
not smug, and she wanted to believe that this place was not where he'd
ended up but rather where he was starting out. Tomorrow, or the day
after that, or sometime very soon, he'd be gone, doing something far

beyond the limited minds in the employee smoking area of Newark International. She looked forward to telling the "haters" what exactly that something was.

She wondered often why he involved himself in her life, why he seemed so motivated to take care of her. She knew he had other responsibilities, his mother, his house, his vast network of friends and family, his long nights dealing drugs, his travel. But very few days passed without at least a text, even if that text originated in Croatia. Most men she'd known, both romantic and platonic, followed the same pattern of being around only until a more attractive situation than the single mother of a plucky adolescent living in an airport-adjacent neighborhood presented itself. Rob wasn't drawing any tangible benefit from her; she wasn't much of a cook, and he certainly wasn't getting laid. Aside from her sense of humor that aligned closely with his, the transaction, as it were, felt lopsided. But still the months passed, and his affection for her family, if anything, grew—as did the weight that seemed to press always downward on his broad shoulders. And Lisa realized that Rob did mine value from her, and that evenings spent in her messy apartment doing fifth-grade homework and watching sitcom reruns were an escape for him. An escape from what, exactly, he would never let her know.

Oswaldo Gutierrez knew. He was almost finished with med school at Penn, and he'd seen Rob plenty over the last few years, as Rob would loop through Philadelphia after visits to the Raymond brothers in Browns Mills. For the most part, these visits were easy. Together for a night, they could smoke and chill and just talk, complaining some, commiserating, thinking out loud. But as 2009 began, Oswaldo noticed a circular aspect to Rob's speech and manners, a narrowing of vision in a man who, in college, had been more curious and knowledgeable than seemingly any of the five thousand Yale undergraduates surrounding him. Like the planes that circled above the airport when the ground crew caused runway delays, he fell into a holding pattern of carping about his life while hunched over a joint on Oswaldo's sofa: tenants, rent, Carl, women, work, money, even his mother. His laments were small and tiresome—*this motherfucker . . . that motherfucker . . . I'm so tired of all this stupid-ass shit, man*—and yet they instilled a deep sadness in Oswaldo as he, in the analytical way of the psychiatrist he was studying to become, isolated the man he had first encountered at Yale and placed him alongside the one bemoaning the annoyances of his life here, now, seven years later.

Oswaldo had been there for Rob through all of the experiences that now separated those two versions of the same man, and unlike most of Rob's current friends, he was linked into the space that college inhabited in Rob's psyche. He could trace the many events and patterns that, though sometimes innocuous in the happening, had accumulated with a rigid scientific surety to produce this man, whose generosity and intelligence were matched only by his flaws.

"All I'm asking for is some numbers. Nothing on you. Just people to call."

Rob was asking Oswaldo for drug contacts in Philadelphia, perhaps classmates of his who smoked, so that he could hustle there.

"Get the fuck out," Oswaldo replied. He opened the door.

"Damn," Rob said. "So it's like this now?"

"Yeah," Oswaldo replied. "It's like this."

And Rob left, rolling his eyes like this scene was just part of a comedy in which he was the focal point of the farcical behavior of those around him. And Oswaldo understood now with a clarity he'd never had before that all of Rob's troubles were self-inflicted—that on Yale graduation day Rob had stood within reach of everything he now didn't have. Maybe Yale hadn't guaranteed fame and wealth and general greatness, but it had ensured, at the very least, stability. Oswaldo had never been as smart as his friend, but he'd sorted his life out with the same odds against him. He was six months from earning an MD and had a probable job waiting for him near Boston counseling abused youths. He'd figured it out. And Rob was still clinging, after all these years, to the idea of being the Man. Oswaldo was no longer interested in seeing what that looked like up close.

*   *   *

TY CANTEY'S DAUGHTER, Akira, was tottering around on the hardwood floor of our dining room in West Hollywood, giggling as she repeatedly attempted to grab hold of our dog's ears.

"Have you heard from Rob lately?" I asked.

Ty, sitting beside his wife, Raina, leaned back and said with low-key regret, "I really haven't, man. It's hard to keep track of him, you know? Because he's always traveling, and he's always changing his fucking phone number."

"Is he on Facebook?" Rebecca asked.

Ty laughed. "Rob would *never* join Facebook. That would be funny, though."

"If you track down his number, would you text it to me?" I asked. "I haven't seen that guy since our wedding."

"That was a fun wedding," Ty said. (I had already roasted him with the story of my bachelor party, when we'd been standing on a street corner debating what to do next, and Ty had made the decision for everyone by saying, "I took the *Fung Wah bus* down here, motherfucker, and I am going to see some *titties*.")

"Not as fun as yours," Rebecca replied. Ty and Raina had had a Hare Krishna ceremony in her hometown of Kansas City, and we recalled the white man, bald except for a two-inch-long gray ponytail, singing endless verses of *"Hare hare kriiiishnaaaa"* as a stall tactic since Ty, when the wedding was supposed to begin, had still been back at his in-laws' house in his underwear, looking for a tie.

Ty and his family were in Los Angeles for Raina's fifth-year reunion at USC, and we'd had them over for dinner at our small one-bedroom. We felt oddly grown-up, having a dinner party with my old roommate: late-night eater of soy burgers, wearer of FUBU, now on the verge of becoming a real doctor. He'd opted out of the PhD component of his degree so he could get out of school and start earning money. Raina, a beauty and a pistol whom he'd met at Harvard Medical School, was pregnant with their second daughter (though that apparently hadn't stopped her from hip-hop dancing for hours at the reunion the night before). I noticed my wife beside me staring at Raina's belly. Attention had already been paid to that particular element, with congratulatory embraces, the females talking about morning sickness and maternity clothes, Ty looking shell-shocked as he tried to imagine a near future surrounded by three women, two of them under twenty months old. I knew very well the unavoidable gloom welling up in my wife, however; after three miscarriages and many tens of thousands of dollars of credit card debt run up for fertility treatments, she had a hard time being in close proximity to people who bore children effortlessly, by accident. The concept of getting "knocked up" was one that my wife would never know.

Life was supposed to be easier. This current ran beneath all our laughter about college and weddings and pregnancy, and it rose to the surface when I mentioned that my second novel had failed to find a publisher—more than two years of work, wasted—and that my third was losing steam (I mentioned this self-effacingly, with a shrug and a smile that suggested old clichés of the journey, not the destination, being what mattered). The side gigs I took copyediting self-published books that would never be read barely contributed to our income, let alone our future that we hoped would involve children. The current rose again when Ty tried to explain the economics of his and Raina's career trajectory: the half million dollars of student debt they now carried between them, the unlikelihood of being placed in residencies in the same city when they graduated, the ultimate aim to open a dermatology practice in Kansas City, so her family could help with child care, which would be difficult because the market there was saturated. We weren't speaking out of self-pity so much as presenting facts, and though none of us mentioned it outright, the facts spoke of something alarming about the world in which we lived and the generation we were a part of: among the four of us we shared over twenty years of education at Ivy League schools, and we were all motivated and hard-working, and none of us were currently able to make life function beyond the short term. As Ty said at one point near the end of dinner, "It's like, *what the fuck?*"

As they left with their daughter, we swore that we would figure out some way to have a reunion with Rob. He was missed that night.

"What would Rob have told us during the pity party?" I asked.

"Rob would have told us to quit being a bunch of bitches," Ty replied.

Before we went to bed later, Rebecca told me, "Make sure you follow up on that reunion with Rob."

"Sure, sure," I replied.

"Seriously, you should do that. It's not right that you haven't seen him in three years."

"I know."

But like so many promises made to oneself, that, too, was quickly forgotten.

*   *   *

ROB AND TAVARUS, after many months of loose-ended talk, came up with a new vision for Peace Realty, which involved the Section 8 housing program in the city. Tavarus knew all about this domain, having grown up in and around its living spaces. In his admittedly biased opinion, the program was nothing more than a scam in which suburban landlords charged the city of Newark premium rents so that struggling families could live in severely neglected apartments. In the meantime, the Great Recession had begun to wreak havoc on the outlying neighborhoods. Just as Jackie had noticed the For Sale signs sprouting weedlike around Newark during the white flight of the '60s and '70s, Tavarus and Rob witnessed a new flourishing of abandoned, foreclosed homes. The encroaching blight was personal to them. These were the blocks they called home. They watched as properties—seven or eight in a block in the poorest stretches—first went dark in the windows, then were stapled with red-inked city housing forms, then grew waist-high weeds in the yard now surrounded by a chain-link fence, then had the windows smashed—by homeless people looking for shelter, or junkies looking for a place to shoot up, or looters scavenging pipes and appliances to sell for scrap—and then, in the final throes of this slow demise, had coffinlike boards replace the windows. The process affected them deeply, particularly when they'd known the former occupants, which they often did, and more so when those occupants had children, which they often had.

In their imaginings, the city would sell Peace Realty a few of these abandoned homes at a wholesale rate in the neighborhood of $20,000. They would themselves invest an additional $15,000 to $20,000 in renovations to bring them to a suitable standard far above the Section 8 code requirements. Once fixed up, they would sell these holdings back to the city at around $50,000 to $75,000, still below market rate, and the properties would be incorporated into the Section 8 program as owned homes rather than rented apartments. The way they saw it, the city would be saving money overall by not having to pay premium rents, a few families would have a chance for stability, and Rob and Tavarus would be making anywhere between $10,000 and $25,000 profit—a negligible amount for a typical real estate firm but a life-changing income for the Burger Boyz. If the first round turned out successfully, they would have leverage to expand the enterprise, and soon they would be making six figures a year. That was a career, and one they could feel good about.

Tavarus was trying to earn a proper living. He'd gotten enough money together to open a small lunch spot in Montclair serving up egg sandwiches and burgers and grilled cheese. His older brother, an ex-con, worked the grill. Tavarus was waking up at five each morning to open the place for the early commuters, and he stayed until seven or eight in the evening, at which point he came back to 34 Smith Street, where he and his family were now living on the second floor, to hang out with his son for a few minutes and then collapse into bed beside Darlene. He knew now what Jackie's life had been like during Rob's youth, spending all day on her feet and the rest of her time parenting. He also knew that it was no way to make a living. The profit margin was 2 percent on fare priced in the $5 range, and he'd been in the red for the first six months. Though he was just now breaking even, and the feeling of running a business that involved interacting with neighborhood people was positive, a café was never going to support his family.

"No one's ever gonna give shit to a nigger like you." So said Flowy, with regard to the real estate proposal Rob and Tavarus were writing together. He wasn't being dismissive; he just wanted to remind his friends that the deck was stacked against them, and stacked high. Flowy still dreamed of saving up a few thousand dollars to move out of Newark. For now, he was most contented when he was just driving around the city in his preciously maintained '96 Ford Bronco. He took pride in knowing all the streets by heart, able to *flow*, as ever.

He wasn't alone in his thinking when it came to the business plan. The majority of the observers in their circle treated Rob and Tavarus's talk of becoming Robin Hood–like figures in the real estate market with a smirk, and maybe a comment such as Flowy's. They pointed to Rob's dreadlocks, Tavarus's scimitar-shaped sideburns, their clothes, their language, their tattoos. The image of these two men sitting in a conference room with the city's urban planners incited laughter. And that meeting could happen only after they'd brought serious investors on board to loan them the seed capital.

"But what you don't understand," Tavarus replied, "is that this isn't even money to people like that. A hundred grand for our first five properties? These people shit a hundred grand. And then there's our ace card."

"What's that?"

"Shawn *Peace*"—in East Orange, Rob was still tagged by his middle name. "He went to *Yale U.* They have no choice but to listen to what he says."

"You don't think they're gonna ask why he works at an airport?" (Rob was not present for this particular exchange; if he had been, the comment would have been phrased more gingerly, or more likely not voiced at all.) "You don't think that's a *red flag*?"

"It's all about the business plan," Tavarus replied. "They just have to read that, meet us, see that we're smart people. No one reads résumés anyway."

"No one reads *business plans.* You're gonna have to sell that shit yourselves."

Tavarus and Rob had already put together a rough list of target investors, most of them St. Benedict's alumni who could be reached through Friar Leahy. And they labored over their written business proposal. They knew that with minimal entrepreneurial experience—a short-order burger joint and a single owned property between the two of them—the document had to be close to perfect. They spent any spare daytime hours in the downtown Hall of Records researching the history of the Section 8 program as well as the property values in target areas. At night, they worked at the kitchen table on Smith Street, writing and revising and haggling over the fine points.

"I don't know if we should use 'exponential' here," Rob said.

"Why not? Exponential is good. That's a word they want to see."

"It'll look naïve. The growth we're aiming for isn't 'exponential' per se. It's a steady increase." Rob drew an exponential curve swooping upward toward infinity, and then, beneath it, drew the actual projection in his mind, a clean line slanting upward with a 30 percent grade.

"Did you just use the term 'per se'?"

Curtis, Drew, and Flowy were heartened to see this despite their doubts regarding the endeavor's viability: the two men hunched over a mat of splayed paper covered in red pen marks, kneading their temples, running on fumes, focused on a goal. They looked activated. The nightly scene reminded them of high school, when all five of them gathered at the table or in the basement to do the same thing, looking just as worn-out while doing it. Back then, they'd worked over Mrs. Gamble's casseroles and cans of grape soda. Now, it was take-out barbeque and vodka. Despite their skepticism, they dared to permit themselves to hope that this idea, after all the past ideas, might work. They would have loved nothing more than for at least two of the five of them to succeed at something.

*　　*　　*

ROB SAT BACK from his third serving of pasta at Raquel's table. She'd just thrown an impromptu dinner party for him and Isabella Peretzian, a classmate from Yale. Mesh trays of cooling cookies and biscotti covered every available surface of the apartment, the baked goods cut and decorated to resemble the legs of burlesque dancers. After giving birth, Raquel had decided not to return to her job at Sony. She was trying to become a professional baker instead, selling artfully crafted desserts.

Isabella's father had worked in foreign service. She was a smart, worldly girl of Armenian descent. While at Yale, she'd chosen to focus much of her academic and social life on black culture, particularly hip-hop music. Now she wrote music reviews for websites like allhiphop.com, and she spent nights dancing at clubs that were out of even Raquel's league. In college, during the few times they'd hung out, Isabella had seen Rob as a reserved and confident man: an authentic representation of the world that, for reasons she couldn't explain, fascinated her. And as they talked through the meal tonight, the admiration she'd tendered in college welled up once more. Whereas Oswaldo had come to see Rob as immobile and in some ways pathetic, Isabella couldn't help seeing him as fundamentally "real," airline job and all, harboring no aspirations to be anyone other than who he was and had always been.

The baby cried, and Rob accompanied Raquel into the nursery to check on Felix. He stroked the tiny head while Raquel reswaddled the blanket, and he said, "It's all good, little man. It's all good." Raquel watched the expression on his face and did not understand why he didn't have a child of his own, a person capable of focusing all the love and caretaking instincts that Rob had always dispersed thinly among his friends and family, many of whom (she felt) didn't necessarily deserve it. She giggled.

"What are you laughing at?" he asked.

"Just you."

"Why me? I'm trying to help."

She lowered her voice to a low grumble. *"I'm Rob, the big man, the tough guy, but deep down I'm a big fat softie."* In fact, she'd laughed because she'd been picturing Rob with a little girl in his arms, crushingly in love even as he complained about no sleep.

"Uh-huh," he said. "Someday there will be some little Robs running around, raising hell. You wait and see."

Later, Isabella and Rob were sitting in his car on 119th Street so that they could listen to a new hard-core rap group called Slaughterhouse without waking the baby. They talked about music. Back in college, Rob had schooled her on songs by M.O.P. and Jay-Z. But that had been years ago, and at this point very few people could keep up with her when it came to the bass lines and turns of phrase in hip-hop. She wanted to impress him with how far she had come in their shared domain. Rob was mostly concerned with the downhill slide of this music in general, the "selling out" of artists who had once nourished him and now were angling hip-hop toward the shallow, popped-out style of Justin Timberlake.

"It's becoming unrelatable," he said.

"Yes," Isabella agreed. "Most of it is wack now."

He sighed. "So, damn, what am I supposed to listen to?" She recommended Roc Marciano, an up-and-comer from Long Island, whom he hadn't heard of. Rob promised to check him out. Then he sat there, staring forward at the dark stretch before them. A block and a half away, headlights flashed past in both directions on the FDR, beyond which the city opened up over the East River, peaceful and at ease.

"You need a ride?" he asked.

"You don't mind?"

"Nah, I got you." He drove her to her boyfriend's apartment in Harlem, which was convenient because he had drop-offs to make in the same neighborhood. He'd begun using a portion of the marijuana he'd been bringing back from Miami for his own dealings, to make a little money through a few long nights.

When neither Isabella nor Ina panned out romantically for Rob, the letdowns occurred despite Raquel's hopes and efforts. When Rene Millien did pan out for him, in the fall of 2010, the relationship blossomed despite Raquel's severe reservations.

They met at Raquel's thirtieth birthday party, at a baroque-style performance space in SoHo complete with a red stiletto leather chair on which PG-13-rated lap dances were given. Rene lived in Clinton Hill, Brooklyn, and worked as a digital artist. She had tight coils of dark hair down past her shoulders and a soft, freckled, light-skinned face. Where Rob's sensibilities trended toward scientific analysis—treating life as an equation to be solved—Rene was visually minded. Whether in spite of or because of their contrasting perceptions, they were in sync that night as Rob "laid down a rap." They remained so when they encountered each other at a dinner on 119th Street later that month, and again at Felix's fifth birthday party. Rob brought Tavarus's son Christopher along with him, and Raquel noticed how good he was to the boy, coaching him about manners and playing with others. She also noticed Rob and Rene pairing off together away from the group, laughing in the corner.

"I'm sorry," Raquel told Rob once he came to her apartment a few weeks later and formally unveiled the relationship. "You know you're like my brother, but Rene is my girl and I'm just very protective of her." Rene's roommate and best friend had recently died of AIDS; she had been beside him in the hospital as he'd drawn his last breaths. She was still hurting deeply, and Raquel didn't think she needed to be "Robbed" in the wake of her loss.

"I'll take care of the woman," Rob said. He was eating soup at Raquel's kitchen table.

"She's been through a lot."

He looked up from the bowl, locked eyes with her for a moment, and said, "So have I." And Raquel saw it then in his face, the briefest reveal of what Rob had strived always to hide from her and so many others: what he'd been through and how it clung to him. She'd known of the weight he carried, but she'd never actually *seen* it until now, after a dozen years of knowing him. Before he left, she gave him her blessing.

Rene lived in a narrow railroad apartment on the second floor of a brownstone. The walls were covered with photos, hundreds of them, colorfully doctored on her sophisticated desktop computer. Some were random street scenes. Others were of her family, Jamaica, friends growing up, designs she created in the vein of Salvador Dalí. Rob loved being in that room with her. And she was struck by his willingness to come there, sometimes driving across Manhattan from Newark in the middle of the night—with the $12 tolls—just to lie beside her for a few hours before he headed down the BQE and over the Verrazano for a seven a.m. shift at the airport. She offered to meet him in New Jersey more than once. She would have an easier time hopping on the Path train than he would inching under and over the rivers.

He always shook his head. "No. This way is better. Except for the fucking parking tickets. What is it with Brooklyn and parking tickets?"

"There are signs, you know, that tell you where to not park."

He made a guttural *uggghh* sound.

More than the time he spent driving to reach her, she was surprised by his tenderness, particularly regarding the friend she had lost. Over the first weeks of their relationship, as she rested her head against Rob's chest with his strong arm wrapped around her, crying sometimes, she spent hours talking about him. And Rob lay beside her, listening always, recording every detail, and every so often offering the perfect word or gentle tightening of his embrace to soften her pain.

*   *   *

"Just move the plane," hissed the dispatcher's voice.

"The luggage crew's not here. I don't know where the hell they are."

"Get it done."

From his seat in the small super tug, Rob was looking up at the massive 777, which more than three hundred international passengers were waiting to board at another gate. The luggage from the previous flight had all been unloaded. The problem was that no one had disengaged "the can"—the giant conveyer belt that carried bags from the loading carts to the cargo hold twenty feet above—from the aircraft. And now the luggage crew seemed to have taken a break; Rob couldn't get a response to his repeated pleas over the radio. His partner that day stood to take care of it, but Rob stopped him and climbed out of the truck himself. "Not like I didn't do this shit for two years."

Thanksgiving of 2010 was not far away, and a cold front had swept over the airport. With his head burrowed into the collar of his jacket, he climbed to the console halfway up the can's stairway and backed the entire machine a few feet away from the aircraft. Then he flicked the switch to close the plane's cargo bay doors. Maybe he realized his mistake right away, maybe he didn't. He'd forgotten to fold down the industrial-strength steel rails that jutted up on either side of the conveyer. Consequently, the outer edge of the plane's bay door descended against one of the upright rails on the can. If he'd backed the luggage machine away two more inches, there would have been enough room to spare. As it was, the hard materials collided, and the hydraulic motor that operated the cargo bay door groaned for a moment before Rob flicked the switch to cut the power.

The door on the plane had kinked only a fraction of an inch. When he pulled the can back farther and once again closed the bay door, everything looked fine. The super tug was already hooked to the nose of the aircraft and facing away at such an angle that his partner hadn't witnessed anything. Rob folded the rails down on the can and returned to his passenger seat.

"Good to go," he said.

Twenty minutes later, the plane idled at the proper gate, and the delayed, disgruntled passengers were boarding while the dispatcher laid into Rob about the holdup. The luggage crew hurriedly loaded the plane, disengaged the can, and closed the cargo bay door. Then the communication paused, and runway workers began gathering beneath the cargo bay door, squinting upward. The pilot had radioed the tower that a warning light was flashing in the cockpit because the luggage compartment had failed to seal properly. The maintenance team arrived with ladders and quickly identified the damage. The plane was put out of commission and towed to a hangar by another team. The passengers would have to wait three hours for the next available plane. The physical replacement of the door would cost roughly $20,000; the labor and service costs associated with interchanging planes and travelers missing connections most likely ended up in the same vicinity. The question became: Who was the last person to handle the door?

Rob came forward. He told them that the door had looked fine when he'd left the last gate, perhaps figuring that the blame would be dispersed among the whole crew, or perhaps, like the child who'd once spilled milk in the kitchen on Chapman Street, he was simply relying on the old reflex of figuring out how this was not his own fault.

The surveillance footage from the tarmac revealed whose fault it was before the day was over.

Accidents like this happened from time to time, and a protocol existed. The very first step of that protocol was a urine sample.

Rob refused to provide one.

He also refused to file the first of three appeals granted him by the union's contract with the airline.

After an afternoon spent getting reamed out by various supervisors, both on the tarmac and in the administrative offices above where his skills had once been sought, he was fired. No one there except Lisa Wingo heard from him again.

* * *

THE FACEBOOK MESSAGE from Rob came in August 2010:

Long time no hear from. Just checking in on u and the family. I hope all is well.

I replied:

Hey Rob! Was talking to Ty and he said you're back home again. Hope we can catch up next time we're in NYC—probably Christmas. Wishing you all the best till then . . . jeff

The previous fall, Rebecca had given birth to our daughter, Lucy. Via Facebook (and in the midst of my disbelief that Rob had created an account), I'd sent him a few pictures. In reply, along with the words, "She's beaooooootiful," he'd attached his own photo, from Rio, backlit by the sunset, each arm around a curvy woman in a thong bikini, all of their respective features obscured by shadow except for the whiteness of Rob's grin. I knew that he'd worked at the airport, but not in what capacity; I'd assumed he'd taken some kind of corporate job. I had no idea that over our last three years of periodic visits to friends and family in New York, on the few instances when we'd calculated that the cheaper flights into Newark International were worth the extra cab fare from there to Brooklyn, Rob might have been the one handling our bags on the tarmac below. His words, "Long time no hear from," were true, and the distance was my fault. Since September 2009, I'd been taken up in my role as more or less a stay-at-home dad, and I was overly prideful about it (a mother walking around with her infant was generally probed for her flaws in the role, while a father seemed to be given undue accolades for showing even minor aptitude). In the mornings I tinkered with a novel revision that, in theory, was supposed to lift our family out of the debt we'd undertaken to have our child. I seemed to spend much of that time changing commas into dashes, then back into commas. Forgotten was the literary success that Yale and a splashy first novel had seemed to promise; all I wanted was for us to be out of the red for a year. Embedded within these anxieties was the larger question of what difference it actually made. In college, immersed in classes taught by famous academic minds on Shakespeare and Faulkner and Dante and Joyce, I'd presumptuously dreamed of being a "writer" who "mattered." Now that I was trying to accomplish that dream and failing to be much of a writer at all, let alone one who mattered, writing began to strike me as inherently selfish. All the highbrow talk of "cultural measuring sticks" that had characterized college writing classes played on rewind in my head and sounded self-gratifying at best.

I began to envy people like Ty and Rob, who had geared their education around science: concrete contributions to the well-being of the people around them. In my small world, the only thing I seemed capable of that had any functional significance was to raise decent children, children who were unfairly difficult for us to have. The multiple miscarriages had familiarized us with the concept of potential, which, politics aside, was really all an unborn child was. With each loss, I'd experienced anew the thousands of footballs I would never be throwing into a son's outstretched arms, the hundreds of ponytails I would never be twisting on a daughter's tangled hair (the image of which called to mind, as it still does when I wrangle Lucy's hair, all those women investing precious hours in Rob's cornrows during college). Ironically, upon losing each fetus, I had wondered with increasing power what kind of father I would be. Now I was a father, and I was determined to be an active one—to participate in the evolving personhood of my daughter, hopefully with some level of competence.

Jackie, when pregnant with Rob, had never imagined that the little kicking body within her would one day be the leader of his class at St. Benedict's before going on to Yale. She'd hoped it, or something like it, but she'd never divined a reality in which it would actually *be*. The reality he seemed destined for, back then, had more to do with the streets in and around East Orange, the task of staying afloat, and a stable job. Now, twenty-nine years later, her son's life was tied to two of those things. The third, his job, had fled him.

Jackie missed her son. The feeling was reminiscent of but more heartbreaking than when he'd left for college. Back then, in the fall of 1998, she'd cried every night for two months. But those tears had been laced with pride, hope, relief, and a litany of positive emotions that had accompanied this pinnacle of all her son's achievements (and, sadly, admission to Yale still remained the pinnacle twelve years later). Now, in the late autumn of 2010, there were no tears. Though Rob was technically living on Chapman Street, spending most afternoons sitting beside Frances in the living room, reading and watching TV and holding his grandmother's hand, he was not *present* there. He didn't listen to her in the same way. He wasn't curious about her days. He still left money on the counter even after losing his job, $100 or $200 a month, but he did so without the pride that had previously fueled him. The gesture was more automated than that, the way a smoker pulls from a cigarette while wishing he could kick the habit. He rarely slept in the house. She didn't know where he slept, or if he slept at all.

In Rob's stead, Carl typically stayed at Chapman Street. Jackie wasn't comfortable spending nights in the house without a male presence, for security purposes, particularly with Frances sleeping on the ground floor. Carl was the only one around without family tying him elsewhere, so he did this to help look out for her, as she'd always looked out for him. On a number of evenings, she'd heard the particular choking of Rob's engine turning off Center Street onto Chapman, and she'd looked out the window as the beater trudged its way down the block, leaning back from the part in the curtain so that he wouldn't notice her watching. When Rob saw Carl's car parked, he accelerated and made a right onto Hickory, and headed back toward East Orange in the dusky light, away from her.

Rob on the "stairway to heaven," below the Cristo Redentor statue in Rio de Janeiro. He would often call this 2003 trip the best time of his life.

Part VI

---◆---

The Gray Area

*Postmeal at one of Raquel Diaz's dinner parties on 119th Street
in Spanish Harlem, during which she typically tried to set Rob up
on dates. "Girl," he told Raquel once, "I wouldn't know what to do
with a good woman even if I found one."*

Chapter 14

———————◆———————

M Y FIRST FOUR YEARS, we led the nation in crime reduction," Cory Booker said in a 2010 interview. This had been one of his top priorities entering office in 2006, and he touted the statistics proudly as he ran for reelection. As with most such claims in the political arena, the raw data existed but the interpretation was less than precise. Murders had fallen over 20 percent, from 104 in 2006 to 80 in 2009. "Shooting hit incidents," the total number of instances in which guns had been fired, had fallen from 435 to 256. "Shooting hit victims," the total number of people actually struck by a bullet in said incidents, had dropped from 502 to 316. But Newark's numbers were also in line with a nationwide downward trend of violent crimes, and the FBI made a point never to rank cities in crime reduction, due to hazy figures in general and geographic variables in particular. The organization denied any affiliation with Booker's claims.

Still, the mayor had without question lived up to his promises to make Newark safer. The police force was bigger and more directed than it had been in decades, with a focus on regular patrols in the most dangerous neighborhoods, an effort called Operation Impact. He'd installed a citywide camera system to monitor high-risk intersections day and night. Massive drug stings had steadily been targeting high-rise hot zones, such as the Garden Spires complex, where in the spring of 2010,

149 arrests were made and $50,000 worth of drugs were confiscated. The operation was a very public triumph that occurred symbolically at the same project towers where Mayor Booker had camped in a tent for months as a city councilman in 1999. But even with the falling statistics and the much-broadcast seizures, large segments of the public remained skeptical. "They can't arrest their way out of the problem," said one by-stander at the Garden Spires. "There need to be alternatives to crime. The root cause of it all is poverty."

The issue of poverty remained as pertinent and divisive as ever, per-haps more so in the context of the Great Recession. With such a large percentage of its population living below the line, paired with high taxes, poor high school graduation rates, and an ever-contracting employment sector, the residents of Newark and its surrounding townships were as vulnerable to the recession's social and economic effects as anywhere else in the country, save perhaps the auto-dependent communities of Michigan and Ohio. The city was also less capable of rebounding once the national "recovery" began. As the foreclosures that inspired Rob and Tavarus's Section 8 proposal proliferated, the city's revenue, so closely linked to property taxes, declined in inverse proportion to the demands that social safety nets placed on its coffers. In the late fall of 2010, more than a year after the Great Recession was proclaimed officially over by the federal government, Mayor Booker made painful budgetary conces-sions. Perhaps the hardest of these was the decision to cut 163 police of-ficers, or 13 percent of the force. Residents, store owners, the remaining police, and public school administrators collectively began to murmur that the milieu in which they lived resembled that of the 1970s. During the ensuing four months, the city's murder rate would spike by 65 per-cent over the same period one year before.

The mayor nevertheless was skilled at inspiring hope among those who listened. "We are brick city," he said in more than one speech. "We are like bricks themselves. We are strong. We are resilient. We are enduring. And like those bricks that build bridges and mighty structures, when we come together, there is nothing that we cannot do, create, or overcome."

* * *

STATEMENT OF PURPOSE

Science has always been my passion. Perhaps it was the first laboratory course I took at Essex County College on Saturday mornings in the early 1990s that engendered my research career. Or maybe it was the summer I spent working with the electron microscope at the University of Medicine and Dentistry of New Jersey during high school. It is impossible to pinpoint the exact moment, but these are the experiences that drew me into the laboratory. Initially I aspired to become a surgeon. My volunteer experience in the emergency room while getting my Emergency Medical Technician certification my senior year of high school made me realize I was more interested in the science behind the treatments, as opposed to the actual practice of medicine. My insatiable curiosity led me to Yale University where I majored in molecular biophysics and biochemistry.

It was at Yale that I studied different branches of chemistry, biology and physics and how they applied to biological molecules. In addition to the various lectures and lab courses I studied to complete my major, I had the opportunity to conduct research in the labs of two principal investigators. I worked with Dr. Diane Krauss during the summer of 1999 while participating in Yale's Science Technology and Research Scholars Program (STARS). It was a critical learning experience as I was able to put into practice many of the molecular biology techniques I learned in class. The project involved determining the genes responsible for stem cell maturation into different cell lines. As I familiarized myself with electrophoresis, northern blotting, and rodent dissections, I realized I enjoyed collecting and analyzing scientific data. The experience left a lasting impression on me and once my water polo season ended in the fall of 1999 I began looking for another lab to gain more experience in.

In February of 2000 I joined the lab of Dr. Elias Lolis, where I was teamed up with a graduate student and was trained on how to use the different equipment. Soon I was adding to the repertoire of skills I had learned previously. Initially, I assayed macrophage inhibitory factor (MIF) for binding affinity to small molecule inhibitors. Next I screened crystallization conditions, trying to find the optimum conditions for co-crystallizing MIF with the small molecule inhibitor that had the highest binding affinity. Although I was able to produce crystals, none of them were of diffraction quality. I learned many important skills and techniques to help me in the laboratory and in life. I regard persistence as the most valuable of these. Day after day, I completed my tasks, interpreted the results, and made changes accordingly. The weekly lab meetings and talks with my advisor helped me maintain my focus and work through the different complications that arose. After I graduated, I continued in the Lolis lab until February 2003.

For the next three months I would return to Rio de Janeiro, Brazil. I secured an apartment, learned to communicate effectively in Portuguese, and overcame my fear of the unfamiliar. The interactions and exchanges that took place there forced me to realize all the possibilities that I never considered before. It was a moment of clarity similar to the peace I found while working in the lab. Just as my understanding of science changed when I began doing research, my understanding of the world changed when I began to see humanity from different perspectives. After viewing poverty in a developing country firsthand, I realized that growing up in Orange, New Jersey was not the worst starting point imaginable. But more importantly, I became aware that my journey had just begun. But before I could continue my formal education I had to first experience more of the world. When I returned to New Jersey in June of 2003 I was more focused than I had ever been in my life.

Over the next four years, I taught biology at St. Benedict's Academy. I would learn twice as much from the students as I thought

I was teaching them. The level of insight offered by some of these young men was matched only by the level of guidance others required. As ideas and dialogue about science and life were exchanged, things began to come into focus. My career as a teacher reinforced what I had come to learn in foreign countries, it is the people I meet and how we influence one another's lives that give me satisfaction. The experience I gained as a teacher influenced my decision to pursue a doctorate degree. I am looking forward to returning to the classroom as both a student and a teacher. Ultimately I would like to teach at the collegiate level, instilling future generations . . .

I became enamored with international travel in 2000 and it has had a major influence on my life for the last 10 years. This would ultimately lead to my employment with Continental Airlines from 2007 to 2010 and would allow me to visit the limestone beaches of Croatia, the beef sushi markets in Seoul, and various other places. With each excursion I learn more about the world and myself.

My goal is to earn my PhD in <INSERT PROGRAM> at <INSERT INSTITUTION NAME> in the <INSERT SPECIACLTY [*sic*] OR PROGRAM>. I have contacted <INSERT RESEARCHERS NAME AND PROJECT IF THIERE [*sic*] IS A SECOND CHOICE NAME THEM ALSO> about his research and have expressed an interest in working with him/her. I would enjoy the opportunity to learn from them and work with them on new discoveries. I also welcome the thought of returning to the classroom as both student and TA. I look forward to learning from some of the brightest minds in the field. Once my core courses were completed, I selected Immunology and Structure and Functions of Nucleic Acids as my electives. These two courses influenced my decision to pursue higher education in the field of <INSERT FIELD OF SPECIFIC PROGRAM>. I am seeking to increase my knowledge in this area for the purpose of addressing diseases like cancer and HIV.

The knowledge I gain from a [*sic*] earning a PhD will help me

achieve my career objectives which include educating future scientists as a professor, becoming a principal investigator and continuing scientific research to better understand the mechanisms
underlying the pathways of life. Given to [*sic*] my academic preparation, research experience, and desire to teach at the college level I
feel that this is an attainable goal that would allow me to both pursue my passion and contribute to the betterment of society.

Isabella Peretzian read the unfinished draft Rob had sent her. He
wouldn't be able to enroll in graduate school for another year, but he
wanted to have a head start on the applications so that they wouldn't fall
by the wayside again, as they had every year since 2007. He'd emailed
the document to her beneath a message that read, *Hey hun, You asked for
it and here it is. Please be as harsh as you can possibly be. I tend to be fallin in love
with sentences and will let shit ride just cuz.* She marked a few typos and then,
in keeping with her task, replied that she felt the references to his foreign travels could be pared down—or cut entirely—because they gave
the impression of a certain wanderlust. Rob called her immediately, and
his voice was testy. While still being perfectly grateful, he argued that
these travels were a fundamental part of who he was, and if a graduate
school program had a problem with that, then so be it. He felt strongly
that altering these sentences would compromise his integrity. Isabella
replied, "Okay, it's fine, it was just a suggestion."

Since his firing, Rob had been living off his rental income, plus unemployment checks of $412 a week. He was ashamed of those checks
and the dependency they represented. But he took them out of their
envelopes, deposited them, bought food for the house, paid attention to
his grandmother, and maintained an uneasy truce with Jackie. On hiatus
were the long nights on Smith Street with Tavarus, poring over their
business proposal and planning a course of action to begin meeting with
investors. Once again, he needed a job.

Jackie silently hoped that his firing from Continental would ultimately prove to be the best thing that had happened to her son since

Charles Cawley approached him more than a decade ago. She knew that she had grounds to tell Rob, "I told you so." She was not above saying such a thing in general, but she kept those inclinations contained. Seeing her son struggle was hard, and made harder by his silent, simmering mood. She would look at his face while he ate, or read, or watched TV and observe this dark, almost cold visage that was no longer capable of concealing his interior. No mother could easily endure watching her child in stasis—and particularly Jackie, who felt unequipped to offer any specific advice that might help him.

Only in groups was Rob fully himself, at least outwardly. To the extent that he could at the end of each day, he surrounded himself with people. On Thanksgiving, just weeks after he lost his job, he performed his usual holiday routine of house-hopping: Shannon Heggins's to Lisa Wingo's to his cousin Nathan's to Victor's aunt's to Oswaldo Gutierrez's family to Jackie's to Smith Street and finally landing at Rene's after midnight, eating full meals at each destination. Laughing throughout the day, he betrayed no trace of the most recent turn in his life, and except for his close friends, no one really knew.

"Cut off your dreads," Oswaldo told him. "Get a suit that fits right, that's not all baggy and hip-hop. Make eye contact. Don't mumble, don't swear, don't talk around the topic. Act interested."

"What does that mean?"

"When you're not one hundred percent into something, you have a tendency to act above it all. Don't do that. Interviewers can tell, and it pisses them off."

Rob had called him in December, wondering why he couldn't get hired. He'd interviewed at a handful of pharmacies along South Orange Avenue, for administrative positions at real estate firms, at a Merck plant in Rahway hiring bench positions, and he hadn't heard back from any of them. He knew the fundamental reason: he was overeducated and underskilled, with a jarring résumé in which a laboratory stint had segued into a high school teaching job which had segued into airport manual labor which had ended in a controversial firing. Even Rob had trouble making sense of it, trying and failing to bend the facts into the representation of himself he desired to project. In the happening, each step had made sense to him; each had held a purpose, even if others had questioned what that purpose had been. But now, when those decisions were condensed into bullet points on a single sheet of white paper, they looked discordant, with none of the texture that had characterized the actual living of his life. In addition, and contrary to Oswaldo's last bit of advice, Rob found it hard to be interested in the people interviewing him or the jobs he was interviewing for. He could avidly talk to any of his friends for hours about the simple minutiae of their lives, but he had trouble sitting through a twenty-minute job interview without becoming bored, and showing it.

And now Oswaldo, who had begun his first job counseling abused, impoverished children and teenagers in the Boston area, was telling him, basically, to stop being himself. What made the advice harder to digest was how sensible it was.

"Yeah," Rob replied in a rare instance of refusing to argue with someone telling him something he didn't want to hear. "Yeah, I get that."

"I'll come down this weekend. I'll help you find a suit."

"I can do that on my own," Rob replied.

"You sure?" Oswaldo was not confident of Rob's capacity to dress himself to code.

"Yeah. You got enough going on without having to shop with me like a girl."

"Spend a little money. None of that discount crap. People can tell."

"Money," Rob replied resignedly.

Rob Peace, more than anyone else I've known, didn't need money to be happy. His needs and wants were basic: sustenance, companionship, sex, music, marijuana, little else. He was content with his unit on Greenwood, during the various stretches in which he lived there. He'd never replaced the leather jacket Zina had given him as a freshman in college eleven years earlier. He liked eating rice and beans—he actually preferred it over heartier fare, when cooked with care, the way Oswaldo's mother made it. At his core, he was indifferent to the American concept of success: owning nice things, vacationing at resorts, being the boss of others. By all accounts, he could have lived a happy life on a teacher's salary, the way Coach Ridley, Friar Leahy, and many of his St. Benedict's colleagues did. But Rob coveted money so that he could help other people materially and in doing so manipulate their perception of him.

He sought money because he wanted to be the Man. And the unemployment checks, which came to Chapman Street in the middle and at the end of each month, made him feel quite the opposite of that.

*   *   *

CHRISTOPHER RODE IN the front seat, which was illegal for a four-year-old, but Rob figured it was safer than the backseat because his car had no passenger-side airbags, and the front seats were the only ones with the diagonal chest straps. Since he wasn't working, Rob had been picking Christopher up from preschool at one thirty each afternoon and taking him back to Smith Street.

Christopher was a sweet, quiet little guy. He was adept at entertaining himself for hours. He enjoyed being surrounded by the men like Rob constantly filing in and out of his home. He knew when he was welcome to hang out with them and when it was time to retreat upstairs. Rob always said that his godson had a "good head." But he worried that the boy was on the soft side.

His worries were confirmed when Christopher confided that there'd been an altercation over a toy truck that morning, the same kind of altercation that occurred daily in thousands of preschools across the country: one kid was playing with something that a more forceful kid wanted to play with, and the forceful kid won out. Christopher asked if he should have hit the kid. The thought had occurred to him, but he'd restrained himself, and now he felt ashamed—not for having been bullied, but for not having fought back.

"Nah," Rob said. "You don't want to be hitting anybody over something like that."

"What should I have done, then, Uncle Shawn? Told the teacher?"

"*Hell* no," Rob replied. "You do not want to be *that* guy."

"So . . . what?"

"I think you did right in the situation by doing nothing, because if you do something, hit the kid or tell the teacher or whatever, it's just going to define you, and then people just be looking at you and saying, 'There's the dude that hits people,' or, 'There's the dude that tells the teacher.' You lost the truck. Who gives a damn? It's a toy truck. The important thing isn't what you do, it's who you are, and who your friends are. This little punkass you told me about, he's not your friend. I know you got other friends, though."

"Yeah."

"Then you stay near them. Watch their backs, and they watch yours. Keep them close. Then nobody's gonna mess with you."

Tavarus laughed when Rob related the story that night.

"He's a good dude," Rob said.

"Yeah, he'll be all right."

"How does it make you feel, as a father, hearing stories like that?" Rob looked at Tavarus with real curiosity, something that had been missing from his face lately.

"You know, you get mad as hell, you want to strangle the little motherfucker that messes with your boy. But you can't. So mostly you just remember what it was like when you were his age and be thankful he's not dealing with anywhere close to what we had to deal with. You know, he doesn't have to worry about getting *stabbed* over whatever truck he's playing with. And then I think, yeah, maybe he could stand to be harder, but being hard doesn't get you anywhere, not really."

Rob recalled aloud the Maine retreat Tavarus had been on after freshman year of high school, and the call he'd made to Chapman Street following the fistfight over his footwear. "You were cussing, groaning, flexing those scrawny-ass chicken wings," Rob said, laughing.

"I was *mad as hell*, man."

"And I told you to calm down, didn't I?"

"Yeah. Good words, too."

"Sometimes," Rob said, "I wish I was as smart now as I was back then."

"You're as smart, smarter even. It's just that life was a lot simpler then."

"Yeah. Didn't seem that way at the time, but I guess it was."

They sat and drank into the night, later joined by Curtis. Soon they were arguing about the identities and powers of certain Greek gods: Curtis thought that Hermes was the god of war; Rob told him that he was thinking of Ares, son of Zeus and Hera. A quick Google search confirmed Rob to be correct, as per usual, and the two friends lauded him for being able to access such useless knowledge after killing at least half a bottle of one-hundred-proof Smirnoff.

Rob drank plenty that fall. At bars like Passion, Slick's, and A.S.H., he made a game of challenging friends to drink as many Long Island iced teas as he put down, which he liked to chase with "little beers," a shot-size mixture of Licor 43 and Baileys. He was staying up late, until three or four in the morning, sometimes for weeks in a row. His friends thought this was fine. In their view, Rob was entitled to a wayward period, and they accommodated him, milking the long nights hanging out in bars or around the kitchen table or over a Monopoly board, with Rob neither rising early for work nor disappearing for weeks to some far-flung country. Outwardly, he seemed at ease, a capable man taking a minute to weigh his options. He did not seem like an unemployed and paralyzed person anesthetizing his problems with alcohol and weed, delaying the inevitable confrontation he would soon have to make with the decisions that had brought him to this circumstance and the decisions that would or would not free him from it.

In Cambridge, Massachusetts, Oswaldo Gutierrez quietly seethed. He talked to Rob often and continually counseled him. But now it was January 2011, two months after Rob's firing, and he still hadn't bought a suit. His voice was more often than not phlegmy and cracked, and he was stiff from sleeping on a friend's couch while Oswaldo had already been working for six hours. Oswaldo knew who these friends were, and he knew that Rob was blinded in too many ways to their negative influence; Oswaldo saw these very same patterns in the teenagers he worked with. He remembered days when Rob had been a teacher and Oswaldo had still been wallowing in Newark himself, doing more or less what Rob was doing now. Back then, Rob's car would break down often, and he'd called on Oswaldo to give him rides to and from work. Oswaldo would pick him up at Smith Street or some other house where people had gathered the night before. Bottles would be overturned on tables. Bodies would be sprawled on couches, some awake and already smoking weed. And later that day, when Oswaldo dropped Rob off again, the same people would be lying on the same couches. The immobility he observed in those moments, the languor that was nearly total, seemed to embody the thing that Rob had always proclaimed to disrespect above all: laziness. But Rob had never been able to see what Oswaldo saw, because he'd considered these people his friends, and his family.

What bothered Oswaldo more than anything else was the way these friends took from Rob, and many of them did so without reciprocating. Money actually concerned Oswaldo the least, because a guy like Rob would always be able to earn more in some capacity no matter how erratically he was behaving. More valuable was Rob's time, and more valuable still was his positive energy. From experience, Oswaldo felt that the people Rob hung out with the most, including the Burger Boyz, took his time and replaced it with negativity, the feeling ingrained over generations that any path taken—whether college, real estate, the opening of a neighborhood café—would only loop back to the kitchen table on Smith Street, a blunt and some liquor to pass around. Their years at St. Benedict's had buoyed this crew above that feeling for a time, but in the end the promise of better things to come had proved too hard to fulfill. In the meantime, Oswaldo remembered when Rob had first bought the house on Greenwood Avenue, the weekends spent fixing it up. Rob had called a lot of his people for help during those months, people he considered his best friends. Oswaldo had been the only one who'd ever shown up. And now he watched from afar as Rob's days became weeks, weeks became months, and soon enough months would become years. The same inexorable movement of time had afflicted Oswaldo during the three years after college graduation. Resurrecting himself had been the hardest decision he'd ever made, but in retrospect it had simply been logical.

Rob had never seen, let alone heeded, that logic, and he wouldn't listen now. Though Rob visited him in Cambridge every couple of weeks (Oswaldo's fellow residents were enamored of him, after a few late nights at Harvard-area bars), Oswaldo still couldn't offer advice deeper than what to wear and what not to say—and even that could make Rob angry.

He wished that Rob's father were still alive, in which case Oswaldo would have sent Skeet a letter in prison framing Rob's situation and explaining what guidance might help him achieve actual progress. If he could have used Skeet as a conduit, he truly believed that he could have motivated his friend to change. Few influences on earth were more powerful than that which a father had on a son.

"I just want to succeed," Rob had told him years earlier, in 2006. They'd been driving up to Boston together. Rob had something like five pounds of marijuana in the trunk, and Oswaldo was composing a fictional short story in his head about what would happen if they were pulled over by police.

"You want to succeed in this new jack, fucked-up way," Oswaldo replied. "You want to succeed in business, and as a dealer. That's never gonna happen. You have to pick one. And I know which I'd choose."

Rob wasn't cold-blooded enough to be a truly successful drug dealer. Oswaldo had known people who were. Growing up, his uncle had been friends with a bona fide kingpin. The man lived in a three-story town house on Bleecker Street, in Manhattan. He had a wife and children and a circle of friends to whom he was kind, loyal, and generous. He also wouldn't have hesitated to put a bullet in the head of anyone who even obliquely crossed him—hence the wealth he possessed and, more important, the respect. Rob cared about people too much to move anywhere near that place. He cared about their stories, their families, their needs. He wasn't dangerous or lethal.

Oswaldo had never said any of this to Rob. He had never said a lot of what he observed. Back then, there might have been a window in Rob's consciousness through which these words could slip inside and gain purchase, illuminating the patterns. Now, five years later, that window seemed to be closed.

*   *   *

HE DIDN'T HAVE the money to invest in his own supply of marijuana. What he did have was the street cred of his Sour Diesel recipe. In December 2010, he leveraged that into a job working for a dealer named Amin, whom he knew through one of his old connects. Amin was Puerto Rican, in his thirties, a successful middleman who lived in a rundown bungalow in Weequahic to mask his considerable earnings, which he spread over a number of small business fronts. He was an Immaculate Heart of Mary alumnus, friendly and intelligent. He was gentle with his two Doberman pinschers, but like the dogs he could become sternly alert and threatening in a moment. For a stipend of $800 a month, Rob converted a few pounds of Amin's weed into his hybrid Sour Diesel and delivered it to one of Amin's supply outposts. This job was time-consuming and solitary but relatively simple. The true stress of it came from relinquishing control. Dealing drugs, while taxing on multiple levels, had always been the one thing Rob felt he could stop and start as he pleased and operate on the level that suited him. The money was earned and owned and spent by him alone. He'd always stayed under the radar, aside from a few very fixable situations. He owed nothing to anyone.

Now he had a boss. Whether he was driving Christopher home from school or watching TV with his grandmother or at a bar listening to a friend DJ, when the call came from Amin, he had to figure out how to be there. Whatever the conversion deadline was, he had to meet it or there would be consequences, typically financial but always carrying the latent menace of something more. He pulled all-nighters in the basement on Smith Street, sometimes two or three in a row, something he'd never had to do in college. This work was fundamentally more dangerous than anything else he'd ever done.

The underworld of drugs, even drugs as relatively benign as marijuana, existed in a complicated hierarchy that paralleled the socioeconomic gradations of the American class system. There were the very small number of individuals at the top who controlled commerce, men like the one Oswaldo had grown up having family dinners with. While extremely dangerous in the power they wielded, these men worked from a calculated distance, like Wall Street titans. They were rarely seen. Their actual workplace dynamics were mysterious. They neither cared much about nor dealt directly with the vast number of people working on the bottom, where Rob had always comfortably resided. These people—the lower class, so to speak—were mostly teenagers, sometimes children, sometimes young adults. They sold drugs on street corners and worked as mules. For a tiny fraction of the overall proceeds—often less than minimum wage, when hours and pay were calculated—these low-level cogs in the machine were the most exposed, and so they carried the bulk of the risk. They, too, were dangerous, particularly the ambitious sorts who desired to make a career of this work. Beefs over territory, women, words, and money—always money—had the capacity to escalate, and indeed that brand of conflict accounted for roughly 20 percent of the violent crime in Newark, a statistic that has remained stable for three decades. Rob had always been able to steer clear of the danger they represented, as Jackie and her family had steered clear of the project towers during their youth. He conducted most of his commerce among friends and friends of friends. His "connects" had always been independent, known quantities without gang ties. He'd made sure that, when necessary, local dealers had been aware of his presence and his methods so that rumors wouldn't work their way up the chain of command to those who actually posed a true threat.

These were the dealers in the middle, a vast and amorphous group of suppliers, creditors, lieutenants, and the like who, in the organized rackets, gave commands to the lower class while taking orders from on high. They were the blood and the muscle of this world. They were the enforcers. They controlled the territory and solved the problems. They had the most to gain and the most to lose. In this uncertain arena, Rob now worked as a kind of chemist on retainer for Amin's corporation—a corporation from which quitting was not as simple as walking away. Rob hated his involvement as much as he relied on it for the short-term future.

"Just be careful," Flowy told him. "You don't want to be in deep, and he's gonna want you in deep, and he's not gonna want to let you loose when that time comes."

"I'm cool with him," Rob replied. "He knows where I'm at."

Rob was confident that because Amin liked and respected him, extricating himself from the operation wouldn't be difficult once he landed a job and went back to school.

He was hoping to lump these two eventualities—job and school—together by applying to a Leadership Development Program at Johnson & Johnson. He was revising the personal statement he'd sent Isabella for the application to this program. If Rob was accepted, he would start at the company as a bench worker—mixing simple chemicals and taking care of lab equipment, which was his first role in the lab at Yale—while concurrently earning a graduate degree at NYU, with the tuition paid for by Johnson & Johnson in return for a long-term contract. He was confident that he would be accepted to the program. He just had to get by until the following September, when the recruitment started, and he was constantly on the lookout for some alternative, viable means that didn't involve working for Amin.

That alternative came through Curtis in early March 2011, just as spring was beginning to penetrate the long, cold winter. The prospect he put forward was ambitious, labor-intensive, and perilous. It also had the potential to solve all of Rob's problems.

Chapter 15

———————◆———————

"THIS WILL BE OUR gray area," Rob said. Flowy, Drew, Tavarus, and Curtis were listening. Three burned-down joints were neatly balanced on the lip of an ashtray, beside the liter of one-hundred-proof Smirnoff nearing its dregs. "There's no great man who doesn't have one, no man who's ever made a difference, anyway. You don't get to the top without compromising something along the way. Jay-Z, Biggie, Tupac—they all hustled early on. Look at politics and presidents: real estate scams, bribes, women. LBJ stuffed a ballot box back in the early days. Kennedy gave syphilis to any girl who came his way. Clinton was a draft dodger among other things. Cory Booker, Obama even—you know they did shady shit to get where they're at."

"Your point?" Drew asked.

"My point is, this right here will be ours. This will be our gray area."

Curtis's eyes brightened. For the last few hours of heavy talk, he'd been waiting for Rob to say something like this: analytical but philosophically resonant enough to bring the group toward an elusive unanimous decision on the matter at hand, still standing at Rob, Curtis, and Tavarus in favor against Flowy and Drew opposed. This matter involved what, to all of them, and to Rob in particular, could be the opportunity of a lifetime: fifty pounds of bulk marijuana that could be obtained, through Curtis's connect, at an up-front cost of $4,000 apiece—less than

351

10 percent of the market rate. All told, they stood to profit in the vicinity of $400,000 in a few months' time—a 2,000 percent return, enough to take care of their mothers, grandmothers, girlfriends, and children for more than a year. Enough to buy suits for job interviews. Enough to not have to hustle for the foreseeable future, and perhaps ever again.

"I don't know," Flowy said, looking down and away. Tonight he had drawn the chair with one leg missing. To stay upright, the corner had to be wedged against the hot radiator, and he was preoccupied with staying balanced without burning his thigh. Flowy was against the idea due to the sheer scope of the enterprise and the unlikelihood of pulling something like this off without the wrong people learning about it.

In a rare rebuttal to a Rob Peace argument, Flowy pointed out that two of the three rappers mentioned had been murdered. Rob countered that Tupac and Biggie were gone because money had made them lazy. "It won't make us that way," he said. At the end of the day, they each stood to clear $76,000 minimum, enough for him and Tavarus to start their housing venture sans investors, enough for Flowy to move out of the hood, enough for Curtis and Drew to do whatever the hell they wanted.

"But how about your house?" Flowy said, to Curtis this time. "If we store the product downstairs—and we have to, there's nowhere else big enough—your house will be a target. Your ma's house. What if we can't hang here anymore? If it gets heavy, where would we go?"

"We'll keep it all quiet," Rob answered. The drugs would be gone before anyone found out they were here. Rob assured him that he was aware of the risks—primarily police and other hustlers—and that he would assume them himself. All he really needed the four other men to do was watch his back.

"Why do you want to do this?" Drew asked Rob bluntly. "Why can't you just get a job, go back to school like you've been talking about?"

"What have I been trying to do for the last four months?" Rob replied loudly, his face kinetic with the question. His friends hadn't seen him this energized in a long time, since before his last trip to Croatia, talking about his six-foot blond-haired girlfriend and his business plan to sell ice makers in Pula. "Looking for a job every damn day. St. Benedict's, Yale—it doesn't mean anything here. That's how it is. So I'm gonna make my own plans happen. C'mon now, aren't you all tired of struggling yet? You and me, the five of us, deserve to be doing more than getting by, doing what we can to keep a roof on our heads, just like everyone else. An opportunity like this doesn't happen every day, and we only have to do it once and, when we have the money, be smart with it. Yeah, there's police, hustlers, lowlifes, but you know the biggest risk in this business? It's trust and not having it. That's the one thing we *do* have right here."

He watched Flowy and Drew exchange a look and a shrug, and he knew that he'd changed their minds.

Outside on Smith Street, the midnight atmosphere was quiet, neighbors having retired from their stoops, the children in bed, the hustlers migrated to adjacent neighborhoods with fewer families and thus more nocturnal action. A car passed every so often outside the barred front door, crunching over haphazardly shoveled snow.

At around one in the morning, the decision was made unanimously to obtain the weed, convert it to Sour Diesel in the basement, and sell it. They would be quick, they would be careful, and when the business was done they would be on their way toward the future they'd begun imagining more than a decade ago, at that dance party near Columbia high school. Rob grinned wide, distributed five glasses of vodka, and they toasted one another as well as a new hope that here, now, felt close enough to grasp.

* * *

"I'LL GIVE IT TO YOU," Oswaldo said. "And after you pay me back, you and I will never speak again."

The pause on the other end of the phone was long even for Rob. Then: "Okay. Thank you."

That weekend, Rob drove the five hours up to Cambridge, frigid and windy in the middle of February, and knocked on Oswaldo's door. His old friend had the manila envelope ready. He handed it over without letting Rob inside. They exchanged very few words. Everything Oswaldo needed to hear had been said over the phone: the excuses and justifications and deflections, the guarantees for a quick turnaround, the assurance of, "I can do this, no problem," the plea of, "I need this, man."

"Thanks again," Rob said. "It means a lot."

Oswaldo shook his head. "Just pay me back. That's a lot of money for me."

"I know."

Oswaldo knew how much pride his old friend had sacrificed to ask for a loan of this size. Oswaldo also knew that the only reason Rob had come to him was that he couldn't go to anyone else: of all the dozens of people he considered his family, Oswaldo Gutierrez was the only one who might have this kind of money, understand what the money was going to be used for, and be willing to part with it. Rob hadn't expected that Oswaldo would also be willing to part with their friendship. In that moment, their last together, Rob's face pointed down to the floor by Oswaldo's feet. The face was impassive, even submissive.

"All right," Rob said. "Later."

Oswaldo watched him walk away, his shoulders nearly spanning the width of the building's narrow hallway. He thought of the time Rob had offered to buy him a ticket to Rio, just to experience a fleeting reprieve from Newark and from life, and Oswaldo had refused out of the conviction that, until he had his own life in order, he was not entitled to a vacation.

Not twenty minutes after getting out of his car, Rob drove five hours back to Newark.

Once the weed—fifty pounds of it, procured at a fire-sale rate from a bulk supplier whose "block got hot"—was safely in the basement, it didn't look like all that much, maybe twenty-five gallons in volume. If Rob still had his snake tank, the entire stash would have fit comfortably inside the glass walls. The disappointingly small heap of drugs didn't resemble the nearly half a million dollars that Rob planned to make in a

few months' time. It didn't appear worth the friendship he had lost, the
risks he had taken in transporting it here, the risks he was going to take
in selling it. The few dozen ziplocked bags looked like so much potting
soil for Curtis's garden. They didn't look like freedom, not yet.

But still, even sealed in plastic, the concentration gave off a powerful
aroma. In preparation for the pickup, Rob had insulated the front door
that opened from the basement onto the sidewalk, as well as the doorway between the basement and the laundry area, with tarps. Without
ventilation, the fumes intensified to the point where his eyes tingled and
watered. Rob stood in the middle of the room and inhaled a deep breath
through his nose. He grinned and told his friends that it wouldn't be so
bad spending the next few weeks shut up down here, even with the gas
mask. That night, the Burger Boyz permitted themselves to feel like kids
again as they sampled the new product and talked and laughed. Smoke
filled the basement, their old retreat. These dense, pungent clouds that
unfurled between them felt, on that night, to be laced with hope.

The levity ended the next morning, when Rob woke up in the basement, hungover and staring at the tremendous amount of work that lay
ahead. With the space and materials he had, the Sour Diesel conversion
process had to be done a fraction of an ounce at a time, using a cylin-
drical sieve smaller than a bicycle pump. Any bigger, and the butane
fumes would rise to the ground floor of the house and make the air
noxious for Christopher to breathe. All told, he had to work about ten
to fifteen hours to process each pound. Fifty pounds added up to more
than five hundred hours. And he was still processing Amin's weed on
the side, in amounts ranging from two to five pounds a week. If he
worked twenty-four hours a day, he would need almost a month to
convert their entire cache. He'd accounted for this from the outset and
had considered the necessary time span a good thing; he would have no
choice but to sell the drugs at a measured pace and thus ensure that no
heads were raised in the neighborhood. But now those hours lay ahead
of him, and the rest of the winter and early spring must have looked
bleak and insular.

He attacked the work ferociously at first, disappearing into the basement for full days at a time, trudging up the back stairs only to eat and use the bathroom, gas mask set on the table. He counteracted the grubbiness of this work by talking constantly about the eventual profits, how they would launder them, what they would do with them. He did this with the same low-key but constant energy that had characterized his last summer in East Orange before heading off to Yale: the idea that ahead of him lay countless hours of work and uncomfortable situations, but beyond that sacrifice a wide canvas of possibility unfurled. Like college, the next phase of his life existed as a necessary passage that must be endured to advance onward toward greater things.

*   *   *

"I'M WORRIED ABOUT YOU."

It was April. He was on the phone with Ina, who was now stationed at the Port Hueneme naval base in Oxnard, California. She'd been home from Afghanistan for almost a year. Her unit was supposed to be heading to the South Pacific, which in contrast to where they'd just served was being treated like a vacation. She'd just learned that, instead, they were being sent back to Kabul. She'd emailed Rob, and he'd called to ask if he could buy her a plane ticket to Florida to see her family before leaving. She couldn't go; her unit was on lockdown for the month preceding departure. She wouldn't have accepted anyway. Rob's generosity, manifesting itself now, was a big reason that he was where he was.

"Don't worry about me," she replied. "I'll be fine." She was aware that she'd said these exact same words to him before. Now she extended them to encompass her experience in the Afghan War, where her unit had worked building infrastructure to accommodate the troop surge. "I worry more about you."

He laughed. "What do you worry about me for?"

"I was there for a year," she said. "And no one I knew was killed or even hurt. Back home, though, a lot of people were killed. Friends of mine. That's why I worry about you." To her, the war being fought abroad, engineered by powerful strangers, did not measure against the wars fought at home by people she knew.

He laughed again, and she hated how he always did that. "I'm cool," he assured her. A few moments later, they said goodbye.

Other than that phone call, Rob hadn't been laughing much that winter. He'd made a rare miscalculation, not in the man-hours required to convert the stash to Sour Diesel but in the logistics of actually moving the product. Each pound divided into roughly 450 dime bags, which meant that there were 22,500 units to sell in total. Tavarus couldn't do any of the driving, because of his prior record of possession. Curtis and Drew weren't comfortable being mules, either. This trepidation hadn't come up during the groupthink that had delivered them to this point; as was often the case in decisions involving money and risk, there had been a lot of nodding heads in the lead-up followed by sheepish backtracking in the follow-through. Surprisingly, Rob didn't turn this into an argument. He'd pledged to carry most of the load, both figurative and literal, and he just wanted to see this through. Only Rob and Flowy could actually make deliveries, and two people working this kind of volume could not conceivably do so without attracting attention. He'd set a ceiling for each of them at ten drop-offs per night, which to anyone keeping track would reflect the one- to two-pound quantities he'd always dealt in the past. He was particularly worried about Amin catching wind of the added commerce and mistakenly believing that Rob was siphoning off his boss's supply. He refused to sell in East Orange at all, where the majority of his friends' contacts resided. Troublingly, he found that many of his friends were reluctant to help him broaden his network. He felt as if people who had always been perfectly happy to have him roll through and get stoned had suddenly grown up, or grown wiser, or grown disinterested in the culture he was depending on for one last good break. Or maybe they were just concerned about him, maybe they'd heard his talk about getting out of the game enough times already.

Exacerbating the problem was the fact that the weed had been relatively old when they'd procured it, at least three months by Rob's analysis. Some bagged clusters were already growing mold due to the humidity in the basement paired with the hash oil integrated into the buds. He could have frozen what he had in order to string out the process over a few extra months or even a year, but doing so affected the quality of the high, which in turn would be bad for his reputation as he tried to keep selling. Above all, he just wanted all this behind him and to have the cash in hand.

"Let's hire," Rob said, his voice resigned, the prospect akin to admitting defeat.

Flowy didn't like it, but there was really no other way. He hadn't been helping much in finding new buyers. Flowy knew intimately every block of the three square miles of East Orange. Looking one direction from his apartment window, he could see east across the Garden State Parkway toward downtown Newark. Looking the other way, he could see the forested incline that rose into South Orange. These lines of sight encompassed fully what he felt to be his domain, but his reach did not extend many blocks beyond it, and he suffered a kind of agoraphobia whenever he ventured beyond Newark, where business could be conducted safely and in higher densities. The opportunity he now had to leave this neighborhood permanently was narrowed by his inability to operate outside it. When he and Rob had begun selling in earnest, they'd shared a proud solidarity in being the only members of the Burger Boyz "hard" enough to go all-in on the enterprise. Now, as the pressure quickly mounted and those dozens of pounds of marijuana rested uneasily in the basement while weeks passed and quality decayed, Rob was assuming the burden almost fully alone. Instead of becoming resentful, he seemed further driven in this role; once again, he was dutifully carrying his friends, the way he'd carried them toward college. But there was more at stake now than there had been then. The Burger Boyz had learned—or they believed they had learned—that at the end of the day education didn't matter. Potential didn't matter. Knowledge didn't matter. Only money mattered. And Rob, once the only one capable of actualizing a full education, was now the only one capable of producing the money—this ability having nothing to do with his intelligence, only his endurance.

He began canvassing for mules. The job description was very specific. Rob wanted young guys who had enough experience to avoid arrest but not so much experience that they'd get greedy and try to negotiate rates. He wanted people connected enough to pad Rob's base but not so connected as to spread rumors. He wanted people with the aspirational drive to be doers but also with the respect to heed his authority. He wanted people desperate enough to work hard for the commissions he offered but secure enough to stay safe and conservative. He wanted people who were smart enough to understand what they were doing but dumb enough to do it anyway. He wanted people like the young man he had been, once. A man like this was hard to find, let alone several of them. In the end, concessions had to be made.

*   *   *

"I JUST WANT to provide for you." Rob was lying in Rene's bed in Brooklyn, repeating words that, consciously or not, had become all but a mantra for him. On the wall above, her photo collages were like a dream, all of life's moments scattered and colored and angled almost at random, a kind of organized chaos that, when looked at closely, told her story. Rob would stare up at it and breathe out smoke and let himself be hypnotized.

Rene was self-sufficient. She worked in a photo artist's studio. She paid her rent. She had a career trajectory, even if it was that of a starving artist. She sometimes felt that she'd been born twenty years too late, and in the '80s she would have thrived as a professional photographer working for glossies. But computer technology had also opened up her profession in new ways, and success simply meant finding a new method by which to apply it. Like Rob in his college labs, she worked through trial and error, constantly experimenting with color and layout. She possessed a buoyant hopefulness that Rob did not. Increasingly, he dwelled on archaic principles of manhood and providing, and his current inability to do so: "I just want to provide for you . . . I just want to provide . . . Soon, real soon, I'll be able."

She didn't need him to provide. She wanted him to replace her roommate and move in with her. Nothing was keeping him in Newark except his mother, and she didn't live too far away from Clinton Hill. For now, Rene's hope remained unvoiced. Rob's equilibrium was off in a way that she hadn't seen before, and not even marijuana seemed to be helping. He would show up at her apartment at all hours and fall backward onto her bed, and she could almost see the pressure sliding off him like some primordial ooze. And she would be overcome by the urge to take care of him—to provide for *him*—not with money but with words and gestures that she could not summon, because right now he would not understand them. Lately, he'd been upset because of a murder on Center Street, right around the corner from his mother's house. The victim was no one he knew, just an anonymous young male Newarker who'd paid the ultimate price for dealing drugs.

*   *   *

"I'VE ALWAYS LOOKED UP to you," Ty Cantey said into the phone. Ty and Raina were living in San Jose for a portion of their residencies. Through an arrangement with the hospital, they were swapping twelve-hour shifts so that one of them could always be with their two children (a third daughter was on the way). The existence was grueling, and made more so by the fact that for months at a time, they saw each other only in passing, just long enough to trade parenting details such as when medicine was to be administered and how much food should be eaten. Spontaneously one afternoon in March, having slept for four hours in the last forty-eight, Ty thought of Rob, and he called him half expecting the cell number to have changed. Rob answered in his deep, brusque voice, and Ty told him why he'd called, simply to say that Rob had always inspired him.

"Uh, thanks, I guess," Rob replied, sounding uncomfortable with this naked emotional sharing between men.

"I'm serious," Ty said. He didn't know why he was so desperate to get his feelings across. "I guess I always wished I could be more like you."

"Eh, grass is always greener. You're a cool dude, too."

Ty tried to recall moments that would illustrate his feelings. He had been troubled for a long time by the dissolution of his memory. He had been the top student in the Yale premed Class of 2002, and very near the top at Harvard Medical School, with unsurpassed memorization skills. But a few years of marriage, fatherhood, and residency had nearly wiped his brain clean of what mattered more and more as time passed: the conversations, the dining hall meals, the small moments that had made him who he was now.

"Anyway," Ty said, "I just wanted to say that to you."

"I appreciate it."

"Gotta get back to the kids now."

"Enjoy them."

And they both hung up.

Around the same time, Nathan met Rob at the Gaslight Brewery in South Orange, its windows peering out onto the beautiful town square bordered by quaint shops and streetlamps, white suburban kids loitering on benches. Nathan asked a question that, by now, Rob had been asked dozens of times by those who cared about him. "What are you doing?"

On this rare instance, Rob confronted the question directly, albeit without providing an actual answer. "I went to Yale," he said. "I know what I'm doing."

"Shawn," Nathan replied, "I hate that I'm the one who has to say this to you, but that was ten years ago. What are you doing *now*?"

This time, Rob didn't answer.

*   *   *

BY MID-APRIL, Rob had four young guys working for him. They were between the ages of eighteen and twenty-two. They worked for stipends of $400 a week, plus gas money, plus commissions. One of them, when hired, actually fell to his knees and wept, saying the job would keep him from becoming homeless. Rob treated them very casually, like a big brother, careful not to give orders in a way that would engender any resentment at all. The only point he was aggressive about was that their cars have up-to-date registrations and functional taillights, and that they obeyed all traffic laws. Otherwise, he cracked jokes and gave them small kickbacks and tried to maintain a smooth dynamic. While careful to keep a certain distance, he presented himself as a mentor figure: *If you handle yourself this way and don't cause problems, you'll be where I'm at soon enough.* To the mules, where Rob was looked pretty good. None of them ever saw the basement on Smith Street or knew any of the specifics of the enterprise; their business was conducted in parks, parking lots, side streets.

For three weeks, the situation worked out well. They were moving the product at almost a pound per day, and money was coming in— less than Rob had originally calculated because of the new overhead of roughly $8,000 a month, but that would ultimately be a small dent. The first profits went to Curtis, Tavarus, Drew, and Flowy to pay down their original investments. The money Rob took in himself, he spent on back mortgage payments for the Greenwood house and Jackie, to whom he hadn't been able to contribute much since last November. The house on Chapman Street needed some radiator repairs. Frances was in her worst condition yet, undergoing dialysis for kidney disease in addition to her emphysema; he began paying off the credit card debts that the family had taken on for those costs. He was once again able to be generous with his friends, helping with rent, car repairs, and marijuana. At their current rate, the stash would be cleared out by midsummer, just in time to prepare for the Johnson & Johnson application process.

Before he could start thinking fully forward, however, Kamar had to be handled.

Kamar was one of the mules. He was nineteen years old, small in stature but able to carry himself like a heavy, complete with a full beard.

At first he'd been very quiet. He listened. He was on time. His car never broke down. He worked harder than the others and never tried to renegotiate his stipend. Rob liked him; he respected the kid's work ethic and follow-through. The latter quality, in particular, was rare. "That one's got a future," Rob told Flowy. "Hopefully not in the game, but somewhere."

Maybe Rob liked him a little too much. Maybe he grew lax during their exchanges. Maybe he allowed Kamar to feel like an associate rather than an underling. Their physical meetings happened one on one, in the dark, so nobody knew. They only knew that by late April, Kamar had become a problem.

Bits of gossip began filtering back from some of the buyers with whom Kamar had been dealing. "Watch out for that one, he's talking shit." Apparently, during drug deals, he'd been making comments about Rob, saying that he was smug, he was a cheat, he didn't know what he was doing. He was also talking about the Yale marker. The natural capacity for Rob's pedigree to draw resentment was at work once again. Overall, these rumors were harmless and had no effect on the business; as in any industry, low-rung workers undermined their bosses all the time. Words were currency, as they always had been, and it was important, careerwise, to present yourself as bigger than you were. The worry was that words would morph into something more serious. Rob's biggest concern was that Kamar would start talking to more people than simply the buyers—that the information would spread wide that he was running his own operation while still working for Amin, and that the operation was far-reaching. The possibility of this coming to pass was remote; Rob had made sure that none of his employees had any history with Amin, the local Bloods, or anyone else capable of intruding. But regardless, Rob had enough on his mind already.

The severance occurred on the sidewalk outside Smith Street. Because Rob was hungover and didn't feel like driving to a more discreet location, he let Kamar pull up right outside the basement door. Curtis was inside playing video games when he heard the shouting. Kamar's voice was high-pitched and, though Curtis had met him only once and not directly, unmistakable. Rob's remained, as ever, low and controlled. The exchange was laced with profanities from Kamar, met with weary platitudes from Rob. Curtis's only real thought was that Rob should have done this somewhere else, because he didn't want the neighbors to complain. After a short time, the car rumbled off, and Rob came back inside. He laughed uneasily and said, "*Damn*, the young 'uns be uppity these days." Curtis laughed and kept playing his game as Rob passed the TV room and returned to the basement.

The talk started almost immediately and intensified fast. People around the neighborhood were worried because Rob's name was coming up in a bad, bad way. In the kitchen of Smith Street, his cell phone would ring constantly, and he would take the calls into the backyard and speak in halting, unheard phrases.

"You need to tell me something?" Flowy asked during the first week of May. He was concerned by how reclusive Rob had become, all but cutting Flowy out of the business transactions. In drug dealing, as at St. Benedict's, disengagement was always the first sign of trouble within.

"No," Rob said, "nothing's going on."

"Seriously, what is it?" Flowy had been in partnerships where the pulling away of another typically meant that he himself was getting screwed somehow. He didn't have to worry about this with Rob. He only had to worry *about* Rob, and the degree to which, unasked, he'd taken the entire enterprise on his shoulders.

"The boy's asleep upstairs," Rob said, referring to Christopher on the second floor. "We'll talk later."

There wasn't any time to talk later, because Rob wasn't around the house much anymore. Usually, neither Flowy nor the others knew where he was. They figured maybe Hrvoje's or Lisa Wingo's, and sometimes they were right. Lana, his Croatian girlfriend, visited that week, and Rob slept with her a couple times on Hrvoje's couch. They made enough noise during their coupling to wake Hrvoje and Marina's infant son, and Rob was told that he couldn't stay there anymore. Rob had no plans to anyway. For the first two weeks of May, he slept in his car in random parking spaces around East Orange so that violence, were it to trail him, would not do so in the homes of anyone he loved. How dark and still and quiet those nights must have been, reclined in the passenger seat with a blanket covering his chest. How he must have thought of the various places he'd slept during his thirty years, the hundreds of different beds: Chapman Street, Smith Street, Lanman-Wright Hall and Pierson College, the apartment with the French doors overlooking Ipanema, Ohio and Florida and Japan and South Korea and Costa Rica and Amsterdam, Hrvoje's and Lisa Wingo's and Ina's and Rene's and the Raymond brothers', various airplanes flying seven miles above the world's oceans. How he must have questioned the decision points that had led to him sleeping here, now, in his chilly car, alone in the streets to which he'd always been drawn.

He wore a Kevlar vest on these nights and during certain segments of the day. He also owned a handgun now, which he kept close. Though there are no accounts of Rob ever following through on his plan to sell weapons on the black market (a plan that, like so many others he had, seems to have fallen by the wayside), he did purchase one.

Amin, the dealer for whom Rob still worked, hadn't in fact learned about his massive dealings, but members of the Double II Set Bloods had. Apparently, Kamar had deduced that what he'd been involved in— and fired from—had involved more than just a few ziplocks of weed, and he'd decided to raise his station by getting in good with the most powerful entity in East Orange. The Yalie was working in secret, Kamar said, and in a big way, in their territory. This was a lie; the essential aspect of Rob's initial instructions to Kamar and the other mules had hinged on the layout of territory in East Orange and the specific blocks they were to venture nowhere near. But fact-checking wasn't a major tenet of gang behavior. Immediate action was.

Rob suspended his dealings for the time being. He spent his time trying to figure out how to plug the freely flowing stream of information. He needed to talk to someone associated with the Double II Sets and do so quietly, safely. He was good at talking. Given the right chance with the right person, he was certain he could explain honestly his intentions and his dealings while outing Kamar as an unreliable source with a petty vendetta. He had two concerns. The first was that he didn't want to get Kamar hurt. The second was that, were he to stage his outreach under the wrong circumstances, there wouldn't be time to talk.

He finally told his friends what had happened. And his admission, while standing in direct contrast to all his initial promises, was received calmly, without anger. The guys had not helped him as much as they'd promised, but they wanted nothing more than to fix this situation.

"We should get rid of the stuff," Drew said. "For real. We're paid out. No harm done."

"No," Rob replied. "I just need a minute to get on top of this."

"C'mon," Curtis said. "It's not worth it."

Rob looked at Tavarus, their real estate vision with its many charts and graphs passing through the eye contact.

"Give me three days," Rob said, nearly a plea. "No one's gonna do anything in three days, certainly not that little punkass Kamar. I can get it right by then."

They'd entered into this dialogue hoping to be reassured by Rob's demeanor if not his words. But Rob looked cold, antsy, the opposite of peaceful.

In the *Newark Star-Ledger* a few days later, a front-page article referenced the previous March, 2010, which had been Newark's first murder-free calendar month in over forty years. The first quarter of 2011 had shown a 71 percent uptick in violent crime compared to the same period of last year.

* * *

"You work until you're sixty-five and your benefits go up almost twenty percent," Rob told his mother.

Jackie was sixty-three and dreaming of retirement. She knew that one of her son's most enduring motivations had always been to allow her to retire early, much earlier than sixty-three. She didn't hold it against him that he was now convincing her, with numeric logic, to hold out until sixty-five. According to the tables he'd found, if she retired now she'd receive $964 per month in Social Security payments as opposed to $1,201 per month if she worked for two more years.

They were sitting across from one another in the parlor. The curtains hung down over the window right behind Rob's head, the same curtains she used to chastise him for poking his face through while waiting for his father to arrive. Jackie took them down twice a year for cleaning. The street was semivisible through the lace. Spring was beginning to manifest in earnest; new weeds in the vacant lot across the street had almost reached the height of the fence. Clusters of children passed by in their navy uniforms walking home from school, looking forward to the summer.

Jackie nodded her head and said, "Yeah, yeah, I know you're right." She hadn't really been serious about retiring this year but had nurtured the idea as a pleasant fantasy. She'd been working at the nursing home for fifteen years. The recession had hit the company hard, and she'd taken a pay cut, but she was still making over $30,000 a year supervising the kitchen, and her pension and benefits would remain intact. The $237 extra per month would make a difference in the long run.

Her son made sense with numbers. He always had. And now he was thirty years old, taking her through the tiers of retirement benefits. She wished that these calculations hadn't always been so challenging, not in terms of the math but its implications. She knew that he wished the same thing. But she didn't fix any anger, as her son did, to that wish. She'd entertained many such wishes during the course of her life and had long since accepted the reality that very few of them would come true. She'd wished that Skeet had been innocent. She'd wished for jackpots with each crank of an Atlantic City slot machine. She'd wished that her boss would slip and fall and hit his head hard enough that he would suddenly become kind. She'd wished that her mother would be able to pass on without further suffering. She'd wished that her son would be able to make his way in the world easily, successfully, and happily. When she'd been thirty, she hadn't yet given birth to him; in retrospect, her life hadn't even begun, because Rob would ultimately become her life. He was still more or less a child. He had time. But she couldn't explain this brand of time to him. She wasn't good with words that way.

By the middle of May, any danger Rob felt himself to be in seemed, at least to his friends, to have subsided. He spent one night at Tamba's house, a DJ friend of his who lived around the corner from Smith Street, playing spades until four in the morning. He told Flowy that he'd talked to someone, a Blood, and it was all on the up-and-up again. Kamar hadn't been seen or heard from in over a week. "Bitch left town, no doubt, now that I outed his lyin' ass." He filled the void left by Kamar himself, spending most nights driving around, selling dimes, music blaring and the window down as his car worked the freeways and bridges and tunnels surrounding New York City. He texted with Lisa Wingo incessantly.

Lisa: u don't visit a sister?
Peace: gotta lay low
Lisa: what u been doing?
Peace: Rippin n runnin
Lisa: b careful
Peace: always
Peace: oh and I started watching glee yesterday
Peace: Don't tell anyone
Lisa: =))
Lisa: N u luuuuuuv it
Peace: More than I thought possible
Peace: Shhhhhhh.....
Lisa: See??? Told ya
Peace: Just watched the episode where they did ceelo song forget u
Lisa: Hahahahahaha
Peace: I know. This is our lil secret though, right?????

Lisa: Who da hell am I gonna tell??!?

Peace: Just making sure

Lisa: Imma blast u on facebook!!!!!!!

Lisa: Just like a man......u like glee, but don't wanna admit it.

   Puuuuunk

Peace: U so mean

He wore the Kevlar vest whenever he was in his car, night and day, but he kept the gun buried in the spare tire compartment of the trunk or else in a ground-floor closet at Smith Street, an afterthought, or maybe a reminder, but nothing more.

"I just can't believe I know someone with a gun in his car," Raquel told him. He had stopped by to give her weed so she could make brownies, which he called Dem Shits. "Who the fuck does that?"

He shook his head and smiled. "It'll be done with soon enough." He gave her a hug and told her to give one to Felix for him when the boy woke the next morning. Then he left. From the window, she watched his shadow cross 119th Street and get in his car and head west toward First Avenue. She imagined him driving over the gorgeously lit George Washington Bridge, alone, with that sober expression on his face that being stoned could no longer mask.

On Thursday, May 12, he took Lisa Wingo and her daughter to Red Lobster for dinner. She gave him a hard time for ordering a pineapple cocktail complete with an umbrella skewering a stack of fruit slices. She argued over the check but ultimately let him pay. His happiness was always the most genuine when he was taking care of her in some mannish way such as this: paying a bill, lifting a heavy box, bringing food to the apartment. They joked sometimes about an alternate world in which they were husband and wife. "You're too pretty for me," he said, "my little Oompa Loompa." After dinner, she asked him where he was going.

"Get some ass."

"Who with?"

"Brooklyn."

"Well, have fun."

"If she's already asleep when I get there, I'll kill her. I ain't paying no twelve-dollar tolls just to go to bed."

Rene was asleep, but he woke her, and they made love, and afterward he talked once again, in that deep refrain, about providing for her someday. She let him talk. His voice was a pleasing sound by which to drift off to sleep, a white noise.

*   *   *

THAT WEEKEND, the Burger Boyz had a cookout in the backyard on Smith Street. Friends came in and out down the side alley between houses. In fold-out chairs along the fence, men and women passed a joint back and forth. Music played, old-school songs like "Ruff Ryders' Anthem" by DMX and "Put It on Me" by Ja Rule. Lisa came, her mousy voice rising high above the men's low tones. Flowy held court, his long arms waving loops above his tall, narrow frame as he talked. Curtis showed off the watermelon vines he'd planted in his garden this year, the tiny buds that in a few months would be monstrous and succulent. Christopher scurried around at waist height until his bedtime, at which point Tavarus and Darlene both took him upstairs to read books.

Rob was in a quiet mood. He worked the grill for hours, slow-roasting his Brazilian pork with a spatula in one hand and a drink in the other. His face lit brightly whenever the rendered fat caused a flare-up out of the charcoal bed; his eyes were angled down into the flames as he carefully scooted the meat toward the edges of the grill. A friend from Mt. Carmel Elementary, Demien, taught karate classes at a local dojo, and Rob had been training with him recently—intense, battering workouts that taught him a specific set of combat moves that leveraged an opponent's power against him. Rob asked Demien how he could live on the minuscule salary he made there. "I don't know." Demien shrugged. "I can pay rent, eat. That's good enough with how much I love what I do."

The night felt happy and old—a return to form no different from the hundreds that had occurred over the years since high school, but also a foreshadowing of times to come.

Tavarus returned to the yard from Christopher's room upstairs. He was drunk and talking loudly about the latest long-term idea he and Rob had conceived. They wanted to establish a kind of training college, in which students would come straight out of high school and learn practical skills like how to interview and dress and work for a corporation. The curriculum would be tiered over three years. The first year would be purely classroom lessons, taught by local business owners. The second year would involve an intensive internship in one's chosen field. The third year would segue into an actual job, with a certain percentage of salary set aside to pay for the full tuition on the back end. Tavarus spoke in big terms about how necessary such an institution would be in this neighborhood, how meaningless the traditional secondary education ultimately was to people like him: loading up on debt in order to study liberal arts with no practical value.

"You talk too much," Rob called from the grill. "This isn't even an idea yet. This is, like, the far future, like, decades away. And who knows what the educational system's gonna look like then. Chill."

On Monday, May 16, Rob showed up at Sherman Feerick's house in Bloomfield. Sherman was a former classmate from Yale, a staple at the Weed Shack. They'd remained good friends over the years, though Sherman did not overlap much with Rob's other friends. He had a seven-year-old daughter and was active in Newark's business sector as a consultant. He was constantly talking on one of his three cell phones, filling the atmosphere around him with business-speak that Rob didn't understand. He had worked off and on as a liaison between the mayor's office and the gang entities of the North Ward, though a murder on the street outside his office in Vailsburg, in the middle of the day when he'd brought his daughter to work, had caused him to rethink his capacity to bring any form of progress to these neighborhoods. He was thinking about moving to Orange County in California to give his little girl a healthier life. In the meantime, his latest venture was a summer camp for at-risk children.

For all Sherman's goings-on, his home was small and barely furnished. Rob sat at the kitchen table, uncharacteristically quiet as he stared down at the nicked wooden surface. He didn't take off his leather jacket.

"I need some work," he said.

"Okay," Sherman replied. He was confused; Rob had never asked him for anything in over a decade of knowing each other.

"I was thinking I could be, like, a counselor at your camp or whatever."

"You'd be great at that," Sherman said.

"So, you got any openings?"

Sherman shook his head. He didn't have the money to pay any actual wages. "Our fund-raiser is in June, I'm putting it together right now. After that, yeah, I'll probably be able to make a spot for you if you can hold out till then."

Rob breathed out and nodded. Sherman felt for him, knowing how hard it had been to come here and ask for a job, wishing he had a job to give. He was also flummoxed by the defeated, desperate expression on his friend's face. Too much time had passed, too many opportunities had come and gone, for Rob Peace to still not have his life figured out. Sherman experienced something close to pity as his old friend left. If Rob had come even a few months earlier, Sherman probably could have figured something out for him. He had the contacts to do so. They were close enough that Rob shouldn't have needed to wait until the last possible moment to ask. He had never understood why Rob had found so much shame in asking.

Two days later, on Wednesday, Rob woke up late after a long night working in the basement. He picked up Christopher from school and brought him back to Smith Street, where he hung out with the boy for two hours in the backyard. When Darlene came home, Rob took a Tupperware container with the leftover pork to Chapman Street. Jackie was working, so he left it in the refrigerator with a note that read,

Ma—Bon apetit. Love, Shawn. That evening he texted some friends and watched TV with Curtis, the two men sprawled on the sofa like college kids in a dorm room. Tavarus was upstairs with his family. Rob was in an upbeat mood, as if beginning to see through to the other side of this task he'd undertaken. After a time, they moved to the kitchen to cook dinner. Curtis washed sweet peppers from his garden in the sink. Before he finished the stir-fry he was preparing, Rob stood up, arched his back severely with his hands locked behind him, and let all those bones pop.

"Hang out and eat," Curtis said. "Then go to bed. You haven't slept in, like, a week."

"I'll hang out later. Gotta do some work downstairs first."

"Come on, just take a break."

"Just want this all done," Rob mumbled, leaving the kitchen through the rear door, turning left down the stairs.

Then they heard the car pull up in the driveway.

Chapter 16

◆

F ROM HIS ANGLE in the kitchen, Curtis couldn't see what happened
in the rear stairwell. He heard Rob open the back door on the landing half a level below the kitchen and above the laundry room, to see
who had pulled up. Rob muttered, "Ah, *shit!*" and began to close the
door, then froze with the door half open. It must have been too late.
In the days following, when Curtis gave his account to the police, he
would guess that at this point, not three seconds after his final exchange
with Rob about eating and sleeping, someone outside already had a gun
trained on his best friend.

The door swung open, and Rob was saying, "Chill, chill, chill . . . ,"
as the footsteps of at least two, possibly three, men seemed to back or
prod him down the stairs toward the basement. Curtis didn't try to get
a clear look into the stairwell, because he was running toward the front
of the house, his diaphragm pressing up against his lungs such that
breathing became difficult. Already, he heard yelling in the basement,
though he could not make out the words. The men who had invaded
his home wanted something, and Curtis did not need to be thinking
coherently—which he was not—to discern what that was. Because they
had pushed Rob immediately downstairs without even checking the rest
of the house, they must have known where Rob did his work, which

meant they had talked to someone with knowledge of both the money and the drugs.

Curtis reached the front door, his plan at this point simply to start yelling outside as loud as he could, draw some bodies out of the neighboring houses and onto the street. During any time of year, during any time of day or night, a street was always safer when people were on it. If neighbors congregated outside wondering what the hell was going on, these men would hear that, and they would leave the way they'd come in. If Curtis was lucky, he wouldn't even have to call the police.

Curtis was not lucky. Before he opened the front door he saw a man—or possibly a teenager—standing watch directly outside, wearing a hoodie and leaning against the wall at the bottom of the front steps so that he could cover the stoop, the sidewalk, and the front basement door simultaneously. His hand was buried allusively in his pocket. His face was hidden.

The basement had been largely cleared since that initial procurement of their stash. The marijuana was hidden in a trunk wedged back on one of the metal storage shelves. The hydroponic planters had been dismantled, as Rob had dried enough plant matter to see him through the remaining poundage of Sour Diesel. Money was down there, maybe a few thousand dollars.

The men had been inside the house for maybe twenty seconds at this point, and they were still yelling—the kind of yelling that indicated something important was at stake, yelling that negated the value of human life. Curtis couldn't pick out Rob's voice, which was alarming, because Rob's voice was so distinctive and it was unlike him to not be taking control of a situation, calming people down, as he'd done with Boobie a few years ago on the sidewalk where the watchman now stood. Talking was Rob's talent.

Curtis moved backward, away from the front door and its guard, toward a storage closet in the hallway. As he did so, his mind cycled through the possible circumstances in play downstairs. They could have been some of Rob's buyers desperate enough to risk ripping them off.

They could have been involved with a threatened local dealer, here to make a statement. They could have been Amin's people responding to rumors. They could have had something to do with Kamar and his recent associations with the Double II Set Bloods. They could have been anyone, really, any of the dozens of people, both local and farther flung, with whom Rob worked now or had in the past, people who Rob had confidently assured the Burger Boyz they would never know anything about. Curtis thought—here, now—of how vastly compartmentalized his best friend's life was, how even with all the hundreds and hundreds of nights he'd spent in this house, he'd spent just as many nights out there in places unknown. For the most part until recently, Rob's shadiness and mysteriousness regarding his conduct outside the realm of 34 Smith Street had been a source of amusement: he was always acting as if he were living a hustler's life, when most likely he'd been home on Chapman Street watching sitcoms with Frances and Jackie, or at some woman's house helping her kid study math, or getting laid in Brooklyn. All of his cumulative dour expressions and weighty sighs and murmured phone calls taken in the other room had always struck them to some extent as being staged by a guy who, hard as he presented himself to be, was just a mama's boy Yalie at heart. They'd always let him play the role, as most people in his life had, believing it to be for the most part simply that: a role. It wasn't real. It wasn't dangerous. It wasn't uncontrollable. It was just marijuana. It was just Rob Peace.

Maybe thirty seconds had passed since the break-in. Curtis was pulling the gun from the closet, the gun Rob had been carrying around town lately. Except for visits to the firing range with Rob and a few other friends, he had no experience with guns. He checked the chamber, which was loaded, and he moved back toward the rear stairway. He cocked the gun, unaware that this motion was unnecessary when a round was already chambered. He heard Rob's voice now, his tone defensive and deflecting and scared, and then Rob stopped speaking abruptly, too abruptly.

Curtis descended the stairs slowly, first to the landing by the back door, then down the last flight into the laundry room. He squatted behind the wooden railing for cover. On the far side of this area, about eight feet away, a very tall, robust black man filled the entire doorway of the basement, facing away from Curtis and into the room. He was wearing a ski mask and holding a gun at his side.

The majority of men figure that, when put in a situation where life hangs in the balance—both your own and that of those you care about—some dormant, primal instinct will activate, and you will be strong and decisive and precise and intelligent with every movement. In this moment, Curtis learned that such an instinct did not exist, or at least not in him. His weapon quavered, as did his voice when he called out to Rob to ask if he was all right.

The man in the doorway turned but didn't seem particularly startled. They exchanged charged words from either end of the laundry room. Curtis wouldn't remember exactly what had been said, only that he'd alternated a few times between ordering the intruders out of his house and pleading for Rob to say something, just one word, to let Curtis know he was okay. But behind the blocked door, Rob remained silent, which signaled that at least one more man was in the basement, most likely with a gun aimed at him.

Then the large man opened fire toward the stairs where Curtis crouched, and Curtis pulled his own trigger, but the gun didn't fire; he'd jammed the chamber when he'd cocked it moments earlier. The large man was advancing now, gaining an angle over the railing, and Curtis bolted back upstairs, crouching low. The back door was closed and locked, so he pivoted 180 degrees on the landing and climbed back toward the kitchen. The large man's weapon was popping off behind him, sounding like the M-80s they'd set off in the yard as boys. On the stairway one level above, Tavarus was standing with a laundry basket. He'd been on his way down to do a load of Christopher's school clothes. Curtis screamed at him to get back upstairs before fleeing behind the refrigerator. He peered around the edge and saw the large man's arm curled around the stair railing on the landing, firing blindly, bullets strafing the side of the refrigerator, the stove, the walls. Then the firing stopped.

Curtis was cornered. If he tried to run across the kitchen, back toward the front of the house, the man would have a line of sight on him. If he stayed here, with a gun that didn't work, he was most likely dead, too. He was breathing fast enough that he couldn't hear very well. He remained huddled against the refrigerator until he heard footsteps on the back stairs, more shouting voices, the back door opening and closing, the car peeling out of the driveway, then silence.

Curtis ran outside; they were already gone. Perhaps two minutes total had elapsed since they'd first entered, maybe less. What his first impulse had been to do, Curtis did now: he screamed to bring the neighbors out of their homes, to make the area safe with people the Burger Boyz had known since high school. But people were already outside in response to the shots. An elderly woman next door—whose bedroom window was not more than six feet away from the back door of 34 Smith Street— had already called the police, who were on their way. Tavarus was outside now, too. Christopher had woken up but was groggy. Darlene was upstairs with him. They were safe. Curtis told Tavarus to call people, as many as he could, just get people over here. And then, since the police were coming, he headed for the basement to see about getting the drugs out of his house. He figured that Rob was already doing the same thing; he figured that Rob, as ever, was one step ahead of everyone else.

Downstairs, beyond the laundry room where Curtis had almost been killed, the tarp had fallen back over the basement door. Curtis lifted it, calling out to his friend.

Rob was lying facedown on the floor, his knees bent and tucked beneath his torso, his arms folded under his chest. He had crumpled forward off the sunken love seat on which he'd been sitting. He wasn't moving. Blood that had pooled underneath him, contained by the position of his limbs, was just beginning to trickle past his face toward the small water drain just off center in the faux-tile floor. Afterward, Curtis wouldn't remember any words he said, or whether he had even been breathing. He just knew that his friend was not. He turned the body over. Rob was a dense man, maybe 175 pounds, but Curtis, still pulsing with adrenaline, didn't register the weight. Rob's shirt, soaked with blood, clung to his chest and stomach. His eyes were closed, and his mouth parted as his head tipped back over Curtis's thigh. He must have been screaming for someone to get down there, because that's what Tavarus did. And he must have been rocking the body, cradling the head in his right elbow, weeping, because that was how the East Orange police officers found him twenty-odd minutes later, before ordering him to stand up and put his hands in the air.

* * *

JACKIE WAS AWAKENED at one thirty by someone knocking on the front door. The knocking was barely audible, which meant it was likely some vagrant testing to see if anyone was home. This had happened before, which was why she refused to sleep in this house without a man present. Carl was there tonight, in Rob's old room. She waited to see if he would rise to take care of it, but he'd been drinking and never stirred. So she got up, put on a housecoat, and went halfway down the stairs, ready to hiss that whoever was out there was about to wake her sick mother and, in the meantime, the phone was in her hand to call the police. But she recognized the tall, long, lanky silhouette outside the front door immediately: Flowy. She turned on the porch light and opened the door.

"Ma," he said. "It's Shawn. We gotta . . . we gotta . . ." He turned away from her, back toward the deserted street, eyes wet and swollen. Tavarus had called Flowy an hour earlier, frantic but not making much sense, and he'd hung up quickly. Flowy had driven to Smith Street, but he hadn't been allowed past the yellow tape. Police cars were lined up at odd angles, flashing rhythmically. He'd seen the ambulance and connected its presence with the one decipherable word Tavarus had said, "Shawn." From the porch where officers were talking to Curtis and Tavarus, Tavarus had managed to call out to him: "Go take care of Ma."

Flowy had driven to Chapman Street, and now all he could say was that they needed to get to Curtis's house.

Jackie remained calm and composed. She imagined that Rob had been arrested for something she'd always convinced herself that he hadn't been involved with, and the days ahead of her would entail hours in precinct waiting rooms, the logistics of bail and lawyers, and the hard but doable task of aligning her vision of her son's life with what that life actually was. "Let me get dressed," she said.

"I'll drive you." He was choking on his words, she assumed out of embarrassment, or because he might be in trouble, too.

"I'll drive myself," she replied, and she turned back into her house, calling to Carl's unhearing ears that she was going out.

Flowy followed her east along Central Avenue, then right onto Telford, down into the dark, narrow gridwork of the neighborhood. Another right on Tremont, then left on Smith, where the red and blue lights spun two hundred yards down the block. Cars were backed up from the house, some belonging to friends who had heard something about the night's events, others just people trying to get through to South Orange Avenue. Jackie was already out of her car and hurrying down the sidewalk when Flowy put his in idle. Walking to the house, he passed policemen asking neighbors if anyone had surveillance footage of the street, as if these people's homes were equipped with modern security systems. He caught up to Jackie. A young, white policeman had met her at the tape barricade.

"You can't pass through this way, ma'am."

"It's my son," she said, "my son is in that house."

"You can't pass through this way."

Flowy towered behind her, his confusion and sadness turning into anger. "It's the boy's mother. Let her through."

The house was crowded with uniformed men clustered around the basement door and the stoop. Two more officers came down from the porch and approached. They consulted with one another and with their radios, then faced Jackie again. "You can't come through here, ma'am."

"Motherfffff—" Flowy began, but Jackie laid her hand against his chest. Her face remained calm, so impossibly calm, amid the lights and uniforms and spectators looking on with the sober, downcast expressions that Flowy had seen surrounding crime scenes growing up on his block, that Jackie had seen on her block, too. These expressions appeared only in reaction to violence, to pointlessness, to tragedy.

"Where is he?" she asked. "Is he still inside there?"

The officers consulted again, this time only with their eyes. They told her that a man had been taken to the hospital, but they refused to give a reason, name, or condition.

Flowy's big hands, so perfect for palming water polo balls, were on her shoulders. Quickly now, he was realizing what he'd known intuitively since he'd answered that call from Tavarus. His friend was either dead or close to it. Police behaved differently when someone had died than when someone had been wounded; they behaved just as they were behaving now, repeating evasive, scripted statements over and over. *You can't come through here, ma'am.* Flowy pulled gently on Jackie's shoulders, and she turned away from the house with him. They went back to their cars, and he followed her again, this time to East Orange Hospital, where she had once spent twelve-hour days cooking meals.

Flowy took over the questioning while Jackie sat in the ER waiting room, hands folded in her lap, eyes pointed at the floor as her body rocked gently forward and backward. Anyone who looked vaguely associated with the hospital, he grabbed and asked where Shawn Peace was. Then he realized that these people wouldn't know Rob's middle name, the name he went by in the hood, and started asking for Robert Peace instead, what Rob had called his *"nom professionnel."* Regardless of the name, nobody could tell him anything. He kept being passed off by doctors and nurses and administrators who seemed to put a special effort into looking harried and important and being needed urgently somewhere else. "It's the man's mother here, and nobody's telling her anything? This is fucked-up . . ." Flowy was not a violent man; his nickname had derived from growing up peacefully in one of the city's most unpeaceful neighborhoods. But he had anger in him that began to rise very fast up his spine. An administrator appeared and threatened to kick him out of the hospital if he couldn't be more patient and less profane. He sat beside Jackie. Finally, almost an hour later, a nurse said that a John Doe had been brought in from 34 Smith Street, nothing more. Another hour passed. Flowy, fuming, noticed that Jackie was crying as quietly as it was possible for a human being to cry.

"Let's go," he said. "You need to rest. Shawn's okay. We'll find that out soon enough."

He followed her home from the hospital and walked her to the front door. The phone had been ringing at the house, and Carl and Frances were awake. It was five in the morning, the first faint glow radiating from the horizon to the east, where the city was. Carl had spoken with Tavarus by now. He knew that Rob was dead. On the front porch of 181 Chapman Street, while Flowy watched from the cracked stairwell by the sidewalk, Carl took Jackie into his arms and whispered into her ear. Frances was wailing faintly inside, her respiratory system not capable of volume. Jackie nodded silently as if she already knew, then moved slowly inside with him.

"Ma," Flowy called, but no one heard him or else didn't respond. He didn't know what he'd meant to say, at any rate. He drove back to his apartment on Munn Avenue. His girlfriend, LaQuisha, was out of town. His cell phone was ringing every few minutes. He didn't answer or call anyone back. He lay in his bed and stared at the ceiling. The room was dark and very quiet aside from the neighborhood sounds that invariably rose to the seventh-floor window: cars passing by with the early-to-work shift, dogs barking in backyards, and the ever-present sirens.

*   *   *

THEY'D CONFISCATED EVERYTHING, including the dismantled planters, and now the basement was a mess of overturned furniture, chalk and fingerprint dust, decades' worth of the Gamble family's stored detritus. They'd searched the entire house for more drugs and money, so the upper floors were a disaster, too. Darlene had taken Christopher to her parents' house, and Curtis had been taken into custody by the police. Tavarus found himself drawn to the basement. The blood remained pooled in and around the chalk outline of Rob's body, lying on his side as he had rolled off Curtis's lap when the police had arrived. The narrow profile drawing didn't look anything like Rob, or any person at all. The red trail that led to the drain had congealed. Tavarus squatted at the trail's midpoint. They would be back before long, maybe even in minutes, and he'd been instructed not to enter the basement or touch anything. He was also aware that there were murderers out there in the hood somewhere, probably laughing about having done the smart-ass Yalie but good. Tavarus didn't care. His friend had been here in the house, with Curtis, talking, laughing, being Rob. And then he was unconscious and bleeding out on the floor. And now he was gone. Rob Peace was gone. He would never come back the way he had from all those trips abroad, coasting through the front door to make himself a drink and catch up on what he'd missed. He was just gone, gone, gone.

*   *   *

THE HOLDING CELL where Curtis waited between questioning sessions was crowded with the vagrants and dealers and johns and drunks of Newark. Curtis had made his phone call, to his mother. She would get him out of here soon. He sat on a bench in the corner, leaning far over so that his head was nearly resting on his knees. For the most part, the other criminals left him alone; each man seemed lost in his own interior. In the basement of his house had been a dead body, dozens of pounds of marijuana, and thousands of dollars of illegally obtained cash. The questioning both at the scene and here at the precinct had been aggressive, beginning with the events directly surrounding the murder and segueing harshly into the circumstances of the basement lab and growhouse. He forgot most of what he'd told them, except that he'd been honest about the home intrusion and his whereabouts during it, but he'd pleaded ignorance regarding the drugs as well as the gun that had jammed on him, which he'd left lying beside the refrigerator. He must have sounded like a fool saying that he never went into the basement, that the basement was Rob's room, that Rob paid rent for it, no one else knew what was going on down there. Charges would be formally filed against him; no universe existed in which they wouldn't be. During the questioning, he'd gotten the impression that he might even be held accountable for the murder itself. These were the immediacies that his mind had no option but to confront, even as they paled in comparison to the life that had been taken tonight. He thought of all those parties in high school, all those cookouts in the backyard, all the nights out at the bars and clubs. He thought mostly of Rob cracking his joints, laughing, calling him a bitch for something he'd said or done. Rob's laugh had been oddly high-pitched compared to his baritone voice, as if his true spirit were released only in those moments, the stupid, humorous ones. Curtis cried, sniveling tears like those cast by a small child, and he feared that as a result these other imprisoned men would be drawn toward him, attuned to the naked weakness and looking to take some kind of advantage. But everyone remained still and quiet as night became morning.

* * *

IN THE MORNING, Jackie received a call from the police, asking if she would be able to go to the city morgue and identify the body thought to belong to Robert DeShaun Peace. She told Carl to stay with Frances, and she drove downtown, nearly the same route she'd taken to St. Benedict's on the days she'd dropped Rob off. She parked and placed one foot in front of the other until she stood in the cold, metallic room that smelled of chemicals, and watched the coroner fold the white sheet down from her son's face. She nodded and said, "Yeah, that's Shawn, that's my son." From there, she drove straight to work.

Chapter 17

◆

From: Facebook
To: Jeff Hobbs
Subject: Victor Raymond sent you a message on Facebook...

Hey Jeff,

You might not remember me but I was your roommate's Rob
Peace's best friend. I came down to visit him at Yale a few times
throughout the years.
Well I regret to inform you that he passed away. I am trying to
figure out a way to notify his Yale friends. The only one I knew
to contact was you. Please let me know if you need further
information.
Sorry to inform you this way!!!
Victor

This message brayed on my phone just before midnight on Thursday, May 19, the day after Rob died. The words wiped away the drowsiness caused by two *Seinfeld* reruns. A few shocked back-and-forths confirmed what I instinctively knew already: my college roommate of four years had died violently. But they did not give much else, not even the minor consolation of knowing he'd made the ultimate transition without pain.

The death of someone you know is so vastly different from reading of the same event happening to a stranger. You are familiar with your friend's face and voice, and so you are haunted, during the overstimulated state of being wide awake at four in the morning, by the very specific expressions and sounds he might have made as a bullet, perhaps more than one, passed into his body. The terrible resoluteness of this passage had likely happened not long after my wife and I, three thousand miles away, had undergone our nightly square dance—one flosses while the other brushes, then switch—padding softly on the floorboards so as not to wake our little girl.

A Yale graduate lost to the drug trade seemed so far-flung and bizarre that the task of relating this to our college community was barely short of incapacitating. But still, the tidy Facebook search-poke-send features provided the necessary distance for me to friend a few dozen people I was no longer—or, in some cases, had never been—friends with in order to inform them that our mutual friend was gone. The responses I received all fell along the lines of, "Jeff it is so great to hear from you but what HORRIBLE news!!! How did this HAPPEN???" The bombardment of questions to which I had no answers only made me feel less fit for the task, particularly when I was corresponding with those who knew him far better than I, such as Raquel and Daniella. Some inquiries were as simple as the when/where of the funeral (I had conflicting times/addresses), while others asked, in the cosmoreligious sense, *Why?* (Being more or less a Christmas and Easter churchgoer, I had no clue.) The answers I did manage to learn in the days preceding the burial remained broad and overearnest and sometimes contradictory: he was dealing only to support his mother; all he wanted was to live in South America; he was broke; he was trying to go back to school; he was going to get out of it soon; he was trying to open up his own pharmacy; what had happened wasn't supposed to have happened. And yet they still rendered the predictable media spin of potential squandered, the gift of education sacrificed to the allure of thug life, etc., not only simplistic but offensively so. Equally unilluminating were the brainy musings of classmates, accompanied by the requisite, almost haughty "borne back ceaselessly into the past" references. The fact was that what he'd been killed over didn't seem any more sinister than what he'd done in college, when the "farmacy" he'd opened in his dorm room had seemed as far removed from lethality as the Ivory Tower itself.

I flew alone from LAX to JFK and arrived at eleven on the night before the funeral. Ty Cantey and a few other Yale classmates were out drinking relatively near my in-laws' house in Brooklyn, so I went straight to the bar, my small suitcase clattering on the sidewalk behind me. This was in Clinton Hill, a kind of in-between neighborhood, and the side streets were dark and intimidating. But I reached the bar without incident and sidled up beside my old roommate. The girl whom Rob had set me up with following my college heartbreak, LaTasha, was also there. She'd majored in MB&B with Rob and was now a veterinarian in Philadelphia. Ty and I talked about our wives and children, the tribulations of last-minute travel arrangements, the logistics of all of us reaching Newark by train in the morning—anything, it seemed, except Rob himself. Our collective information regarding his death was still limited, which brought forward the sadder fact that, at the end of it all, none of us had actually known Rob as well as we thought we did, as well as we should have, as well as—with just a little more effort—we could have. But we were here. We'd spent the money and made the arrangements and undergone the hassle of gathering to commemorate his death. That, at least, meant something, as did our subdued toasts to Rob having been a "good dude."

The next morning I showed up at the apartment where Ty and LaTasha were crashing on Eastern Parkway, across the street from the Brooklyn Museum. Ty, as he'd been on his wedding day, was late getting dressed. We boarded the subway a half hour later than we'd planned, got all turned around trying to find the Path station at the World Trade Center (wondering why, a decade after the towers had fallen in our senior year of college, they didn't seem to be building anything yet), disembarked from the Path at the wrong stop, and were swindled by the Newark cabdrivers who charged a flat $20 to take us to the funeral less than a mile from the train station. The trip ended up being so long and error filled, our laughter over the general incompetence of us Yale graduates so constant, that at a certain point we almost forgot that we were heading to the funeral of someone we'd known and loved. Then we arrived and saw the people gathered outside. The ceremony was at St. Mary's Church, which adjoined the St. Benedict's campus. None of us had ever been to an open-casket funeral before. The line for the viewing was two blocks long and one of the most diverse collections of people I'd ever seen: Yale students and professors, people conversing in Portuguese and Croatian and Spanish, young and old residents of all the boroughs of New York City and all the townships surrounding Newark. More than four hundred people were there.

For us, the achingly slow-moving line along Martin Luther King Jr. Boulevard took on the aspect of a college reunion without alcohol. Some faces I recognized vaguely as Rob's customers from a decade ago, men and women who'd constantly filed through our common room, wearing hoodies and piercings—uniform in their aversion to uniformity—to sit with Rob in giggly plumes of smoke, railing against university robo-culture while feeding live mice to his python. Now they were lawyers and investment bankers, with faces creased and drawn by the skirmish of daily life. Others I'd known well, and as we inched perilously closer to the casket, our talk evidenced a shared fondness for Rob but also something else shared in our own receding dreams. There was Ty and his dermatology career, me and my struggles to publish a second novel, former history majors who were doing their best to remain in school forever. Nobody, it seemed, was making the money he'd thought he would make, inhabiting the home he'd thought he would inhabit, doing the thing he'd thought he would do in life. Nobody was fulfilling the dreams harbored on graduation day almost ten years earlier.

These uncomfortable observations closely preceded the limbo moments, maybe fifteen seconds' worth, during which we finally filed inside and faced the embalmed body. Rob's hair had been tightly braided by his cousin Diandra that morning. He was dressed in a black suit, with his hands folded at his waist. His head was tipped backward slightly. His skin was waxen, shrunken, scentless, insufficient, and so very still. I'd expected that Rob would look somewhat at ease—peaceful even. But if anything, he looked uncomfortable, like maybe he needed to crack his joints one last time to relieve some pressure inside him.

The day was muggy and hot, and the crowded church was stifling. Between the series of hymns and as the occasional cracked sob sent a stab of pain through the atmosphere, Friar Leahy gave a long and fiery sermon about the value of human life. I didn't really listen to much of it, because I was trying to figure out what I would say when Ty and I went up to the lectern later. Victor had mentioned to me in an email that there would be something like an "open mike" at the end of the ceremony, and anyone could speak, but that comments should be kept under two minutes if possible. Ty went before me and promised to establish a scholarship to St. Benedict's and to Yale in Rob's name, to resonant applause. (There would ultimately be two separate efforts in this regard, and neither would gain any traction at all; donors weren't prone to give money in the name of a drug dealer.) Then I was standing there, my gaze panning across those hundreds of faces, every one of whom Rob had known but only a very few of whom I did. The coffin was beneath the lectern and to the left. Rob's face was obscured by a flower arrangement. I said something about the kung fu movies we used to watch in our dorm room, and something else about his grin and how we were all lucky to have known someone with a grin like that. After I stepped down, a funeral-crashing evangelist who had seen the obituary spoke extensively about the Lord's judgment and how we all needed to go to church more often and pray more devoutly. Then Raquel climbed the three steps to the microphone and, through a curtain of tears, spoke of what a gentleman Rob was, what a good friend, what a role model to her son Felix ("He taught my son how to shake hands like a *man* instead of this Puerto Rican kissy-kiss-on-the-cheek thing we do when we greet people . . ."), and how he'd always instilled her with confidence:

first when she'd been a student, then a young woman, and then, most
important, a mother. She said, in reference to Jackie, "He knows a good
mama when he sees one." Then she concluded:

> I don't know where I heard it first but "It takes a long time to grow
> an old friend." In that way, Rob was like a redwood tree looming
> large in my life. His life was cut short before it could reach the full
> heights of its glory. But as I look around this room, I take solace in
> the fact that so many others thrived and found refuge in his shade
> while he was with us. I miss you, Rob. I always will.

Only a small contingent made it to the burial following the service, maybe two dozen people or so. In a small lawn on the fringe of
the sprawling Rosedale Cemetery, Rob was buried in his father's plot,
which still had no headstone. After a curiously labor-intensive process
of straps and pulleys managed by two grunting, sweaty workers, his coffin was set literally on top of Skeet Douglas's. From a heap of flowers at
the foot of the plot, we each pulled a lily or a rose and dropped it on the
bowed, dark wood. I noticed that there were a lot of pretty women our
age weeping, none of whom seemed to know one another. I watched
Jackie throughout the burial. She did not cry, though almost all the family members surrounding her did. She was tucked in the middle of them
all, like a pillar covered in vines. She looked as she had in our dorm
room that day in September of 1998, sullen and impassive and not yet
accepting the sheer degree to which she would miss her son.

After that, a luncheon was held in St. Benedict's bright and airy cafeteria, aluminum vats of chicken, rice, and greens. People were laughing
and telling stories, some of which involved Rob, some of which didn't.
At one point Friar Leahy approached the table where the remaining
Yale contingent sat. Ty and I stood and shook his hand. He told us
about the school and its philosophy while showing us a plaque bearing
Rob's name as the 1998 Presidential Award winner. He seemed very
happy to have a collection of Yale grads in his school, happy that we

were there because a boy he had once taught had gone to Yale, had once stood on the cusp of achieving everything that word called to mind. I imagined Rob sitting over his own food in this very room so many hundreds of mornings, as both a student and a teacher. I imagined the particular way he ate, hunched over, mouth close to the plate while his left forearm made a rampart around it, as if someone lurking nearby would try to snatch his meal away. Outside the windows stretched a pristine turf field where he had played lacrosse with Victor for one season. Beyond that, the Newark skyline cut an industrial picture against the overcast sky.

Like college graduation, there always seemed to be another event. The last of the day was at a bar in Bloomfield called A.S.H., one of Rob's haunts. I took a ride from one of Rob's East Orange friends who, while swerving sharply through the labyrinth of merging Newark streets, told me about the travails of his job selling cars, the lousy commissions. Once we reached the bar, he ordered me a "little beer," one of Rob's favorite drinks, which was disgusting, and we had our own toast, though I never even learned the guy's name. Most of the people there, myself included, drank aggressively. Men I didn't recognize were paying hundreds of dollars for bottles of vodka to bring to the tables, as if we were at a nightclub. I talked to Raquel, whom I barely knew, for a while about how weird it was that we were all adults. Oswaldo Gutierrez was there. He was the only one who still looked sober and grim, the expression that a day like this seemed to call for. I didn't know how involved he had been in Rob's life after college; I didn't know how angry he was that day because Rob had never listened to him, because he had enabled Rob to not listen, because Rob had died owing him the $4,000 that had indirectly caused his death. Oswaldo knew better than to blame himself. Rob would have found that money one way or another, and that was one of the hardest things for many of us to accept: that no matter how loosely or intimately intertwined we had been with the life of Rob Peace, our ineffectuality extended far enough to encompass the living and dying of others. *So fucking smart, but so fucking dumb.* That was how

Oswaldo had always characterized his friend, to his face as well as in his consciousness. The words were a refrain in his head that would play on and on and on.

*   *   *

THE BURGER BOYZ did not attend the funeral or any of the festivities that followed. Jackie requested their absence, and Nathan communicated this wish to them two days after Rob's death. Flowy and Drew were mad at first, especially when they learned that the funeral was going to be at St. Benedict's. The placement and their nonattendance made them look culpable, they felt, in a community that remained important to them. They planned to go anyway.

"No, you're not doing that," Tavarus told them. The day before, Tavarus had taken a sponge and a bucket downstairs. On his knees, using both hands to scrub deep into the textured flooring, he'd washed away Rob's blood.

"How are we gonna lose our boy and not go to his funeral?" Flowy asked. "I've seen that boy most every day of my life since we were fourteen."

"Because this is a mother who lost her son, and she wants answers that none of us have, and we are going to do whatever the hell she wants," Tavarus replied. "That's how."

On the day of the funeral, they had their own small ceremony in the backyard, just a few yards from where Rob died. Police were still in and out, though less so as the days passed. They still hadn't filed charges against Curtis, who'd been released after three nights in the cell, but charges were imminent. The house was nearly clean of the mess left in the wake of the police search; this had taken days of work. No one ventured to comment on their surreal capacity to remain in the house, to eat and sleep there, and, now, to share a mournful blunt and toast to Rob. They still could not fully process the vacancy following Rob's death, the space that was not occupied by his broad shoulders, the silence that was not punctured by his voice. Christopher was riding his bike, the one

Rob had given him years earlier, around the driveway. The bike was the perfect size for him now.

They couldn't avoid talking about that night. Whether or not those men had shown up with the intent to kill Rob would always remain unclear. That no one remembered hearing the shots that killed him meant that they must have been discharged as Curtis was running upstairs from the large man firing on him. They figured that during Curtis's failed intervention, whoever had a gun on Rob—a teenage neighbor who'd seen them leave said the second intruder had been a small, light-skinned guy with dreadlocks—must have turned around, and Rob must have made a move on him, perhaps thinking that his recent martial arts training gave him a better-than-average chance of gaining the upper hand. The Burger Boyz would never know if this had been the case, either. What Curtis did know was that if Rob hadn't been shot, then the intruders wouldn't have fled so quickly, and he would most likely be dead instead of—or in addition to—Rob. Tavarus, Darlene, and Christopher would have been vulnerable, too. Rob saved their lives. This was what they told themselves that night.

Curtis didn't contribute much to the dialogue. He abstained from alcohol and drugs in the event that the police showed up, and he spent most of that long afternoon rooted in the moment four nights earlier when he'd held and cradled his friend's lifeless body, a moment he would never leave.

The state medical examiner had pulled two .18 caliber bullets from Rob's torso. The first shot had entered his abdomen and lacerated the liver. The second had struck him squarely in the chest, pierced a coronary artery, and lodged in the back of his rib cage. Blood had immediately begun filling his chest cavity, causing a very painful buildup of pressure. Rob was most likely conscious for ninety seconds or so, but his brain, which he had strived to dull so many thousands of times with marijuana, would have begun shutting down into a foggy state almost immediately from the drop in blood pressure. He had clearly suffered severely in the moments before he closed his eyes for the last time, but he suffered silently; Curtis had heard neither a cry nor a groan following the gunshots. Maybe, even then, he was thinking about his friends and contained his pain, as he'd always managed to do, so as not to draw them down to the basement and into harm's way.

*   *   *

Killed in apparent drug-related shooting,
Yale alumnus remembered for leadership

Wherever he went, Robert Peace was a star.

His intellect and athletic skill carried him from the modest apartment he shared with his mother in Orange, to the halls of Newark's venerable St. Benedict's Academy, where he won the school's highest honor, and then to Yale University, where he graduated with a degree in molecular biochemistry.

Even when he was shot to death in a Newark house Wednesday, police say, he was not your garden variety drug dealer.

The 30-year-old Yale scientist was using his knowledge of biochemistry to bring in $1,000 a day selling marijuana grown in the basement of the Smith Street home where he was killed, said law enforcement officials with knowledge of the investigation. They requested anonymity because they were not authorized to discuss the case. . . .

Flowy's cell phone rang all morning the day the article was published in the *Newark Star-Ledger*; almost everyone he knew was telling him not to read it. They weren't worried so much about the article itself, the remainder of which briefly described police speculation regarding Rob's alleged drug distribution network, followed by a longer recap of all his past achievements at St. Benedict's and Yale. They were more concerned about Flowy seeing the online public comments that followed, which over the day of the article's release had degenerated into a kind of class warfare.

From opieisback: How you go from Yale to this, I don't know.

From drphil1: One word—MONEY. Not everyone who graduates from Yale becomes a success. Peace saw that he could make hundreds of thousands of dollars manufacturing rather than working in a lab for peanuts. Of course he had to establish a distribution system that brought in more people including those that wanted a big piece of the action. His demise means his manufacturing operation is defunct and the distribution network he supported is disrupted.

From LADYFROMNJ30: This man was a loyal friend to many! This article was written by two idiots that have no clue as to what actually took place in this house . . . I have been to this home many times and know for a fact there was no 'lab' in the basement . . . come on now are you serious? He didn't even live at this house!!!! At the end of the day, I am not here to go back and forth in an argument with anyone here. It's just sad that he lost his life, his family and friends have lost someone and this man is not even here to defend himself. The police monopolize on any opportunity to exploit the black man in Newark, and ANYONE with real common sense would know this and not post these ignorant comments about 'education' being thrown away . . .

From Yo: *The police monopolize on any opportunity to exploit the black man in Newark* . . . Huh? Don't think because he was black that he was destined to be a criminal.

From FactsDon'tMatter: To the rest of the people here that THINK they know everything about Robert. You don't. You don't know that he was raised by a single mother that worked in a kitchen; you don't know the hardships he had to overcome, like having a father in prison. You don't know that he tried his hardest to get his dad out of that prison when he was terminally ill with cancer only to be turned down and then having to watch his father waste away and die behind bars. You don't know the many young men he inspired by being there for them and with them. You don't know the many young men he taught to swim. You don't know how he made chemistry assessable to those same kids. . . . You only know anecdotal clichés about drugs and fast money and consequences . . . I didn't know Robert well, but I knew of him as my son's Water Polo coach, a guy who pushed and cared for those kids that he coached. I know that I am saddened that a great light has been extinguished. I'm sad because he died alone. I'm sad because he'll no longer be there to inspire another young gifted Black man to aspire to Yale and beyond. The rest of you can be happy, but those of us that knew Robert in any way at all are devastated. RIP ROB . . . Another Grey Bee gone too soon. WHATEVER HURTS MY BROTHER HURTS ME.

From SUMMITNJ1: This deceased drug-dealing character Robert Peace would have instantaneously shot *anyone* here who would have threatened his illegal (yet lucrative) source of dirty income. He was a thug through and through.

From njresident80: Who the heck is from Summit NJ?

Charles Cawley was staying at his Maine estate when he learned of Rob's death via an email from Friar Leahy. He took his coffee outside into the gray, temperate northeastern spring. He sat on his patio and gazed down the lawn, which sloped steeply toward the rocky shore of Lincolnville Beach. He had a dock and assorted boats moored there. Tavarus had once gone fishing in the harbor during his St. Benedict's retreat. Later this summer, twelve boys from the current St. Benedict's student body would arrive to do the same. Mr. Cawley remained sitting there for a time, long after he'd finished his coffee, surprised by how unsurprised he was by the news of Rob's passing. He was saddened, regretful, angry—but not surprised. Soon his wife joined him and patted his hand. He thought back to Friar Leahy's introduction of Rob during the senior banquet in 1998. He thought of what he'd given the boy, not in terms of money but rather in choices, and he wondered how a person as bright and deserving as Rob Peace could have made the choices, beginning on the night of that banquet, that had resulted in this. And he figured that the choices hadn't necessarily begun on that night. Most likely, they'd begun on the night he was born, and not all of them had been his to make.

The police, with so little information to go on, had rooted around the neighborhood but found little. They had no suspects, no prints, no evidence. The forty-eight-hour window in which the vast majority of violent crimes are solved had long since passed. Most likely, the murderers had fled town for a while, and the investigators' ongoing hope was that one of them would be picked up on a moving violation or drug charge in Philadelphia or Baltimore or some other troubled urban clime. When Charlene and Estella Moore had been killed in 1987, the police had found a gun, an address, and a suspect armed with the murder weapon within twenty-eight hours. When Rob Peace had been killed in 2011, the police had found nothing.

Raquel was using Facebook in order to solicit donations from as many friends of Rob's as she could in order to help pay Jackie's funeral costs. She ultimately raised $5,000 but was disappointed by the fact that so many former classmates, many of them wealthy and many of whom had bought weed from Rob regularly in college, either failed to respond or outright refused due to the circumstances of his death. At the same time, Curtis was using the same platform in a brief and unsuccessful effort to hire his own private mercenaries to track down the killers and repay them in kind. The vendetta obsessed him as his own legal snarls carried on with hearings linking him with the commerce in his basement. Tavarus, who himself was incapacitated to the point of closing down his restaurant and getting a job as a telemarketer, convinced him to stop. Violence wasn't going to solve violence. Rob was dead. That was the end of the story, punctuated by the tattoo Flowy had inked on his arm: "Real Peace Never Die BB4Life." More important was trying to mend the break that had occurred between them and Jackie, at least to the point where she would talk to them again. They each tried calling, only to be rebuffed by the aunts and uncles who were still answering Jackie's phone. That they would ever again know the woman they'd all called "Ma" began to feel hard to imagine, more so by far than the murderers being brought to justice. As of the publication of this book, neither has come to pass.

Jackie never took a day off work, and when she wasn't at the nursing home, she was on Chapman Street taking care of Frances, who soon entered hospice care for kidney failure. Frances was in and out of her senses and often asked when Rob would be coming around to eat and watch TV. Jackie would tell her that Rob was on one of his trips, and she didn't know when exactly he was coming back. His cousin had made a large poster for the funeral, with pictures of Rob as a kid holding a football on the sidewalk, after a water polo game with a towel slung over his neck, in Brazil, smiling in all of them. The pictures orbited a gold star, like an enlarged version of those handed out to elementary school students for work well done, in which was written his name and the years of his birth and death. Unframed, the arrangement stood propped on the back of the sofa in the parlor, facing the front window, that boyhood waiting place. In the evenings between cigarettes on the front porch, Jackie would sit in the dusky light and stare at the pictures. Thirty years of her son's life had been reduced to those pictures, which had not been printed on glossy paper and so would fade and yellow with time. Whenever anyone visited, which was often in the months following her son's death, she would nod her head and offer soft-sounding "yeah"s and "uh-huh"s as they conversed, conspicuously not about Rob most of the time. When he did come up and someone inferred directly or indirectly what a good boy he had been, what a tender and compassionate and intelligent soul he'd possessed, she would think of all his accomplishments as well as all he failed to accomplish, and she would say, "Yeah, I think he influenced a lot of people; I really do believe that . . ."

* * *

ASIDE FROM THE private grief coursing through many of its inhabitants, the neighborhood didn't change in the wake of Rob's death. Cory Booker continued to give eloquent speeches about how he was accomplishing something that no one before him had thought possible: he was revitalizing Newark (until two years later, when he was elected to the U.S. Senate). Crime statistics continued to be a centerpiece of these proclamations. Gangs continued to form and expand. Drugs continued to be sold on the corners and in the homes and in Orange Park, where

Sundays were still reserved for children. People, many of whom were involved with gangs or drugs or both, continued to be killed. Babies were born to young mothers who formed sisterhoods together and could be found on temperate afternoons perched on stoops nursing their infants. Young men, many of them fathers, went to jail—including Curtis Gamble, one year and two months after Rob's death. Children walked home from elementary schools in their various uniforms, laughing and swapping candy and listening to rap music. Seasons changed. Cars swooshed east and west on the I-280 beneath Mt. Carmel. Boys herded in the St. Benedict's entrance each morning for convocation at eight o'clock. A percentage of these boys that far exceeded that of the surrounding populace went off to college in the fall. Planes flew in and out of Newark International. People got through their lives, navigating the socioeconomic boundaries that made interesting geometrical shapes across Newark and the Oranges. Those living in the impoverished districts spent their days tending to the immediate obligations of family and money and their nights dreaming of not living there anymore someday, most knowing these were only dreams: incorporeal constructs formed by imaginative and hopeful minds. Jackie made the seven-minute drive to the nursing home each morning and came back each night, careful to keep her car doors locked and her windows raised once she crossed from South Orange into East Orange. She did this until she retired at the end of December 2012, thinking that she would use her nephew Nathan's Continental buddy pass to visit Brazil. The grass that surrounded the small earthen depression around plot 54, row 7, of Rosedale Cemetery grew thick in the summer and yellowed in the fall and was covered by snow in the winter. Sometimes a bunch of flowers could be found tucked within it, or a mix CD, or a short note. Most of the time the receptacle remained empty, hidden, there only to people who knew where to look, no different in appearance or texture from all the grass around it.

On what would have been Rob's thirty-first birthday in June, just over a month after his murder, Raquel and Rene arrived at 181 Chapman Street in the early evening. Neither had ever been to his home before, and Rene had never met his mother. She was surprised by the life, the spark, contained in the bereaved woman's eyes, which reminded her of Rob even though all she'd ever heard from him was how much he looked like his father. Raquel was remembering her crazy thirtieth birthday party in SoHo last fall, where at one point Rob had called out, "My birthday's on June twenty-fifth!" as if to say that he wouldn't object if she were to throw him a party akin to the one she'd thrown herself. Instead, in the parlor, she gave Jackie an envelope packed with checks that had come from all over the world to help allay the monetary cost of his death. She'd worked almost full-time for a month accumulating them. Some were for $10 or $20. Others were for $100, $200, $250. All in all, they added up to about $5,000. To the same degree that she was grateful to those who had contributed, Raquel remained angry with those who had refused.

"Thank you," Jackie said softly.

As they embraced, Raquel replied, "It's not enough. Nothing will ever be enough."

Later that night, his friends and family gathered at Passion. Though not a strip club, the bar had once been something like one, back when Jackie had met Skeet for the first time there. Poles and platforms stood behind the bar. Jackie brought three of her girlfriends and was determined to smile through it all. Victor and Lisa Wingo and Sherman Feerick and Dexter Lopina and Coach Ridley and Carl and Shannon Heggins and Nathan were there. Tamba DJ'd. Guests drank blue Long Island iced teas and little beers in Rob's honor and the music grew louder and a pleasant drunkenness settled on the crowd. Before long people were dancing on the platforms, twisting themselves around the poles, all of this behavior silly and raucous—a night Rob would have enjoyed observing from off to the side, commenting on the gleeful idiocy on display. Jackie found herself able to channel her son and laugh authentically until the cake was brought out. That moment was the only one in which Jackie had cried since the early morning after Rob's death when, while waiting for the call that would confirm what a night of driving around the police stations and hospitals of East Orange had already told her was her new reality, she had permitted herself a few moments of outward, solitary grief.

At the same time, in the backyard of 34 Smith Street, the Burger Boyz had congregated once again with a few packages of floating lanterns, lightweight paper balloons with a small combustible carbon cube suspended beneath the open bottom. These contraptions were hard to unfold and harder to light. The first few ripped, and the next few caught fire and had to be stomped out, and they joked about how frustrated Rob would have been watching their mechanical ineptitude. Ultimately they engineered a two-man system in which one held the balloon open and aloft while the other lit the charcoal, and one by one the lanterns began to rise slowly, gracefully above the yard, their gathering place for almost two decades as they'd grown from boys to young men to something more than young men but not quite old men, that gray in-between area during which most of their mistakes had been made. The lanterns accelerated and began to drift with the breeze, above the salutes sent from below, the toasting plastic cups of liquor and raised marijuana joints and the "East Side" hand gestures and cries of "Happy born day" and avowals of "You gonna live forever, Shawn Peace." Soon they were just glimmering specks a few hundred feet above drifting east toward downtown, over the darkened side streets of East Orange where they had all inhabited various residences over the years, over the streaming headlights along the I-280 and the Garden State Parkway and Central Avenue and South Orange Avenue and the other thoroughfares that radiated like spokes from downtown Newark to the nether regions, over Bloomfield and Vailsburg and Irvington, over St. Benedict's Preparatory Academy for Boys and the Passaic River and the rusty yet mighty bridges spanning it, a vantage point Rob had seen leaving for and returning from all his trips, from which the city looked so serene and sometimes, at the right angle and at the right time of night, even beckoning. At a certain point, the lights disappeared from view beyond the trees and eaves of the neighboring homes, leaving the Burger Boyz to sit down once again in the plastic fold-out chairs and wonder how long it would be before the flames flickered out and the lanterns began their descent. And once that happened, they wondered where each would fall.

Curtis Gamble's house at 34 Smith Street. The black door at the base of the stairs leads directly down to the basement, where Rob Peace was shot twice and killed on the night of May 18, 2011.

ACKNOWLEDGMENTS

◆

REBECCA, REBECCA, REBECCA. Thank you for each of the thousands of hours of nightly conversation. Thank you for your mind, your work ethic, your patience, your way of connecting with people, your editing, your confidence, your humor, your insights, your eyes. Thank you for our children and for your love. YAMAAF.

My baby boy, Whitman Peace Hobbs: we are so happy that you came to us, and we hope that you grow up with Rob's intelligence, generosity, loyalty, humor—and with much more peace in your life.

Lucy: I love you to the moon and back and back to the moon and back again and back to the moon and back again . . .

Sara Nelson is the smartest and kindest person I know. Thank you for your time, advocacy, generosity, and spirit.

David Black read a very short and insufficient outline of an idea, and he saw what, with a few thousand hours of work, that idea could become. In the process, he taught me how to shape a very hard-to-wrangle narrative, and—most important—how to ask the questions that haven't been asked and are thus the easiest to avoid asking. He did so insightfully, patiently, and with unceasing belief in the importance of Rob's story. I will always be grateful.

Rob's many, many friends from his hometown of Newark have spent many, many hours rendering their memories to me: the joyful, the funny, the touching, and the tremendously painful. None of it was easy, and all of you dug deep. Jason, Demien, Tamba, Shannon, Lisa, Dawn, Julio, LaQuisha, Hrvoje, Marina, Roy, Darlene, Ina, Lana, Rene,

403

Mrs. Gamble, Big Steve, Victor, and of course the Burger Boyz: Curtis, Tavarus, Drew, Flowy—and the youngest member, Christopher.

I am equally grateful to Rob's friends from Yale: Daniella, Lamar, Simon, Danny, Sherman, Alejandra, Yesenia, Laurel, Arthur, Helen, Ty, Dan, Phil, Albert, Tasha, Adanna, Anthony, Isabella, Nevine, Cliff, Nick, Pablo, Armando, Zina, Katrina, Jacinta, Anwar, and Mike.

At Yale, Dean Jeffrey Brenzel contributed greatly to my understanding of not only the minority experience in college, but of the larger role a college such as Yale aims to have in the shaping of its students' minds. My sister Lindsay, Amin Gonzalez, Harvey Goldblatt, Christa Dove, Derrick Gilbert, Dr. Iona Black, Dr. Elias Lolis, Nelson Donegan— thank you all for giving your time and insights into Rob's years in New Haven.

Friar Edwin Leahy, Coach Wayne Ridley, Marc Onion, Truman Fox, Dexter Lopina, Charles Cawley—one of the greatest pleasures of this book has been the window it gave into St. Benedict's and the devotion with which you treat your special school.

Mike Pallardy, Cory Booker, Ron Howell, Carl Herman, Thomas Lechliter, Albert Kapin, Mary Gibbons, Leroy Franklin, John Armeno, Louis Seppola—whether you were explaining the logistics of governing a city such as Newark, sharing with me how you police it, guiding me through New Jersey's largest prison (as a guard or as an inmate), or recalling the intricacies of a murder trial that took place twenty-three years ago, you have all helped me—and, hopefully, the reader—understand the environment in which Rob grew up.

Mom, Dad, Bryan, Kelly, Lindsay, Michael, Andy, Clare, Grandma— I do not forget for a moment how fortunate I am to be a part of such a big, kind, funny family.

Nor do I forget the fortune I have in being married to one. Martin and Ruth Goldstein, Emily Learnard, Batab, Lanie, Ann-Marie, Pixie, Ruthie, Matt—thank you all for your support and love through all things.

Many others have helped bring this book to completion in both direct and indirect ways: Daniel Riley, Corrie and Ken Nolan, Sam Radin, Alyssa Bachner, Marty Scott, Bellinda Scott, Rawson Thurber, Sarah Koplin, Sarah Treem, Jay Carson, Michelle Weiner, Joy Gorman, Nick Wettels, Jess Lappin, Andy Wuertele, Russell Hollander, Sarah Smith, Lisa Rivlin, Cynthia Merman, Katrina Diaz, and Kate Lloyd.

I have relied on a few books to illuminate the broader canvas that Rob's life traversed, most notably *How Newark Became Newark: The Rise, Fall, and Rebirth of an American City* by Brad R. Tuttle, *The Shape of the River: Long-Term Consequences of Considering Race in College and University Admissions* by William G. Bowen and Derek Bok, and *Race and Class Matters at an Elite College* by Elizabeth Aries. Also the documentaries *Brick City*, created by Mark Benjamin and Marc Levin, and *Street Fight* by Marshall Curry are both very powerful and multilayered views of modern-day Newark.

Oswaldo Gutierrez toured me through the physical and emotional landmarks of his hometown of Newark, as well as those of his alma mater, Yale University. More than anyone else, he helped me build a kind of bridge between these two worlds, and to capture the largely invisible burden that inhabiting both of them places on the individuals who are able to do so.

This entire endeavor began with what was intended to be a short, cathartic visit with Raquel Diaz not long after Rob's funeral, which turned into an eight-hour-long conversation in her living room in Spanish Harlem while the rain poured down outside. Raquel, you have remained almost as close to this book as I have, and the insightfulness of your questions has never ceased (nor have the questions themselves).

My editor, Colin Harrison, is just about perfect at doing what he does. Whether you were answering my questions, asking me your much smarter questions, steering both my research and my writing with a gentle yet unrelenting hand, editing text with attention paid to every single word, or simply leaving me alone to work—I don't believe the editorial experience could have been more satisfying or that I could be more thankful. Your "Nice job" means more to me than you know. Above all, I thank you for believing that Rob Peace's story was worth telling in this form, for having the sensitivity to want to understand who he was and why he made the decisions he did.

Nathan, Carl, Diandra, Cory, Dante, Garcia, Camilla—and all members of the Peace family—you have invited me into your homes and trusted me with your memories. My greatest aspiration in writing this book has been to earn that trust.

Jackie Peace, you have spent dozens of hours talking to me during the hardest years of your life, and about the man whose loss has made them so. You are a truly great woman, and I am a lucky man to have been able to call your son my friend.

To donate to the Robert Peace Scholarship at St. Benedict's Preparatory School, visit www.lifeofrobertpeace.com/scholarship.

The Short and Tragic Life of Robert Peace

JEFF HOBBS

BOOK DESCRIPTION

WHEN JEFF HOBBS arrived at Yale University, he became fast friends with the man who would be his college roommate for four years, Robert Peace. Rob's life was rough from the beginning in the crime-ridden streets of Newark in the 1980s, with his father in jail and his mother barely scraping by as a cafeteria worker. But Rob was a brilliant student, and everything was supposed to get easier when he was accepted to Yale. But nothing got easier. Rob carried with him the difficult dual nature of his existence, "fronting" at Yale and at home.

As Jeff pieces together Rob's life story through his relationships—with his struggling mother, his incarcerated father, his teachers and friends and fellow drug dealers—*The Short and Tragic Life of Robert Peace* comes to encompass the most enduring conflicts in America: race, class, drugs, community, imprisonment, education, family, friendship, and love. Rob's story is about the collision of two fiercely insular worlds—the ivy-covered campus of Yale University and Newark, New Jersey—and the difficulty of going from one to the other and then back again. It's about trying to live a decent life in America. But most all, the book is about the life and death of one brilliant man.

TOPICS & QUESTIONS FOR DISCUSSION

1. The title of *The Short and Tragic Life of Robert Peace* reveals its ending. What was it like to read Peace's life story, knowing how it would end? Was the tragedy present in your mind throughout the reading experience, or were you able to forget it at any point?

2. When Jackie first asked Skeet for tuition to send their son to private school, Skeet called her "uppity" (pp. 22–23). How does the term "uppity" capture the possibilities and pitfalls of Jackie's aspirations for Rob?

3. Throughout his short life, Rob "strove to project confidence and strength while refusing to show weakness and insecurity" (p. 57). Why do you think Rob refused to ask for help during his many moments of need? What were the direct and indirect consequences of Rob's projection of confidence?

4. Discuss Rob's methods of "Newark-proofing": code-switching to protect himself in the streets of his hometown. According to Rob, how is Newark-proofing compatible with authenticity? How does Newark-proofing compare to "fronting," a type of role-play that Rob disdained? Do you agree with Rob's distinction between Newark-proofing and fronting? Why or why not?

5. Consider Rob's relationship to the drug trade, as both user and seller. How did marijuana affect his intellect, his emotions, and his relationships? Do you think a different legal policy toward marijuana might have affected his life course? Why or why not?

6. Discuss Rob's attitudes toward money, poverty, and class. In what ways did Rob seek to escape or fix the deprived circumstances of his upbringing? In what ways did he replicate or revert to the cycle of poverty?

7. Consider the complicated journey of Skeet's conviction, appeals, illness, and death. What were the injustices of Skeet's experience? How do these injustices mirror larger issues of America's justice system? How might the crime and its punishment be considered ambiguous or complicated?

8. Jeff Hobbs doesn't enter the story until almost a third of the way through the book, when he and Rob Peace were matched as college roommates. What was it like to begin this book without "meeting" its narrator? How does the narrative change when Jeff steps onto the page?

9. Discuss the universal and particular elements of Rob's college experience. What are some of the typical college milestones that Rob experienced at Yale? What was extraordinary or singular about his Yale years? In what ways does Rob's experience point to larger questions about the value of a college degree today, particularly from an Ivy League school?

10. Consider Oswaldo Gutierrez, Rob's friend who also traveled from Newark to New Haven and back again. Which of Oswaldo and Rob's obstacles were similar, and which were different? How does Oswaldo's current success shed light on Rob's life choices?

11. Revisit Rob's "statement of purpose" drafted for graduate school applications, printed in full near the end of the book (pp. 337–40). Why do you think Hobbs chose to print the statement in full—typos and all? What is the effect of reading this rough draft?

12. Jeff Hobbs orchestrates dozens of voices on the life and death of Robert Peace. Of all the perspectives in the book, whose felt most objective? Who, if anyone, might have offered a biased view of Peace's history?

13. How did you feel when the Burger Boyz were disallowed from attending Rob's funeral (pp. 392–93)? Could you sympathize with this decision? Do you think these young men deserve forgiveness for any connection with Rob's death?

14. At Rob's funeral, in front of four hundred mourners, Raquel compared her friend to a redwood tree, and took "solace in the fact that so many others thrived and found refuge in his shade while he was with us" (p. 390). Why do you think Rob had such a towering influence on so many people? How might that influence extend to the people who "meet" Rob by reading this book?

ENHANCE YOUR BOOK CLUB

1. Listen to a short interview with Jeff Hobbs on KCRW, the Los Angeles–based radio station: http://blogs.kcrw.com/whichwayla/2014/09/two-unlikely-friends-one-tragic-ending.

2. Watch the Academy Award–nominated PBS documentary *Street Fight*, about Cory Booker's 2002 campaign for mayor of Newark. Learn more about the film and find websites that stream it at: http://www.streetfightfilm.com/index.html.

3. Mourners have left mix CDs on Rob Peace's grave site. Using your favorite music-streaming service, compile a mix in tribute to Peace, including some of the songs mentioned in the book: "Southern Hospitality" by Ludacris, "Ride wit Me" by Nelly, "Put It on Me" by Ja Rule, "It Wasn't Me" by Shaggy, "Forget You" by Cee Lo Green, and "Ruff Ryders' Anthem" by DMX. Add songs by Tupac Shakur, Biggie Smalls, Nas, and even two of the "prog rock" bands Rob discovered through his friend Hrvoje: the Misfits and Black Flag.

4. Try your hand at Jeff Hobbs's research methods: choose any friend or loved one as a research subject. Interview three of your subject's friends or relatives, asking the same two or three questions about the subject's personal history. Do you get similar versions of the same story, or completely different stories? Discuss your research results with your book club.

AUTHOR Q&A

Why did you decide to write this book?

On a Wednesday night in May 2011, while in the midst of brushing my teeth, I learned that my best friend from college had died violently, pointlessly, and painfully. I did what anyone does upon losing someone dear: flew to the funeral, said a few words during the service, bowed my head during the burial, made toasts to Rob having been a "good dude," mourned, tried to move on. Except that I couldn't move on; I returned home and found myself spending full workdays staring at the knotty wall planking in the garage where I work, mostly remembering good times had with Rob. I wrote a bunch of personal essays, weaving together college memories with weak attempts at insight, as well as stabbing at the guilt of having allowed our friendship to grow distant over the decade since we'd graduated. I reached out to mutual friends, spent hours talking on the phone and in person, asking each other, of course, why? A community formed around this question, many people from the various spaces of his life connecting with one another. And at some point it became important to people that some record exist—of his life, not only his death.

In the end, there was not so much a specific decisive moment of, "I am going to write a book about Rob," but rather a process of being caught in this wave of loss and curiosity—of needing to know more—which only gathered strength as weeks and months passed. To some degree, no matter the medium or intention, everyone writes about what conflicts them, and nothing has ever conflicted me more than the death of Rob Peace.

How did Rob's friends and family react to your intention to write his biography?

To say that Jackie Peace had given all of herself in order to nurture Rob's intelligence and curiosity in a neighborhood in which neither trait had much currency would be a vast understatement. When she lost him, she lost not only her only child but all those decades of sacrifice—she lost her identity and her hope. I didn't know Jackie well at all when I first sat down in her living room to speak formally about the book. She told me that her lone consolation after his death was, "I think my son influenced a lot of people, I really do believe that." Feeling very small in proximity to this woman and her grief, I replied that, if she was willing, I wanted to write a book—a book about Rob's life, not his death. I told her that there was very little chance of it being published, but I was driven to work to piece his story together, and that if this effort were in fact successful, perhaps he might continue to influence a few people for the better—and might even spare another mother the anguish that she has endured and will endure for the rest of her life. The blessing she gave to this project was courageous and selfless.

As for his friends—and he had an awful lot of friends—reactions were varied. Most were extremely enthusiastic and giving. Some were still too captured by grief to process it. A small few were doubtful of my ability to tell Rob's story, which was of course a valid doubt.

What were some of the difficulties you faced putting the book together?

Foremost among challenges was the process of exploring a neighborhood foreign to me, and in which my presence was not generally welcome. An inherent discomfort lies in a white guy—a Yale graduate no less—entering the homes of mostly black, mostly struggling people and asking for their stories as they related to a man we both cared for and missed. But that was perhaps the most affecting part of this experience: once we started talking about Rob and exchanging stories filled with humor and warmth, those walls between us tended to come down pretty quickly. Dialogue streamed out of the past and, at times, Rob seemed to spring back into being.

Also challenging was the emotional freight that reporting out this story carried, not only on me personally but on all participants. Positive intention charged all of our efforts, but it was depleting to inhabit such a tragedy day in and day out. I experienced guilt as the details of Rob's life came out of the dark—guilt that even though I lived with him for four years in a small space and had hundreds of conversations with him, I had never become aware of his whole story. In truth, no one had, not even his mother.

What would you say is the impact of Yale on Rob's life? If you were advising a teenager in his position, would you recommend Yale?

What Rob said somewhat often was, "I don't hate Yale, I just hate Yalies." The entitlement bothered him the most, the blithe energy that coursed through classrooms and parties that we deserved this rare experience more than those who weren't here. There was this outrage kind of underneath his skin that made him resent his own presence there. That was unhealthy, and if I could go back in time and talk to that version of him, I'd say, "Dude, there are entitled assholes *everywhere*. They might be more concentrated at Yale for obvious reasons, but wherever you live, wherever you work, there will always be entitlement. The key to living successfully in any environment is to keep from being contaminated by it." His anger, I think, was a kind of contamination.

I risk painting the picture of this brooding Hamlet figure. Rob was not that. He was a bright light. He became a true scientist there and he made fantastic friendships, lifelong friendships that he took with him. And yes, I think he would advise anyone with the opportunity to go to Yale to go to Yale—to go and take advantage of the plentiful resources available, be they academic or social or emotional resources. Let people in despite your biases against what they may represent. Ask people for help. Yes, it's a lot to ask of an eighteen- or nineteen-year-old experiencing such a drastic and all-encompassing change to have that level of maturity, but listen, college is the last time in your life where you have a stable of people—intelligent people—professors, advisers, upperclassmen—whose *job* it is to help you. If this book has any influence on college-aged kids, I hope it would be that there is no shame in receiving help, even the simplest kind of help, such as sitting with a friend and permitting them to listen, because never again will help be so close by.

What did you learn about Robert Peace that most surprised you? Troubled you?

You didn't have to know Rob well to understand that he inhabited two vastly different, fiercely insular worlds: the streets he'd come from and the classrooms his abilities allowed him to enter. That was his broad narrative as reported in the newspaper following his death, that Rob Peace was "two people" (having lived in a small room with him for four years, I can assure you that he was absolutely one person). But what I began to learn even before writing this book was that he didn't live in two worlds. He lived in ten, fifteen, more. He made communities for himself in Rio and Croatia. He spent much of his life, unbeknown to anyone, working to free his father from prison—writing letters, studying in legal libraries, filing appeals. He mentored hundreds of kids as a high school teacher and coach. He all but carried his friends through the travails of life—academically, emotionally, financially. He lived firmly in the center of all these many spheres, shouldered the dependence of so many people, strived to carry all these various pressures with order and grace—and steadfastly refused help in any form along the way. This dynamic was exacerbated by a pattern that emerged in which none of his friends at Yale felt comfortable or capable of offering advice because of the hard way he'd grown up in Newark, and none of his friends in Newark felt comfortable doing the same because this was the guy who'd graduated from Yale. He was heartbreakingly isolated, even in the midst of his closest friends.

So Rob's life overall was nothing if not surprising and troubling—all that he achieved, all that he failed to achieve, the manner in which he was killed and all the hundreds of decisions, most of them innocuous in the happening, that brought him to that moment. But even in that context, I encountered so much positivity that I do hope courses through these pages. He faced so many challenges, many self-wrought, many induced by the relentless algorithms of poverty, and he never wilted, he never stopped caring about others and, as his mother told me, influencing others.

Why do you think what happened, happened?

My young daughter, clued in to what I've been working on for more than half her life, asked me once: "Why did your friend Rob Peace pass away?" I replied, "He had a lot of bad luck, and he made a lot of bad decisions." This answer is tailored to a child, but I think it remains the most accurate answer. The fact is, we all experience bad luck, we all make bad decisions. I certainly have. Most of mine have been insignificant. But Rob's bad decisions—because of the circumstances he was born into and those he wrought for himself—were life-ending.

What was the "meaning of Rob's life"?

The meaning of Rob's life is closely linked with the staggering contrasts that life encapsulated. Here is a man who made communities all over the world when he traveled, but couldn't leave his old neighborhood. A man who aspired to be free of the harried, fiscally based existences that most of us lead, yet ended up bound to one of the most harried, fiscally based occupations there is. A man who performed X-ray crystallography in a cancer research lab but couldn't own an E-ZPass for fear of being traced by police, and so spent much of his brief life in cash-only toll lines between Newark and Manhattan. A man whose ambition was to teach college chemistry and cook out with his friends and family on weekends, who bled to death in the basement beside a gas mask, a butane tank he used for THC extraction, and the Kevlar vest he wore whenever he went outside.

This is the story of a boy from Orange, New Jersey, who earned his way to Yale, flourished there, and then did what almost everyone in his life told him not to do: he came back. He came back and he taught high school, and he was present for his family, and he traveled, and he loved, and he hustled marijuana, and he stumbled through his twenties the way almost everyone stumbles through their twenties, dwelling on greater purpose and ultimately placing himself within the ever-lurking orbit of ruthless urban violence. That's a messy story. Because it's messy being a person, and having a consciousness, and having values, often conflicting values. But it's also a story about love, and not just the standard associations of grace and depth, but the trickier components, the ones that are hard to confront let alone wrap your head around: the warped logic and impossible loyalties and invisible burdens that love can and does generate.

In a broader cultural sense, what would you hope readers take away from this story?

This is the story of one man's life, a relatively anonymous man who died because he sold drugs—and that stark fact can be and has been sufficient for any given person to dismiss his story as one of potential wasted in the service of thuggery. And if that's your reaction, you're perfectly entitled to it. But this book is about details, it's about empathy—about remembering that everyone does not experience each moment the same way. It's about getting to know and understand a remarkable, flawed young man. Yes, his life touches on race and class in this country; yes, it illuminates education and entitlement and access; and yes, it speaks to the fact that living a decent life in America can be tremendously difficult. These issues are quite subjective, and they are best served to remain that way; my intent is not to make statements but simply to tell what happened.

I've mentioned the idea of seeking out help. Yale has a comprehensive infrastructure in place, geared primarily toward students whose upbringings haven't necessarily prepared them for college life—academic, emotional, social. There are guidance counselors and writing tutors and cultural advisers, all free and readily available. But it turns out that the kids most likely to take advantage of these resources are those who need it the least: the Exeter graduates, the future Rhodes Scholars, the affluent students who from the day they were born were primed to believe that adults existed almost exclusively to help them. I've cited Rob's aversion to seeking out help as an admission of not belonging. But what do you do about that gap? Who's most culpable—the students falling behind or the administration unable to pull them forward?

These are questions that lie under the shadow of broader and more bombastic debates. I don't know the answers, but I do feel like awareness—and empathy—is where anyone's potential to do good, maybe even cause change, maybe even save a friend's life, begins.

ABOUT THE AUTHOR

—————◆—————

Jeff Hobbs grew up in Kennett Square, Pennsylvania. He attended Yale University, where he won the Meeker Prize for his writing and the Gardner Millett Award for his running. After graduating with a BA in English language and literature, he spent three years living alternately in New York City and Tanzania while working as executive director for the African Rainforest Conservancy. His first novel, *The Tourists*, was published in 2007 by Simon & Schuster. He lives in Los Angeles with his wife and two children.

Winner, Los Angeles Times Book Prize

Named a best book of the year by *The New York Times Book Review*, Amazon, Apple, *The Washington Post*, NPR, and *Entertainment Weekly*

Robert Peace was born outside Newark, in a neighborhood known as "Illtown," to an unwed mother who worked long hours in a kitchen. Peace's intellectual brilliance and hard-won determination earned him a full scholarship to Yale University. At college, while majoring in molecular biophysics and biochemistry, he straddled the world of academia and the world of the street, never revealing his full self in either place. Upon graduation from Yale, he went home to teach at the Catholic high school he'd attended, slid into the drug trade, and was brutally murdered at age thirty.

That's the short version of Robert Peace's life. The long version, the complete version, is this remarkable tour de force by Jeff Hobbs, a talented young novelist who was Peace's college roommate. Hobbs attended Peace's funeral, reached out to his friends from both Yale and Newark, and ultimately decided to write this harrowing and beautiful account of his life.

What does the untimely death of one man mean? [barcode] esn't reduc ions. Throu and remarkable writing, we learn the cost of moving between the world Peace was born into and the one he achieved. We see him work, love, fail, succeed, give to others, care for his mother, travel, and dream. We witness the decisions he made for himself and the ones that life forced upon him. Most important, we come to understand the sheer complexity of Robert Peace's existence and are irrevocably changed by his fascinating, devastating, and unforgettable life.

"Necessary, relevant, and urgent."
—*Grantland*

"Devastating." —*The Boston Globe*

"Intimate . . . By the end, the reader, like the author, desperately wishes that Peace could have had more time."
—*The New Yorker*

© NICOLE CALDWELL 2013

JEFF HOBBS graduated with a BA in English language and literature from Yale in 2002. The author of *The Tourists*, a national bestselling novel, Hobbs lives with his wife and two children in Los Angeles, where he is working on his second book of nonfiction while also speaking to high school and college students across the country.

INCLUDES A READING GROUP GUIDE AND Q&A WITH THE AUTHOR

SCRIBNER

MEET THE AUTHORS, WATCH VIDEOS AND MORE AT
SimonandSchuster.com
COVER DESIGN BY RODRIGO CORRAL
COVER PHOTOGRAPH BY YESENIA VASQUEZ, 2005

0715

ISBN 978-1-4767-3191-9 $16.00 U.S./$21.00 Can.

51600

9 781476 731919

PRINTED IN THE U.S.A.